THE COMPLETE WORKS OF ROBERT BROWNING

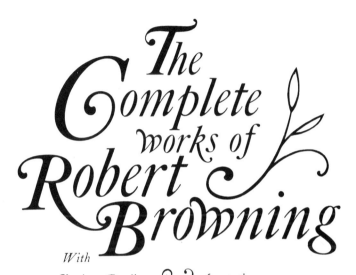

The Complete Works of Robert Browning

With Variant Readings & Annotations

EDITORIAL BOARD

Roma A. King, Jr., *General Editor*

MORSE PECKHAM

PARK HONAN

GORDON PITTS

OHIO UNIVERSITY PRESS

ATHENS, OHIO 1969

CONTENTS

		Page Number
Preface		
I	Contents	vii
II	General Textual Principles	vii
III	Specific Problems in Editing Browning's Works	x
IV	Choice of Text	xiii
V	Presentation of Variants	xiii
	Table of Signs	xiv
VI	Collation	xv
VII	Annotations	xvi
	Table of Abbreviations Used in Annotations	xvi
VIII	Table of Manuscripts	xvii
IX	Request for Corrections	xviii
X	Acknowledgments	xix
Table of Editions Referred to in Volume One		xx

	Page Number	Page Number in Original Edition
PAULINE	3	
Sonnet: "Eyes calm beside thee"	53	
PARACELSUS	59	
Part One	69	1
Part Two	108	42
Part Three	139	72
Part Four	190	124
Part Five	224	157
Browning's Note to *Paracelsus*	267	203
Editorial Notes		
Pauline	279	
Paracelsus	285	

I CONTENTS

This edition of the works of Robert Browning is intended to be complete. It is expected to run to thirteen volumes and will contain:

1. The full contents of the first editions of Browning's work, arranged in chronological order. The poems included in *Dramatic Lyrics, Dramatic Romances and Lyrics,* and *Men and Women* appear in the order of their first publication rather than the order in which Browning rearranged them for later publication.

2. All prefaces, dedications, and advertisements which Browning wrote for his own works or for those of Elizabeth Barrett Browning and others.

3. The two known prose essays which Browning published: the review of a book on Tasso, generally referred to as "The Essay on Chatterton," and the preface for a collection of letters supposed to have been written by Percy Bysshe Shelley, generally referred to as "The Essay on Shelley."

4. The front matter and the table of contents of each of the collected editions (1849, 1863, 1868, 1888–89a, and 1889) which Browning himself saw through the press. The table of contents will include both the pagination of the original volume and of this edition.

5. Poems by Browning published during his lifetime but not collected by him.

6. Unpublished poems by Browning which have come to light since his death.

7. John Forster's *Thomas Wentworth, Earl of Strafford* to which Browning contributed significantly, though to what precise extent cannot be determined.

II GENERAL TEXTUAL PRINCIPLES

The assumptions on which we have prepared the text are, we think, reasonably straightforward, if not entirely conventional. Our principal departure from current textual theory is that we question the conventional meanings of *text* and *author*. For a work which varies in a series of documents and editions, there is no such empirical entity as the *text*. Consequently, the problem of *the transmission of the text* is not a real one; rather, the real problem is to understand the character of the decisions which were responsible for the successive and varying states of the work. Conventionally, it is assumed that only those texts should be used for which evidence of authorial control can be demonstrated, but, as with *text*, the *author* is a constructed entity; not only is it the fact that the *author* (conceived as a static entity) no longer exists; it is equally the case that the *author* (so conceived) never did exist. Our focus, therefore, shifts from *text* and *author* conceived as static metaphysical entities to the dynamic process of creating and editing involved in the compilation of a series of documents.

Any writer's work consists of two processes: he generates an utterance and he corrects that utterance by balancing his current conception of the coherence of what he has so far written, and his grasp of the conventions applicable to the kind of discourse he is composing as they then obtain and as he understands them. Thus, instead of making a distinction between *author* and *editor,* we make a distinction between *authorial function* and *editorial function*. It appears to us that in exercising his editorial functions the author's basis for his activity is continually changing, and may continue to change throughout his life. His grasp of both the coherence of his work and of the conventions may improve or deteriorate; he may come to feel that the conventions are either more or less binding on him. *Author* refers, then, not to a stable entity but to an unstable and continuously innovating continuum.

Furthermore, a writer's attitude towards the exercise of the editorial function may vary from an insistence that he alone has the right to exercise it to an acceptance of virtually any editorial decision made by another. The explanation for this phenomenon is that the author, as every practicing author knows, is not necessarily the one best equipped to balance the two demands at work in the editorial decision-making process. If he is unusually intelligent and richly cultivated at the high cultural level, however, the probability that he is best equipped increases, especially if his cultural situation is relatively limited and stable and imposes upon him a demanding notion of the editorial function. Consequently, there is no logical difference between an author's exercise of the editorial function and an editor's, who is also an unstable and continuously innovating continuum, but whose editorial function is precisely the same as the author's.

Other individuals also exercise the editorial function: the compositor, the printer, and the copyreader. In the history of printing, each of these has been responsible for variants, and insofar as such variants reflect a grasp of the coherence of the work and of current conventions, they cannot be classified as errors. An error is a variant which self-evidently damages the coherence of the text and departs from the conventions as the textual critic himself understands both factors as they were at work in the historical situation from which the work emerged. The history of printing has moved in the direction of trying to limit the printer to errors, to train the compositor to set only what is before him, and to restrict the copyreader to the detection of errors by requiring him to refer questionable variants to the editor and author. Actual practice varies from house to house, within 'the history of each house, and according to the kind of discourse.

We also depart from one line of current textual theory by assuming that punctuation is not to be categorized as an accidental. An accidental, we maintain, is a variant that cannot alter the semantic function of the semiotic data. Spelling, for example, can delay the recognition of a semantic function, but if the current standard spelling can be unequivocally substituted, then it is truly an accidental, and so with word divisions and the like. But whatever the semantic function of punctuation may be—and it is a matter which is little understood—everyone feels it, though some feel it more than others, and this instability of semiotic response is also true of authors. Punctuation, under which we include paragraphing, does not merely *affect* the semantic continuum; it is part of that continuum. Thus, the study of a series of editorial decisions in a passage involving only punctuational variants can, and usually does, have both an interesting and an important effect upon the interpretation of a passage. It seems to us, therefore, that particularly in a nineteenth or twentieth century work, punctuational variants must be considered as substantive changes and so recorded.

The problem, then, is this. Given a work which varies in a series of documents and editions, which document exhibits evidence of the most adequate exercise of the editorial function, and on what grounds is this decision to be made? Or, given a work which so varies but apparently has never had adequate editing, to what degree should the textual editor carry out the task? The textual editor must recognize that he is not restoring or establishing a text, but is continuing the editorial function initiated by the author. When it comes to what variants to record and what emendations to make, the textual critic cannot console himself by falling back on a nonexistent metaphysical entity, the *author*.

The works of Browning offer few problems (though some are of genuine interest) and provide a great redundance of data. Aside from a handful of uncollected poems, all short, everything but *Asolando* went through two or more editions during Browning's lifetime. Except for *Pauline, Strafford,* and *Sordello,* everything published before 1849 was republished in newly edited form in the 1849 collection. *Strafford* and *Sordello* were newly edited for the collection of 1863, as were all other works in that edition. The 1868 collection added a newly edited *Pauline* and *Dramatis Personae* to the other works, which were themselves re-edited. The 1888–89a collection in sixteen volumes included everything so far published in volumes (certain poems published only in periodicals were not included; *Asolando* was added as Volume XVII after Browning's death). The printing of this edition was completed in July, 1889, and the exhaustion of some of the early volumes led Browning to correct the first ten volumes before he left for Italy in late August. The second edition of this sixteen volume collection is dated 1889 on the titlepages; the first eight volumes of the first edition are dated 1888, the rest, 1889. We have designated Volumes IX to XVI of the first edition 1889a.

We have designated the existing manuscripts and editions either as primary or secondary materials. The primary materials include:

1. The manuscript of each volume (when such exists; see table at the end of preface);

2. The proof sheet (when such exists);

3. The original edition of each volume (and subsequent separate editions where such exist);

4. The collected editions over which Browning exercised editorial control:

1849–*Poems by Robert Browning.* Two Volumes. London: Chapman and Hall.

1863–*The Poetical Works.* Three Volumes. London: Chapman and Hall.

1868–*The Poetical Works.* Six Volumes. London: Smith, Elder and Company.

1888–*The Poetical Works.* Volumes 1–8. London: Smith, Elder and Company.

1889a–*The Poetical Works.* Volumes 9–16. London: Smith, Elder and Company.

1889–*The Poetical Works.* Volumes 1–16. London: Smith, Elder and Company. (Vols. 1–10, a revision of 1888–1889a; Vols. 11–16, a reprint of 1889a).

All other relevant materials now known to exist or which may be discovered while this edition is being prepared will be called secondary. Examples of such materials are: the copy of the first edition of *Pauline* which contains annotations by Browning and John Stuart Mill; the copy of the first edition of *Paracelsus* which contains corrections in Browning's hand; Elizabeth Barrett's suggestions for the revision of *A Soul's Tragedy* and certain of the short poems which composed *Dramatic Romances and Lyrics* (1845); and the edition of *Strafford* by Miss Emily Hickey for which Browning made suggestions.

Given all these diverse materials, our first problem is to determine the nature of the decisions for the variants. We are concerned, of course, with all kinds of substantive variants, not only of word and line but also of punctuation. That Browning was responsible for changes of words and lines seems obvious. As far as our records indicate, no one other than Elizabeth Barrett recommended specific changes in the actual wording of Browning's poems. Of the numerous suggestions which she made for changes in the poems which composed *Dramatic Romances and Lyrics* (1845), he accepted some and rejected others. In the case of *Paracelsus,* for example, there are no differences in wording or lines between Browning's corrected manuscript and the printed first edition which suggest that an editor other than Browning was responsible for word changes in the text. Here, then, we need ask only if he were also responsible for changes in punctuation, or if these were imposed upon his poems by the publisher.

To begin with available evidence, the practice of Tennyson and of Swinburne, for example, suggests there was a strong tendency in the nineteenth century to allow a poet general control over the punctuation of his own work. Byron (not very typically) sought editorial help in punctuating; but, as a rule, English poets seem to have been able to insist that even their eccentricities in pointing be followed by compositors—both before the 1840's, when punctuation practice tended to be more anarchic, as well as after the publication of John Wilson's comprehensive, systematic, and highly influential *A Treatise on Grammatical Punctuation* (Manchester, 1844). Thus, the general practice today of publishers deferring to the editorial function of the author according to his literary status seems already to have been in existence, and the similar practice of ascribing high status to a poet, or at least higher than that granted to a novelist, seems to have been obtained.

We do know that for the final 1889 edition Browning had full control over all variants, including punctuation. Indeed, the probabilities indicate that by at least 1863 Browning had principal control over the editorial function. Moreover, in writing to Chapman in the 1850's he shows concern for punctuation. ("I attach importance to the mere stops . . . ." *New Letters of Robert Browning*, eds. William Clyde DeVane and Kenneth Knickerbocker, New Haven, 1950, p. 83.)

Still earlier, the history of the *Paracelsus* texts is of the highest interest and importance. The manuscript of that poem exhibits either an ignorance of punctuation conventions or a refusal to consider them very seriously. For whatever reason, Browning exhibits in this manuscript a wide latitude of innovation even from a variety of conflicting current punctuational conventions. The manuscript shows, however, housestyling, or the exercise of the editorial function by someone other than Browning for one leaf in Act I and all but the first and last pages of Act III. Several other pages show editorial changes in punctuation which may be Browning's. What precisely happened to the styling of some of the manuscript before it was finally printed is uncertain. Either a new manuscript was prepared, or proof was set up from the manuscript as it stood after partial editing and was then thoroughly revised. The manuscript shows signs of heavy use, indications for the signatures (corrected for one signature), and what are evidently compositors' names. The second possibility, then, seems the more likely. The results are significant. First, although the printed punctuation of the edited portions of the manuscript does not correspond with that editing, it is in the same style as that editing. Second, the printed punctuation of the unedited portions is in the same style as the printed versions of the edited portions, and thus of the editing in the manuscript. Third, subsequent published works for which no manuscript exists are in the same style as the printed 1835 *Paracelsus*. Finally, the next available manuscript of major significance, that for *Christmas Eve and Easter Day,* prepared for the printer by Elizabeth and Robert, shows virtually no variation from the first edition of 1850. Everything leads to the probability that Browning exercised final control of the punctuation from the printed 1835 *Paracelsus* through the rest of his career. Indeed, we are aware of Mrs. Sutherland Orr's statement (*Life and Letters of Robert Browning,* London, 1891) that Browning invariably sent proof sheets of his work to his French friend Joseph Milsand for corrections. There is no indication, however, that, in seeking such help, Browning relinquished his own final editorial function.

All evidence, then, indicates that from 1835 onward Browning was responsible for all substantive variants to be found in the several editions of his works over which he had nominal supervision.

(There were indeed during his lifetime a number of editions and selections over which he exercised no control and which, as a result, we have eliminated from consideration here.)

IV CHOICE OF TEXT

By 1889, Browning was the most experienced editor of his own poetic discourse. It seems to us, therefore, that the 1889 edition of his works provides the most satisfactory basic text, not just because it is chronologically the last one he worked on. Rather, the probability is that in 1888 and 1889 he had a better grasp of the coherence of individual works and of this particular style of the conventions, including the conventions of punctuation, than anyone else. The text we have presented is the 1889 text for the contents of the first ten volumes, emended only to correct a few obvious compositor's or printer's errors; the 1888 text for the contents of the last six volumes, emended in the same way; and the 1889 first edition of *Asolando,* similarly emended for the contents of that volume. The text for the uncollected material is based on the original publication. Compared with the textual critic of an Elizabethan play, the textual critic of Browning has on the whole an easy decision to make about what edition to select as the basis for his own text and what further editorial functions are to be exercised.

V PRESENTATION OF VARIANTS

The presentation of the variants is not conventional. Indeed, there is no standard way to offer variants. Initially, we attempted to follow a system sometimes adhered to but, because of the nature of the materials, found it inadequate. We were forced therefore to improvise. We believe that the style we have adopted, which is explained in detail below, has the advantage of presenting the history of the variants in the order in which they appeared, from the first form through the final one, and in a way in which the full text of each line of each edition is most accurately and readily reconstructed.

In presenting the variants from the 1889 text we print at the bottom of the page variants found in the manuscripts, when available, and in the first and subsequent editions—that is, variants found in the primary materials. It seems to us that we can give a clearer, more concise notion of Browning's editorial function if we separate primary materials from secondary materials. Moreover, we must assume that additional manuscripts may become available between now and the time the last volume of this edition is published, making a supplemental volume of variants necessary. We have decided, therefore, that it would be logical to place all variants derived from secondary materials together in a final volume. This final volume will also include *Thomas Wentworth, Earl of Strafford* by John Forster, to which Browning's contribution was considerable but indeterminable.

TABLE OF SIGNS

All signs used by Browning himself have been avoided. The symbols essential to an understanding of the variant notes are set out in the following table of signs:

§ . . . §	Editor's note
< >	Words omitted
/	Line break
//,///, . . .	Line break plus one or more
	lines without internal variants

All variants are placed at the bottom of the page of text to which they refer. A variant is generally preceded and followed by a pickup and a drop word *(a)*. No note terminates with a punctuation mark unless the punctuation mark comes at the end of a line. If a variant drops or adds a punctuation mark, the next word is added *(b)*. If the normal pickup word has appeared previously in the same line, the note begins with the word preceding it. If the normal drop word appears subsequently in the line, the next word is added *(c)*. A single capitalized pickup word indicates the beginning of a line of poetry. When a capitalized pickup word occurs within the line, it is accompanied by the preceding word *(d)*.

No pickup word, however, is used for any variant consisting of an internal change, for example, a hyphen in a compounded word, an apostrophe, a tense change, or a spelling change. Nor is a drop word used when the variant comes at the end of a line *(e)*. Illustrations from *Pauline:*

a ^{47}| *1833:* thee, and   *1868:* thee and
b ^{130}| *1833:* hope, or part, or care, in   *1868:* hope or part or care in
    ^{131} | *1833:* cares, and strife, and toil,   *1868:* cares and strife and toil   *1888:* care
c ^{654}| *1833:* selfishness, this still decaying   *1888:* selfishness, the still-decaying
    ^{24}| *1833:* altars, and stand   *1868:* altars and stand

d **166|** *1833:* And creatures of my own were mixed with
them,   *1888:* And with them creatures of my own were
mixed,
34| *1833:* on Fancy's wings, and   *1868:* on fancy's wings
and
e **215|**   *1833:* tho'   *1868:* though

Each recorded variant will be assumed to be incorporated in
the next edition if there is no indication otherwise.

Punctuational variants (the use of parentheses rather than
square brackets, and of abbreviation rather than full spelling and
other such genuine accidentals) which occur in the presentation of
casts of characters, place locations, stage directions, and character des-
ignations are not listed.

Two kinds of variants which we regard as genuine accidentals
have been emended and not recorded. For a time during Browning's
career it was the practice, as every student of Victorian literature is
aware, to precede every line of a quotation with a quotation mark.
We have eliminated all but the first and last quotation mark, in
accordance with modern practice and with the practice of some of
the original Browning editions. Secondly, during most of his career, a
space was left in contractions of two words; thus "it's" was printed
"it 's." These we have closed up, in accordance with modern practice.

VI COLLATION

Finally, there remains the question of collation within an edi-
tion. In the first place all printings of the 1868 edition except the
first have been eliminated. Those volumes were evidently sold sepa-
rately, for some of them were reprinted, according to the dates on
the title pages, a number of times. There is also evidence that,
though the edition may have been stereotyped, there was some reset-
ting. Since there is no indication that Browning had anything to do
with the resetting and since, for the reasons given above, we have
decided that his editorial decisions are to be preferred when known,
we have disregarded these versions. In any case, it would be impossi-
ble to be sure that all of them had been discovered, even a represent-
ative sampling. As for the other editions, Browning was not a popu-
lar author and the editions were small. A sampling of various
exemplars of several editions has not revealed a significant yield
among them. However, in case of doubt about incomplete inking and
dropped endline punctuation and letters, a sample collation with
other exemplars of the same edition has been undertaken.

Browning scholarship is not yet fully mature. The notes we have presented, therefore, are not intended to be exhaustive or final. The format of the edition has been planned to allow for revision of the notes without disturbing the text. If the text prove satisfactory, it can be reprinted indefinitely with new sets of notes.

As a general principle, we have annotated proper names, phrases that function as proper names, and words or groups of words the full meaning of which require factual, historical, or literary background. Thus, we have attempted to hold interpretation to a minimum, although we realize that the act of selection itself is to some extent interpretative.

Specifically, we have annotated the following: (1) proper names; (2) geographical locations; (3) allusions to Biblical and other literature; (4) words not included in *Webster's Collegiate Dictionary,* Seventh Edition (since some limits must be imposed upon our work and because this dictionary is generally accepted and readily available; we annotate words either not in or used by Browning in a sense other than that given in the desk dictionary; for a more accurate understanding of the meaning which Browning gives to words we have relied heavily upon Samuel Johnson's dictionary); other items requiring factual information which is not of current common knowledge or easily available. All passages in a language other than English are translated into English. Occasional quotations from Browning's sources are included when such source quotations seem especially pertinent and are of difficult access.

For notes, particularly on historical figures and events, we have tended to prefer fullness and even to risk the tangential and unessential. As a result, some of the information provided may be perhaps unnecessary for the mature scholar. On the other hand, it is impossible to assume that all who use this edition—the ordinary reader and the undergraduate and graduate students, for example—will be fully equipped to assimilate unaided all of Browning's copious literary, historical, and mythological allusions. Thus we have directed our efforts toward an audience conceived as a continuum from the relatively uninformed to the trained.

TABLE OF ABBREVIATIONS USED IN ANNOTATIONS

B	Browning
Orr *Hbk*	*Handbook to The Works of Robert Browning.* Mrs. Sutherland Orr, London, 1885.
P-C	*The Complete Works of Robert Browning.* Eds. Charlotte Porter and Helen A. Clarke. 12 Volumes. New York, 1900.

The following manuscripts are known to exist in the locations indicated:

Paracelsus
 Forster and Dyce Collection,
 Victoria and Albert Museum, Kensington

Christmas Eve and Easter Day
 Forster and Dyce Collection,
 Victoria and Albert Museum, Kensington

Dramatis Personae
 Pierpont Morgan Library, New York

The Ring and the Book
 British Museum

Balaustion's Adventure
 Balliol College Library, Oxford

Prince Hohenstiel-Schwangau
 Balliol College Library, Oxford

Fifine at the Fair
 Balliol College Library, Oxford

Red Cotton Night-Cap Country
 Balliol College Library, Oxford

Aristophanes' Apology
 Balliol College Library, Oxford

The Inn Album
 Balliol College Library, Oxford

Of Pacchiarotto and How He Worked in Distemper
 Balliol College Library, Oxford

The Agamemnon of Aeschylus
 Balliol College Library, Oxford

La Saisaiz and The Two Poets of Croisic
 Balliol College Library, Oxford

Dramatic Idyls First Series
 Balliol College Library, Oxford

Dramatic Idyls   Second Series
     Balliol College Library, Oxford
Jocoseria
     Balliol College Library, Oxford
Ferishtah's Fancies
     Balliol College Library, Oxford
Parleyings With Certain People of Importance in Their Day
     Balliol College Library, Oxford
Asolando
     Pierpont Morgan Library, New York
     Each manuscript is fully described in this edition in the section given to annotations on the corresponding text.

The following manuscripts are not known to be extant:

Pauline	*A Blot in the 'Scutcheon*
Strafford	*Colombe's Birthday*
Sordello	*Dramatic Romances and Lyrics*
Pippa Passes	*Luria*
King Victor and King Charles	*A Soul's Tragedy*
"The Essay on Chatterton"	"The Essay on Shelley"
Dramatic Lyrics	*Men and Women*
The Return of the Druses	

We should like to request that anyone with information about any of the manuscripts which are presently unknown to the scholarly world communicate with the Director of the Ohio University Press, Athens, Ohio.

IX REQUEST FOR CORRECTIONS

We have tried to make this edition free from error, but we know that the history of printing proves that such an ambition is impossible of fulfillment. We urgently request that whoever discovers errors will report them to the Ohio University Press, Athens, Ohio, where a file of such errors will be kept so that any future printings can take advantage of such reports.

We express our appreciation especially to the following: the Ohio University Press, the Ohio University Library, and the Ohio University English Department for providing money and services which have made it possible for us to assemble the vast materials required for preparation of this edition; The Armstrong Browning Library, Baylor University, Waco, Texas, and its director Professor Jack Herring for various favors including permission to use and to reproduce the 1835 silver-copper daguerreotype of Robert Browning, the original of which is in the Baylor collection (see *Robert Browning's Portraits, Photographs and Other Likenesses* by Grace Elizabeth Wilson, Baylor University Interests, Series Fourteen, 1943); The Victoria and Albert Museum, Kensington, England, for permission to reproduce and use the manuscript of *Paracelsus*. We have also received valuable assistance in securing and preparing materials to appear in later volumes from the British Museum; Balliol College Library, Oxford; Mr. Philip Kelley, New York; and Mr. John Murray, London. We also gratefully acknowledge the assistance of Mr. Marshall Lee, New York, for helping to design the format of the edition.

The Editors
Athens, Ohio
1969

1833   *Pauline: A Fragment of a Confession.*
        London: Saunders and Otley.
1835   *Paracelsus.*
        London: Effingham Wilson.
1849   *Poems.* Two Volumes.
        London: Chapman and Hall.
1863   *The Poetical Works.*
        Three Volumes. London: Chapman and Hall.
1868   *The Poetical Works.*
        Six Volumes. London: Smith, Elder, and Company.
1888   *The Poetical Works.*
        Volumes 1–8. London: Smith, Elder, and Company.
1889a   *The Poetical Works.*
        Volumes 1–16. London: Smith Elder, and Company.
1889   *The Poetical Works.*
        Sixteen Volumes. London: Smith Elder, and Company.

A full description of each of these may be found in Section A, pp. 1–60 of *Robert Browning: A Bibliography, 1830–1950.* Compiled by Leslie Nathan Broughton, Clark Sutherland Northup, and Robert Pearsall: Cornell University Press, 1953.

PAULINE

Edited by John Berkey

"Eyes calm beside thee"

PARACELSUS

Edited by Morse Peckham

PAULINE

Edited by John Berkey

PAULINE;

A FRAGMENT OF A CONFESSION.

Plus ne suis ce que j'ai été,
Et ne le sçaurois jamais être.—Marot.

Non dubito, quin titulus libri nostri raritate sua quamplurimos alliciat ad legendum: inter quos nonnulli obliquæ opinionis, mente languidi, multi etiam maligni, et in ingenium nostrum ingrati accedent, qui temeraria sua ignorantia, vix conspecto titulo clamabunt. Nos
5 vetita docere, hæresium semina jacere: piis auribus offendiculo, præclaris ingeniis scandalo esse: . . . . adeo conscientiæ suæ consulentes, ut nec Apollo, nec Musæ omnes, neque Angelus de cœlo me ab illorum execratione vindicare queant: quibus et ego nunc consulo, ne scripta nostra legant, nec intelligant, nec meminerint: nam noxia sunt, venenosa sunt: Acherontis ostium est in hoc libro, lapides loquitur, caveant,
10 ne cerebrum illis excutiat. Vos autem, qui æqua mente ad legendum venitis, si tantam prudentiæ discretionem adhibueritis, quantam in melle legendo apes, jam securi legite. Puto namque vos et utilitatis haud parum et voluptatis plurimum accepturos. Quod si qua repereritis, quæ vobis non placeant, mittite illa, nec utimini. NAM ET EGO
15 VOBIS ILLA NON PROBO, SED NARRO. Cætera tamen propterea non respuite. . . . . Ideo, si quid liberius dictum sit, ignoscite adolescentiæ nostræ, qui minor quam adolescens hoc opus composui.—*Hen. Corn. Agrippa, De Occult. Philosoph. in Præfat.*

20 London: January 1833.
V. A. XX.

[This introduction would appear less absurdly pretentious did it apply, as was intended, to a completed structure of which the poem was meant for only a beginning and remains a fragment.]

1| *1833:* suâ *1868:* sua 4| *1833:* temerariâ suâ ignorantiâ vix < >
clamabunt: Nos *1868:* temeraria sua ignorantia, *1888:* clamabunt Nos *1889:*
clamabunt. Nos 6| *1833:* adeò *1868:* adeo 8| *1833:* execrationè
1868: execratione 11| *1833:* æquâ *1868:* æqua 14| *1833:* parùm < >
plurimùm *1868:* parum < > plurimum. 17| *1833:* uite . . . . Ideo *1868:*
uite . . . . . . Ideo *1888:* uite . . . . . Ideo, 18| *1833: H. Cor.* *1868: Hon.
Corn.* 19| *1833: Phil.* *1868: Philosoph. in Prefat.* *1888: Philosoph. in
Præfat.* 20| *1833: London, January, 1833.* *1888:* LONDON: *January 1833.*
§ Bracketed passage omitted in 1833, 1868. §

PAULINE

1833

Pauline, mine own, bend o'er me—thy soft breast
Shall pant to mine—bend o'er me—thy sweet eyes,.
And loosened hair and breathing lips, and arms
Drawing me to thee—these build up a screen
5 To shut me in with thee, and from all fear;
So that I might unlock the sleepless brood
Of fancies from my soul, their lurking-place,
Nor doubt that each would pass, ne'er to return
To one so watched, so loved and so secured.
10 But what can guard thee but thy naked love?
Ah dearest, whoso sucks a poisoned wound
Envenoms his own veins! Thou art so good,
So calm—if thou shouldst wear a brow less light
For some wild thought which, but for me, were kept
15 From out thy soul as from a sacred star!
Yet till I have unlocked them it were vain
To hope to sing; some woe would light on me;
Nature would point at one whose quivering lip
Was bathed in her enchantments, whose brow burned
20 Beneath the crown to which her secrets knelt,
Who learned the spell which can call up the dead,
And then departed smiling like a fiend
Who has deceived God,—if such one should seek

---

§ Ed. 1833, 1868, 1888, 1889. §   3| *1833:* hair, and breathing   *1868:* hair and breathing   5| *1833:* fear,   *1868:* fear;   7| *1833:* lurking place,   *1868:* lurking-place   9| *1833:* loved, and   *1868:* loved and   11| *1833:* dearest! whoso   *1868:* dearest, whoso   12| *1833:* veins,—thou   *1868:* veins! Thou   13| *1833:* should'st   *1888:* shouldst   15| *1833:* soul, as < > star.   *1868:* soul as < > star!   17| *1833:* me,   *1868:* me;   18| *1833:* one, whose   *1868:* one whose   19| *1833:* enchantments—whose   *1868:* enchantments, whose   20| *1833:* crown, to < > knelt;   *1868:* crown to < > knelt,   22| *1833:* departed, smiling   *1868:* departed smiling   23| *1833:* deceived God. If   *1868:* deceived God,—if

Again her altars and stand robed and crowned
25   Amid the faithful! Sad confession first,
Remorse and pardon and old claims renewed,
Ere I can be—as I shall be no more.

I had been spared this shame if I had sat
By thee for ever from the first, in place
30   Of my wild dreams of beauty and of good,
Or with them, as an earnest of their truth:
No thought nor hope having been shut from thee,
No vague wish unexplained, no wandering aim
Sent back to bind on fancy's wings and seek
35   Some strange fair world where it might be a law;
But, doubting nothing, had been led by thee,
Thro' youth, and saved, as one at length awaked
Who has slept through a peril. Ah vain, vain!

Thou lovest me; the past is in its grave
40   Tho' its ghost haunts us; still this much is ours,
To cast away restraint, lest a worse thing
Wait for us in the dark. Thou lovest me;
And thou art to receive not love but faith,
For which thou wilt be mine, and smile and take
45   All shapes and shames, and veil without a fear
That form which music follows like a slave:
And I look to thee and I trust in thee,
As in a Northern night one looks alway
Unto the East for morn and spring and joy.

24| *1833:* altars, and stand   *1868:* altars and stand   **25**| *1833:* faithful:
sad   *1888:* faithful! Sad   **26**| *1833:* pardon, and   *1868:* pardon and
28| *1833:* shame, if < > sate   *1868:* shame if < > sat   **29**| *1833:* ever,
from   *1868:* ever from   **31**| *1833:* truth.   *1868:* truth: **32**| *1833:*
hope, having   *1868:* hope having   **33**| *1833:* unexplained—no   *1868:*
unexplained, no   ' **34**| *1833:* Fancy's wings, and   *1868:* fancy's wings
and   **35**| *1833:* world, where   *1868:* world where   **36**| *1833:* But
doubting   *1888:* But, doubting   **37**| *1833:* awaked,   *1868:* awaked
38| *1833:* thro' < > Ah! vain   *1868:* through < > Ah vain   **39**| *1833:*
me—the < > grave,   *1868:* me; the < > grave   **40**| *1833:* us—still   *1868:*
us; still   **42**| *1833:* darkness < > me,   *1868:* me;   *1888:* dark
43| *1833:* love, but   *1868:* love but   **44**| *1833:* smile, and   *1868:* smile
and   **45**| *1833:* shapes, and   *1868:* shapes and   **46**| *1833:* slave;
1868: slave: **47**| *1833:* thee, and   *1868:* thee and   **49**| *1833:* morn,
and spring   *1868:* morn and spring

50 Thou seest then my aimless, hopeless state,
And, resting on some few old feelings won
Back by thy beauty, wouldst that I essay
The task which was to me what now thou art:
And why should I conceal one weakness more?

55 Thou wilt remember one warm morn when winter
Crept aged from the earth, and spring's first breath
Blew soft from the moist hills; the black-thorn boughs,
So dark in the bare wood, when glistening
In the sunshine were white with coming buds,
60 Like the bright side of a sorrow, and the banks
Had violets opening from sleep like eyes.
I walked with thee who knew'st not a deep shame
Lurked beneath smiles and careless words which sought
To hide it till they wandered and were mute,
65 As we stood listening on a sunny mound
To the wind murmuring in the damp copse,
Like heavy breathings of some hidden thing
Betrayed by sleep; until the feeling rushed
That I was low indeed, yet not so low
70 As to endure the calmness of thine eyes.
And so I told thee all, while the cool breast
I leaned on altered not its quiet beating:
And long ere words like a hurt bird's complaint
Bade me look up and be what I had been,
75 I felt despair could never live by thee:
Thou wilt remember. Thou art not more dear
Than song was once to me; and I ne'er sung

51| *1833:* And resting < > feelings, won   *1868:* And, resting < > feelings
won   52| *1833:* would'st   *1868:* wouldst   53| *1833:* task, which
1868: task which   55| *1833:* morn, when Winter   *1868:* morn when
winter   56| *1833:* Spring's   *1868:* spring's   57| *1833:* hills—the
1868: hills; the   58| *1833:* wood; when   *1868:* wood, when   60| *1833:*
sorrow—and   *1868:* sorrow, and   61| *1833:* eyes—   *1868:* eyes.
62| *1833:* thee, who knew   *1868:* thee who   *1888:* knew'st   63| *1833:*
words, which   *1868:* words which   64| *1833:* it—till < > mute;   *1868:* it till
< > mute,   68| *1833:* sleep—until   *1868:* sleep; until   70| *1833:*
eyes;   *1888:* eyes.   72| *1833:* beating;   *1868:* beating,   *1888:*
beating: 73| *1833:* words, like < > complaint,   *1868:* words like < >
complaint   75| *1833:* thee.   *1868:* thee: 76| *1833:* remember:—thou
1868: remember. Thou

11

But as one entering bright halls where all
Will rise and shout for him: sure I must own
80 That I am fallen, having chosen gifts
Distinct from theirs—that I am sad and fain
Would give up all to be but where I was,
Not high as I had been if faithful found,
But low and weak yet full of hope, and sure
85 Of goodness as of life—that I would lose
All this gay mastery of mind, to sit
Once more with them, trusting in truth and love
And with an aim—not being what I am.

Oh Pauline, I am ruined who believed
90 That though my soul had floated from its sphere
Of wild dominion into the dim orb
Of self—that it was strong and free as ever!
It has conformed itself to that dim orb,
Reflecting all its shades and shapes, and now
95 Must stay where it alone can be adored.
I have felt this in dreams—in dreams in which
I seemed the fate from which I fled; I felt
A strange delight in causing my decay.
I was a fiend in darkness chained for ever
100 Within some ocean-cave; and ages rolled,
Till through the cleft rock, like a moonbeam, came
A white swan to remain with me; and ages
Rolled, yet I tired not of my first free joy
In gazing on the peace of its pure wings:
105 And then I said "It is most fair to me,
Yet its soft wings must sure have suffered change

78| *1833:* halls, where   *1868:* halls where   79| *1833:* him. Sure   *1868:* him:
sure   80| *1833:* fallen—having   *1868:* fallen, having   81| *1833:*
sad—and   *1868:* sad and   82| *1833:* was;   *1868:* was,   83| *1833:*
been, if < > found—   *1868:* been if < > found,   84| *1833:* weak; yet
1868: weak yet   87| *1833:* love,   *1888:* love   88–89| § no space in
1833, 1868. §   89| *1833:* Oh, Pauline! I am ruined! who   *1868:* Oh Pauline, I
am ruined who   90| *1833:* tho'   *1868:* though   91| *1833:* Of wide
dominion   *1868:* Of wild dominion   92| *1833:* ever:—   *1868:* ever!
98| *1833:* decay;   *1888:* decay.   99| *1833:* fiend, in   *1868:* fiend in
101| *1833:* thro'   *1868:* through   103| *1833:* first joy   *1888:* first free
joy   104| *1833:* wings.   *1868:* wings: 105| *1833:* said, "It   *1868:* said
"It

From the thick darkness, sure its eyes are dim,
Its silver pinions must be cramped and numbed
With sleeping ages here; it cannot leave me,
110 For it would seem, in light beside its kind,
Withered, tho' here to me most beautiful."
And then I was a young witch whose blue eyes,
As she stood naked by the river springs,
Drew down a god: I watched his radiant form
115 Growing less radiant, and it gladdened me;
Till one morn, as he sat in the sunshine
Upon my knees, singing to me of heaven,
He turned to look at me, ere I could lose
The grin with which I viewed his perishing:
120 And he shrieked and departed and sat long
By his deserted throne, but sunk at last
Murmuring, as I kissed his lips and curled
Around him, "I am still a god—to thee."

Still I can lay my soul bare in its fall,
125 Since all the wandering and all the weakness
Will be a saddest comment on the song:
And if, that done, I can be young again,
I will give up all gained, as willingly
As one gives up a charm which shuts him out
130 From hope or part or care in human kind.
As life wanes, all its care and strife and toil
Seem strangely valueless, while the old trees
Which grew by our youth's home, the waving mass
Of climbing plants heavy with bloom and dew,

107| *1833:* darkness—sure < > dim— *1868:* darkness, sure < > dim,
110| *1833:* light, beside *1868:* light beside 111| *1833:* Withered—tho'
1868: Withered, tho' 112| *1833:* witch, whose *1868:* witch whose
114| *1833:* god—I *1868:* god; I *1888:* god: I 115| *1833:* radiant—and
1868: radiant and *1888:* radiant, and 119| *1833:* perishing. *1868:*
perishing: 120| *1833:* departed, and *1868:* departed and 121| *1833:*
throne—but < > last, *1868:* throne, but < > last 123-124| § No space in
1833, 1868. § 125| *1833:* For all *1888:* Since all 126| *1833:* song.
1868: song: 128| *1833:* gained as *1868:* gained, as 130| *1833:* hope,
or part, or care, in *1868:* hope or part or care in 131| *1833:* cares, and strife,
and toil, *1868:* cares and strife and toil *1888:* care 133| *1833:*
home—the *1868:* home, the 134| *1833:* plants, heavy < > dew— *1868:*
plants heavy < > dew,

135   'The morning swallows with their songs like words,
     All these seem clear and only worth our thoughts:
     So, aught connected with my early life,
     My rude songs or my wild imaginings,
     How I look on them—most distinct amid
140   The fever and the stir of after years!

     I ne'er had ventured e'en to hope for this,
     Had not the glow I felt at His award,
     Assured me all was not extinct within:
     His whom all honour, whose renown springs up
145   Like sunlight which will visit all the world,
     So that e'en they who sneered at him at first,
     Come out to it, as some dark spider crawls
     From his foul nets which some lit torch invades,
     Yet spinning still new films for his retreat.
150   Thou didst smile, poet, but can we forgive?

     Sun-treader, life and light be thine for ever!
     Thou art gone from us; years go by and spring
     Gladdens and the young earth is beautiful,
     Yet thy songs come not, other bards arise,
155   But none like thee: they stand, thy majesties,
     Like mighty works which tell some spirit there
     Hath sat regardless of neglect and scorn,
     Till, its long task completed, it hath risen
     And left us, never to return, and all
160   Rush in to peer and praise when all in vain.

135| *1833:* words,—   *1868:* words,   **136|**   *1833:* thoughts.   *1868:* thoughts: **137|**   *1833:* So aught < > life — — § Long dash after life §   *1868:* So, aught < > life,   **141|**   *1868:* ventured e'er to < > this;   *1888:* ventured e'en to < > this,   **143|**   *1833:* within.   *1868:* within: **144|**   *1833:* HIM < > honor—whose   *1868:* HIS < > honor, whose   *1888:* honour   **145|**   *1833:* world;   *1868:* world,   **148|**   *1833:* nets, which   *1868:* nets which   **149|**   *1833:* retreat.—   *1868:* retreat.   **150|**   *1833:* poet,—but, can *we*   *1868:* poet, but can we   **150–151|**   § No space in 1868 §   **151|**   *1833:* Sun-treader—life < > ever;   *1868:* Sun-treader, life < > ever!   **152|**   *1833:* us—years go by—and   *1868:* us; years go by and   **153|**   *1833:* Gladdens, and < > beautiful,   *1868:* not, other   **155|**   *1833:* thee—they stand—thy   *1868:* thee: they stand, thy   **156|**   *1833:* Spirit   *1868:* spirit   **159|**   *1833:* return: and   *1868:* return, and

The air seems bright with thy past presence yet,
But thou art still for me as thou hast been
When I have stood with thee as on a throne
With all thy dim creations gathered round
165 Like mountains, and I felt of mould like them,
And with them creatures of my own were mixed,
Like things half-lived, catching and giving life.
But thou art still for me who have adored
Tho' single, panting but to hear thy name
170 Which I believed a spell to me alone,
Scarce deeming thou wast as a star to men!
As one should worship long a sacred spring
Scarce worth a moth's flitting, which long grasses cross,
And one small tree embowers droopingly—
175 Joying to see some wandering insect won
To live in its few rushes, or some locust
To pasture on its boughs, or some wild bird
Stoop for its freshness from the trackless air:
And then should find it but the fountain-head,
180 Long lost, of some great river washing towns
And towers, and seeing old woods which will live
But by its banks untrod of human foot,
Which, when the great sun sinks, lie quivering
In light as some thing lieth half of life
185 Before God's foot, waiting a wondrous change;
Then girt with rocks which seek to turn or stay
Its course in vain, for it does ever spread
Like a sea's arm as it goes rolling on,
Being the pulse of some great country—so
190 Wast thou to me, and art thou to the world!

162| *1833:* me, as *1868:* me as   163| *1833:* thee, as *1868:* thee as
156| *1833:* mountains,—and *1868:* mountains, and   166| *1833:* And creatures of my own were mixed with them, *1888:* And with them creatures of my own were mixed, 168| *1833:* me, who have adored, *1868:* adored *1888:* me who   169| *1833:* name, *1868:* name   171| *1833:* wert < > men— *1868:* wast < > men!   174| *1833:* droopingly, *1888:* droopingly—   175| *1833:* won, *1868:* won   176| *1833:* rushes—or *1868:* rushes, or   177| *1833:* boughs—or *1868:* boughs, or   178| *1833:* air, *1868:* air: 180| *1833:* river—washing *1868:* river washing 182| *1833:* banks, untrod *1868:* banks untrod   185| *1833:* foot—waiting < > change *1868:* foot, waiting < > change;   186| *1833:*—Then *1868:* Then   190| *1833:* Wert < > me—and < > world. *1868:* Wast < > me, and < > world!

And I, perchance, half feel a strange regret
That I am not what I have been to thee:
Like a girl one has silently loved long
In her first loneliness in some retreat,
195 When, late emerged, all gaze and glow to view
Her fresh eyes and soft hair and lips which bloom
Like a mountain berry: doubtless it is sweet
To see her thus adored, but there have been
Moments when all the world was in our praise,
200 Sweeter than any pride of after hours.
   Yet, sun-treader, all hail! From my heart's heart
I bid thee hail! E'en in my wildest dreams,
I proudly feel I would have thrown to dust
The wreaths of fame which seemed o'erhanging me,
205 To see thee for a moment as thou art.

And if thou livest, if thou lovest, spirit!
Remember me who set this final seal
To wandering thought—that one so pure as thou
Could never die. Remember me who flung
210 All honour from my soul, yet paused and said
"There is one spark of love remaining yet,
For I have nought in common with him, shapes
Which followed him avoid me, and foul forms
Seek me, which ne'er could fasten on his mind;

191| *1833:* regret, *1888:* regret   193| *1833:* has loved long silently, *1868:* silently *1888:* has silently loved long   194| *1833:* first loveliness, in *1868:* loveliness in *1888:* first loneliness in   195| *1833:* When first emerged *1868:* When, first *1888:* When, late emerged   196| *1833:* eyes, and soft hair, and lips which bleed *1868:* eyes and soft hair and *1888:* which bloom 197| *1833:* berry. Doubtless *1868:* berry: doubtless   198| *1833:* adored—but *1868:* adored, but   199| *1833:* Moments, when < > in his praise, *1868:* Moments when *1888:* in our praise,   201| *1833:* Sun-treader, all hail!—from *1868:* sun-treader, all hail! From   202| *1833:* hail!—e'en *1868:* hail! E'en   203| *1833:* I am proud to feel < > thrown up all *1888:* I proudly feel < > thrown to dust   204| *1833:* wreathes *1868:* wreaths 205| *1833:* To have seen thee, for a moment, as *1868:* thee for a moment as *1888:* To see thee   205–206| § No space in 1868 §   206| *1833:* livest—if *1868:* livest, if   207| *1833:* me, who *1868:* me who   209| *1833:* me, who *1868:* me who   210| *1833:* honor < > soul—yet < > said, *1868:* soul, yet *1888:* honour < > said   212| *1833:* him—shapes *1868:* him, shapes

215 And though I feel how low I am to him,
Yet I aim not even to catch a tone
Of harmonies he called profusely up;
So, one gleam still remains, although the last."
Remember me who praise thee e'en with tears,
220 For never more shall I walk calm with thee;
Thy sweet imaginings are as an air,
A melody some wondrous singer sings,
Which, though it haunt men oft in the still eve,
They dream not to essay; yet it no less
225 But more is honoured. I was thine in shame,
And now when all thy proud renown is out,
I am a watcher whose eyes have grown dim
With looking for some star which breaks on him
Altered and worn and weak and full of tears.

230 Autumn has come like spring returned to us,
Won from her girlishness; like one returned
A friend that was a lover, nor forgets
The first warm love, but full of sober thoughts
Of fading years; whose soft mouth quivers yet
235 With the old smile, but yet so changed and still!
And here am I the scoffer, who have probed
Life's vanity, won by a word again
Into my own life—by one little word
Of this sweet friend who lives in loving me,
240 Lives strangely on my thoughts and looks and words,
As fathoms down some nameless ocean thing

215| *1833:* tho' *1868:* though   217| *1833:* Of all the harmonies which he
called up, *1868:* called up; *1888:* Of harmonies he called profusely up;
218| *1833:* So one <> altho' *1868:* So, one <> although   219| *1833:*
me—who *1868:* me who   222| *1833:* melody, some wond'rous *1868:* melody
some wondrous   224| *1833:* less, *1868:* less   225| *1833:* honored
1888: honoured   227| *1833:* watcher, whose *1868:* watcher whose
228| *1833:* star—which <> him, *1868:* star which <> him   229| *1833:*
Altered, and worn, and weak, and *1868:* Altered and worn and weak and
230| *1833:* come—like Spring *1868:* come like spring   231| *1833:*
girlishness—like *1868:* girlishness; like   232| *1833:* lover—nor *1868:*
1888: lover, nor   235| *1833:* smile—but *1868:* smile but *1888:* smile,
but   238| *1833:* life—for one *1888:* life—by one   239| *1833:* friend,
who *1868:* friend who   240| *1833:* thoughts, and looks, and *1868:* thoughts
and looks and

Its silent course of quietness and joy.
O dearest, if indeed I tell the past,
May'st thou forget it as a sad sick dream!
245 Or if it linger—my lost soul too soon
Sinks to itself and whispers we shall be
But closer linked, two creatures whom the earth
Bears singly, with strange feelings unrevealed
Save to each other; or two lonely things
250 Created by some power whose reign is done,
Having no part in God or his bright world.
I am to sing whilst ebbing day dies soft,
As a lean scholar dies worn o'er his book,
And in the heaven stars steal out one by one
255 As hunted men steal to their mountain watch.
I must not think, lest this new impulse die
In which I trust! I have no confidence:
So, I will sing on fast as fancies come;
Rudely, the verse being as the mood it paints.

260 I strip my mind bare, whose first elements
I shall unveil—not as they struggled forth
In infancy, nor as they now exist,
When I am grown above them and can rule
But in that middle stage when they were full
265 Yet ere I had disposed them to my will;
And then I shall show how these elements
Produced my present state, and what it is.

243| *1833:* if, indeed, I *1868:* if indeed I 244| *1833:* dream; *1868:* Mayst
< > dream! *1888:* May'st 246| *1833:* itself, and whispers, we *1868:* itself
and *1888:* whispers we 247| *1833:* linked—two *1868:* linked, two
248| *1833:* singly—with < > feelings, unrevealed *1868:* singly, with < > feelings
unrevealed 249| *1833:* But to *1888:* Save to 250| *1833:* some Power,
whose *1868:* power whose 251| *1833:* in God, or < > world, *1868:* in
God or < > world. 252| *1833:* sing; whilst *1868:* sing whilst
253| *1833:* dies, worn *1868:* dies worn 254| *1833:* by one, *1868:* by
one 256| *1833:* think—lest *1868:* think, lest 257| *1833:* trust. I < >
confidence, *1868:* trust; I < > confidence: 258| *1833:* So I < > on—fast
< > come *1868:* So, I < > on fast < > come; 259| *1833:* Rudely—the
1868: Rudely, the § period omitted by error in 1888, 1889 § 260| *1833:*
bare—whose *1868:* bare, whose 263| *1833:* That I < > them, and can rule
them, *1868:* them and can rule— *1888:* When I < > rule 264| *1833:*
stage, when < > full, *1868:* stage when < > full 267–268| § Space §

I am made up an intensest life,
Of a most clear idea of consciousness
270 Of self, distinct from all its qualities,
From all affections, passions, feelings, powers;
And thus far it exists, if tracked, in all:
But linked, in me, to self-supremacy,
Existing as a centre to all things,
275 Most potent to create and rule and call
Upon all things to minister to it;
And to a principle of restlessness
Which would be all, have, see, know, taste, feel, all—
This is myself; and I should thus have been
280 Though gifted lower than the meanest soul.

And of my powers, one springs up to save
From utter death a soul with such desire
Confined to clay—of powers the only one
Which marks me—an imagination which
285 Has been a very angel, coming not
In fitful visions but beside me ever
And never failing me; so, though my mind
Forgets not, not a shred of life forgets,
Yet I can take a secret pride in calling
290 The dark past up to quell it regally.

A mind like this must dissipate itself.
But I have always had one lode-star; now,
As I look back, I see that I have halted
Or hastened as I looked towards that star—
295 A need, a trust, a yearning after God:

270| *1833:* self—distinct *1868:* self, distinct   272| *1833:* tracked in all,
1868: all: *1888:* tracked, in   273| *1833:* linked in *1868:* linked, in
275| *1833:* create, and rule, and *1868:* create and rule and   279| *1833:*
been, *1868:* been   282| *1833:* desires *1868:* desire   283| *1833:*
clay—which is the *1888:* clay—of powers the   285| *1833:* been an angel to
me—coming *1868:* me, coming *1888:* been a very angel, coming
286| *1833:* visions, but < > ever, *1868:* visions but < > ever   287| *1833:*
so tho' *1868:* so, though   288| *1833:* not—not < > forgets— *1868:* not, not
< > forgets,   290| *1833:* up—to *1868:* up to   291| *1833:* itself,
293| *1833:* have wasted, *1868:* wasted *1888:* have halted   294| *1833:* Or
progressed as < > toward *1868:* towards *1888:* Or hastened as   295| *1833:*
after God, *1868:* after God:

19

A feeling I have analysed but late,
But it existed, and was reconciled
With a neglect of all I deemed his laws,
Which yet, when seen in others, I abhorred.
300 I felt as one beloved, and so shut in
From fear: and thence I date my trust in signs
And omens, for I saw God everywhere;
And I can only lay it to the fruit
Of a sad after-time that I could doubt
305 Even his being—e'en the while I felt
His presence, never acted from myself,
Still trusted in a hand to lead me through
All danger; and this feeling ever fought
Against my weakest reason and resolve.

310 And I can love nothing—and this dull truth
Has come the last: but sense supplies a love
Encircling me and mingling with my life.

These make myself: I have long sought in vain
To trace how they were formed by circumstance,
315 Yet ever found them mould my wildest youth
Where they alone displayed themselves, converted
All objects to their use: now see their course!

They came to me in my first dawn of life
Which passed alone with wisest ancient books
320 All halo-girt with fancies of my own;

301| *1833:* fear—and   *1868:* fear: and   302| *1833:* omens—for < > every
where;   *1868:* omens, for < > everywhere;   305| *1833:* being—having always
felt   *1888:* being—e'en the while I felt   306| *1833:* presence—never acting
1868: presence, never   *1888:* acted   307| *1833:* trusting < > hand that
leads   *1888:* trusted < > hand to lead   308| *1833:* feeling still has fought
1888: feeling ever fought   309| *1833:* resolves.   *1868:* resolve.
311| *1833:* last—but   *1868:* last: but   313| *1833:* myself—for I have sought
1868: myself: for   *1888:* myself: I have long sought   315| *1833:* For I still
find them—turning my wild youth   *1868:* them turning   *1888:* Yet ever found them
mould my wildest youth   316| *1833:* converting   *1888:* converted
317| *1833:* use—now   *1868:* use: now < > course.   *1888:* course!
318| *1833:* life,   *1868:* life   319| *1833:* books,   *1868:* books
320| *1833:* own,   *1868:* own;

And I myself went with the tale—a god
Wandering after beauty, or a giant
Standing vast in the sunset—an old hunter
Talking with gods, or a high-crested chief
325 Sailing with troops of friend to Tenedos.
I tell you, nought has ever been so clear
As the place, the time, the fashion of those lives:
I had not seen a work of lofty art,
Nor woman's beauty nor sweet nature's face,
330 Yet, I say, never morn broke clear as those
On the dim clustered isles in the blue sea,
The deep groves and white temples and wet caves:
And nothing ever will surprise me now—
Who stood beside the naked Swift-footed,
335 Who bound my forehead with Proserpine's hair.

And strange it is that I who could so dream
Should e'er have stooped to aim at aught beneath—
Aught low or painful; but I never doubted:
So, as I grew, I rudely shaped my life
340 To my immediate wants; yet strong beneath
Was a vague sense of power though folded up—
A sense that, though those shades and times were past,
Their spirit dwelt in me, with them should rule.

Then came a pause, and long restraint chained down
345 My soul till it was changed. I lost myself,

321| *1833:* god, *1868:* god   322| *1833:* beauty—or a giant, *1868:* beauty, or a giant   323| *1833:* hunter, *1868:* hunter   324| *1833:* gods—or < > chief, *1868:* gods, or *1888:* chief   325| *1833:* friends to Tenedos;— *1868:* Tenedos.   327| *1833:* lives. *1868:* lives: 329| *1833:* beauty, nor *1868:* beauty nor   331| *1833:* sea: *1868:* sea,   332| *1833:* groves, and white temples, and wet caves— *1868:* groves and white temples and wet caves: *1888:* caves   336| *1833:* An' < > is, that < > dream, *1868:* And < > is that < > dream   338| *1833:* low, or painful, but < > doubted; *1868:* painful; but < > doubted, *1888:* low or < > doubted: 339| *1833:* So as *1868:* So, as   340| *1833:* wants, yet *1868:* wants; yet   341| *1833:* powers folded *1888:* power though folded   342| *1833:* that tho' those shadowy times *1868:* though < > past *1888:* that, though those shades and times were past,   343| *1833:* me, and I should *1888:* me, with them should   345| *1833:* soul, till *1868:* soul till

And were it not that I so loathe that loss,
I could recall how first I learned to turn
My mind against itself; and the effects
In deeds for which remorse were vain as for
350 The wanderings of delirious dream; yet thence
Came cunning, envy, falsehood, all world's wrong
That spotted me: at length I cleansed my soul.
Yet long world's influence remained; and nought
But the still life I led, apart once more,
355 Which left me free to seek soul's old delights,
Could e'er have brought me thus far back to peace.

As peace returned, I sought out some pursuit;
And song rose, no new impulse but the one
With which all others best could be combined.
360 My life has not been that of those whose heaven
Was lampless save where poesy shone out;
But as a clime where glittering mountain-tops
And glancing sea and forests steeped in light
Give back reflected the far-flashing sun;
365 For music (which is earnest of a heaven,
Seeing we know emotions strange by it,
Not else to be revealed,) is like a voice,
A low voice calling fancy, as a friend,
To the green woods in the gay summer time:
370 And she fills all the way with dancing shapes
Which have made painters pale, and they go on

346| *1833:* loathe that time,   *1888:* loathe that loss,   348| *1833:* effects,
1868: effects   349| *1833:* vain, as   *1868:* vain as   351| *1833:*
falsehood, which so long   *1888:* falsehood, all world's wrong   352| *1833:* Have
spotted me—at < > I was restored,   *1868:* me: at < > restored.   *1888:* That
spotted < > I cleansed my soul.   353| *1833:* long the influence   *1888:* long
world's influence   354| *1833:* apart from all,   *1888:* apart once more,
355| *1833:* left my soul to seek its old   *1888:* left me free to seek soul's old
356–357| § No space in 1833, 1868 §   357| *1833:* pursuit: *1868:*
pursuit;   358| *1833:* rose—no new impulse—but   *1868:* rose, no new impulse
but   361| *1833:* lampless, save   *1868:* lampless save   362| *1833:* clime,
where < > mountain-tops,   *1868:* clime where < > mountain-tops
363| *1833:* sea, and < > light,   *1868:* sea and < > light   365| *1833:* music,
(which   *1868:* music (which   367| *1833:* is as a   *1888:* is like a
368| *1833:* Fancy   *1868:* fancy   369| *1833:* time.   *1868:* time:
370| *1833:* shapes,   *1868:* shapes   371| *1833:* pale; and   *1868:* pale, and

Till stars look at them and winds call to them
As they leave life's path for the twilight world
Where the dead gather. This was not at first,
375 For I scarce knew what I would do. I had
An impulse but no yearning—only sang.

And first I sang as I in dream have seen
Music wait on a lyrist for some thought,
Yet singing to herself until it came.
380 I turned to those old times and scenes where all
That's beautiful had birth for me, and made
Rude verses on them all; and then I paused—
I had done nothing, so I sought to know
What other minds achieved. No fear outbroke
385 As on the works of mighty bards I gazed,
In the first joy at finding my own thoughts
Recorded, my own fancies justified,
And their aspirings but my very own.
With them I first explored passion and mind,—
390 All to begin afresh! I rather sought
To rival what I wondered at than form
Creations of my own; if much was light
Lent by the others, much was yet my own.

I paused again: a change was coming—came:

372| 1833: While stars < > them, and < > to them,   1868: them and < > to
them   1888: Till stars   373| 1833: world,   1868: world   376| 1833:
No wish to paint, no yearning—but I sang.   1868: yearning; but   1888: An impulse
but no yearning—only sang.   377| 1833: sang, as < > seen,   1868: sang as
< > seen   380| 1833: scenes, where   1868: scenes where   384| 1833:
What mind had yet achieved. No fear was mine   1888: What other minds achieved.
No fear outbroke   385| 1833: As I gazed on < > bards,   1888: As on < >
bards I gazed,   387| 1833: Recorded, and my powers exemplified,   1868:
Recorded and   1888: Recorded, my own fancies justified,   388| 1833: And
feeling their aspirings were my own.   1888: And their aspirings but my very
own.   389| 1833: And then I < > mind;   1888: With them I < >
mind,—   390| 1833: And I began afresh; I   1888: All to begin afresh! I
391| 1833: at, than   1888: at than   392| 1833: own; so much   1868: so,
much   1888: own; if much   393| 1833: Lent back by others, yet much was
my   1888: Lent by the others, much was yet my   394| 1833: ¶ I < >
again—a < > coming on,   1868: I < > again, a   1888: again: a < >
coming—came:

395 I was no more a boy, the past was breaking
Before the future and like fever worked.
I thought on my new self, and all my powers
Burst out. I dreamed not of restraint, but gazed
On all things: schemes and systems went and came,
400 And I was proud (being vainest of the weak)
In wandering o'er thought's world to seek some one
To be my prize, as if you wandered o'er
The White Way for a star.

And my choice fell
Not so much on a system as a man—
405 On one, whom praise of mine shall not offend,
Who was as calm as beauty, being such
Unto mankind as thou to me, Pauline,—
Believing in them and devoting all
His soul's strength to their winning back to peace;
410 Who sent forth hopes and longings for their sake,
Clothed in all passion's melodies: such first
Caught me and set me, slave of a sweet task,
To disentangle, gather sense from song:
Since, song-inwoven, lurked there words which seemed
415 A key to a new world, the muttering
Of angels, something yet unguessed by man.

395| *1833:* boy—the *1868:* boy, the   396| *1833:* the coming, and *1868:*
coming and *1888:* the future and   397| *1833:* I first thought on myself—and
here my *1868:* myself, and *1888:* I thought on my new self, and all my
398| *1868:* out: I < > restraint but *1888:* out. I < > restraint, but
400| *1833:* weak), *1868:* weak)   401| *1833:* o'er them, to seek out some
1868: them to *1888:* o'er thought's world to seek some   402| *1833:* my own;
as one should wander o'er *1868:* own, as *1888:* my prize, as if you wandered
o'er   403| *1833:* white way *1888:* White Way   403–405| *1833:* star. /
° ° ° ° / On *1868:* star. § space § ¶ And my choice fell / Not so much on a system
as a man— / On   406| *1833:* beauty—being *1868:* beauty, being
407| *1833:* Pauline, *1868:* Pauline,—   408| *1833:* them, and *1868:* them
and   411| *1833:* melodies, which first *1888:* melodies: such first
412| *1833:* me, and set me, as to a *1868:* me and *1888:* me, slave of a
413| *1833:* To gather every breathing of his songs. *1868:* songs: *1888:* To
disentangle, gather sense from song: 414| *1833:* And woven with them there
were words, which *1868:* words which *1888:* Since, song-inwoven, lurked there
words   415| *1833:* world; the *1868:* world, the   416| *1833:* angels, of
some thing unguessed *1868:* angels of *1888:* angels, something yet unguessed

How my heart leapt as still I sought and found
Much there, I felt my own soul had conceived,
But there living and burning! Soon the orb
420 Of his conceptions dawned on me; its praise
Lives in the tongues of men, men's brows are high
When his name means a triumph and a pride,
So, my weak voice may well forbear to shame
What seemed decreed my fate: I threw myself
425 To meet it, I was vowed to liberty,
Men were to be as gods and earth as heaven,
And I—ah, what a life was mine to prove!
My whole soul rose to meet it. Now, Pauline,
I shall go mad, if I recall that time!

430   Oh let me look back ere I leave for ever
The time which was an hour one fondly waits
For a fair girl that comes a withered hag!
And I was lonely, far from woods and fields,
And amid dullest sights, who should be loose
435 As a stag; yet I was full of bliss, who lived
With Plato and who had the key to life;
And I had dimly shaped my first attempt,
And many a thought did I build up on thought,

417| *1833:* heart beat, as I went on, and   *1868:* beat as < > on and   *1888:* heart
lept as still I sought and   418| *1833:* there! I < > own mind had   *1868:*
there, I   *1888:* own soul had   419| *1833:* burning; soon the whole   *1868:*
burning! Soon   *1888:* the orb   420| *1833:* me; their praise   *1888:* me; its
praise   421| *1833:* Is in < > men; men's   *1868:* men, men's   *1888:* Lives
in   422| *1833:* pride;   *1868:* pride,   423| *1833:* So my weak hands may
< > to dim   *1868:* So, my   *1888:* weak voice may < > to shame
424| *1833:* What then seemed my bright fate   *1888:* What seemed decreed my
fate   425| *1833:* it. I   *1868:* it, I   426| *1833:* gods, and < > heaven.
1868: gods and < > heaven,   427| *1833:* ah! what < > to be,   *1868:* ah,
what < > be!   *1888:* to prove!   429| *1833:* time.   *1868:* time!
429-430| § *1833:* space with ° ° ° ° Later editions: space §   430| *1833:* O < >
back, e'er   *1868:* Oh < > back e'er   *1888:* ere   431| *1833:* time, which < >
hour, that one waits   *1868:* time which < > hour that one waits   *1888:* hour one
fondly waits   432| *1833:* girl, that < > hag.   *1868:* girl that < > hag!
433| *1833:* lonely,—far   *1868:* lonely, far   435| *1833:* stag—yet < > of
joy—who   *1868:* stag; yet < > joy, who   *1888:* of bliss, who   436| *1833:*
With Plato—and < > life.   *1868:* With Plato and < > life;

As the wild bee hangs cell to cell; in vain,
440 For I must still advance, no rest for mind.

'Twas in my plan to look on real life,
The life all new to me; my theories
Were firm, so them I left, to look and learn
Mankind, its cares, hopes, fears, its woes and joys;
445 And, as I pondered on their ways, I sought
How best life's end might be attained—an end
Comprising every joy. I deeply mused.

And suddenly without heart-wreck I awoke
As from a dream: I said "'Twas beautiful,
450 Yet but a dream, and so adieu to it!"
As some world-wanderer sees in a far meadow
Strange towers and high-walled gardens thick with trees,
Where song takes shelter and delicious mirth
From laughing fairy creatures peeping over,
455 And on the morrow when he comes to lie
For ever 'neath those garden-trees fruit-flushed
Sung round by fairies, all his search is vain.
First went my hopes for perfecting mankind,

439| *1833:* cell—in vain; *1868:* cell; in vain, **440|** *1833:* still go on: my mind rests not. *1868:* on, my. *1888:* still advance, no rest for mind.
441| *1868:* life *1888:* life, **442|** *1833:* Which was all *1888:* The life all **443|** *1833:* so I left them, to look upon *1888:* so them I left, to look and learn **444|** *1833:* Men, and their cares, and hopes, and fears, and *1868:* Men and their cares and hopes and fears and *1888:* Mankind, its < > its woes and **445|** *1833:* on them all, I *1868:* And as < > all I *1888:* And, as < > on their ways, I **448|** *1833:* suddenly, without heart-wreck, I *1868:* suddenly without heart-wreck I **449|** *1833:* dream—I said, 'twas *1868:* dream: I said "'Twas beautiful *1888:* beautiful, **450|** *1833:* dream; and < > it. *1868:* dream, and < > it!" **452|** *1833:* towers, and walled gardens, thick *1868:* towers and < > gardens thick *1888:* and high-walled gardens **453|** *1833:* Where singing goes on, and < > mirth, *1868:* on and *1888:* Where song takes shelter and < > mirth **454|** *1833:* And laughing *1888:* From laughing **455|** *1833:* morrow, when < > to live *1868:* morrow when *1888:* to lie **456|** *1833:* ever by those springs, and trees, fruit-flushed *1868:* springs and trees fruit-flushed *1888:* ever 'neath those garden-trees fruit-flushed **457|** *1833:* And fairy bowers—all *1868:* bowers, all *1888:* Sung round by fairies, all **457–458|** *1833:* vain. / Well I remember ° ° ° ° / First

Next—faith in them, and then in freedom's self
460 And virtue's self, then my own motives, ends
And aims and loves, and human love went last.
I felt this no decay, because new powers
Rose as old feelings left—wit, mockery,
Light-heartedness; for I had oft been sad,
465 Mistrusting my resolves, but now I cast
Hope joyously away: I laughed and said
"No more of this!" I must not think: at length
I looked again to see if all went well.

My powers were greater: as some temple seemed
470 My soul, where nought is changed and incense rolls
Around the altar, only God is gone
And some dark spirit sitteth in his seat.
So, I passed through the temple and to me
Knelt troops of shadows, and they cried "Hail, king!
475 We serve thee now and thou shalt serve no more!
Call on us, prove us, let us worship thee!"
And I said "Are ye strong? Let fancy bear me
Far from the past!" And I was borne away,
As Arab birds float sleeping in the wind,
480 O'er deserts, towers and forests, I being calm.
And I said "I have nursed up energies,
They will prey on me." And a band knelt low

459| *1833:* And faith in them—then freedom in itself, *1868:* them, then < > itself
1888: Next—faith in them, and then in freedom's self 460| *1833:* And virtue in
itself—and then my motives' end, *1868:* itself, and < > motives, ends *1888:* And
virtue's self, then my own motives 461| *1833:* And powers and loves; and
1868: loves, and *1888:* And aims and loves 463| *1868:* mockery *1888:*
mockery, 464| *1833:* And happiness; for *1888:* Lightheartedness; for
465| *1833:* resolves: but *1868:* resolves, but 466| *1833:* away—I < >
said, *1868:* away: I < > said 467| *1833:* this"—I < > think; at *1868:*
this!" I < > think: at 468| *1833:* look'd < > see how all went on. *1868:*
looked *1888:* see if all went well. 470| *1833:* changed, and *1868:* changed
and 471| *1833:* altar—only < > gone, *1868:* altar, only < > gone
472| *1833:* seat! *1868:* seat. 473| *1833:* So I < > temple; and *1868:* So,
I < > temple and 474| *1833:* shadows; and they cried, "Hail, *1868:*
shadows, and they cried "Hail, 475| *1833:* now, and *1868:* now and
477| *1833:* said, "Are ye strong—let *1868:* said "Are ye strong? Let
478| *1833:* past."—And < > away *1868:* past!" And < > away, 480| *1833:*
towers, and < > calm; *1868:* towers and *1888:* calm. 481| *1833:* said,
"I *1868:* said "I 482| *1833:* low, *1868:* low

And cried "Lord, we are here and we will make
Safe way for thee in thine appointed life!
485 But look on us!" And I said "Ye will worship
Me; should my heart not worship too?" They shouted
"Thyself, thou art our king!" So, I stood there
Smiling—oh, vanity of vanities!
For buoyant and rejoicing was the spirit
490 With which I looked out how to end my course;
I felt once more myself, my powers—all mine;
I knew while youth and health so lifted me
That, spite of all life's nothingness, no grief
Came nigh me, I must ever be light-hearted;
495 And that this knowledge was the only veil
Betwixt joy and despair: so, if age came,
I should be left—a wreck linked to a soul
Yet fluttering, or mind-broken and aware
Of my decay. So a long summer morn
500 Found me; and ere noon came, I had resolved
No age should come on me ere youth was spent,
For I would wear myself out, like that morn
Which wasted not a sunbeam; every hour

483| *1833:* cried, "Lord, < > here, and   *1868:* cried "Lord, < > here and
484| *1833:* A way for thee—in < > life   *1868:* thee in < > life!   *1888:* Safe
way   485| *1833:* O look < > said, "Ye   *1868:* said "Ye   *1888:* But
look   486| *1833:* Me; but my heart must worship too." They shouted,   *1868:*
shouted   *1888:* Me; should my heart not worship too?" They   487| *1833:*
"Thyself—thou < > So I   *1868:* "Thyself, thou < > So, I   488| *1833:* Smiling
° ° ° ° ° § only word in line. Space between lines §   *1868:* Smiling . . . . . § only
word in line. No space between lines §   *1888:* Smiling—oh, vanity of vanities! § no
space §   489| *1833:* And buoyant   *1888:* For buoyant   490| *1833:* my
days;   *1888:* my course;   491| *1833:* myself—my powers were mine;   *1868:*
myself, my   *1888:* powers—all mine;   492| *1833:* I found that youth or health
< > me,   *1868:* me   *1888:* I knew while youth and health   493| *1833:* life's
vanity, no   *1888:* life's nothingness, no   494| *1833:* me—I   *1868:* me,
I   495| *1833:* this feeling was   *1888:* this knowledge was   496| *1833:*
Betwixt me and < > so if   *1868:* so, if   *1888:* Betwixt joy and   497| *1833:*
be as a   *1888:* be left—a   498| *1833:* mind-broken, and   *1868:* mind-broken
and   500| *1833:* e'er   *1888:* ere   501| *1833:* me, ere youth's hopes
went,   *1868:* me ere   *1888:* ere youth was spent,   502| *1833:* out—like
1868: out, like   503| *1833:* sunbeam—every joy   *1868:* sunbeam; every

I would make mine, and die.

And thus I sought
505 To chain my spirit down which erst I freed
For flights to fame: I said "The troubled life
Of genius, seen so gay when working forth
Some trusted end, grows sad when all proves vain—
How sad when men have parted with truth's peace
510 For falsest fancy's sake, which waited first
As an obedient spirit when delight
Came without fancy's call: but alters soon,
Comes darkened, seldom, hastens to depart,
Leaving a heavy darkness and warm tears.
515 Bùt I shall never lose her; she will live
Dearer for such seclusion. I but catch
A hue, a glance of what I sing: so, pain
Is linked with pleasure, for I ne'er may tell
Half the bright sights which dazzle me; but now
520 Mine shall be all the radiance: let them fade
Untold—others shall rise as fair, as fast!
And when all's done, the few dim gleams transferred,"—
(For a new thought sprang up how well it were,

504| *1833:* die; and *1868:* die. And § no space or half-line division in 1833,
1868 §   505| *1833:* down, which I had fed *1868:* down which *1888:* which
erst I freed   506| *1833:* With thoughts of fame. I said, the *1868:* fame: I said
"The *1888:* For flights to fame   507| *1833:* genius seen so bright when
1868: genius, seen *1888:* genius seen so gay when   508| *1833:* end, seems
sad, when all in vain— *1868:* sad when *1888:* end, grows sad when all proves
vain—   509| *1833:* Most sad, when < > with all joy *1868:* sad when *1888:*
How sad < > with truth's peace   510| *1833:* For their wild fancy's < >
first, *1868:* first *1888:* For falsest fancy's   511| *1833:* spirit, when *1868:*
spirit when   512| *1833:* Came not with her alone, but *1868:* alone; but
1888: Came without fancy's call: but   513| *1833:* Coming < > hasting *1868:*
Comes < > hastening *1888:* hastens   514–515| § space in 1833 §
516| *1833:* Brighter for < > seclusion—I *1868:* seclusion. I *1888:* Dearer
for   517| *1833:* sing, so pain *1868:* so, pain *1888:* sing: so
519| *1833:* The radiant sights *1888:* Half the bright sights   520| *1833:* They
shall be all my own, and let *1868:* own; and *1888:* Mine shall be all the radiance:
let   521| *1833:* fast. *1868:* fast!   522| *1833:* transferred,— *1868:*
transferred,"—   523| *1833:* sprung up—that it were well *1868:* up that
1888: sprang up how well it were,

Discarding shadowy hope, to weave such lays
525   As straight encircle men with praise and love,
So, I should not die utterly,—should bring
One branch from the gold forest, like the knight
Of old tales, witnessing I had been there)—
"And when all's done, how vain seems e'en success—
530   The vaunted influence poets have o'er men!
'Tis a fine thing that one weak as myself
Should sit in his lone room, knowing the words
He utters in his solitude shall move
Men like a swift wind—that tho' dead and gone,
535   New eyes shall glisten when his beauteous dreams
Of love come true in happier frames than his.
Ay, the still night brings thoughts like these, but morn
Comes and the mockery again laughs out
At hollow praises, smiles allied to sneers;
540   And my soul's idol ever whispers me
To dwell with him and his unhonoured song:
And I foreknow my spirit, that would press
First in the struggle, fail again to make
All bow enslaved, and I again should sink.

545   "And then know that this curse will come on us,
To see our idols perish; we may wither,

524| *1833:* To leave all shadowy hopes, and weave   *1868:* hope   *1888:* Discarding shadowy hope, to weave   **525|**   *1833:* As would encircle me with < > love;   *1868:* love,   *1888:* As straight encircle men with   **526|**   *1833:* So I < > utterly—I should   *1868:* So. I < > utterly, I   *1888:* utterly,—should   **528|**   *1833:* there,)—   *1868:* there)—   **529|**   *1833:* And < > success,   *1868:* "And < > success   *1888:* success—   **530|**   *1833:* And all the influence   *1888:* The vaunted influence   **531|**   *1833:* one, weak as myself,   *1868:* one weak as myself   **534|**   *1833:* tho' he be forgotten,   *1888:* tho' dead and gone,   **535|**   *1833:* Fair eyes   *1888:* New eyes   **537|**   *1833:* brought   *1888:* brings   **538|**   *1833:* Came, and < > laughed   *1888:* Comes and < > laughs   **539|**   *1833:* praises, and smiles, almost sneers;   *1868:* smiles almost   *1888:* praises, smiles allied to sneers;   **540|**   *1833:* idol seemed to whisper   *1888:* idol ever whispers   **541|**   *1833:* unhonoured name—   *1868:* name: *1888:* unhonoured song: **542|**   *1833:* I well knew my < > would be   *1888:* I foreknow my < > would press   **543|**   *1833:* struggle, and again would make   *1888:* struggle, fail again to make   **544|**   *1833:* bow to it; and I would sink again.   *1868:* it, and I should sink   *1888:* bow enslaved, and I again should sink.   **544–545|**   *1833:* § space with ° ° ° ° ° Later editions: space §   **546|**   *1833:* perish—we   *1868:* perish; we

No marvel, we are clay, but our low fate
Should not extend to those whom trustingly
We sent before into time's yawning gulf
550 To face what dread may lurk in darkness there.
To find the painter's glory pass, and feel
Music can move us not as once, or, worst,
To weep decaying wits ere the frail body
Decays! Nought makes me trust some love is true,
555 But the delight of the contented lowness
With which I gaze on him I keep for ever
Above me; I to rise and rival him?
Feed his fame rather from my heart's best blood,
Wither unseen that he may flourish still."

560 Pauline, my soul's friend, thou dost pity yet
How this mood swayed me when that soul found thine,
When I had set myself to live this life,
Defying all past glory. Ere thou camest
I seemed defiant, sweet, for old delights
565 Had flocked like birds again; music, my life,
Nourished me more than ever; then the lore

547| *1833:* Nor marvel—we are clay; but   *1868:* marvel, we are clay, but   *1888:* No marvel   **548|** *1833:* extend them, whom   *1868:* extend to them   *1888:* to those whom   **549|** *1833:* Time's < > gulf,   *1868:* time's < > gulf   **550|** *1833:* what e'er may < > there—   *1868:* whate'er might < > there.   *1888:* what dread may lurk   **551|** *1833:* To see the painters'   *1888:* To find the painter's   **552|** *1833:* Sweet music move < > or worst,   *1868:* or, worst,   *1888:* Music can move   **553|** *1833:* To see decaying   *1888:* To weep decaying   **554|** *1833:* Decays. Nought < > trust in love so really,   *1868:* Decays! Nought   *1888:* trust some love is true,   **555|** *1833:* As the delight   *1888:* But the delight   **556|** *1833:* on souls I'd keep   *1888:* on him I keep   **557|** *1833:* In beauty—I'd be sad to equal them;   *1868:* beauty; I'd   *1888:* Above me; I to rise and rival him?   **558|** *1833:* I'd feed their fame e'en from   *1888:* Feed his fame rather from   **559|** *1833:* Withering unseen, that they might flourish still.   *1868:* unseen that < > still."   *1888:* Wither unseen that he may flourish   **559–560|** § *1833:* space with ° ° ° ° Later editions: space §   **560|** *1833:* my sweet friend thou dost not forget   *1888:* my soul's friend thou dost pity yet   **561|** *1833:* me, when thou first wert mine,   *1868:* me when < > wast   *1888:* when that soul found thine,   **563|** *1833:* all opinion. Ere   *1888:* all past glory. Ere   **564|** *1833:* I was most happy, sweet,   *1888:* I seemed defiant, sweet,   **565|** *1833:* Had come like   *1888:* Had flocked like   **566|** *1833:* I nourished more than ever, and old lore   *1888:* Nourished me more than ever; then the lore

Loved for itself and all it shows—that king
Treading the purple calmly to his death,
While round him, like the clouds of eve, all dusk,
570 The giant shades of fate, silently flitting,
Pile the dim outline of the coming doom;
And him sitting alone in blood while friends
Are hunting far in the sunshine; and the boy
With his white breast and brow and clustering curls
575 Streaked with his mother's blood, but striving hard
To tell his story ere his reason goes.
And when I loved thee as love seemed so oft,
Thou lovedst me indeed: I wondering searched
My heart to find some feeling like such love,
580 Believing I was still much I had been.
To soon I found all faith had gone from me,
And the late glow of life, like change on clouds,
Proved not the morn-blush widening into day,
But eve faint-coloured by the dying sun
585 While darkness hastens quickly. I will tell
My state as though 'twere none of mine—despair
Cannot come near us—this it is, my state.

Souls alter not, and mine must still advance;
Strange that I knew not, when I flung away
590 My youth's chief aims, their loss might lead to loss

567| *1833:* itself, and < > shows—the king   *1868:* itself and   *1888:* shows—that king   569| *1833:*—While   *1868:* While   571| *1833:* doom,   *1868:* doom;   572| *1833:*—And < > blood, while   *1868:* And < > blood while   573| *1833:* boy,   *1868:* boy   577| *1833:* thee, as I've loved so   *1868:* thee as   *1888:* as love seemed so   578| *1833:* me, and I wondered, and looked in   *1868:* wondered and   *1888:* me indeed: I wondering searched   580| *1833:* still what I had been;   *1888:* still much I had been.   581| *1833:* And soon   *1888:* Too soon   582| *1833:* life—changing like clouds,   *1868:* life, changing   *1888:* life, like change on clouds,   583| *1833:* 'Twas not   *1888:* Proved not   584| *1833:* But evening, coloured   *1868:* evening coloured   *1888:* But eve faint-coloured   585| *1833:* darkness is quick hastening:—I   *1868:* hastening. I   *1888:* darkness hastens quickly. I   587| *1833:* near me—thus it is with me.   *1888:* near us—this it is, my state.   587–588| § no space in 1833, 1868 §   588| *1833:* must progress still;   *1888:* must still advance;   589| *1833:* And this I knew not when   *1888:* Strange that I knew not, when   590| *1833:* aims. I ne'er supposed the loss   *1888:* aims, their loss might lead to loss

Of what few I retained, and no resource
Be left me: for behold how changed is all!
I cannot chain my soul: it will not rest
In its clay prison, this most narrow sphere:
595 It has strange impulse, tendency, desire,
Which nowise I account for nor explain,
But cannot stifle, being bound to trust
All feelings equally, to hear all sides:
How can my life indulge them? yet they live,
600 Referring to some state of life unknown.

My selfishness is satiated not,
It wears me like a flame; my hunger for
All pleasure, howsoe'er minute, grows pain;
I envy—how I envy him whose soul
605 Turns its whole energies to some one end,
To elevate an aim, pursue success
However mean! So, my still baffled hope
Seeks out abstractions; I would have one joy,
But one in life, so it were wholly mine,
610 One rapture all my soul could fill: and this
Wild feeling places me in dream afar
In some vast country where the eye can see

591| *1833:* retained; for no   *1868:* retained, for   *1888:* retained, and no
592| *1833:* Awaits me—now behold the change of all.   *1868:* me: now   *1888:* Be
left me: for behold how changed is all!   593| *1833:* soul, it   *1888:* soul:
it   594| *1833:* prison; this < > sphere—   *1868:* prison, this < >
sphere: 595| *1833:* strange powers, and feelings, and desires,   *1868:* powers
and feelings and   *1888:* strange impulse, tendency, desire,   596| *1833:* Which
I cannot account for, nor   *1868:* for nor   *1888:* Which nowise I account
597| *1833:* But which I stifle not, being   *1888:* But cannot stifle, being
598| *1833:* equally—to   *1868:* equally, to   599| *1833:* Yet I cannot indulge
them, and they   *1888:* How can my life indulge them? yet they   600| *1833:*
state or life unknown . . . . .   *1868:* unknown.   *1888:* state of life   603| *1833:*
is pain;   *1888:* grows pain;   604| *1833:* whose mind   *1888:* whose
soul   605| *1833:* Turns with its energies < > end!   *1868:* end,   *1888:* Turns
its whole energies   606| *1833:* elevate a sect, or a pursuit,   *1868:* sect or a
pursuit   *1888:* elevate an aim, pursue success   607| *1833:* mean—so my < >
hopes   *1868:* mean! So, my   *1888:* hope   608| *1833:* Seek < > have but
one   *1888:* Seeks < > have one   609| *1833:* Delight on earth, so < >
mine;   *1868:* mine,   *1888:* But one in life, so   610| *1833:* fill—and   *1868:*
fill: and   611| *1833:* afar,   *1868:* afar   612| *1833:* some wide country,
where   *1868:* some wild country where   *1888:* some vast country

No end to the far hills and dales bestrewn
With shining towers and towns, till I grow mad
615 Well-nigh, to know not one abode but holds
Some pleasure, while my soul could grasp the world,
But must remain this vile form's slave. I look
With hope to age at last, which quenching much,
May let me concentrate what sparks it spares.

620 This restlessness of passion meets in me
A craving after knowledge: the sole proof
Of yet commanding will is in that power
Repressed; for I beheld it in its dawn,
The sleepless harpy with just-budding wings,
625 And I considered whether to forego
All happy ignorant hopes and fears, to live,
Finding a recompense in its wild eyes.
And when I found that I should perish so,
I bade its wild eyes close from me for ever,
630 And I am left alone with old delights;
See! it lies in me a chained thing, still prompt
To serve me if I loose its slightest bond:
I cannot but be proud of my bright slave.

How should this earth's life prove my only sphere?
635 Can I so narrow sense but that in life

614| *1833:* and dwellings. I   *1868:* dwellings: I   *1888:* and towns, til I
616| *1833:* pleasure—for my < > grasp them all,   *1868:* pleasure, for < > all
1888: pleasure, while my < > grasp the world,   617| *1833:* remain with this
vile form. I   *1888:* remain this vile form's slave. I   619| *1833:* concentrate the
sparks   *1888:* concentrate what sparks   622| *1833:* Of a   *1888:* Of yet
624| *1833:* That sleepless harpy, with its budding wings   *1868:* harpy with   *1888:*
The sleepless harpy with just-budding wings   625| *1833:* whether I should
yield   *1888:* whether to forego   626| *1833:* All hopes < > live alone with
it,   *1888:* All happy ignorant hopes < > live,   627| *1833:* eyes;   *1888:*
eyes.   629| *1833:* ever;—   *1868:* ever,   630| *1833:* with my
delights,—   *1868:* delights;   *1888:* with old delights;   631| *1833:* So it < >
thing—still ready   *1868:* So, it < > thing, still   *1888:* See! it < > still
prompt   632| *1833:* me, if < > bond—   *1868:* me if < > bond:
634| *1833:* And thus I know this earth is not my sphere,   *1888:* How should this
earth's life prove my only sphere?   635| *1833:* For I cannot so narrow me,
but   *1868:* me but   *1888:* Can I so narrow sense but

Soul still exceeds it? In their elements
My love outsoars my reason; but since love
Perforce receives its object from this earth
While reason wanders chainless, the few truths
640 Caught from its wanderings have sufficed to quell
Love chained below; then what were love, set free,
Which, with the object it demands, would pass
Reason companioning the seraphim?
No, what I feel may pass all human love
645 Yet fall far short of what my love should be.
And yet I seem more warped in this than aught,
Myself stands out more hideously: of old
I could forget myself in friendship, fame,
Liberty, nay, in love of mightier souls;
650 But I begin to know what thing hate is—
To sicken and to quiver and grow white—
And I myself have furnished its first prey.
Hate of the weak and ever-wavering will,
The selfishness, the still-decaying frame . . .
655 But I must never grieve whom wing can waft
Far from such thoughts—as now. Andromeda!
And she is with me: years roll, I shall change,
But change can touch her not—so beautiful

636| *1833:* I still exceed it; in   *1868:* it: in   *1888:* Soul still exceeds it? In
637| *1833:* love would pass my reason—but since here   *1868:* reason; but
1888: love outsoars my < > since love   638| *1833:* Love must receive its
objects < > earth,   *1868:* earth   *1888:* Perforce receives its object
639| *1833:* reason will be chainless,   *1888:* reason wanders chainless,
641| *1833:* All love below;—then what must be that love   *1868:* below; then
1888: Love chained below; then what were love, set free,   642| *1833:* would
quell   *1888:* would pass   643| *1833:* Reason, tho' it soared with the   *1868:*
Reason tho'   *1888:* Reason companioning the   644| *1833:* No—what < >
love,   *1868:* No, what < > love   645| *1833:* be: *1868:* be.
647| *1833:* For here myself stands < > hideously.   *1868:* hideously: *1888:* Myself
< > hideously: of old   648| *1833:* I can forget   *1888:* I could forget
649| *1833:* Or liberty, or love of mighty souls. § space with ° ° ° ° §   *1868:* souls;
1888: Liberty, nay in love of mightier souls;   651| *1833:* sicken, and to quiver,
and grow white,   *1868:* sicken and to quiver and grow white—   653| *1833:* All
my sad weaknesses, this wavering will,   *1888:* Hate of the weak and ever-wavering
will,   654| *1833:* selfishness, this still decaying   *1888:* selfishness, the still-
decaying   655| *1833:* grieve while I can pass   *1888:* grieve whom wing can
waft   656| *1833:* now—Andromeda!   *1868:* now, Andromeda!   *1888:* now,
Andromeda!   657| *1833:* me—years   *1868:* me: years

With her fixed eyes, earnest and still, and hair
660 Lifted and spread by the salt-sweeping breeze,
And one red beam, all the storm leaves in heaven,
Resting upon her eyes and hair, such hair,
As she awaits the snake on the wet beach
By the dark rock and the white wave just breaking
665 At her feet; quite naked and alone; a thing
I doubt not, nor fear for, secure some god
To save will come in thunder from the stars.
Let it pass! Soul requires another change.
I will be gifted with a wondrous mind,
670 Yet sunk by error to men's sympathy,
And in the wane of life, yet only so
As to call up their fears; and there shall come
A time requiring youth's best energies;
And lo, I fling age, sorrow, sickness off,
675 And rise triumphant, triumph through decay.

And thus it is that I supply the chasm
'Twixt what I am and all I fain would be:
But then to know nothing, to hope for nothing,
To seize on life's dull joys from a strange fear
680 Lest, losing them, all's lost and nought remains!

There's some vile juggle with my reason here;

659| *1833:* her dark eyes, *1888:* her fixed eyes, 660| *1833:* breeze; *1868:* breeze, 661| *1833:* red-beam, *1868:* red beam, 662| *1833:* eyes and face and hair, *1868:* hair *1888:* and hair, such hair, 663| *1833:* beach, *1868:* beach 664| *1833:* rock, and *1868:* rock and 665| *1833:* alone,—a *1868:* alone; a 666| *1833:* You doubt < > secure that God *1888:* I doubt < > secure some god 667| *1833:* Will come in thunder from the stars to save her. *1888:* To save will come in thunder from the stars. 668| *1833:* pass—I will call another *1868:* pass! I *1888:* pass! Soul requires another 669| *1833:* wond'rous soul, *1868:* wondrous *1888:* wondrous mind, 671| *1833:* life; yet *1868:* life, yet 672| *1833:* fears, and *1868:* fears; and 674| *1833:* And strait I *1888:* And lo, I 675| *1833:* And I rise triumphing over my decay. *1888:* And rise triumphant, triumphant through decay. 675–676| § space with ° ° ° ° in 1833 § 677| *1833:* all that I would be. *1868:* be: *1888:* all I fain would 678| *1833:* nothing—to hope for nothing— *1868:* nothing, to hope for nothing, 679| *1833:* fear, *1868:* fear 680| *1833:* lost, and nought remains. *1868:* lost and nought remains! 680–681| § space with ° ° ° ° in 1833 § 681| *1833:* here— *1868:* here;

I feel I but explain to my own loss
These impulses: they live no less the same.
Liberty! what though I despair? my blood
685 Rose never at a slave's name proud as now.
Oh sympathies, obscured by sophistries!—
Why else have I sought refuge in myself,
But from the woes I saw and could not stay?
Love! is not this to love thee, my Pauline?
690 I cherish prejudice, lest I be left
Utterly loveless? witness my belief
In poets, though sad change has come there too;
No more I leave myself to follow them—
Unconsciously I measure me by them—
695 Let me forget it: and I cherish most
My love of England—how her name, a word
Of hers in a strange tongue makes my heart beat!

Pauline, could I but break the spell! Not now—
All's fever—but when calm shall come again,
700 I am prepared: I have made life my own.
I would not be content with all the change
One frame should feel, but I have gone in thought
Thro' all conjuncture, I have lived all life
When it is most alive, where strangest fate

683| *1833:* impulses—they   *1868:* impulses; they   *1888:* impulses; they
684| *1833:* despair—my   *1868:* despair? my   685| *1833:* Rose not at < >
proudlier than now,   *1888:* Rose never at < > proud as now.   686| *1833:* And
sympathy < > sophistries.   *1868:* sympathy, < > sophistries!   *1888:* Oh
sympathies, < > sophistries!—   687| *1833:* Why have not I   *1888:* Why else
have I   688| *1833:* But for the < > stay—   *1868:* stay?   *1888:* But from
the   689| *1833:* And love!—do I not love   *1868:* love! do   *1888:* Love! is not
this to love   689-690| § space with ° ° ° ° in 1833 §   691| *1833:*
loveless—witness this belief   *1888:* loveless? witness my belief   692| *1833:* tho'
< > too   *1868:* though < > too;   693| *1833:* them: *1868:* them—
694| *1833:* them.   *1868:* them—   695| *1833:* it; and   *1868:* it: and
696| *1833:* name—a   *1868:* name, a   697| *1833:* her's < > beat! . .   *1868:*
beat!   *1888:* hers   697-698| § space with ° ° ° ° in 1833 §   698| *1833:*
Pauline, I could do any thing—not   *1888:* Pauline, could I but break the spell!
Not   699| *1833:* again—   *1868:* again,   700| *1833:* prepared—I < >
own—   *1868:* prepared: I < > own.   702| *1833:* feel—but   *1868:* feel,
but   703| *1833:* conjuncture—I   *1868:* conjuncture, I   704| *1833:*
alive—where   *1868:* alive, where

705 New-shapes it past surmise—the throes of men
    Bit by some curse or in the grasps of doom
    Half-visible and still-increasing round,
    Or crowning their wide being's general aim.

    These are wild fancies, but I feel, sweet friend,
710 As one breathing his weakness to the ear
    Of pitying angel—dear as a winter flower,
    A slight flower growing alone, and offering
    Its frail cup of three leaves to the cold sun,
    Yet joyous and confiding like the triumph
715 Of a child: and why am I not worthy thee?
    I can live all the life of plants, and gaze
    Drowsily on the bees that flit and play,
    Or bare my breast for sunbeams which will kill,
    Or open in the night of sounds, to look
720 For the dim stars; I can mount with the bird
    Leaping airily his pyramid of leaves
    And twisted boughs of some tall mountain tree,
    Or rise cheerfully springing to the heavens;
    Or like a fish breathe deep in the morning air
725 In the misty sun-warm water; or with flower
    And tree can smile in light at the sinking sun
    Just as the storm comes, as a girl would look
    On a departing lover—most serene.

    Pauline, come with me, see how I could build
730 A home for us, out of the world, in thought!

705| *1833:* New Shapes < > the tales of   *1888:* New-shapes < > the throes
of   706| *1833:* curse—or   *1868:* curse or   707| *1833:* still increasing
1888: still-increasing   708| *1833:* aim . . . .   *1868:* aim.
708–709| § space with ° ° ° ° in 1833 §   711| *1833:* flower;   *1868:*
flower,   714| *1833:* confiding, like   *1868:* confiding like   715| *1833:*
child—and   *1868:* child: and   715–716| § space with ° ° ° ° in 1833 §
720| *1833:* bird,   *1868:* bird   723| *1833:* heavens—   *1868:* heavens;
724| *1833:* breathe in the   *1868:* breathe-in   *1888:* breathe deep the
725| *1833:* water—or with flowers   *1868:* water; or   *1888:* flower
726| *1833:* And trees can < > sun,   *1868:* sun   *1888:* And tree can < >
sun   727| *1833:* comes—as   *1868:* comes, as   729| *1833:* me—see
730| *1833:* world; in thought—   *1868:* world, in thought!

38

I am uplifted: fly with me, Pauline!

Night, and one single ridge of narrow path
Between the sullen river and the woods
Waving and muttering, for the moonless night
735 Has shaped them into images of life,
Like the uprising of the giant-ghosts,
Looking on earth to know how their sons fare:
Thou art so close by me, the roughest swell
Of wind in the tree-tops hides not the panting
740 Of thy soft breasts. No, we will pass to morning—
Morning, the rocks and valleys and old woods.
How the sun brightens in the mist, and here,
Half in the air, like creatures of the place,
Trusting the element, living on high boughs
745 That swing in the wind—look at the silver spray
Flung from the foam-sheet of the cataract
Amid the broken rocks! Shall we stay here
With the wild hawks? No, ere the hot noon come.
Dive we down—safe! See this our new retreat
750 Walled in with a sloped mound of matted shrubs,
Dark, tangled, old and green, still sloping down
To a small pool whose waters lie asleep
Amid the trailing boughs turned water-plants:
And tall trees overarch to keep us in,
755 Breaking the sunbeams into emerald shafts,
And in the dreamy water one small group
Of two or three strange trees are got together
Wondering at all around, as strange beasts herd

731| _1833:_ am inspired—come with   _1868:_ inspired: come   _1888:_ am uplifted: fly
with   **734|** _1833:_ muttering—for   _1868:_ muttering, for   **737|** _1833:_
fare.   _1868:_ fare: **740|** _1833:_ breasts; no—we   _1868:_ breasts. No, we
741| _1833:_ Morning—the rocks, and vallies, and   _1868:_ Morning, the rocks and
valleys and   **742|** _1833:_ here,—   _1868:_ here,   **743|** _1833:_
element—living   _1868:_ element, living   **745|** _1833:_ the golden spray.   _1868:_
spray   _1888:_ the silver spray   **746|** _1833:_ cataract,   _1868:_ cataract
747| _1833:_ rocks—shall   _1868:_ rocks! Shall   **748|** _1833:_ hawks?—no, ere < >
come   _1868:_ hawks? No, ere < > come,   **749|** _1833:_ safe;—see   _1868:_ safe!
See   **751|** _1833:_ green—still   _1868:_ green, still   **753|** _1833:_ water-
plants   _1868:_ water-plants: **754|** _1833:_ over-arch   _1888:_ overarch
757| _1833:_ together,   _1868:_ together   **758|** _1833:_ around—as   _1868:_ around,
as

Together far from their own land: all wildness,
760   No turf nor moss, for boughs and plants pave all,
And tongues of bank go shelving in the lymph,
Where the pale-throated snake reclines his head,
And old grey stones lie making eddies there,
The wild-mice cross them dry-shod. Deeper in!
765   Shut thy soft eyes—now look—still deeper in!
This is the very heart of the woods all round
Mountain-like heaped above us; yet even here
One pond of water gleams; far off the river
Sweeps like a sea, barred out from land; but one—
770   One thin clear sheet has overleaped and wound
Into this silent depth, which gained, it lies
Still, as but let by sufferance; the trees bend
O'er it as wild men watch a sleeping girl,
And through their roots long creeping plants out-stretch
775   Their twined hair, steeped and sparkling; farther on,
Tall rushes and thick flag-knots have combined
To narrow it; so, at length, a silver thread,
It winds, all noiselessly through the deep wood
Till thro' a cleft-way, thro' the moss and stone,
780   It joins its parent-river with a shout.

Up for the glowing day, leave the old woods!
See, they part like a ruined arch: the sky!
Nothing but sky appears, so close the roots
And grass of the hill-top level with the air—
785   Blue sunny air, where a great cloud floats laden

759| *1833:* land—all wildness—   *1868:* land: all wildness,   **761|** *1833:* the
waters,   *1888:* the lymph,   **763|** *1833:* there;   *1868:* there,
764| *1833:* wild mice < > dry-shod—deeper in—   *1868:* dry-shod: deeper in!
1888: wild-mice < > dry-shod. Deeper in!   **765|** *1833:* in: *1868:* in!
766| *1833:* woods—all round,   *1868:* woods all round   **767|** *1833:* Mountain-
like, heaped   *1868:* Mountain-like heaped   **768|** *1833:* gleams—far   *1868:*
gleams; far   **770|** *1833:* over-leaped   *1888:* overleaped   **774|** *1833:*
thro' < > plants stretch out   *1868:* through   *1888:* through < > plants out-
stretch   **777|** *1833:* thread   *1868:* thread,   **778|** *1833:* noiselessly, thro'
< > wood,   *1868:* noiselessly through < > wood   **779|** *1833:* cleft way,
1888: cleft-way,   **780–781|** § no space in 1833, 1868 §   **781|** *1833:*
day—leave < > woods: *1868:* day, leave < > woods!   **782|** *1833:* part, like
< > arch, the   *1868:* arch: the   **783|** *1833:* root   *1868:* roots
785| *1833:* floats, laden   *1868:* floats laden

With light, like a dead whale that white birds pick,
Floating away in the sun in some north sea.
Air, air, fresh life-blood, thin and searching air,
The clear, dear breath of God that loveth us,
790 Where small birds reel and winds take their delight!
Water is beautiful, but not like air:
See, where the solid azure waters lie
Made as of thickened air, and down below,
The fern-ranks like a forest spread themselves
795 As though each pore could feel the element;
Where the quick glancing serpent winds his way,
Float with me there, Pauline!—but not like air.

Down the hill! Stop—a clump of trees, see, set
On a heap of rock, which look o'er the far plain:
800 So, envious climbing shrubs would mount to rest
And peer from their spread boughs; wide they wave, looking
At the muleteers who whistle on their way,
To the merry chime of morning bells, past all
The little smoking cots, mid fields and banks
805 And copses bright in the sun. My spirit wanders:
Hedgerows for me—those living hedgerows where
The bushes close and clasp above and keep

788| *1833:* Air, air—fresh life-blood—thin < > air—   *1868:* Air, air, fresh life-blood, thin < > air,   **789|** *1833:* God, that loveth us: *1868:* God that loveth us,   **790|** *1833:* delight.   *1868:* delight!   **791|** *1833:* air.   *1868:* air: **792|** *1833:* lie,   *1868:* lie   **794** *1833:* fern-ranks, like < > themselves,   *1868:* fern-ranks like < > themselves   **795|** *1833:* tho'   *1868:* though   **796** *1833:* way—   *1868:* way,   **797|** *1833:* Pauline, but   *1868:* Pauline!—but   **797–798|** § no space in 1833, 1868 §   **798|** *1833:* hill—stop   *1868:* hill! Stop   **799|** *1833:* rocks < > plains,   *1888:* rock < > plain: **800|** *1833:* And envious < > rest,   *1868:* rest   *1888:* So, envious   **801|** *1833:* boughs. There they   *1868:* boughs; there   *1888:* boughs; wide they   **802|** *1833:* muleteers, who whistle as they go   *1868:* muleteers who   *1888:* whistle on their way,   **803|** *1833:* of their morning bells, and all   *1888:* of morning   **804|** *1833:* cots, and fields, and blanks,   *1868:* cots and fields and banks   *1888:* cots, mid fields   **805|** *1833:* copses, bright < > sun; my spirit wanders.   *1868:* copses bright < > sun. My spirit wanders: **806|** *1833:* Hedge-rows for me—still, living, hedge-rows, where   *1868:* living hedge-rows where   *1888:* Hedgerows for me—those living hedgerows   **807|** *1833:* close, and clasp above, and   *1868:* close and clasp above and

Thought in—I am concentrated—I feel;
But my soul saddens when it looks beyond:
810 I cannot be immortal, taste all joy.

O God, where do they tend—these struggling aims?*

1   *Je crains bien que mon pauvre ami ne soit pas toujours parfaitement compris
dans ce qui reste à lire de cet étrange fragment, mais il est moins propre que
tout autre à éclaircir ce qui de sa nature ne peut jamais être que songe et
confusion. D'ailleurs je ne sais trop si en cherchant à mieux coordonner certaines
5   parties l'on ne courrait pas le risque de nuire au seul mérite auquel une
production si singulière peut prétendre, celui de donner une idée assez précise
du genre qu'elle n'a fait qu'ébaucher. Ce début sans prétention, ce remuement
des passions qui va d'abord en accroissant et puis s'apaise par degrés, ces élans
de l'âme, ce retour soudain sur soimême, et par-dessus tout, la tournure d'esprit
10   tout particulière de mon ami, rendent les changemens presque impossibles. Les
raisons qu'il fait valoir ailleurs, et d'autres encore plus puissantes, ont fait trouver
grâce à mes yeux pour cet écrit qu'autrement je lui eusse conseillé de jeter au
feu. Je n'en crois pas moins au grand principe de toute composition—à ce
principe de Shakespeare, de Rafaelle, de Beethoven, d'où il suit que la concen-
15   tration des idées est due bien plus à leur conception qu'à leur mise en exécution:
j'ai tout lieu de craindre que la première de ces qualités ne soit encore étrangère
à mon ami, et je doute fort qu'un redoublement de travail lui fasse acquérir la
seconde. Le mieux serait de brûler ceci; mais que faire?
Je crois que dans ce qui suit il fait allusion à un certain examen qu'il fit
20   autrefois de l'âme, ou plutôt de son âme, pour découvrir la suite des objets
auxquels il lui serait possible d'atteindre, et dont chacun une fois obtenu devait
former une espèce de plateau d'où l'on pouvait apercevoir d'autres buts, d'autres
projets, d'autres jouissances qui, à leur tour, devaient être surmontés. Il en

2| *1833:* fragment—mais   *1868:* fragment, mais   6| *1833:* singuliere   *1868:*
singuliére   6| *1833:* prétendre—celui   *1868:* prétendre, celui   7| *1833:*
que' ébaucher.—Ce   *1868:* qu'ébaucher. Ce   8| *1833:* puis s'appaise par
1888: puis s'apaise par   9| *1833:* soi-même.—Et par dessus <> ami rendent
1868: soi-même, et par-dessus <> ami, rendent   12| *1833:* feu—Je   *1868:*
feu. Je   13| *1833:* Shakspeare, de Raffaelle, <> d'où   *1868:* Shakespeare, de
Rafaelle, <> 'ou   *1888:* Shakespeare, de Rafaelle, <> d'où   15| *1833:* est
dûe bien <> conception, qu'à   *1868:* conception qu'à   *1888:* est due bien <>
conception qu'à   15-16| *1833:* execution . . . j'ai   *1868:* execution: j'ai
17| *1833:* ami—et   *1868:* ami, et   17| *1833:* de bruler   *1868:* de brûler
20| *1833:* l'âme ou plutot <> la suité   *1868:* l'âme ou plutôt <> la
suite   *1888:* l'âme, ou plutot <> la suite   21| *1833:* d'attèndre, et   *1888:*
d'atteindre, et   22| *1833:* aperçevoir   *1888:* apercevoir   808| *1833:*
feel;—   *1868:* feel;   809| *1833:* beyond;   *1868:* beyond: 810| *1833:*
immortal, nor taste all.   *1868:* immortal nor   *1888:* immortal, taste all joy.
810-811| § no space in 1833, 1868 §   811| *1833:* O God! where does this tend—
<> aims!°   *1868:* O God, where <> aims?°   *1888:* O God, where do they—these

résultait que l'oubli et le sommeil devaient tout terminer. Cette idée, que je ne
25 saisis pas parfaitement, lui est peut-être aussi inintelligible qu'à moi.

PAULINE.

What would I have? What is this "sleep" which seems
To bound all? can there be a "waking" point
Of crowning life? The soul would never rule;
815 It would be first in all things, it would have
Its utmost pleasure filled, but, that complete,
Commanding, for commanding, sickens it.
The last point I can trace is—rest beneath
Some better essence than itself, in weakness;
820 This is "myself," not what I think should be:
And what is that I hunger for but God?

My God, my God, let me for once look on thee
As though nought else existed, we alone!
And as creation crumbles, my soul's spark
825 Expands till I can say,—Even from myself
I need thee and I feel thee and I love thee.
I do not plead my rapture in thy works
For love of thee, nor that I feel as one
Who cannot die: but there is that in me
830 Which turns to thee, which loves or which should love.

23| *1833:* idée que < > parfaitement lui   *1868:* idée, que < > parfaitement,
lui   24| *1833:* peutêtre aussi intelligible   *1868:* peutêtre aussi inintelligible
1888: peu-être aussi inintelligible   812| *1833:* have? what < > "sleep,"
which   *1868:* have? What < > "sleep" which   814| *1833:* rule—   *1868:*
rule;   815| *1833:* things—it   *1868:* things, it   816| *1833:* filled,—but the
complete   *1868:* filled, but, that complete,   817| *1833:* Commanding for
commanding sickens   *1868:* Commanding, for commanding, sickens
818| *1833:* point that I < > is, rest   *1868:* point I < > is, rest, beneath   *1888:*
is—rest beneath   819| *1833:* itself—in   *1868:* itself, in   820| *1833:*
"myself"—not < > be,   *1868:* "myself," not < > be: 821–822| § no space in
1833, 1868 §   822| *1833:* my God! let   *1868:* my God, let   823| *1833:*
tho' < > existed: we alone.   *1868:* though < > existed, we alone!
825| *1833:* say, "Even   *1868:* say,—Even   826| *1833:* thee, and I feel thee,
and < > thee;   *1868:* thee and < > thee and < > thee: *1888:* love thee.
828| *1833:* thee—or   *1868:* thee, nor   829| *1833:* die—but   *1868:* die:
but   830| *1833:* loves, or < > love."   *1868:* loves or < > love.
830–831| § space in 1833, 1888, 1889; no space in 1868 §

Why have I girt myself with this hell-dress?
Why have I laboured to put out my life?
Is it not in my nature to adore,
And e'en for all my reason do I not
835 Feel him, and thank him, and pray to him—now?
Can I forego the trust that he loves me?
Do I not feel a love which only ONE . . .
O thou pale form, so dimly seen, deep-eyed!
I have denied thee calmly—do I not
840 Pant when I read of thy consummate power,
And burn to see thy calm pure truths out-flash
The brightest gleams of earth's philosophy?
Do I not shake to hear aught question thee?
If I am erring save me, madden me,
845 Take from me powers and pleasures, let me die
Ages, so I see thee! I am knit round
As with a charm by sin and lust and pride,
Yet though my wandering dreams have seen all shapes
Of strange delight, oft have I stood by thee—
850 Have I been keeping lonely watch with thee
In the damp night by weeping Olivet,
Or leaning on thy bosom, proudly less,
Or dying with thee on the lonely cross,
Or witnessing thine outburst from the tomb.

855 A mortal, sin's familiar friend, doth here
Avow that he will give all earth's reward,
But to believe and humbly teach the faith,
In suffering and poverty and shame,

835| *1833:* to him?—*Now.* *1868:* to him—now? 837| *1833:* ONE . . . . .
1888: ONE . . . 838| *1833:* deep-eyed, *1868:* deep-eyed! 840| *1833:*
consummate deeds, *1888:* consummate power, 841| *1833:* calm, pure *1868:*
calm pure 843| *1833:* thee? . . . . *1868:* thee? 843–844| § space in
1833 § 845| *1833:* powers, and pleasures—let *1868:* powers and pleasures,
let 846| *1833:* thee: I *1868:* thee! I 847| *1833:* charm, by *1868:*
charm by 848| *1833:* tho' *1868:* though 850| *1833:* thee, *1868:*
thee 852| *1833:* less— *1868:* less, 853| *1833:* cross— *1868:*
cross, 854| *1833:* witnessing thy bursting from the tomb! *1888:* witnessing
thine outburst from the tomb. 855| *1833:* friend doth *1868:* friend,
doth 858| *1888:* suffering, and poverty, and *1868:* suffering and poverty and

Only believing he is not unloved.

860 And now, my Pauline, I am thine for ever!
I feel the spirit which has buoyed me up
Desert me, and old shades are gathering fast;
Yet while the last light waits, I would say much,
This chiefly, it is gain that I have said
865 Somewhat of love I ever felt for thee
But seldom told; our hearts so beat together
That speech seemed mockery; but when dark hours come,
And joy departs, and thou, sweet, deem'st it strange
A sorrow moves me, thou canst not remove,
870 Look on this lay I dedicate to thee,
Which through thee I began, which thus I end,
Collecting the last gleams to strive to tell
How I am thine, and more than ever now
That I sink fast: yet though I deeplier sink,
875 No less song proves one word has brought me bliss,
Another still may win bliss surely back.
Thou knowest, dear, I could not think all calm,
For fancies followed thought and bore me off,
And left all indistinct; ere one was caught
880 Another glanced; so, dazzled by my wealth,

859| *1833:* unloved .... *1868:* unloved.   862| *1833:* Deserting me: and old
shades gathering on;   *1868:* me, and   *1888:* Desert <> shades are gathering
fast;   863| *1833:* while its last   *1888:* while the last   864| *1833:* And
chiefly, I am glad that   *1888:* This chiefly, it is gain that   865| *1833:* That love
which I have ever <> thee,   *1868:* thee   *1888:* Somewhat of love I ever
866| *1833:* together,   *1868:* together   867| *1833:* speech is mockery, but <>
come;   *1868:* mockery; but <> come,   *1888:* speech seemed mockery
868| *1833:* And I feel sad; and <> strange;   *1868:* sad, and <> strange   *1888:*
And joy departs, and   869| *1833:* remove.   *1868:* remove,   871| *1833:*
thro' <> began, and which I   *1868:* through   *1888:* which thus I
873| *1833:* That I <> now—   *1868:* now   *1888:* How I   874| *1833:* That I
am sinking fast—yet tho' I sink,   *1868:* fast: yet though   *1888:* That I sink fast <> I
deeplier sink,   875| *1833:* less I feel that thou hast   *1868:* bliss   *1888:* less
song proves one word has <> bliss,   876| *1833:* And that I still may hope to
win it back.   *1888:* Another still may win bliss surely back.   877| *1833:*
know'st, dear friend, I   *1868:* knowest   *1888:* dear, I   878| *1833:* For wild
dreams followed me, and   *1868:* me and   *1888:* For fancies followed thought
and   879| *1833:* And all was indistinct. Ere   *1868:* indistinct; ere   *1888:* And
left all indistinct   880| *1833:* glanced: so dazzled   *1868:* glanced; so, dazzled

45

I knew not which to leave nor which to choose,
For all so floated, nought was fixed and firm.
And then thou said'st a perfect bard was one
Who chronicled the stages of all life.
885 And so thou bad'st me shadow this first stage.
'Tis done, and even now I recognize
The shift, the change from last to past—discern
Faintly how life is truth and truth is good.
And why thou must be mine is, that e'en now
890 In the dim hush of night, that I have done,
Despite the sad forebodings, love looks through—
Whispers,—E'en at the last I have her still,
With her delicious eyes as clear as heaven
When rain in a quick shower has beat down mist,
895 And clouds float white above like broods of swans.
How the blood lies upon her cheek, outspread
As thinned by kisses! only in her lips
It wells and pulses like a living thing,
And her neck looks like marble misted o'er
900 With love-breath,—a Pauline from heights above,
Stooping beneath me, looking up—one look

881| *1833:* Knowing not   *1888:* I knew not   **882|** *1833:* For all my thoughts so < > fixed—   *1868:* fixed.   *1888:* For all so < > fixed and firm.
884| *1833:* Who shadowed out the < > life,   *1888:* Who chronicled the   *1889:* life.   **885|** *1833:* badest me tell this my first stage;—   *1868:* bad'st < > stage.   *1888:* me shadow this first   **886|** *1833:* done: and < > I feel all dim the shift   *1868:* done, and   *1888:* I recognize   **887|** *1833:* Of thought. These are my last thoughts; I discern   *1868:* thought; these   *1888:* The shift, the change from last to past—discern   **888|** *1833:* Faintly immortal life, and truth, and good.   *1868:* life and truth and   *1888:* Faintly how life is truth and truth is good.   **889|** *1833:* now,   *1868:* now   **890|** *1833:* night—that < > done—   *1868:* night, that < > done,   **891|** *1833:* With fears and sad forebodings: I look thro'   *1868:* forebodings, I look through   *1888:* Despite the sad forebodings, love looks through—   **892|** *1833:* And say, "E'en   *1868:* say,—E'en   *1888:* Whispers,—E'en   **893|** *1833:* heaven,   *1868:* heaven   **895|** *1833:* white in the sun like < > swans."   *1868:* swans.   *1888:* white above like.   **896|** *1833:* cheek, all spread   *1888:* cheek, outspread   **897|** *1833:* kisses; only   *1868:* kisses! only   **899|** *1833:* looks, like   *1868:* looks like   **900|** *1833:* love-breath; a dear thing to kiss and love,   *1868:* love-breath,—a   *1888:* a Pauline from heights above,   **901|** *1833:* Standing beneath me—looking out to me,   *1868:* me, looking   *1888:* Stooping beneath me, looking up—one look

46

As I might kill her and be loved the more.

So, love me—me, Pauline, and nought but me,
Never leave loving! Words are wild and weak,
905 Believe them not, Pauline! I stained myself
But to behold thee purer by my side,
To show thou art my breath, my life, a last
Resource, an extreme want: never believe
Aught better could so look on thee; nor seek
910 Again the world of good thoughts left for mine!
There were bright troops of undiscovered suns,
Each equal in their radiant course; there were
Clusters of far fair isles which ocean kept
For his own joy, and his waves broke on them
915 Without a choice; and there was a dim crowd
Of visions, each a part of some grand whole:
And one star left his peers and came with peace
Upon a storm, and all eyes pined for him;
And one isle harboured a sea-beaten ship,
920 And the crew wandered in its bowers and plucked
Its fruits and gave up all their hopes of home;
And one dream came to a pale poet's sleep,
And he said, "I am singled out by God,
No sin must touch me." Words are wild and weak,
925 But what they would express is,—Leave me not,
Still sit by me with beating breast and hair

902| *1833:* loved for it.   *1888:* loved the more.   903| *1833:* Love me—love
me, Pauline, love nought but me;   *1868:* but me,   *1888:* So, love me—me,
904| *1833:* Leave me not. All these words are   *1868:* not! All   *1888:* Never leave
loving! Words   905| *1833:* Pauline. I stooped so low   *1868:* Pauline! I   *1888:*
Pauline! I stained myself   907| *1833:* breath—my life—a   *1868:* breath, my life,
a   908| *1833:* Resource—an   *1868:* Resource, an   909| *1833:* look to
thee, nor   *1868:* look to thee; nor   *1888:* look on thee   910| *1833:* for me.
1868: me!   *1888:* for mine!   912| *1833:* course. There   *1868:* course;
there   913| *1833:* isles, which   *1868:* isles which   915| *1833:* choice.
And   *1868:* choice; and   916| *1833:* of the dim whole.   *1868:* whole:
1888: of some grand whole: 917| *1833:* And a star   *1868:* And one
star   918| *1833:* him.   *1868:* him;   920| *1833:* bowers, and   *1868:*
bowers and   921| *1833:* fruits, and <> hopes for home.   *1868:* fruits and
<> home;   *1888:* hopes of home;   924| *1833:* me." I am very weak,   *1868:*
weak   *1888:* me." Words are wild and weak,   925| *1833:* what I would
1888: what they would   926| *1833:* me—with beating breast, and   *1868:* me
with beating breast and

Loosened, be watching earnest by my side,
Turning my books or kissing me when I
Look up—like summer wind! Be still to me
930 A help to music's mystery which minds fails
To fathom, its solution, no mere clue!
O reason's pedantry, life's rule prescribed!
I hopeless, I the loveless, hope and love.
Wiser and better, know me now, not when
935 You loved me as I was. Smile not! I have
Much yet to dawn on you, to gladden you.

No more of the past! I'll look within no more.
I have too trusted my own lawless wants,
Too trusted my vain self, vague intuition—
940 Draining soul's wine alone in the still night,
And seeing how, as gathering films arose,
As by an inspiration life seemed bare
And grinning in its vanity, while ends
Foul to be dreamed of, smiled at me as fixed
945 And fair, while others changed from fair to foul
A young witch turns an old hag at night.

927| *1833:* Loosened—watching *1868:* Loosened, be watching 928| *1833:*
books, or *1868:* books or 929| *1833:* wind. Be *1868:* wind! Be
930| *1833:* A key to music's mystery, when mind fails, *1868:* mystery when *1888:*
A help to music's mystery which mind fails 931| *1833:* A reason, a solution and
a clue. *1868:* clue! *1888:* To fathom, its solution, no mere clue! 932| *1833:*
You see I have thrown off my prescribed rules: *1888:* O reason's pedantry, life's rule
prescribed! 933| *1833:* I hope in myself—and hope, and pant, and love—
1868: hope and pant and love. *1888:* I hopeless, I the loveless, hope and
love. 934| *1833:* You'll find me better—know me more than when *1868:*
better, know *1888:* Wiser and better, know me now, not when 935| *1833:*
not; I *1868:* not! I 936| *1833:* to gladden you—to dawn on you. *1868:* you,
to *1888:* to dawn on you, to gladden you. 936-937| § no space in
1868 § 937| *1833:* past—I'll < > more— *1868:* past! I'll < > more.
938| *1833:* trusted to my own wild wants— *1868:* wants, *1888:* trusted my own
lawless wants, 939| *1833:* trusted to myself—to intuition. *1868:* myself, to
intuition— *1888:* trusted my vain self, vague intuition— 940| *1833:* Draining
the wine *1888:* Draining soul's wine 941| *1833:* how—as *1868:* how,
as 943| *1833:* vanity, and ends *1888:* vanity, while ends 944| *1833:*
Hard to < > of, stared at < > fixed, *1888:* Foul to < > of, smiled at < >
fixed 945| *1833:* And others suddenly became all foul, *1868:* foul *1888:*
And fair, while others changed from fair to foul 946| *1833:* a fair witch turned
an *1888:* As a young witch turns an

No more of this! We will go hand in hand,
I with thee, even as a child—love's slave,
Looking no farther than his liege commands.

950 And thou hast chosen where this life shall be:
The land which gave me thee shall be our home,
Where nature lies all wild amid her lakes
And snow-swathed mountains and vast pines begirt
With ropes of snow—where nature lies all bare.

955 Suffering none to view her but a race
Or stinted or deformed, like the mute dwarfs
Which wait upon a naked Indian queen.
And there (the time being when the heavens are thick
With storm) I'll sit with thee while thou dost sing

960 Thy native songs, gay as a desert bird
Which crieth as it flies for perfect joy,
Or telling me old stories of dead knights;
Or I will read great lays to thee—how she,
The fair pale sister, went to her chill grave

965 With power to love and to be loved and live:
Or we will go together, like twin gods
Of the infernal world, with scented lamp
Over the dead, to call and to awake,
Over the unshaped images which lie

970 Within my mind's cave: only leaving all,
That tells of the past doubt. So, when spring comes

947| *1833:* this—we   *1868:* this! We   948| *1833:* I will go with < > child,
love's   *1888:* I with < > child—love's   949| *1833:* no further than thy sweet
commands.   *1868:* no farther than commands,   *1888:* than his liege
commands.   949–950| § no space in 1833, 1868 §   950| *1833:* be—
1868: be: 953| *1833:* mountains, and vast pines all girt   *1868:* mountains
and   *1888:* pines begirt   956| *1833:* Most stinted and deformed—like   *1868:*
deformed, like   *1888:* Or stinted or deformed, like   959| *1833:* storms   *1888:*
storm   961| *1833:* Who crieth as he flies   *1888:* Which crieth as it flies
962| *1833:* knights.   *1868:* knights;   963| *1833:* read old lays   *1888:* read
great lays   965| *1833:* love, and < > loved, and live.   *1868:* love and to be
loved and live: 968| *1833:* dead—to call < > awake—   *1868:* dead, to call
< > awake,   970| *1833:* cave—only leaving all *1868:* cave: only leaving
all,   971| *1833:* doubts. So when spring comes,   *1868:* So, when   *1888:*
doubt < > comes

49

With sunshine back again like an old smile,
And the fresh waters and awakened birds
And budding woods await us, I shall be
975 Prepared, and we will question life once more,
Till its old sense shall come renewed by change,
Like some clear thought which harsh words veiled before;
Feeling God loves us, and that all which errs
Is but a dream which death will dissipate.
980 And then what need of longer exile? Seek
My England, and, again there, calm approach
All I once fled from, calmly look on those
The works of my past weakness, as one views
Some scene where danger met him long before.
985 Ah that such pleasant life should be but dreamed!

But whate'er come of it, and though it fade,
And though ere the cold morning all be gone,
As it may be;—tho' music wait to wile,
And strange eyes and bright wine lure, laugh like sin
990 Which steals back softly on a soul half saved,
And I the first deny, decry, despise,

972| *1833:* And sunshine comes again   *1888:* With sunshine back again
973| *1833:* waters, and awakened birds,   *1868:* waters and awakened birds
974| *1833:* us—I   *1868:* us, I   975| *1833:* will go and think again,   *1888:*
will question life once more,   976| *1833:* And all old loves shall come to
us—but changed   *1868:* us, but   *1888:* Till its old sense shall come renewed by
change,   977| *1833:* As some sweet thought   *1888:* Like some clear
thought   978| *1833:* errs,   *1868:* errs   979| *1833:* Is a strange dream
< > dissipate;   *1868:* dissipate.   *1888:* Is but a dream   980| *1833:* then
when I am firm we'll seek again   *1868:* firm, we'll   *1888:* then what need of longer
exile? Seek   981| *1833:* My own land, and again I will approach   *1888:* My
England, and, again there, calm approach   982| *1833:* My old designs, and
calmly look on all   *1888:* All I once fled from, calmly look on those
985| *1833:* Ah! that   *1868:* Ah that   986| *1833:* it—and tho'   *1868:* it, and
though   987| *1833:* tho' < > gone   *1868:* though < > gone,
988| *1833:* wait for me,   *1888:* wait to wile,   989| *1833:* And fair eyes < >
wine, laughing like sin,   *1868:* wine laughing like sin   *1888:* And strange eyes < >
wine lure, laugh like   990| *1833:* saved;   *1868:* saved,   991| *1833:* And
I be first to deny all, and despise   *1888:* And I the first deny, decry, despise,

With this avowal, these intents so fair,—
Still be it all my own, this moment's pride!
No less I make an end in perfect joy.
995 E'en in my brightest time, a lurking fear
Possessed me: I well knew my weak resolves,
I felt the witchery that makes mind sleep
Over its treasure, as one half afraid
To make his riches definite: but now
1000 These feelings shall not utterly be lost,
I shall not know again that nameless care
Lest, leaving all undone in youth, some new
And undreamed end reveal itself too late:
For this song shall remain to tell for ever
1005 That when I lost all hope of such a change,
Suddenly beauty rose on me again.
No less I make an end in perfect joy,
For I, who thus again was visited.
Shall doubt not many another bliss awaits,
1010 And, though this weak soul sink and darkness whelm,
Some little word shall light it, raise aloft,
To where I clearlier see and better love,
As I again go o'er the tracts of thought
Like one who has a right, and I shall live
1015 With poets, calmer, purer still each time,
And beauteous shapes will come for me to seize,
And unknown secrets will be trusted me

992| *1833:* This verse, and these intents which seem so fair; *1868:* fair,— *1888:*
With this avowal, these intents so fair,— 993| *1833:* Still this is all < >
pride, *1888:* Still be it all < > pride! 996| *1833:* me. I *1868:* me:
I 998| *1833:* treasures—as *1868:* treasure, as 999| *1833:*
definite—but *1868:* definite: but 1001| *1833:* care, *1868:* care
1002| *1833:* Lest leaving *1868:* Lest, leaving 1004| *1833:* ever, *1868:*
ever 1006| *1833:* Beauty *1868:* beauty 1008| *1833:* I, having thus
again been visited, *1888:* I, who thus again was visited, 1010| *1833:* And
tho' < > sink, and darkness come, *1868:* And, though < > sink and *1888:*
darkness whelm, 1011| *1833:* it up again, *1888:* it, rise aloft,
1012| *1833:* And I shall see all clearer and love better; *1868:* better, *1888:* To
where I clearlier see and better love, 1013| *1833:* I shall again < > thought,
1868: thought *1888:* As I again 1014| *1833:* As one < > right; and *1868:*
right, and *1888:* Like one 1015| *1833:* poets—calmer—purer *1868:* poets,
calmer, purer 1016| *1833:* come to me again, *1888:* come for me to
seize, 1017| *1833:* me, *1868:* me

51

Which were denied the waverer once; but now
I shall be priest and prophet as of old.

1020 Sun-treader, I believe in God and truth
And love; and as one just escaped from death
Would bind himself in bands of friends to feel
He lives indeed, so, I would lean on thee!
Thou must be ever with me, most in gloom
1025 If such must come, but chiefly when I die,
For I seem, dying, as one going in the dark
To fight a giant: but live thou for ever,
And be to all what thou hast been to me!
All in whom this wakes pleasant thoughts of me
1030 Know my last state is happy, free from doubt
Or touch of fear. Love me and wish me well.

RICHMOND:
October **22**, 1832.

1018| *1833:* were not mine when wavering—but   *1868:* wavering; but   *1888:* were
denied the waverer once; but   1019| *1833:* and lover, as   *1868:* lover as
1888: and prophet as   1020| *1833:* in God, and truth,   *1868:* in God and
truth   1023| *1833:* indeed—so < > thee;   *1868:* indeed, so < > thee!
1024| *1833:* me—most   *1868:* me, most   1025| *1833:* When such shall
come—but   *1868:* come, but   *1888:* If such must come   1026| *1833:* seem
dying   *1868:* seem, dying   1027| *1833:* giant—and live   *1868:* giant: and
1888: giant: but live   1028| *1833:* me—   *1868:* me!   1029| *1833:* me,
1888: me   1030| *1833:* happy—free from doubt,   *1868:* happy, free from
doubt   1031| *1833:* well!   *1888:* well.

"Eyes calm beside thee"

SONNET

"Eyes calm beside thee"

SONNET

EYES, calm beside thee, (Lady couldst thou know!)
   May turn away thick with fast-gathering tears:
I glance not where all gaze: thrilling and low
   Their passionate praises reach thee—my cheek wears
5 Alone no wonder when thou passest by;
Thy tremulous lids bent and suffused reply
To the irrepressible homage which doth glow
   On every lip but mine: if in thine ears
Their accents linger—and thou dost recall
10 Me as I stood, still, guarded, very pale,
Beside each votarist whose lighted brow
Wore worship like an aureole, 'O'er them all
   My beauty,' thou wilt murmur, 'did prevail
Save that one only:'—Lady couldst thou know!
August 17, 1834

---

§ Monthly Repository, New Series, VIII, Oct., 1834, p. 712. §

PARACELSUS

Edited by Morse Peckham

PARACELSUS

INSCRIBED TO

AMÉDÉE DE RIPERT-MONCLAR

BY HIS AFFECTIONATE FRIEND

R. B.

LONDON: *March* 15, 1835

1835: INSCRIBED / TO / THE COMTE A. DE RIPART-MONCLAR, / BY HIS AFFECTIONATE FRIEND, / ROBERT BROWNING 1849: § omitted §   *1863:* INSCRIBED TO / AMÉDÉE DE RIPERT-MONCLAR, / BY HIS AFFECTIONATE FRIEND, / R.B. *March* 15*th*, 1835.   *1868:* RIPERT-MONCLAR / < > FRIEND R.B. / *London, March* 15, 1835.

I am anxious that the reader should not, at the very outset—mistaking my performance for one of a class with which it has nothing in common—judge it by principles on which it was never moulded, and subject it to a standard to which it was never meant to conform.

5 I therefore anticipate his discovery, that it is an attempt, probably more novel than happy, to reverse the method usually adopted by writers whose aim it is to set forth any phenomenon of the mind or the passions, by the operation of persons and events; and that, instead of having recourse to an external machinery of incidents to

10 create and evolve the crisis I desire to produce, I have ventured to display somewhat minutely the mood itself in its rise and progress, and have suffered the agency by which it is influenced and determined, to be generally discernible in its effects alone, and subordinate throughout, if not altogether excluded: and this for a reason. I

15 have endeavoured to write a poem, not a drama; the canons of the drama are well known, and I cannot but think that, inasmuch as they have immediate regard to stage representation, the peculiar advantages they hold out are really such only so long as the purpose for which they were at first instituted is kept in view. I do not very

20 well understand what is called a Dramatic Poem, wherein all those restrictions only submitted to on account of compensating good in the original scheme are scrupulously retained, as though for some special fitness in themselves—and all new facilities placed at an author's disposal by the vehicle he selects, as pertinaciously rejected.

25 It is certain, however, that a work like mine depends more immediately on the intelligence and sympathy of the reader for its success—indeed were my scenes stars it must be his co-operating fancy which, supplying all chasms, shall connect the scattered lights into one constellation—a Lyre or a Crown. I trust for his indulgence towards

30 a poem which had been imagined six months ago; and that even should he think slightingly of the present (an experiment I am in

---

§ Introduction in MS and 1835 only § § MS variants from 1835: §
¹| Reader   ¹¹| Mood   ¹⁴| throughout, if   ¹⁵| Poem < >
Drama;—the canons of the   ¹⁶| Drama   ¹⁷| stage-representation
²²| scheme, are < > retained as tho'   ²³| themselves,—and
²⁶| Reader   ²⁹| constellation -a Lyre

no case likely to repeat) he will not be prejudiced against other productions which may follow in a more popular, and perhaps less difficult form.

15th March, 1835.

PERSONS.

AUREOLUS PARACELSUS, *a student.*
FESTUS *and* MICHAL, *his friends.*
APRILE, *an Italian poet.*

1835: AUREOLOUS PARACELSUS. / FESTUS & MICHAL, his friends. / APRILE. / N.B.—*For the localities and dates, see the note at the end.*   1849: APRILE, an Italian Poet. §
N.B. omitted through 1889. §   1863: AUREOLUS PARACELSUS, a student.

PARACELSUS

1835

PART I. PARACELSUS ASPIRES

S C E N E—*Würzburg; a garden in the environs.* 1512.

FESTUS, PARACELSUS, MICHAL.

PARACELSUS Come close to me, dear friends; still closer; thus!
Close to the heart which, though long time roll by
Ere it again beat quicker, pressed to yours,
As now it beats—perchance a long, long time—
5   At least henceforth your memories shall make
Quiet and fragrant as befits their home.
Nor shall my memory want a home in yours—
Alas, that it requires too well such free
Forgiving love as shall embalm it there!
10   For if you would remember me aright,
As I was born to be, you must forget
All fitful strange and moody waywardness
Which e'er confused my better spirit, to dwell
Only on moments such as these, dear friends!
15   —My heart no truer, but my words and ways
More true to it: as Michal, some months hence,

---

§ Ed. 1835, 1849, 1863, 1868, 1888, 1889. MS in Forster-Dyce Bequest, Victoria and
Albert Museum. For description of MS see Notes. §   SCENE| *MS:* 1507   *1849:*
1512   1| *MS:* Friends < > closer—thus;   *1835:* friends   *1849:* closer;
thus!   2| *MS:* which,—tho'   *1835:* which, though   3| *1835:* press'd
1849: pressed   4| *MS:* beats . . . perchance < > time . . .   *1835:*
beats—perchance < > time—   7| *MS:* yours:—   *1835:* yours.—   *1849:*
yours—   8| *1835:* Alas! that   *1849:* Alas, that   10| *MS:*—For < >
aright . .   *1835:* For < > aright—   *1863:* aright,   11| *MS:*— —As < > be . .
you   *1835:* As < > be—you   *1863:* be, you   12| *MS:* fitful, strange   *1835:*
strange, and < > waywardness,   *1849:* waywardness   *1863:* strange and   *1868:*
fitful strange   13| *MS:* spirit . . . to   *1835:* spirit, to   14| *MS:*
Friends;   *1835:* friends;   *1849:* friends!   15| *MS:* My heart no truer . . . but
1835: truer, but   *1849:*—My heart

Will say, "this autumn was a pleasant time,"
For some few sunny days; and overlook
Its bleak wind, hankering after pining leaves.
20 Autumn would fain be sunny; I would look
Liker my nature's truth: and both are frail,
And both beloved, for all our frailty.

MICHAL   Aureole!

PARACELSUS Drop by drop! she is weeping like a child!
Not so! I am content—more than content;
25 Nay, autumn wins you best by this its mute
Appeal to sympathy for its decay:
Look up, sweet Michal, nor esteem the less
Your stained and drooping vines their grapes bow down,
Nor blame those creaking trees bent with their fruit,
30 That apple-tree with a rare after-birth
Of peeping blooms sprinkled its wealth among!
Then for the winds—what wind that ever raved
Shall vex that ash which overlooks you both,
So proud it wears its berries? Ah, at length,
35 The old smile meet for her, the lady of this
Sequestered nest!—this kingdom, limited
Alone by one old populous green wall
Tenanted by the ever-busy flies,
Grey crickets and shy lizards and quick spiders,

---

¹⁷| *MS:* say this Autumn < > time   *1835:* say, this autumn   *1849:* say, "this < >
time,"   ¹⁸| *MS:* days—and   *1835:* days; and   ¹⁹| *MS:* leaves:—
1835: leaves.   ²⁰| *MS:* sunny — — *I*   *1835:* sunny—*I*   *1863:* sunny;
I   ²¹| *MS:* truth . . . and   *1835:* truth; and   *1863:* truth: and
²²| *MS:* beloved for all their frailty! . . / Aureole! . .   *1835:* frailty! / Aureole! . . .
1849: Aureole!   *1863:* beloved, for   ²³| *MS:* by drop! . . . she   *1835:* by
drop!—she   *1863:* by drop! she   ²⁴| *MS:* so . . . I am content . . . more than
content . . .   *1835:* so . . . I am content—more than content—   *1849*| so! I   *1863:*
than content;   ²⁵| *MS:* Nay Autumn   *1849:* Nay, Autumn   *1863:*
autumn   ²⁶| *MS:* decay . . .   *1849:* decay!   *1863:* decay: ²⁸| *MS:*
The stained < > down—   *1835:* stain'd   *1849:* Your stained < > down,
²⁹| *MS:* Those < > fruit . . . and see   *1835:* fruit—and   *1849:* Nor blame those
< > fruit,   ³¹| *MS:* among—   *1835:* among;   *1849:* among!   ³²| *MS:*
And for the winds . . what   *1835:* winds—what   *1849:* Then for   ³³| *MS:* ash
that overlooks the rest   *1835:* rest,   *1849:* overlooks you both,   *1863:* ash which
overlooks   ³⁴| *MS:* berries . . . Ah! at   *1835:* berries. Ah   *1849:* berries?
Ah   ³⁶| *MS:* kingdom limited   *1835:* Sequester'd nest! This kingdom,
limited   *1849:* Sequestered   *1863:* nest!—this   ³⁷| *1835:* wall,   *1863:*
wall   ³⁹| *MS:* crickets, and shy lizards, and   *1863:* crickets and shy
lizards and

40 Each family of the silver-threaded moss—
    Which, look through near, this way, and it appears
    A stubble-field or a cane-brake, a marsh
    Of bulrush whitening in the sun: laugh now!
    Fancy the crickets, each one in his house,
45 Looking out, wondering at the world—or best,
    Yon painted snail with his gay shell of dew,
    Travelling to see the glossy balls high up
    Hung by the caterpillar, like gold lamps.
    MICHAL In truth we have lived carelessly and well.
50 PARACELSUS And shall, my perfect pair!—each, trust me, born
    For the other; nay, your very hair, when mixed,
    Is of one hue. For where save in this nook
    Shall you two walk, when I am far away,
    And wish me prosperous fortune? Stay: that plant
55 Shall never wave its tangles lightly and softly,
    As a queen's languid and imperial arm
    Which scatters crowns among her lovers, but you
    Shall be reminded to predict to me
    Some great success! Ah see, the sun sinks broad
60 Behind Saint Saviour's: wholly gone, at last!
    FESTUS Now, Aureole, stay those wandering eyes awhile!
    You are ours to-night, at least; and while you spoke

40| MS: All families <> moss . . .   1835: moss—   1849: Each family
41| MS:—Which look thro', near, this way,—and   1835: Which <> through <>
way, and   1849: Which, look   1863: through near, this   42| MS: stubble-field,
or a cane-brake . . . a   1835: crane-brake—a   1849: cane-brake   1863: stubble-field or
a cane-brake, a   45| MS: out and wondering <> world: . . or best,   1835:
world—or   1849: out, wondering   46| MS: The painted snail, with   1849:
Yon painted   1863: snail with   48| 1849: lamps!   1863: lamps.
49| MS: truth, we <> well!   1835: truth we   1863: well.   50| MS: Pair!
. . each   1835: pair—each   1863: pair!—each   51| MS: other — — nay your
very hair when mixed   1835: other—nay <> hair, when mixed,   1849: other; nay,
your   52| MS: hue — — for where beside this   1835: hue. For   1849: where
save in this   54| MS: fortune? — — stay,—that   1835: fortune? . . . Stay! that
1849: fortune? Stay! Whene'er   1863: Stay: that plant   55| MS: softly   1835:
softly,   1849: That plant shall wave   1863: Shall never wave   56| MS:
Queen's   1835: queen's   57| MS: lovers, . . but   1835: lovers, but   1849:
lovers, you   1863: lovers, but you   58| MS: predict some great   1849:
predict to me   59| MS: Success to me: . . . Ah, see! the   1835: to me. Ah
1849: Some great success! Ah   1863: see, the   1868: Ah see   60| MS: St.
Saviour's — — wholly   1835: Saviour's . . . wholly   1849: Saviour's: wholly   1863:
Saint   61| MS: awhile—   1835: awhile: 1849: awhile!   62| MS:—You
<> least—and   1835: You <> to-night at least; and

Of Michal and her tears, I thought that none
Could willing leave what he so seemed to love:
65 But that last look destroys my dream—that look
As if, where'er you gazed, there stood a star!
How far was Würzburg with its church and spire
And garden-walls and all things they contain,
From that look's far alighting?

PARACELSUS   I but spoke
70 And looked alike from simple joy to see
The beings I love best, shut in so well
From all rude chances like to be my lot,
That, when afar, my weary spirit,—disposed
To lose awhile its care in soothing thoughts
75 Of them, their pleasant features, looks and words,—
Needs never hesitate, nor apprehend
Encroaching trouble may have reached them too,
Nor have recourse to fancy's busy aid
And fashion even a wish in their behalf
80 Beyond what they possess already here;
But, unobstructed, may at once forget
Itself in them, assured how well they fare.
Beside, this Festus knows he holds me one

63| *MS:* tears, § illegible by crossing out § that § replaced by § tears, I thought
1849: tears, the thought came back   *1863:* tears, I thought that none   64| *MS:*
love . . .   *1835:* seem'd   *1849:* That none could leave < > seemed to love: *1863:*
Could willing leave   65| *MS:* dream . . . that look!   *1835:* dream—that   *1863:*
look   66| *MS:* if where'er you gazed there   *1849:* if, where'er you gazed,
there   67| *MS:* — — How   *1835:* How < > Würzburg, with < > spire,
1863: Würzburg with < > spire   68| *MS:* all that they   *1835:* garden-walls,
and   *1849:* all things they   *1863:* garden-walls and   70| *1835:*
look'd < > joy, to   *1849:* looked   *1863:* joy to   71| *MS:* I best love, so well
shut in   *1835:* love so   *1849:* I love best, shut in so well   72| *1835:*
lot;   *1849:* lot,   73| *MS:* That, far from them, my < > spirit, disposed
1849: That, when afar, my < > spirit,—disposed   74| *MS:* cares   *1849:*
care   75| *MS:* looks, and words — — —   *1835:* words,   *1849:*
words,—   *1863:* looks and   76| *MS:* hesitate—nor   *1835:* hesitate, nor   *1849:*
Need   *1863:* Needs   77| *MS:* Incroaching < > too, . . . § written over by §
too,—   *1835:* Encroaching < > reach'd < > too;   *1849:* reached < > too,
78| *MS:* Fancy's   *1863:* fancy's   79| *MS:* Even to frame a   *1849:* To fashion
even a   *1863:* And fashion   80| *MS:* here, . . . § written over by §
here,—   82| *MS:* them,—assured < > they are.   *1835:* them—assured   *1849:*
them, assured   *1863:* they fare.   83| *MS:* — — This Festus knows, beside, he
1835: This < > knows; beside   *1849:* Beside, this Festus knows, he thinks me
1863: knows he holds me

Whom quiet and its charms arrest in vain,
85 One scarce aware of all the joys I quit,
Too filled with airy hopes to make account
Of soft delights his own heart garners up:
Whereas behold how much our sense of all
That's beauteous proves alike! When Festus learns
90 That every common pleasure of the world
Affects me as himself; that I have just
As varied appetite for joy derived
From common things; a stake in life, in short,
Like his; a stake which rash pursuit of aims
95 That life affords not, would as soon destroy;—
He may convince himself that, this in view,
I shall act well advised. And last, because,
Though heaven and earth and all things were at stake,
Sweet Michal must not weep, our parting eve.
100 FESTUS True: and the eve is deepening, and we sit
As little anxious to begin our talk
As though to-morrow I could hint of it
As we paced arm-in-arm the cheerful town
At sun-dawn; or could whisper it by fits
105 (Trithemius busied with his class the while)
In that dim chamber where the noon-streaks peer

84| MS: vain— 1835: vain; 1849: charms attract in vain, 1863: charms arrest
in 85| MS: joys he quits . . . 1835: quits; 1849: joys I quit,
86| 1835: fill'd 1863: filled 87| MS: up . . . . 1835: up: 1849: delights
which free hearts garner 1863: delights his own heart garners 88| MS: . .
Whereas 1835: Whereas, behold 1868: Whereas behold 89| MS: That's
beautiful, is one!—and when he learns 1835: one! And 1849: That's beauteous
proves alike! When Festus learns 90| MS: common sight he can enjoy 1849:
common pleasure of the world 91| MS: himself—that 1835: himself;
that 92| MS: joys 1849: appetites for joy 1863: appetite 93| MS:
things—a 1835: things; a 94| MS: his—and which a rash 1835: his; and
1849: his; a stake which rash 95| MS: That it affords not would < > destroy—
— — — 1835: destroy;— 1849: That life affords not, would 96| MS: himself,
that, knowing this, 1849: that, this in view, 1863: himself that 97| MS:
advised: and last, because 1835: because, 1863: advised. And 98| MS:
Tho' Heaven < > stake 1835: Though heaven and earth, and all things, were at
stake, 1863: earth and all things were 99| MS: Eve. 1835: weep our < >
eve. 1849: weep, our < > eve! 100| MS: True:—and < > deepening, and
1835: True: and < > deepening, and 102| MS: tho' tomorrow 1835: though
to-morrow 1849: could open it 1863: could hint of it 103| MS: arm in
arm 1863: arm-in-arm 104| MS: sundawn—or 1835: sun-dawn; or 1849:
sun-dawn; and continue it 1863: sun-dawn; or could whisper it 105| 1849:
(Old Tritheim 1863: (Trithemius

Half-frightened by the awful tomes around;
Or in some grassy lane unbosom all
From even-blush to midnight: but, to-morrow!
110 Have I full leave to tell my inmost mind?
We have been brothers, and henceforth the world
Will rise between us:—all my freest mind?
'Tis the last night, dear Aureole!

PARACELSUS   Oh, say on!
Devise some test of love, some arduous feat
115 To be performed for you: say on! If night
Be spent the while, the better! Recall how oft
My wondrous plans and dreams and hopes and fears
Have—never wearied you, oh no!—as I
Recall, and never vividly as now,
120 Your true affection, born when Einsiedeln
And its green hills were all the world to us;
And still increasing to this night which ends
My further stay at Würzburg. Oh, one day
You shall be very proud! Say on, dear friends!
125 FESTUS In truth? 'Tis for my proper peace, indeed,
Rather than yours; for vain all projects seem

107| MS: Half frightened < > around— 1835: frighten'd < > around; 1849: frightened 1868: Half-frightened 108| MS:—Or 1835: Or 1849: And here at home unbosom all the rest 1863: Or in some grassy lane unbosom all 109| MS: midnight . . . . but to-morrow 1835: midnight . . . but to-morrow! . . . 1849: midnight: but, to-morrow! . . . 1863: to-morrow! 110 | MS: — — I have full 1835: I 1849: Have I full 111| MS:—We < > brothers and 1835: We < > brothers, and 1849: We two were brothers 1863: We have been brothers 112| MS: Will be between us; — — all < > mind? — — 1835: us . . . . all < > mind? . . . 1849: Will rise between us:—all < > mind? 113| MS: Tis 1835: 'Tis 114| MS:—Devise < > love — — some § written over by § love—some 1835: Devise 1863: love, some 115| MS: you . . . say on, . . . if § written over by § you—say on,—if 1835: perform'd for you—say on; if 1849: performed < > on! If 1863: you: say 116| MS: better: . . . recall § written over by § better:—recall 1835: better: recall 1849: better! Recall 117| 1835: plans, and dreams, and hopes, and fears, 1863: plans and dreams and hopes and fears 118| MS: you . . oh, no! . . as 1835: you . . . oh, no! . . . as 1863: you, oh, no!—as 120| MS: affection born 1835: affection, born 121| MS: us,— 1835: us, 1863: us; 122| 1835: night, which 1863: night which 123| MS: Würzburg . . . Oh you shall 1849: Oh, one day 1863: Würzburg. Oh 124–125| MS: Be very proud one day! . . . say < > Friend; / Talk volumes, I shall still be in arrear. / FESTUS In truth? . . . 'tis 1835: friend; < > truth? 'Tis 1849: You shall be very proud! Say < > friends! / FESTUS 126| MS: yours . . for vain it looks, to seek 1835: yours—for < > looks to 1849: yours; for vain all projects seem

To stay your course: I said my latest hope
Is fading even now. A story tells
Of some far embassy despatched to win
130 The favour of an eastern king, and how
The gifts they offered proved but dazzling dust
Shed from the ore-beds native to his clime.
Just so, the value of repose and love,
I meant should tempt you, better far than I
135 You seem to comprehend; and yet desist
No whit from projects where repose nor love
Has part.

PARACELSUS Once more? Alas! As I foretold.

FESTUS A solitary briar the bank puts forth
To save our swan's nest floating out to sea.

140 PARACELSUS Dear Festus, hear me. What is it you wish?
That I should lay aside my heart's pursuit,
Abandon the sole ends for which I live,
Reject God's great commission, and so die!
You bid me listen for your true love's sake:
145 Yet how has grown that love? Even in a long
And patient cherishing of the self-same spirit
It now would quell; as though a mother hoped
To stay the lusty manhood of the child

127| MS: course — — the last hopes I conceived   1835: course—the   1849: course:
I said my latest hope   128| MS: Are fading < > now:—old stories tell   1835:
now. Old   1849: Is fading < > now. A story tells   129| 1835: despatch'd
1849: despatched to buy   1863: dispatched to win   1888: despatched
130| MS: Eastern king,—and   1835: eastern king, and   131| MS: gifts it
proffered were but   1835: proffer'd   1849: gifts they offered proved but
132| MS: to the clime;—   1835: clime;   1849: to his clime;   1863: clime.
133| MS: — Just < > love   1835: Just < > love,   134| MS: you .. better
§ written over by § you—better   1835: you, better   135| MS: comprehend ...
and still desist   1835: comprehend—and   1849: and yet desist   1863: comprehend;
and   136| MS: where they have no part: 1835: part.   1849: where repose
nor love   137–138| MS: PARACELSUS Alas! as I forbode; this weighty talk / Has for
its end no other than to revive ...... / FESTUS   1835: forbode, this < > revive ...
1849: Have part. PARACELSUS Once more? Alas! as I forbode! FESTUS / 1888: Has
140| MS: me;— — what § edited? to § me.— — What   1835: me. What
141| MS: pursuit— § over §,   1835: pursuit,   142| MS: live— § over §,   1835:
live,   143| MS: commission ... and   1835: commission—and   1863:
commission, and   144| MS: .. And still I listen < > sake.   1835: And   1849:
sake: 145| MS: even   1835: Even   146| 1835: selfsame   1888: self-
same   147| MS: quell ... as tho' a mother should hope   1835: quell—as
though   1849: quell; as < > mother hoped

Once weak upon her knees. I was not born
150 Informed and fearless from the first, but shrank
From aught which marked me out apart from men:
I would have lived their life, and died their death,
Lost in their ranks, eluding destiny:
But you first guided me through doubt and fear,
155 Taught me to know mankind and know myself;
And now that I am strong and full of hope,
That, from my soul, I can reject all aims
Save those your earnest words made plain to me,
Now that I touch the brink of my design,
160 When I would have a triumph in their eyes,
A glad cheer in their voices—Michal weeps,
And Festus ponders gravely!

FESTUS   When you deign
To hear my purpose . . .

PARACELSUS   Hear it? I can say
Beforehand all this evening's conference!
165 'Tis this way, Michal, that he uses: first,
Or he declares, or I, the leading points
Of our best scheme of life, what is man's end
And what God's will; no two faiths e'er agreed

149| *MS:* knees; I   *1835:* knees. I   **150|** *1835:* Inform'd   *1849:*
Informed   **151|** *MS:* Men . . § edited? to § Men.   *1835:* mark'd < > men.
1849: marked   **152|** *MS:* life, and striven their strife,   *1835:* strife—   *1849:*
life, and died their death,   **153|** *MS:* Eluding Destiny, if that might be, . . .
§ written over by § be,—   *1835:* be—   *1849:* Lost in their ranks, eluding
destiny;   **154|** *MS:* thro'   *1835:* through   **155|** *MS:* And taught < >
know them and < > myself; . . . § written over by § myself;—   *1835:* myself;   *1849:*
Taught me to know mankind and   **156|** *MS:* hope § edited? to § hope—   *1835:*
hope;   *1849:* hope,   **157|** *MS:*—That I can from my soul reject   *1835:*
aims,   *1849:* That, from my soul, I can reject all aims   **158|** *MS:* me; . .
§ written over by § me;—   *1835:* me;   **159|** *MS:* Now, that < > design,—
1835: design,   *1863:* Now that   **160|** *MS:*—When   *1835:* When
161| *MS:* voices . . . Michal   *1835:* voices—Michal   **162|** *MS:* you shall
1849: you deign   **163|** *MS:* Have learned my purpose . . . . PARACELSUS Learned
it? . . . I   *1835:* learn'd my purpose . . . PARACELSUS Learn'd it? I   *1849:* To hear my
< > PARACELSUS Hear it   **164|** *MS:* this conference will produce:—   *1835:*
produce.   *1849:* this evening's conference!   **165|** *MS:* . . 'Tis § written over
by § —'Tis < > uses; . . . first, § written over by § uses;—first,   *1835:* 'Tis < > uses:
first,   **167|** *MS:* our belief in what is Man's true End   *1835:* man's < > end
1849: our best scheme of life, what is man's end,   *1868:* end   **168|** *MS:* And
God's apparent will . . . no < > ever   *1835:* will—no   *1849:* And what God's will—no
< > e'er   *1863:* will; no

As his with mine. Next, each of us allows
170 Faith should be acted on as best we may;
Accordingly, I venture to submit
My plan, in lack of better, for pursuing
The path which God's will seems to authorize.
Well, he discerns much good in it, avows
175 This motive worthy, that hope plausible,
A danger here to be avoided, there
An oversight to be repaired: in fine
Our two minds go together—all the good
Approved by him, I gladly recognize,
180 All he counts bad, I thankfully discard,
And nought forbids my looking up at last
For some stray comfort in his cautious brow.
When, lo! I learn that, spite of all, there lurks
Some innate and inexplicable germ
185 Of failure in my scheme; so that at last
It all amounts to this—the sovereign proof
That we devote ourselves to God, is seen
In living just as though no God there were;

169-170| *MS:* Agreed as ours agree:—next, each allows / These points are no mere
visionary truths: / But, once determined, it remains alone / To act upon them straight
as < > may:— *1835:* agree: next < > determin'd < > may: *1849:* As his with
mine: next, each of us allows / Faith should be acted on as *1863:* mine. Next
may; 172| *1849:* A plan *1863:* My plan 173-174| *MS:* authorize . . . /
. . A broad plan, vague and ill defined enough, / But courting censure and imploring
aid: . . . / Well . . . he < > it—avows § written over by § aid:— *1835:* authorize—/
A < > aid: Well—he < > it, avows *1849:* authorize: / Well *1863:* Well,
he 175| *MS:* plausible,— *1835:* plausible, 176| *MS:* —A danger, here,
to be avoided—there, *1835:* A danger here *1863:* here to be avoided, there
177| *MS:* repaired . . in fine, § written over by § repaired—in *1835:* repair'd: in
fine *1849:* repaired: at last *1863:* repaired: in fine 178| *MS:* Our minds
go every way together . . all good *1835:* together—all *1849:* Our two minds go
together—all the good 179| *1835:* recognize; *1863:* recognize,
180| *MS:* discard; *1863:* discard, 181| *MS:* forbids me to look *1849:*
forbids my looking 182| *MS:* brow——— *1835:* brow— *1863:*
brow. 185| *MS:* schemes . . so § written over by § schemes—so *1835:*
schemes; so *1863:* scheme 186| *MS:* this . . . the § written over by §
this—the 187| *MS:* ourselves wholly to God *1849:* ourselves to God
188| *MS:* Is in a life as tho' < > were:— *1835:* though < > were: *1849:* In living
just as though there were no God: *1863:* though no God there were;

A life which, prompted by the sad and blind
190 Folly of man, Festus abhors the most;
But which these tenets sanctify at once,
Though to less subtle wits it seems the same,
Consider it how they may.
MICHAL   Is it so, Festus?
He speaks so calmly and kindly: is it so?
195 PARACELSUS Reject those glorious visions of God's love
And man's design; laugh loud that God should send
Vast longings to direct us; say how soon
Power satiates these, or lust, or gold; I know
The world's cry well, and how to answer it.
200 But this ambiguous warfare . . .
FESTUS   . . . Wearies so
That you will grant no last leave to your friend
To urge it?—for his sake, not yours? I wish
To send my soul in good hopes after you;
Never to sorrow that uncertain words
205 Erringly apprehended, a new creed
Ill understood, begot rash trust in you,
Had share in your undoing.
PARACELSUS   Choose your side,

189| *MS:* . . A < > which prompted   *1835:* which, prompted   190| *MS:* Man
< > most,   *1835:* man < > most—   *1849:* Lusts of the world,
Festus   *1863:* Folly of man, Festus   191| *1835:* once—   *1849:* once;   *1863:*
once,   192| *MS:* Tho' < > same   *1835:* Though < > same,   193| *MS:*
may: *1835:* may.   *1888:* Festus   *1889:* Festus?   194| *MS:* kindly . . is
1835: kindly—is   *1863:* kindly: is   196| *MS:* Man's design—laugh < > that he
should   *1835.* man's design; laugh   *1849:* that God should   197| *MS:*
us; . . or find out   *1835:* us; or   *1849:* us; say how soon   198–200| *MS:* How
else they may be satiated: . . but § written over by § satiated:—but this / Ambiguous
warfare wearies: — FESTUS Not so much   *1835:* satiated: but / wearies . . . FESTUS
1849: Power satiates these, or lust, or gold; I know / The world's cry well, and how
to answer it! / But this ambiguous warfare . . . FESTUS . . . Wearies so   *1863:* lust or
1868: lust, or   201| *1835:* friend,   *1849:* friend   202| *MS:*—And for his
own sake, not for your's? — I   *1835:* And < > yours? I   *1849:* To urge it?—for his
sake, not yours   203| *MS:* you . . . § written over by § you—   *1849:* you;
204| *1835:* words,   *1868:* words   205| *MS:* apprehended—a   *1835:* creed,
1863: apprehended, a new creed   206| *MS:* you . . . § written over by § you—
1835: understood—begot   *1849:* you,   *1863:* understood, begot   207| *MS:*
undoing— — — π PARACELSUS Choose your party: . . § written over by § party:—   *1835:*
undoing. π PARACELSUS < > party: *1849:* And shared < > your side: *1863:* Had
share < > side,

Hold or renounce: but meanwhile blame me not
Because I dare to act on your own views,
210 Nor shrink when they point onward, nor espy
A peril where they most ensure success.
FESTUS Prove that to me—but that! Prove you abide
Within their warrant, nor presumptuous boast
God's labour laid on you; prove, all you covet
215 A mortal may expect; and, most of all,
Prove the strange course you now affect, will lead
To its attainment—and I bid you speed,
Nay, count the minutes till you venture forth!
You smile; but I had gathered from slow thought—
220 Much musing on the fortunes of my friend—
Matter I deemed could not be urged in vain;
But it all leaves me at my need: in shreds
And fragments I must venture what remains.
MICHAL Ask at once, Festus, wherefore he should scorn . . .
225 FESTUS Stay, Michal: Aureole, I speak guardedly
And gravely, knowing well, whate'er your error,
This is no ill-considered choice of yours,
No sudden fancy of an ardent boy.
Not from your own confiding words alone
230 Am I aware your passionate heart long since

208| MS: renounce: . . but § written over by § renounce:—but   1835: renounce:
but   209| MS: views   1835: views—   1849: views,   210| MS:—Nor
< > onward . . nor § written over by § onward—nor spy out   1835: Nor shrink   1849:
onward, nor espy   211| MS: success: . . . § written over by § success:— 1835:
success . . .   1849: success.   212| MS: that:—that you   1835: that: that   1849:
that! Prove you   213| MS: warrant—nor   1849: warrant, nor   214| MS:
you; . . . that § written over by § you;—that all   1835: you; that   1849: you; prove,
all   215| MS: expect;—and most of all   1835: expect; and, most of all,
216| MS: That the   1849: Prove the   217| MS: attainment . . . and < >
speed!   1835: attainment—and   1849: speed,   218| MS: And count < > 'till
< > forth.   1835: till   1849: Nay, count < > forth!   219| MS: You will
smile,—but < > thought,   1835: smile; but < > gather'd < > thought—   1849:
You smile; but < > gathered   220| MS: friend,   1835: friend—
221| 1835: deem'd   1849: deemed   222| MS: need—in   1835: need: in
223| MS: remains: . . . § written over by § remains:—   1835: remains.
225| MS: Michal;—Aureole   1835: Michal: Aureole   226| MS: gravely, . .
knowing   1835: gravely, knowing   227| MS: your's,   1835: ill-consider'd
< > yours—   1849: ill-considered   228| MS: boy:—   1835: boy.
229| MS: ——Not   1835: Not   230| MS: heart has long   1849: heart long
since

Gave birth to, nourished and at length matures
This scheme. I will not speak of Einsiedeln,
Where I was born your elder by some years
Only to watch you fully from the first:
235 In all beside, our mutual tasks were fixed
Even then—'twas mine to have you in my view
As you had your own soul and those intents
Which filled it when, to crown your dearest wish,
With a tumultuous heart, you left with me
240 Our childhood's home to join the favoured few
Whom, here, Trithemius condescends to teach
A portion of his lore: and not one youth
Of those so favoured, whom you now despise,
Came earnest as you came, resolved, like you,
245 To grasp all, and retain all, and deserve
By patient toil a wide renown like his.
Now, this new ardour which supplants the old
I watched, too; 'twas significant and strange,
In one matched to his soul's content at length

231-232| MS: Nourished, and has at length matured a plan / To give yourself up
wholly to one End: . . . . / . . . I < > Einsiedeln,—'twas as 1835: Nourish'd < >
matured, a plan / < > end / I < > Einsiedeln; 'twas 1849: Gave birth to,
nourished, and at length matures / This scheme. I < > Einsiedeln, 1868:
nourished and 233| MS: I had been born 1849: Where I was born
234| MS: first:— 1835: first: 235| 1835: fix'd 1849: fixed
236| MS: then . . . 'twas § written over by § then— 'twas 237-238| MS: soul;
. . accordingly §written over by § soul;—accordingly / I could go further back, and
trace each bough / Of this wide-branching tree even to its birth . . § written over by §
birth— / . . Each § written over by §—Each fullgrown passion to its outspring faint, —
— / But I shall only dwell upon the intents / Which filled you when 1835: soul:
accordingly // < > birth; / Each full-grown < > faint; // < > fill'd 1849: soul
and those intents / Which filled it when 239| MS: heart you 1835: heart,
you 240| MS: childhoods' 1835: favour'd 1849: childhood's < >
favoured 241| MS: Whom famed Trithemius 1849: Whom, here at
Würzburg, Tritheim deigns to 1863: here, Trithemius condescends to
242| MS: lore . . . . and not the dullest 1835: lore—and 1849: lore: and not the
best 1863: not one youth 243| MS: favoured—whom < > despise 1835:
favour'd, whom < > despise, 1849: favoured 244| MS: Was earnest as you
were, . . resolved § written over by § were,—resolved like you 1835: were; resolved,
like you, 1849: Came earnest as you came; resolved 1863: you came, resolved
246-247| MS: his: . . . / . . . Now, just as well have I descried the growth / Of this
< > old: . . § written over by § old:— 1835: his. / Now < > / < > old: 1849:
his. / And this < > old, 1863: Now, this 1888: old 248| MS: watched it
. . 'twas § written over by § it—'twas < > strange 1835: watch'd < > strange,
1849: watched, too; 'twas 249| MS: one, matched 1835: one match'd
1849: matched

250 With rivals in the search for wisdom's prize,
    To see the sudden pause, the total change;
    From contest, the transition to repose—
    From pressing onward as his fellows pressed,
    To a blank idleness, yet most unlike
255 The dull stagnation of a soul, content,
    Once foiled, to leave betimes a thriveless quest.
    That careless bearing, free from all pretence
    Even of contempt for what it ceased to seek—
    Smiling humility, praising much, yet waiving
260 What it professed to praise—though not so well
    Maintained but that rare outbreaks, fierce and brief,
    Revealed the hidden scorn, as quickly curbed.
    That ostentatious show of past defeat,
    That ready acquiescence in contempt,
265 I deemed no other than the letting go
    His shivered sword, of one about to spring
    Upon his foe's throat; but it was not thus:
    Not that way looked your brooding purpose then.
    For after-signs disclosed, what you confirmed,
270 That you prepared to task to the uttermost
    Your strength, in furtherance of a certain aim

250| *MS:* Wisdom's *1863:* wisdom's 251| *MS:* pause— — the § written over
by § pause—the < > change— — — § written over by § change— *1835:* pause, the
< > change, *1849:* change; 252| *MS:* contest that transition to repose
. . . *1835:* contest, that < > repose— *1849:* contest, the transition
253| *MS:* pressed *1835:* press'd, *1849:* pressed, 254| *1835:* idleness; yet
1863: idleness, yet 255| *MS:* soul content, *1835:* content— *1849:* soul,
content, 256| *MS:* quest; *1835:* foil'd—to *1849:* foiled, to < >
quest. 258| *MS:* seek . . . § written over by § seek— 259| *MS:*—Smiling
< > much yet *1835:* Smiling < > much, yet 260| *MS:* praise . . yet not
1835: profess'd to praise . . . yet *1849:* professed to praise—though not
261| *MS:* Secured but < > outbreaks—fierce and brief *1835:* outbreaks, fierce and
brief, *1849:* Maintained but < > fierce as brief, *1863:* fierce and brief
262| *MS:* scorn—as < > curbed . . . *1835:* Reveal'd < > curb'd . . . *1849:*
Revealed < > scorn, as < > curbed— *1863:* curbed. 263| *MS:* . . That < >
defeat— *1835:* That *1849:* defeat, 264| *MS:* contempt . . . . . . § written over
by § contempt— — *1835:* contempt— *1849:* contempt, 265| *1835:* deem'd
1849: deemed 266| *1835:* shiver'd *1849:* shivered 267| *MS:* throat . . .
but < > thus: — — § written over by § thus:— *1835:* thus: *1849:* throat; but
268| *MS:* then;— *1835:* look'd *1849:* looked < > then. 269| *MS:* But after-
signs disclosed, and you *1835:* confirm'd, *1849:* For after-signs disclosed, what you
confirmed, 271| *1835:* aim, *1863:* aim

81

Which—while it bore the name your rivals gave
Their own most puny efforts—was so vast
In scope that it included their best flights,
275 Combined them, and desired to gain one prize
In place of many,—the secret of the world,
Of man, and man's true purpose, path and fate.
—That you, not nursing as a mere vague dream
This purpose, with the sages of the past,
280 Have struck upon a way to this, if all
You trust be true, which following, heart and soul,
You, if a man may, dare aspire to KNOW:
And that this aim shall differ from a host
Of aims alike in character and kind,
285 Mostly in this,—that in itself alone
Shall its reward be, not an alien end
Blending therewith; no hope nor fear nor joy
Nor woe, to elsewhere move you, but this pure
Devotion to sustain you or betray:
290 Thus you aspire.
    PARACELSUS   You shall not state it thus:
I should not differ from the dreamy crew
You speak of. I profess no other share
In the selection of my lot, than this

272| *MS:* Which— § above § , while   *1835:* Which—while   273| *MS:* To their
most < > efforts, was   *1835:* efforts—was   *1849:* Their own most   276| *MS:*
many—the Secret < > World   *1835:* secret < > world—   *1849:* many,—the < >
world,   277| *MS:* Of Man, and Man's < > path, and fate:—   *1835:* Of man,
and man's < > fate: *1863:* fate.   278| *MS:* That you, . . not < > as a
lovely dream   *1835:* you, not   *1849:*—That < > a mere vague dream
279| *MS:* Sages of old Time . . .   *1835:* sages < > Time,   *1845:* of the Past,
1868: past,   282| *MS:* Know: . . . § in large print; written over by §
Know:—   *1835:* KNOW: 284| *1835:* kind—   *1849:* kind,   285| *MS:*
this;—that   *1835:* this; that   *1849:* this,—to seek its own reward   *1863:* this,—that
in itself alone,   *1868:* alone   286| *MS:* be . . . not   *1835:* be—not   *1849:* In
itself only, not   *1863:* Shall its reward be, not   287| *MS:* therewith . . no
1835: therewith—no hope, nor fear, nor joy,   *1849:* To blend therewith; no   *1863:*
Blending therewith   *1868:* hope nor fear nor joy   288| *MS:* woe shall
elsewhere   *1835:* woe, shall < > you; but   *1849:* woe, to elsewhere < > you,
but   289| *MS:* Devotion shall sustain or shall undo you,—   *1835:* you: *1849:*
Devotion to sustain you or betray: 290| *MS:*—This you intend;—PARACELSUS
< > thus . . .   *1835:* This you intend. PARACELSUS < > thus: *1849:* Thus you
aspire. PARACELSUS   291| *MS:* . . I   *1835:* I   292| *MS:* of:—I   *1835:* of.
I   293| *MS:* than in   *1849:* than this,   *1863:* this

My ready answer to the will of God
295 Who summons me to be his organ. All
Whose innate strength supports them shall succeed
No better than the sages.

FESTUS   Such the aim, then,
God sets before you; and 'tis doubtless need
That he appoint no less the way of praise
300 Than the desire to praise; for, though I hold
With you, the setting forth such praise to be
The natural end and service of a man,
And hold such praise is best attained when man
Attains the general welfare of his kind—
305 Yet this, the end, is not the instrument.
Presume not to serve God apart from such
Appointed channel as he wills shall gather
Imperfect tributes, for that sole obedience
Valued perchance! He seeks not that his altars
310 Blaze, careless how, so that they do but blaze.
Suppose this, then; that God selected you

294| *1835:* God, *1849:* A ready < > God *1863:* My ready   295| *MS:*
organ——he § written over in pencil by § organ—he   *1835:* organ: he   *1849:* organ:
all   *1863:* His organ. All   *1868:* his   296| *MS:* supports him shall   *1849:*
supports them shall   297| *MS:* Sages;— FESTUS Such the aim § *the* written
above the line §   *1835:* sages. FESTUS   *1849:* than your sages   *1868:* than the
sages   298| *MS:* you;— § written over by pencil as § you; and 'tis, doubtless,
need   299| *MS:* Praise   *1835:* praise   *1863:* He   *1868:* he   300| *MS:*
praise;—for, tho'   *1835:* praise; for, though   302| *MS:* Man,—   *1834:* man—
1849: man,   303| *MS:* And that such praise seemed best attained when he
1835: attain'd   *1849:* And think such praise is best attained when man   *1863:* And
hold such   304| *MS:* kind, ... § written over by § Kind, ...   *1835:*
kind—   305–306| *MS:* Yet, *that,* the *instrument,* is not the *end:*— / There is a
curse upon the earth—let Man / Presume   *1835:* end. / < > earth; let man   *1849:*
Yet, this, the end, is not the instrument / Presume   307| *1849:* He   *1868:*
he   308| *MS:* tributes—for   *1863:* tributes, for   309| *MS:*
perchance:—He   *1835:* perchance. He   *1849:* Valued, perchance   *1863:* that His
altars   *1868:* Valued perchance < > that his altars   *1888:* perchance! He
310–311| *MS:* Blaze—careless < > but blaze . . . . / Tho' I doubt much if he consent that
we / Discover this great secret . . . I § written over by § secret—I know well / You will
allege no other comprehends / The work in question save its labourer: / —I shall
assume the Aim approved—and you / That I am implicated in the issue / Not simply
as your friend, but as yourself— / —As tho' it were my task, that you perform, / And
some plague dogged my heels till it were done . . . . / ——Suppose this owned,
then,—you are born to Know,— § in large print §   *1835:* blaze. / —Though < > /
< > secret I < > /// < > aim improved; and you /// As though < > task that you
perform, / < > plague dogg'd < > done. / Suppose this own'd then; you < > KNOW.

To KNOW (heed well your answers, for my faith
Shall meet implicitly what they affirm)
I cannot think you dare annex to such
315   Selection aught beyond a steadfast will,
An intense hope; nor let your gifts create
Scorn or neglect of ordinary means
Conducive to success, make destiny
Dispense with man's endeavour. Now, dare you search
320   Your inmost heart, and candidly avow
Whether you have not rather wild desire
For this distinction than security
Of its existence? whether you discern
The path to the fulfilment of your purpose
325   Clear as that purpose—and again, that purpose
Clear as your yearning to be singled out
For its pursuer. Dare you answer this?
PARACELSUS [*after a pause*] No, I have nought to fear! Who will may know
The secret'st workings of my soul. What though
330   It be so?—if indeed the strong desire
Eclipse the aim in me?—if splendour break
Upon the outset of my path alone,
And duskest shade succeed? What fairer seal
Shall I require to my authentic mission
335   Than this fierce energy?—this instinct striving

1849: but blaze. / Suppose this, then; that God selected you   *1863:* Blaze, careless
312| *MS:* (You will heed < > answers for   *1835:* (You will heed < > answers,
for   *1849:* To KNOW (heed   **313|**   *MS:* affirm)—   *1849:* affirm)   **314|**   *MS:*
you have annexed   *1835:* annex'd   *1849:* you dare annex   **316|**   *MS:* intense
purpose . . . gifts § written over by § purpose—gifts that would induce   *1849:* intense
hope, nor let your gifts create   *1863:* hope; nor   **318|**   *MS:* And instruments of
success; no destiny   *1849:* Conducive to success—make destiny   *1863:* success,
make   **319|**   *MS:* Dispenses with endeavour: . . now § written over by §
endeavour:— now   *1835:* endeavour. Now   *1849:* Dispense with man's endeavour
322| *MS:* distinction, than a full assurance   *1849:* distinction, than security   *1868:*
distinction than   **323|**   *MS:* That it exists,—or whether   *1835:* exists; or   *1849:*
Of its existence; whether   *1863:* existence? whether   **325|**   *MS:* purpose, and
1835: purpose—and   **327|**   *MS:* For its possessor— — dare   *1835:* possessor.
Dare   *1849:* its pursuer.   Dare   **328|**   *MS:* pause] . . No § written over by §
pause]—No   *1835:* pause] No; I   *1849:* No, I   **329|**   *MS:* of my soul — —
what § *my* written above the line §   *1835|*   *MS:* soul. What   **331|**   *MS:*
Eclipse the true aim § *true* cancelled; *in me* added above the line to read § Eclipse the
aim in me? . . if   *1835:* me?—if   **333|**   *MS:* succeed:? What   *1835:* succeed?
What   **335|**   *MS:* energy . . . this § written over by § energy—this   *1835:*
energy?—this

Because its nature is to strive?—enticed
By the security of no broad course,
Without success forever in its eyes!
How know I else such glorious fate my own,
340 But in the restless irresistible force
That works within me? Is it for human will
To institute such impulses?—still less,
To disregard their promptings! What should I
Do, kept among you all; your loves, your cares,
345 Your life—all to be mine? Be sure that God
Ne'er dooms to waste the strength he deigns impart!
Ask the geier-eagle why she stoops at once
Into the vast and unexplored abyss,
What full-grown power informs her from the first,
350 Why she not marvels, strenuously beating
The silent boundless regions of the sky!
Be sure they sleep not whom God needs! Nor fear
Their holding light his charge, when every hour
That finds that charge delayed, is a new death.
355 This for the faith in which I trust; and hence
I can abjure so well the idle arts
These pedants strive to learn and teach; Black Arts,
Great Works, the Secret and Sublime, forsooth—

336| *MS:* strive . . . enticed § written over by § strive—enticed   *1835:*
strive?—enticed   **337|** *MS:* course   *1835:* course—   *1849:* course,
338| *MS:* Where error is not, but success is sure . . .   *1835:* sure.   *1849:* With no
success forever in its eyes!   *1863:* Without success   **339|** *MS:*—How < >
own   *1835:* How < > own,   **341|** *MS:* me—is   *1835:* me? Is
342| *MS:* less   *1849:* less,   **343|** *MS:* promptings . . . what   *1835:*
promptings? What   *1868:* Promptings! What   **344|** *MS:* all—your loves, your
cares   *1835:* all; your loves, your cares,   **345|** *MS:* life— —all   *1835:*
life—all   **346|** *MS:* impart— — — — —   *1835:* impart.   *1849:* impart!   *1863:*
He   *1868:* he   **347|** *MS:* gier-eagle why she stoops § *she* written above the
line §   *1888:* geier-eagle   **348|** *MS:* abyss—   *1835:* abyss!   *1849:*
abyss,   **349|** *MS:* fullgrown   *1835:* first!   *1849:* full-grown < > first,
351| *MS:* sky! — — § written over by § sky!—   *1835:* sky!   **352|** *MS:*
needs;—nor   *1835:* needs; nor   *1849:* needs! Nor   **353|** *1863:* His   *1868:*
his   **354|** *MS:* delayed is < > death: *1835:* delay'd < > death.   *1849:*
delayed, is   **355|** *MS:*— —Thus for < > trust;—and   *1835:* Thus < > trust;
and   *1849:* This for   **356|** *MS:* the secret Arts   *1835:* arts   *1849:* the idle
arts   **357|** *MS:* learn—the Magic they   *1849:* learn and teach: Black
Arts,   **358|** *MS:* So reverence— —I shall scarcely seek to know   *1835:*
reverence. I   *1849:* Great Works, the Secret and Sublime, forsooth—

85

Let others prize: too intimate a tie
360 Connects me with our God! A sullen fiend
To do my bidding, fallen and hateful sprites
To help me—what are these, at best, beside
God helping, God directing everywhere,
So that the earth shall yield her secrets up,
365 And every object there be charged to strike,
Teach, gratify her master God appoints?
And I am young, my Festus, happy and free!
I can devote myself; I have a life
To give; I, singled out for this, the One!
370 Think, think! the wide East, where all Wisdom sprung;
The bright South, where she dwelt; the hopeful North,
All are passed o'er—it lights on me! 'Tis time
New hopes should animate the world, new light
Should dawn from new revealings to a race
375 Weighed down so long, forgotten so long; thus shall
The heaven reserved for us at last receive
Creatures whom no unwonted splendours blind,
But ardent to confront the unclouded blaze
Whose beams not seldom blessed their pilgrimage,
380 Not seldom glorified their life below.

359| *MS:* If it exist: too   *1849:* Let others prize: too   **360**| *MS:* God: . . a
§ written over by § God:—a   *1835:* God. A sullen friend   *1849:* God! A sullen
fiend   **361**⌈ *MS:* bidding——fallen § written over by § bidding—fallen   *1849:*
bidding, fallen   **362**| *MS:* me——what   *1835:* me—what   **363**| *MS:* God
every where— § above §, sustaining and directing   *1835:* where, sustaining   *1849:*
God helping, God directing everywhere,   **364**| *MS:* up   *1849:* up,
365| *MS:* object shall be   *1863:* object there be   **366**| *MS:* To teach, to
gratify, and to suggest——— § written over by § suggest?—   *1835:* suggest?   *1849:*
Teach, gratify, her master God appoints?   *1863:* gratify her   **367**| *MS:* young,
Festus,—happy   *1835:* Festus happy   *1849:* young, my Festus   **368**| *MS:*
myself I   *1835:* myself; I   **369**| *MS:* give— I who am singled out for this . . .
§ written over by § this——— give; I, who < > this.   *1849:* I, singled out for this, the
One!   **370**⌈ *MS:* Think, think,—the < > where old wisdom sprung   *1835:*
Think, think; the wide east < > Wisdom sprung;   *1863:* wide East, where all Wisdom
1888: Think, think! the   **371**| *MS:*—The < > South where she dwelt—the
populous North   *1835:* The < > south, where she dwelt; the < > north,   *1849:*
dwelt; the hopeful north,   *1863:* South < > North,   **372**| *MS:*——All < >
me!—'tis   *1835:* All < > me. 'Tis   *1849:* me! 'Tis   **373**| *MS:* world——new
§ written over by § world—new   *1849:* world, new   **376**| *MS:* The Heaven
< > last, receive   *1835:* heaven < > last receive   *1849:* us, at   *1868:* us at
377| *MS:* No creatures whom unwonted   *1849:* Creatures whom no unwonted
378| *1888:* blaze.   *1889:* blaze   **379**| *MS:* seldom lit their   *1849:* seldom
blessed their

FESTUS My words have their old fate and make faint stand
Against your glowing periods. Call this, truth—
Why not pursue it in a fast retreat,
Some one of Learning's many palaces,
385 After approved example?—seeking there
Calm converse with the great dead, soul to soul,
Who laid up treasure with the like intent
—So lift yourself into their airy place,
And fill out full their unfilled careers,
390 Unravelling the knots their baffled skill
Pronounced inextricable, true!—but left
Far less confused. A fresh eye, a fresh hand,
Might do much at their vigour's waning-point;
Succeeding with new-breathed new-hearted force,
395 As at old games the runner snatched the torch
From runner still: this way success might be.
But you have coupled with your enterprise,
An arbitrary self-repugnant scheme

382–383| *MS:* Beside § cancelled by § Against your < > periods I renounce / All
hope of learning further on this head, / And what I next advance holds good as well /
With one assured that all these things are true; / For might not such seek out a fast
retreat   *1835:* periods: I < > / < > head; / < > /// < > retreat—   *1849:*
periods. Call this, truth— / Why not pursue it in a fast retreat,   *1863:* a vast retreat
1868: a fast retreat,   383–385| *MS:* retreat / After < > example, there § written
over by § example? there to have   *1835:* retreat— / example—there   *1849:* retreat, /
Some one of Learning's many palaces, / After < > example; seeking there   *1863:*
example ?—seeking   386| *MS:* Dead   *1835:* dead—soul to soul—   *1849:* dead,
soul to soul,   387| *MS:*—Who < > intent,— — — § written over by § intent,—
1835: Who < > intent?   388| *MS:* To lift himself < > place—   *1835:* place,
1849:—So lift yourself into   389| *MS:* To fill < > careers—   *1835:* unfulfill'd
careers,   *1849:* And fill < > unfulfilled   390| *MS:*— —Unraveling   *1835:*
Unravelling   391| *MS:* inextricable, but surely left   *1849:* inextricable,
true!—but left   392| *MS:* confused—a fresh eye,< > hand   *1835:* confused?
A fresh eye   *1863:* confused. A fresh eye   393| *MS:* much— —at < > waning-
point   *1835:* much at < > waning-point—   *1849:* waning-point;   394| *MS:*
new-breathed and untired force   *1835:* force—   *1849:* and earnest force,   *1863:*
and untired force,   *1868:* new-breathed new-hearted force,   395| *MS:* games a
runner   *1835:* snatch'd   *1849:* snatched   *1868:* games the runner   396| *MS:*
still:— —such one might well do this: *1835:* still? Such < > this.   *1849:* still: this
way success might be.   397| *MS:*— —But you have linked to his your
enterprize   *1835:* But < > link'd to this, your enterprize,   *1849:* have coupled with
your enterprise,   398| *MS:* arbitrary and most perplexing scheme   *1849:*
arbitrary self-repugnant scheme

87

Of seeking it in strange and untried paths.
400 What books are in the desert? Writes the sea
The secret of her yearning in vast caves
Where yours will fall the first of human feet?
Has wisdom sat there and recorded aught
You press to read? Why turn aside from her
405 To visit, where her vesture never glanced,
Now—solitudes consigned to barrenness
By God's decree, which who shall dare impugn?
Now—ruins where she paused but would not stay,
Old ravaged cities that, renouncing her,
410 She called an endless curse on, so it came:
Or worst of all, now—men you visit, men,
Ignoblest troops who never heard her voice
Or hate it, men without one gift from Rome
Or Athens,—these shall Aureole's teachers be!
415 Rejecting past example, practice, precept,
Aidless 'mid these he thinks to stand alone:
Thick like a glory round the Stagirite
Your rivals throng, the sages: here stand you!
Whatever you may protest, knowledge is not
420 Paramount in your love; or for her sake
You would collect all help from every source—

399-415| *MS:* paths,— / Rejecting   *1835:* paths; / < > precept—   *1849:* paths. /
What books are in the desert? writes the sea / The secret of her yearning in vast caves
/ Where yours will fall the first of human feet? / Has Wisdom sate there and recorded
aught / You press to read? Why turn aside from her / To visit, where her vesture never
glanced, / Now—solitudes consigned to barrenness / By God's decree, which who shall
dare impugn? / Now—ruins where she paused but would not stay, / Old ravaged cities
that, renouncing her, / She called an endless curse on, so it came— / Or, worst of all,
now—men you visit, men, / Ignoblest troops that never heard her voice, / Or hate it,
men without one gift from Rome / Or Athens,—these shall Aureole's teachers be! /
Rejecting < > precept,   400| *1868:* desert? Writes   403| *1863:* sat
1868: Has wisdom   410| *1863:* came: 411| *1868:* Or worst
412| *1868:* troops who never < > voice   416-418| *MS:* That so you may stand
aidless and alone— — § written over by § alone: / —If in this wild rejection you regard
/ Mankind and their award of fame,—'tis clear   *1835:* fame—'tis clear,   *1849:* Aidless
'mid these he thinks to stand alone: / Thick like a glory round the Stagyrite / Your
rivals throng, the sages: here stand you!   *1863:* Stagirite   419| *MS:* Whate'er
1868: Whatever   420| *MS:* love—or   *1835:* love; or   421| *MS:* source;
1835: source—

Rival, assistant, friend, foe, all would merge
In the broad class of those who showed her haunts,
And those who showed them not.

PARACELSUS   What shall I say?

425 Festus, from childhood I have been possessed
By a fire—by a true fire, or faint or fierce,
As from without some master, so it seemed,
Repressed or urged its current: this but ill
Expresses what would I convey: but rather

430 I will believe an angel ruled me thus,
Than that my soul's own workings, own high nature,
So became manifest. I knew not then
What whispered in the evening, and spoke out
At midnight. If some mortal, born too soon,

435 Were laid away in some great trance—the ages
Coming and going all the while—till dawned
His true time's advent; and could then record
The words they spoke who kept watch by his bed,—
Then I might tell more of the breath so light

440 Upon my eyelids, and the fingers light
Among my hair. Youth is confused; yet never
So dull was I but, when that spirit passed,

422| *MS:*—Friend, foe assistant, rival, all   *1835:* Friend   *1849:* Rival or helper, friend, foe, all   *1863:* Rival, assistant, friend   **423|** *MS:* shewed her haunts   *1835:* show'd   *1849:* showed her haunts,   **424|** *MS:* shewed it § cancelled by § them not:—PARACELSUS < > say?——   *1835:* show'd them not. PARACELSUS < > say?   *1849:* showed   **425|** *MS:*—Festus   *1835:* Festus   **426|** *MS:* fire——by § written over by § fire—by < > fire——or faint or fierce   *1835:* true fire, or faint or fierce,   **427|** *MS:* Master   *1835:* master < > seem'd,   *1849:* seemed,   **428|** *MS:* current;—this   *1835:* Repress'd < > current: this   *1849:* Repressed   **429|** *MS:* convey——but   *1835:* convey—but   *1863:* convey: but   *1888:* what would I convey   *1889:* what I would convey   **430|** *MS:* Angel   *1835:* angel   **431|** *MS:* nature   *1835:* nature,   **432|** *MS:* manifest;——I § written over by § manifest;—   *1835:* manifest. I   **433|** *MS:* evening and   *1835:* whisper'd < > evening, and   *1849:* whispered   **434|** *MS:* midnight:——if § written over by § might:—if   *1835:* midnight. I   **435|** *MS:* trance— § above §, the   *1835:* trance—the   **436|** *MS:* while,—until   *1835:* while—until   *1849:* while—till dawned   **437|** *MS:* advent—and   *1835:* advent, and   *1863:* advent;—   **438|** *MS:* They < > bed,   *1835:* they   *1849:* bed,—   **440|** *MS:* eyelids——and § written over by § eyelids—and   *1835:* eyelids, and   *1849:* fingers warm   *1868:* fingers light   **441|** *MS:* hair;——youth § written over by § hair;—youth is confused, yet   *1835:* hair. Youth is confused; yet   **442|** *MS:* I, but when < > Spirit passed   *1835:* I but < > pass'd   *1849:* but, when < > passed,

I turned to him, scarce consciously, as turns
A water-snake when fairies cross his sleep.
445 And having this within me and about me
While Einsiedeln, its mountains, lakes and woods
Confined me—what oppressive joy was mine
When life grew plain, and I first viewed the thronged,
The everlasting concourse of mankind!
450 Believe that ere I joined them, ere I knew
The purpose of the pageant, or the place
Consigned me in its ranks—while, just awake,
Wonder was freshest and delight most pure—
'Twas then that least supportable appeared
455 A station with the brightest of the crowd,
A portion with the proudest of them all.
And from the tumult in my breast, this only
Could I collect, that I must thenceforth die
Or elevate myself far, far above
460 The gorgeous spectacle. I seemed to long
At once to trample on, yet save mankind,
To make some unexampled sacrifice
In their behalf, to wring some wondrous good
From heaven or earth for them, to perish, winning

443| _1835:_ turn'd   _1849:_ turned   **444|** _MS:_ sleep:— — § written over by §
sleep:—   _1835:_ sleep: _1849:_ sleep.   **445|** _MS:_—And   _1835:_ And
446| _MS:_ When Einsiedeln, its hills and lakes and plains   _1835:_ hills, and lakes,
and   _1849:_ While Einsiedeln, its mountains, lakes, and woods   _1863:_ lakes
and   **447|** _MS:_ me, what   _1835:_ me—what   **448|** _MS:_ plain—and < >
thronged   _1835:_ plain, and < > view'd the throng'd,   _1849:_ viewed the
thronged,   **449|** _MS:_ The evermoving concourse of mankind! . . .   _1835:_ ever-
moving, concourse of mankind!   _1849:_ ever-moving concourse   _1863:_ The
everlasting concourse   **450|** _MS:_ them,—ere   _1835:_ join'd them—ere   _1849:_
joined   _1863:_ them, ere   **451|** _MS:_ pageant— — —or § written over by §
pageant—or   _1835:_ pageant, or   **452|** _MS:_ Consigned to me within its
ranks,—while yet   _1835:_ Consign'd < > ranks—while   _1849:_ Consigned   _1863:_
Consigned me in its < > while, just awake   **453|** _MS:_ pure, . . .   _1835:_
pure—   **454|** _MS:_ . . . 'Twas   _1835:_ 'Twas < > appear'd   _1849:_
appeared   **455|** _1835:_ crowd;   _1849:_ crowd,   **456|** _MS:_ all!— —   _1835:_
all!   _1863:_ all.   **457|** _MS:_ . . And § written over by §—And   _1835:_ And
458| _MS:_ collect . . . that   _1835:_ collect—that   _1863:_ collect, that   **460|** _MS:_
spectacle;—what seemed a longing   _1835:_ spectacle; what seem'd   _1849:_ spectacle. I
seemed to long   **461|** _MS:_ To trample on yet save Mankind at once . . . . . .
§ written over by § once—   _1835:_ mankind   _1849:_ At once to trample on, yet save
mankind—   _1863:_ mankind,   **462|** _MS:_—To   _1835:_ To   **463|** _MS:_
behalf—to   _1863:_ behalf, to   **464|**   _MS:_ Heaven < > them . . to § written over
by § them—to   _1835:_ heaven   _1863:_ them, to

465 Eternal weal in the act: as who should dare
      Pluck out the angry thunder from its cloud,
      That, all its gathered flame discharged on him,
      No storm might threaten summer's azure sleep:
      Yet never to be mixed with men so much
470 As to have part even in my own work, share
      In my own largess. Once the feat achieved,
      I would withdraw from their officious praise,
      Would gently put aside their profuse thanks.
      Like some knight traversing a wilderness,
475 Who, on his way, may chance to free a tribe
      Of desert-people from their dragon-foe;
      When all the swarthy race press round to kiss
      His feet, and choose him for their king, and yield
      Their poor tents, pitched among the sand-hills, for
480 His realm: and he points, smiling, to his scarf
      Heavy with riveled gold, his burgonet
      Gay set with twinkling stones—and to the East,
      Where these must be displayed!
      FESTUS   Good: let us hear
      No more about your nature, "which first shrank
485 From all that marked you out apart from men!"
      PARACELSUS I touch on that; these words but analyse

465| *MS:* act . . as   *1835:* act: as   466| *MS:* cloud   *1835:* cloud,
467| *1835:* gather'd   *1849:* gathered   468| *MS:* Summer's azure weather . . . :
§ : added in pencil §   *1835:* summer's < > weather—   *1849:* azure sleep:
469| *MS:*—Yet < > with them, so   *1835:* Yet < > mix'd < > them so   *1849:*
mixed with men so   470| *MS:* work,—share   *1835:* work—share
471| *MS:* largess, . . once § written over by § largess,—once < > achieved   *1835:*
largess. Once < > achieved,   473| *MS:*—Would < > thanks   *1835:* Would
< > thanks,   *1849:* thanks: *1863:* thanks.   474| *MS:*—Like < >
wilderness   *1835:* Like < > wilderness,   476| *MS:* Desert-people < > dragon-
foe,   *1835:* desert-people < > dragon-foe;   477| *MS:* Race   *1835:*
race   478| *MS:* feet and < > King   *1835:* feet and < > king
479| *MS:* tents pitched < > sand-hills for   *1835:* tents, pitch'd < > sand-hills, for
1849: pitched   480| *MS:* realm— —and he points smiling to   *1835:* realm; and
he points, smiling to his scarf,   *1863:* scarf   481| *1835:* rivel'd gold—his
burgonet,   *1849:* riveled gold, his   *1863:* burgonet   482| *MS:* East   *1835:*
east,   *1863:* East,   483| *MS:* displayed . . . FESTUS Good: . . let § written over
by § Good:—   *1835:* display'd . . . FESTUS Good: let us   *1849:* displayed!
FESTUS   484| *MS:* nature "which   *1835:* nature, "which   485| *MS:*
men."   *1849:* men!"   486| *MS:* on it:—I would but   *1835:* it: I   *1849:* on
that: these words but

The first mad impulse: 'twas as brief as fond,
For as I gazed again upon the show,
I soon distinguished here and there a shape
490 Palm-wreathed and radiant, forehead and full eye.
Well pleased was I their state should thus at once
Interpret my own thoughts:—"Behold the clue
To all," I rashly said, "and what I pine
To do, these have accomplished: we are peers.
495 They know and therefore rule: I, too, will know!"
You were beside me, Festus, as you say;
You saw me plunge in their pursuits whom fame
Is lavish to attest the lords of mind,
Not pausing to make sure the prize in view
500 Would satiate my cravings when obtained,
But since they strove I strove. Then came a slow
And strangling failure. We aspired alike,
Yet not the meanest plodder, Tritheim counts
A marvel, but was all-sufficient, strong,
505 Or staggered only at his own vast wits;
While I was restless, nothing satisfied,
Distrustful, most perplexed. I would slur over
That struggle; suffice it, that I loathed myself

487| *MS:* That first mad impulse . . 'twas < > fond; *1835:* impulse—'twas *1863:*
The first mad impulse: 'twas **488|** *MS:* show *1835:* show, **489|** *1835:*
distinguish'd *1849:* distinguished **490|** *MS:* eye:— *1835:* eye.
493| *MS:* all—"I rashly said—" and all I *1835:* all," I rashly said, "and *1849:* and
what I **494|** *MS:* These < > accomplished—we are peers! *1835:* these < >
accomplish'd: we *1849:* accomplished *1863:* peers. **495|** *MS:* know
§ written over by § Know < > rule— —I too will know!" § written over by § Know!"
1835: know, and < > rule . . . I *1849:* rule: I, too, will **496|** *MS:*—You < >
say— — *1835:* You < > say; **497|** *1835:* Fame *1863:* fame
498| *MS:* Lords of Mind, *1835:* lords of mind, *1849:* mind; *1868:* mind,
500| *MS:* obtained . . *1835:* obtain'd— *1849:* obtained— *1863:* obtained,
501| *MS:*— —But as they strove, I strove . . then § written over by § strove:—then
1835: But < > strove I strove: then *1849:* But since they < > I strove. Then
502| *MS:* failure— —we < > alike *1835:* failure. We < > alike, **503|** *MS:*
plodder Tritheim deems *1849:* Tritheim schools *1863:* plodder, Tritheim
counts **504|** *MS:* all-sufficient, well content, *1849:* But faced me, all-sufficient,
all-content *1863:* A marvel, but was all-sufficient, strong, **505|** *MS:* And
staggered < > own strong wits, *1835:* stagger'd < > wits; *1849:* Or staggered
1863: own vast wits; **506|** *MS:*—While *1835:* While **507|** *MS:*
perplexed— — —I *1835:* perplex'd. I *1849:* perplexed **508|** *MS:* struggle—
—suffice *1835:* struggle; suffice

As weak compared with them, yet felt somehow
510 A mighty power was brooding, taking shape
Within me; and this lasted till one night
When, as I sat revolving it and more,
A still voice from without said—"Seest thou not,
Desponding child, whence spring defeat and loss?
515 Even from thy strength. Consider: hast thou gazed
Presumptuously on wisdom's countenance,
No veil between; and can thy faltering hands,
Unguided by the brain the sight absorbs,
Pursue their task as earnest blinkers do
520 Whom radiance ne'er distracted? Live their life
If thou wouldst share their fortune, choose their eyes
Unfed by splendour. Let each task present
Its petty good to thee. Waste not thy gifts
In profitless waiting for the gods' descent,
525 But have some idol of thine own to dress
With their array. Know, not for knowing's sake,
But to become a star to men for ever;
Know, for the gain it gets, the praise it brings,
The wonder it inspires, the love it breeds:
530 Look one step onward, and secure that step!"

511| *MS:* me— —and § written over by § me—and   *1835:* me; and   *1849:* me:
and   *1863:* me; and   512| *MS:* sate   *1863:* sat   513| *MS:* said "See'st
thou not   *1835:* said—"See'st thou not,   514| *MS:* springs   *1849:* whence
came defeat   *1863:* whence spring defeat   515| *MS:*—Even < >
strength:—know better: hast   *1835:* Even < > strength. Know   *1849:* strength.
Consider: hast   516| *MS:* Presumptuous on Wisdom's   *1849:* Presumptuously
1868: wisdom's   517–520| *MS:* between, and < > hands / Pursue as well the toil
their earnest blinking, / Whom < > distracts, so clear descries?   *1835:* between;
and   *1849:* thy hands which falter / Unguided by thy brain the mighty sight /
Continues to absorb, pursue their task / On earth like these around thee—what their
sense/ Which radiance ne'er distracted, clear   *1863:* thy faltering hands / < > the
sight absorbs / Pursue their task as earnest blinkers do / Whom radiance ne'er
distracted? Live their life   *1868:* by the brain the sight absorbs,   521| *MS:*—If
1835: If < > eyes   *1849:* choose their life,   *1863:* choose their eyes
522| *MS:* splendor— —let § written over by § splendor;—let   *1835:* splendour.
Let   523| *MS:* thee . . waste § written over by § thee—waste   *1835:* thee.
Waste   524| *MS:* God's   *1835:* gods'   526| *MS:* array:—Know   *1835:*
array. Know   527| *MS:* Men   *1835:* men for ever.   *1868:* ever;
528| *MS:* Know! for   *1835:* Know, for   529| *MS:* breeds— — —   *1835:*
breeds.   *1868:* breeds: 530| *MS:* onward and < > step"— — — — § above §
step" . . .   *1835:* onward, and < > step."   *1868:* step!"

And I smiled as one never smiles but once,
Then first discovering my own aim's extent,
Which sought to comprehend the works of God,
And God himself, and all God's intercourse
535 With the human mind; I understood, no less,
My fellows' studies, whose true worth I saw,
But smiled not, well aware who stood by me.
And softer came the voice—"There is a way:
'Tis hard for flesh to tread therein, imbued
540 With frailty—hopeless, if indulgence first
Have ripened inborn germs of sin to strength:
Wilt thou adventure for my sake and man's,
Apart from all reward?" And last it breathed—
"Be happy, my good soldier; I am by thee,
545 Be sure, even to the end!"—I answered not,
Knowing him. As he spoke, I was endued
With comprehension and a steadfast will;
And when he ceased, my brow was sealed his own.
If there took place no special change in me,
550 How comes it all things wore a different hue
Thenceforward?—pregnant with vast consequence,
Teeming with grand result, loaded with fate?

531| 1835: once;   1868: once,   532| MS: my aim's extent   1835: extent,
1849: my own aim's extent   534| MS:—And God himself——and § written over
by § himself—and   1835: And God himself, and   535| MS: With our own
mind;——and § written over by § mind;—and how such shewed beside   1835: mind;
and < > show'd   1849: With the human mind; I understood, no less,
536| MS: fellow's studies—whose < > saw   1835: studies, whose < > saw,   1863:
fellows'   537| MS: me——   1835: me.   1863: Who   1868: who
538| MS: Voice < > is a way—   1835: voice   1849: is   1863: way:
539| MS:—Tis   1835: 'Tis   540| MS: With weakness——hopeless   1835:
weakness—hopeless   1849: With frailty—hopeless   541| MS: inborn sins to
strength——wilt thou   1835: ripen'd   1849: ripened inborn germs of sin to
strength: 542| MS: Adventure for my sake and for thy kind's § written over
by § Kind's   1835: kind's,   1849: Wilt thou adventure < > and man's,
543| MS: Apart for all reward?"——and < > breathed   1835: reward?" And < >
breathed—   1849: Apart from all   544| MS: soldier—I   1835: soldier;
I   545| MS: end!"——I   1835: end!" . . . I answer'd   1849: end!"—I
answered   546| MS: Him——as § written over by § Him:—as he spoke I
1835: him. As he spoke, I   1849: Him   1868: him   547| MS: will,   1835:
will;   548| MS: ceased, my fate was sealed forever:—   1835: seal'd for ever.
1849: He ceased, my brow was sealed His own.   1868: he < > his   549| MS:
me   1835: me,   551| 1835: consequence—   1863: consequence,
552| MS: results,—loaded with fate,—   1835: results—loaded < > fate;   1863:
results, loaded < > fate?   1868: result

So that when, quailing at the mighty range
Of secret truths which yearn for birth, I haste
555 To contemplate undazzled some one truth,
Its bearing and effects alone—at once
What was a speck expands into a star,
Asking a life to pass exploring thus,
Till I near craze. I go to prove my soul!
560 I see my way as birds their trackless way.
I shall arrive! what time, what circuit first,
I ask not: but unless God send his hail
Or blinding fireballs, sleet or stifling snow,
In some time, his good time, I shall arrive:
565 He guides me and the bird. In his good time!
MICHAL Vex him no further, Festus; it is so!
FESTUS Just thus you help me ever. This would hold
Were it the trackless air, and not a path
Inviting you, distinct with footprints yet
570 Of many a mighty marcher gone that way.
You may have purer views than theirs, perhaps,
But they were famous in their day—the proofs
Remain. At least accept the light they lend.
PARACELSUS Their light! the sum of all is briefly this:
575 They laboured and grew famous, and the fruits

553| MS: when quailing 1868: when, quailing 554| MS: truths yearning
1849: truths which yearn 555| MS: Truth— 1835: truth, 556| MS:
alone— § above §, at 1835: alone, at 1849: alone—at 557| MS: star—
1835: star, 558| MS: Demanding life to be explored alone,— 1835: alone—
1849: Asking a life to pass exploring thus, 559| MS: craze . . I § written over
by § craze:—I 1835: craze. I 560| MS: trackless way 1835: Trackless
way— 1863: trackless way. 561| MS:——I < > arrive——what § written over
by § arrive!—what time 1835: I < > arrive! what 562| MS: not——but
1835: not: but 1863: His 1868: his 563| MS: fire-balls 1835: sleet, or
1863: sleet or 1868: fireballs 564| MS: arrive:— 1835: time—his < >
time—I 1863: time, His < > time, I 1868: his 565| MS: bird— — — in
§ written over by § bird—in 1835: bird. In 1863: His 1868: his 566| MS:
Festus—it 1835: Festus; it 567| MS: you answer ever——this 1835: ever.
This 1849: you help me ever. 568| MS: it the trackless air and § the inserted
above the line § 1849: air, and 569| MS: foot-prints 1835: footprints
570| MS: mighty spirit gone < > way— — 1835: way. 1863: mighty marcher
gone 571| MS: views, for aught I know 1835: know; 1849: views than
theirs, perhaps, 573| MS: Remain— —at § written over by § Remain:—at 1835:
Remain. At 574| MS: light!—the 1835: light! the 1863: this;
575| MS: laboured after their own fashion— —the 1835: labour'd < > fashion; the
1849: laboured, and grew famous; and the 1863: laboured and < > famous, and

Are best seen in a dark and groaning earth
Given over to a blind and endless strife
With evils, what of all their lore abates?
No; I reject and spurn them utterly
580 And all they teach. Shall I still sit beside
Their dry wells, with a white lip and filmed eye,
While in the distance heaven is blue above
Mountains where sleep the unsunned tarns?
FESTUS   And yet
As strong delusions have prevailed ere now.
585 Men have set out as gallantly to seek
Their ruin. I have heard of such: yourself
Avow all hitherto have failed and fallen.
MICHAL Nay, Festus, when but as the pilgrims faint
Through the drear way, do you expect to see
590 Their city dawn amid the clouds afar?
PARACELSUS Ay, sounds it not like some old well-known tale?
For me, I estimate their works and them
So rightly, that at times I almost dream
I too have spent a life the sages' way,
595 And tread once more familiar paths. Perchance
I perished in an arrogant self-reliance
Ages ago; and in that act, a prayer
For one more chance went up so earnest, so

576| 1835: earth,   1863: earth   578| MS: evils their best lore cannot abate— —
— 1835: abate.   1849: evils, which of all you Gods bates?   1863: evils, what of all
their lore bates?   579| MS:— —No, I   1835: No; I < > utterly,   1863:
utterly   580| MS: teach— —shall § written over by § teach:—   1835: teach.
Shall   581| MS: with white < > eye   1835: lips   1849: with a white lip < >
eye,   583| MS: tarns— — FESTUS § written over by § tarns?—FESTUS   1835:
unsunn'd tarns? FESTUS   1849: unsunned   584| MS: now . . . § written over by §
now—   1835: prevail'd ere now: 1849: prevailed   1863: now.
585| MS:—Men   1835: Men   586| MS: ruin— —I < > such— —yourself
1835: ruin; I < > such—yourself   1863: ruin. I < > such; yourself   587| MS:
fallen, . . . § written over by § fallen,—   1835: fail'd and fallen.   1849: failed
589| MS: For the   1849: Through the   590| MS: afar!   1849: dawn afar amid
the clouds?   1863: dawn amid the clouds afar?   591| MS:—Ay < > well
known   1835: Ay < > well-known   592| MS:—For   1835: For
593| MS: I wellnigh dream   1835: well nigh   1849: I almost dream
594| MS: the selfsame way— § above §,   1835: way—   1849: the sages' way,
595| MS:—Treat once again an old life's course—perchance   1835: Tread < > course.
Perchance   1849: And tread once more familiar paths. Perchance   596| 1835:
perish'd   1849: perished   597| MS: And age ago— —and   1835: ago; and
1863: Ages ago   598| MS: earnest,—so   1835: earnest—so   1849: earnest, so

Instinct with better light let in by death,
600 That life was blotted out—not so completely
But scattered wrecks enough of it remain,
Dim memories, as now, when once more seems
The goal in sight again. All which, indeed,
Is foolish, and only means—the flesh I wear,
605 The earth I tread, are not more clear to me
Than my belief, explained to you or no.
FESTUS And who am I, to challenge and dispute
That clear belief? I will divest all fear.
MICHAL Then Aureole is God's commissary! he shall
610 Be great and grand—and all for us!
PARACELSUS   No, sweet!
Not great and grand. If I can serve mankind
'Tis well; but there our intercourse must end:
I never will be served by those I serve.
FESTUS Look well to this; here is a plague-spot, here,
615 Disguise it how you may! 'Tis true, you utter
This scorn while by our side and loving us;
'Tis but a spot as yet: but it will break
Into a hideous blotch if overlooked.
How can that course be safe which from the first
620 Produces carelessness to human love?

599-600| *MS:* Imbued with < > Death, / So free from all past sin— —that it was
heard: / —That < > out— —not   *1835:* Death— / < > sin—that < > heard . . . /
That out—not   *1849:* Instinct with < > Death, / That   *1863:* death,
601| *MS:* enough remain to wake   *1835:* scatter'd   *1849:* scattered < > enough of
it remain,   602| *MS:* memories; as   *1849:* when seems once more   *1863:*
memories, as   *1868:* when once more seems   603| *MS:* again: . . All which is
foolish   *1835:* again: all   *1849:* which, indeed,   *1863:* again. All   604| *MS:*
Indeed and < > means the form I bear   *1835:* indeed, and < > means—the
1849: Is foolish, and < > the flesh I wear,   605-607| *MS:* me. / And < > I
to   *1849:* me / Than my belief, explained to you or no. / And   *1863:* I, to
608| *MS:* belief?— —I < > devest   *1835:* belief? . . . I   *1849:* belief? I put away
all   *1863:* I will divest all   610| *MS:* grand— —and   *1835:* grand—and
1863: Sweet!   *1868:* sweet!   611| *MS:* great or grand:—if   *1835:* grand. If
1849: great and grand If   *1863:* grand. If   612| *MS:* 'Tis well— —but < >
end:—   *1835:* 'Tis well—but < > end: *1863:* well; but   613| *MS:* serve!
1835: serve.   614| *MS: here* < > plague-spot, veil it,   *1835:* this; *here*
1849: here < > plague-spot, here,   615| *MS:* you will:—'tis   *1835:* will: 'tis
1849: you may! 'Tis   616| *MS:* us— —   *1835:* us—   *1849:* us;
617| *MS:* yet;—but   *1835:* yet; but   *1863:* yet: but   618| *MS:*
overlooked:—   *1835:* overlook'd.   *1849:* overlooked.

97

It seems you have abjured the helps which men
Who overpass their kind, as you would do,
Have humbly sought; I dare not thoroughly probe
This matter, lest I learn too much. Let be
625 That popular praise would little instigate
Your efforts, nor particular approval
Reward you; put reward aside; alone
You shall go forth upon your arduous task,
None shall assist you, none partake your toil,
630 None share your triumph: still you must retain
Some one to cast your glory on, to share
Your rapure with. Were I elect like you,
I would encircle me with love, and raise
A rampart of my fellows; it should seem
635 Impossible for me to fail, so watched
By gentle friends who made my cause their own.
They should ward off fate's envy—the great gift,
Extravagant when claimed by me alone,
Being so a gift to them as well as me.
640 If danger daunted me or ease seduced,
How calmly their sad eyes should gaze reproach!
MICHAL O Aureole, can I sing when all alone,
Without first calling, in my fancy, both

621| MS:—I know:—you 1835: I know you 1849: It seems you   623| MS:
sought—I 1835: sought. I 1849: sought—I 1863: sought; I   624| MS:
much:—let be, 1835: much: let be 1849: be, 1863: much. Let   626| MS:
efforts——or particular 1835: efforts—or 1849: efforts, nor   627| MS:
aside;—you shall 1835: aside; you 1849: aside; alone   628| MS: Go < >
task alone, 1849: You shall go < > task,   629| MS: you—none < > toil——
§ written over by § toil— 1849: you, none < > toil,   630| MS:
triumph:—still 1835: triumph—still 1863: triumph: still   631| MS: to trust
your glory to,—to 1835: to; to 1849: to cast your glory on, to   632| MS:
with;—had I been chosen like you 1835: with. Had 1849: with. Were I elect
like you,   633| MS: I should encircle me with love—should raise § me
inserted above the line § 1849: I would encircle < > love, and raise
634| MS: of kind wishes——it 1835: wishes; it 1849: of my fellows; it
635| MS: Impossible for me § for inserted above the line § 1835: watch'd 1849:
watched   636| MS: own; 1863: own.   637| MS:—They < > envy—the
great boon, 1835: Fate's envy—the 1849: great gift, 1863: fate's
638| 1835: claim'd 1849: claimed   639| MS: Being a < > me: . . . § written
over by § me:— 1835: me. 1849: Being so a   640| MS: If ease seduced or
danger < > me, 1849: If danger < > me or ease seduced,   641| MS:
reproach!—— 1835: reproach!   642| MS: sing, tho' all 1835: sing though
1849: sing when all

To listen by my side—even I! And you?
645 Do you not feel this? Say that you feel this!
PARACELSUS I feel 'tis pleasant that my aims, at length
Allowed their weight, should be supposed to need
A further strengthening in these goodly helps!
My course allures for its own sake, its sole
650 Intrinsic worth; and ne'er shall boat of mine
Adventure forth for gold and apes at once.
Your sages say, "if human, therefore weak:"
If weak, more need to give myself entire
To my pursuit; and by its side, all else . . .
655 No matter! I deny myself but little
In waiving all assistance save its own.
Would there were some real sacrifice to make!
Your friends the sages threw their joys away,
While I must be content with keeping mine.
660 FESTUS But do not cut yourself from human weal!
You cannot thrive—a man that dares affect
To spend his life in service to his kind
For no reward of theirs, unbound to them
By any tie; nor do so, Aureole! No—
665 There are strange punishments for such. Give up

644| *MS:* side——even I! —and you—— § written over by § you?— *1835:*
side—even I! And you? 645| *MS:* this?—say < > this!— *1835:* this! *1863:*
this? Say 646| *MS:* pleasant, that *1835:* pleasant that 647| *MS:*
Allow'd *1849:* Allowed 648-649| *MS:* helps! / Once more (since I am forced
to speak as one / Who has full liberty at his discretion) / My < > sake———its
1835: sake—its *1849:* helps! / My *1868:* sake, its 650| *MS:* worth, and
1835: worth; and 651| *MS:* once . . . § written over by § once:— *1835:*
once: 652| *MS:* say "if < > weak:"—— § written over by § weak:"— *1835:*
weak:" *1849:* say, "if 654| *MS:* pursuit;—and < > else—— § above § . .
1835: pursuit; and < > else . . . 655| *MS:*——No matter:—I *1835:* No
matter: I *1849:* matter! I 656| *MS:* own, *1835:* own— *1863:*
own. 657| *MS:* And I regret it;—there's no sacrifice *1835:* it; there's
1849: Would there were some real sacrifice to make! 658| *MS:* To make:—the
sages threw so much away *1835:* make; the *1849:* Your friends the sages threw
their joys away, 659| *MS:* with gaining all. *1849:* with keeping mine.
660| *MS:* weal! . . *1835:* weal! *1849:* weal? *1863:* weal!
661| *MS:* . . You < > thrive ———a *1835:* You < > thrive—a 662| *1835:*
kind, *1868:* kind 663| *MS:* theirs—nor bound *1835:* theirs, nor *1868:*
theirs, unbound 664| *MS:* tie——nor § written over by § tie!—nor < >
Aureole! *1835:* tie; nor *1849:* Aureole! No— 665| *MS:* for such . . .
although *1835:* such; although *1849:* such. Give up

(Although no visible good flow thence) some part
Of the glory to another; hiding thus,
Even from yourself, that all is for yourself.
Say, say almost to God—"I have done all
670 For her, not for myself!"
PARACELSUS   And who but lately
Was to rejoice in my success like you?
Whom should I love but both of you?
FESTUS   I know not:
But know this, you, that 'tis no will of mine
You should abjure the lofty claims you make;
675 And this the cause—I can no longer seek
To overlook the truth, that there would be
A monstrous spectacle upon the earth,
Beneath the pleasant sun, among the trees:
—A being knowing not what love is. Hear me!
680 You are endowed with faculties which bear
Annexed to them as 'twere a dispensation
To summon meaner spirits to do their will
And gather round them at their need; inspiring
Such with a love themselves can never feel,
685 Passionless 'mid their passionate votaries.
I know not if you joy in this or no,

666| MS: thence, give up some   1849: (Although no < > thence) some part
667| MS: Of your renown to another;—so you shall   1835: another: so   1849: Of
the glory to another; hiding thus,   668| MS: Hide from yourself that < >
yourself: 1835: for yourself.   1849: Even from yourself, that   669| MS: Say—
§ above §, say   1835: Say, say < > God "I   1849: God—"I   670| MS: her.—
—not for myself!"— — PARACELSUS < > late,   1835: her—not for myself!"   1849:
who, but lately,   1863: her, not   1868: who but lately   672| MS: but you?
FESTUS Nay, I   1849: but both of you? FESTUS I   673| MS: tis   1835: 'tis
1849: no wish of   1863: no will of   674| MS: make   1835: make;
675| MS:—And < > cause . . . I will no   1835: And < > cause—I   1849: Although
I can no longer seek, indeed,   1863: And this the cause—I   676| MS: truth . . .
that   1835: truth; that   1849: truth, that there will be   1863: there would
be   677| MS: earth— — § written over by § earth,—   1835: earth,
678| MS: sun— —among § written over by § sun,—among the trees—   1849: sun,
among the trees,   1849: trees: 679| MS: A < > is:—hear me;—   1835: is. Hear
me;   1849:—A < > me!   680| MS: which have   1835: endow'd   1849:
endowed < > which bear   681| 1835: Annex'd   1849: Annexed
682| MS: will,   1868: will   683| MS: To gather < > need,—inspiring
1835: need; inspiring   1849: And gather   684| MS: love which they can
1835: feel—   1849: love themselves can   1863: feel,   685| MS: midst < >
votaries;— — —   1835: votaries.   1849: 'mid

Or ever dream that common men can live
On objects you prize lightly, but which make
Their heart's sole treasure: the affections seem
690 Beauteous at most to you, which we must taste
Or die: and this strange quality accords,
I know not how, with you; sits well upon
That luminous brow, though in another it scowls
An eating brand, a shame. I dare not judge you.
695 The rules of right and wrong thus set aside,
There's no alternative—I own you one
Of higher order, under other laws
Than bind us; therefore, curb not one bold glance!
'Tis best aspire. Once mingled with us all . . .
700 MICHAL Stay with us, Aureole! cast those hopes away,
And stay with us! An angel warns me, too,
Man should be humble; you are very proud:
And God, dethroned, has doleful plagues for such!
—Warns me to have in dread no quick repulse,
705 No slow defeat, but a complete success:
You will find all you seek, and perish so!
PARACELSUS [after a pause] Are these the barren firstfruits of my quest?
Is love like this the natural lot of all?
How many years of pain might one such hour

687| *MS:* men live wholly   *1849:* men can live   688| *MS:* you so lightly
prize, which   *1849:* you prize lightly, but which   689| *MS:* sole wealth:—the
soft affections   *1835:* wealth: the   *1849:* sole treasure; the affections
690| *MS:* which they must   *1849:* which we must   691| *MS:* accords   *1835:*
accords,   692| *MS:* how, with you . . . sits § written over by § you—sits   *1835:*
you; sits   693| *MS:* brow——tho' in < > it were   *1835:* brow: though
1849: brow, though < > it scowls   694| *MS:* brand—a shame:——I § written
over by § shame:—I < > not blame you   *1835:* shame. I   *1849:* not judge you:
1863: brand, a   695| *MS:* aside   *1835:* aside,   696| *MS:* alternative . . .
I judge you   *1835:* alternative. I   *1849:* alternative—I own you   697| *MS:*
order—under   *1849:* order, under   698| *MS:* us, . . therefore § written over
by § us,—therefore curb   *1835:* us; therefore   *1849:* therefore, curb   699| *MS:*
'Tis < > aspire——once < > all . . . . .   *1835:* 'Tis < > aspire. Once < > all . . . .
1863: all . . .   700| *MS:* away   *1835:* us Aureole < > away,   *1849:* us,
Aureole   701| *MS:* us—an   *1835:* us; an   *1849:* us! An   702| *MS:*
humble . . . you < > proud!   *1835:* humble; you   *1849:* proud: 703| *1835:*
God dethroned has   *1849:* God, dethroned, has   704| *MS:* Warns < >
repulse   *1835:* repulse,   *1849:* He warns me not to dread a quick   *1863:*—Warns
me to have in dread no quick   705| *MS:* defeat——but   *1835:* defeat, but
1849: Nor slow   *1863:* No slow   707| *MS:*—Are < > first fruits
I should fear   *1835:* Are   *1849:* fruits of my life?   *1863:* firstfruits of my
quest?   709| *MS:* of hate might   *1849:* of pain might

710 O'erbalance? Dearest Michal, dearest Festus,
What shall I say, if not that I desire
To justify your love; and will, dear friends,
In swerving nothing from my first resolves.
See, the great moon! and ere the mottled owls
715 Were wide awake, I was to go. It seems
You acquiesce at last in all save this—
If I am like to compass what I seek
By the untried career I choose; and then,
If that career, making but small account
720 Of much of life's delight, will yet retain
Sufficient to sustain my soul: for thus
I understand these fond fears just expressed.
And first; the lore you praise and I neglect,
The labours and the precepts of old time,
725 I have not lightly disesteemed. But, friends,
Truth is within ourselves; it takes no rise
From outward things, whate'er you may believe.
There is an inmost centre in us all,
Where truth abides in fulness; and around,
730 Wall upon wall, the gross flesh hems it in,
This perfect, clear perception—which is truth.

710| *MS:* dearest Michal, dearest § corrected in pencil to § Dearest Michal, dearest **712|** *MS:* Well to deserve that love, and will < > Friends, *1835:* friends, *1849:* To merit this your love; and *1863:* To justify your love **713|** *MS:* my high resolves: § corrected in pencil to § resolves. *1849:* my first resolves. **714|** *MS:* See—the *1835:* See, the < > 'ere *1863:* ere **715–716|** *MS:* awake, I should have made all sure / For my departure that remains to do; / So answer not, while I run lightly o'er / The topics you have urged to-night:—it § corrected in pencil to § to-night. It seems / We acquiesce < > all, save only *1849:* awake, I was to go. It seems / You acquiesce < > all save this— **718|** *MS:* In the < > chuse *1849:* By the *1863:* choose **720|** *MS:* will offer joys *1849:* will yet retain **721|** *MS:* soul . . . for § corrected in pencil to § soul—for *1868:* soul: for **722|** *MS:* expressed: § corrected in pencil to § express'd. *1849:* expressed. **723|** *MS:* first;—the § corrected in pencil to § first; the **724|** *MS:* old sages, *1849:* old time, **725|** *MS:* not slightly disesteemed——but § corrected in pencil to § disesteem'd. But *1849:* disesteemed. But, friends, *1863:* not lightly disesteemed **726|** *MS:* ourselves—it *1835:* ourselves; it **727|** *MS:* believe; § corrected in pencil to § believe *1863:* believe. **728|** *MS:* all *1835:* all, **729|** *MS:* truth § corrected to § Truth *1835:* truth *1849:* around *1868:* around, **730|** *MS:* Wall within wall < > in— *1835:* in, *1849:* Wall upon wall **731|** Perfect and true Perception < > Truth;— § corrected in pencil to § Truth; *1835:* perception < > truth; *1849:* This perfect, clear perception *1863:* truth.

A baffling and perverting carnal mesh
Binds it, and makes all error: and to KNOW
Rather consists in opening out a way
735 Whence the imprisoned splendour may escape,
Than in effecting entry for a light
Supposed to be without. Watch narrowly
The demonstration of a truth, its birth,
And you trace back the effluence to its spring
740 And source within us; where broods radiance vast,
To be elicited ray by ray, as chance
Shall favour: chance—for hitherto, your sage
Even as he knows, not how those beams are born,
As little knows he what unlocks their fount:
745 And men have oft grown old among their books
To die case-hardened in their ignorance,
Whose careless youth had promised what long years
Of unremitted labour ne'er performed:
While, contrary, it has chanced some idle day,
750 To autumn loiterers just as fancy-free
As the midges in the sun, gives birth at last
To truth—produced mysteriously as cape
Of cloud grown out of the invisible air.

733| *MS:* Which blinds it, and makes Error: and, "to *know*" § corrected in pencil to §
to know" *1835:* error *1849:* Blinds it, and makes all error *1868:* and, to
KNOW, *1888:* Binds it 735| *MS:* splendor § corrected in pencil to § splendour
may dart forth, *1849:* inprisoned < > may escape, *1863:* imprisoned
736| *MS:* for the light *1849:* for a light 737| *MS:* without; watch
§ corrected in pencil to § without. Watch 738| *MS:* Truth *1835:* truth
739| *MS:* you shall trace the Effluence *1835:* effluence *1849:* you trace back
the 740| *MS:* us, where *1863:* us; where 742| *MS:* favour;—*chance*
§ corrected in pencil to § favour; *chance*—for hitherto, *1835:* favour: *chance* *1849:*
chance—for hitherto, your sage 743| *MS:* as we know *1849:* as he
knows 744| *MS:* know we what < > their lair;— § corrected in pencil to §
lair; *1849:* knows he what < > their fount; *1863:* fount. *1888:* fount;
745| *MS:* For Men *1835:* men *1849:* And men 746| *MS:* And died, case-
hardened § corrected in pencil to § case-harden'd *1849:* To die, case-hardened
1868: die case-hardened 749| *MS:* day *1835:* day, *1863:* day *1868:*
day, 750| *MS:* loiterers just § corrected in pencil to § loiterers, just *1835:*
loiterers just *1849:* That autumn *1863:* To autumn 751| *MS:* sun, has
§ corrected in pencil to § have oft brought forth *1835:* has *1849:* have oft given
vent *1863:* sun, gives birth at last 752| *MS:* A Truth, produced § corrected
in pencil to § Truth—produced *1835:* truth *1849:* To truth 753| *MS:*
invisible mist:— § corrected in pencil to § mist. *1849:* invisible air.

Hence, may not truth be lodged alike in all,
755 The lowest as the highest? some slight film
The interposing bar which binds a soul
And makes the idiot, just as makes the sage
Some film removed, the happy outlet whence
Truth issues proudly? See this soul of ours!
760 How it strives weakly in the child, is loosed
In manhood, clogged by sickness, back compelled
By age and waste, set free at last by death:
Why is it, flesh enthrals it or enthrones?
What is this flesh we have to penetrate?
765 Oh, not alone when life flows still, do truth
And power emerge, but also when strange chance
Ruffles its current; in unused conjuncture,
When sickness breaks the body—hunger, watching,
Excess or languor—oftenest death's approach,
770 Peril, deep joy or woe. One man shall crawl
Through life surrounded with all stirring things,
Unmoved; and he goes mad: and from the wreck
Of what he was, by his wild talk alone,

754| *MS:* Truth   *1835:* truth   755| *MS:* highest?—some   *1835:* highest?
some   756-758| *MS:* soul,— § corrected in pencil to § soul?— / Some < >
removed the   *1835:* soul?   *1849:* binds it up / And makes the idiot, just as makes
the sage / Some < > removed, the   *1863:* binds a soul   759-760| *MS:* It issues
proudly? seeing that the soul / Is deathless, we know well— —but § written over by §
deathless (we know well)—but oftener cooped § corrected in pencil to § coop'd / A
prisoner and a thrall, than a throned Power,— § corrected in pencil to § Power; / That
it < > child—is § corrected in pencil to § child; is   *1835:* well) but < > / < >
power; / < > child, is   *1849:* Truth < > proudly? See this soul of ours! / How
it   761| *1835:* clogg'd   *1849:* clogged   762-765| *MS:* waste—set
§ corrected in pencil to § waste, set < > death;— — — § written over by § death,—
§ corrected in pencil to § death— / That not < > still do Truth   *1835:* death: / < >
truth   *1849:* death: / Why is it, flesh enthralls it or enthrones? / What is this flesh
we have to penetrate? / Oh, not   *1863:* still, do   766| *MS:* Power   *1835:*
power   767| *MS:* Affects it   *1849:* Ruffles its   768| *MS:*
hunger—watching, § corrected in pencil to § hunger, watching   *1835:* Where
sickness   *1849:* When sickness   769| *MS:* Excess, or < > approach—   *1863:*
approach,   *1868:* Excess or   770| *MS:* joy or woe;—one § corrected in pencil
to § joy, or woe. One   *1868:* joy or   771| *MS:* Thro' § corrected in pencil to §
Through life, surrounded   *1868:* life surrounded   772| *MS:* Unmoved— —and
§ corrected in pencil to § Unmoved—and < > mad—and § corrected in pencil to §
mad; and   *1868:* unmoved; and < > mad: and

You first collect how great a spirit he hid.
775 Therefore, set free the soul alike in all,
Discovering the true laws by which the flesh
Accloys the spirit! We may not be doomed
To cope with seraphs, but at least the rest
Shall cope with us. Make no more giants, God,
780 But elevate the race at once! We ask
To put forth just our strength, our human strength,
All starting fairly, all equipped alike,
Gifted alike, all eagle-eyed, true-hearted—
See if we cannot beat thine angels yet!
785 Such is my task. I go to gather this
The sacred knowledge, here and there dispersed
About the world, long lost or never found.
And why should I be sad or lorn of hope?
Why ever make man's good distinct from God's,
790 Or, finding they are one, why dare mistrust?
Who shall succeed if not one pledged like me?
Mine is no mad attempt to build a world

---

⁷⁷⁴⁻⁷⁷⁵| *MS:* hid— § corrected in pencil to § hid. / —Seeing all this, why should I
pine in vain / Attempts to win some day the august form / Of Truth to stand before
me, and compel / My dark unvalued frame to change its nature / And straight become
suffused with light— — at § corrected in pencil to § light—at best / For my sole
good—leaving the world to seek / Salvation out as it best may—or §written over by §
may, or follow / The same long thorny course: No § corrected in pencil to § course.
No, I will learn / How to set < > All,   *1835:* hid. / Seeing all this why < > ///
< > nature, /// < > course? No < > / < > in all,   *1849:* hid. / Therefore,
set   ⁷⁷⁶| *MS:* By searching out the laws < > Flesh § corrected in pencil to §
flesh   *1849:* Discovering the true laws   ⁷⁷⁷| *MS:* Spirit——we § corrected in
pencil to § Spirit. We < > doomed § corrected in pencil to § doom'd   *1849:* Bars in
the spirit! We < > doomed   *1863:* Accloys the   ⁷⁷⁹| *MS:* us—make < >
Giants, God!   *1835:* us. Make < > giants   *1863:* God,   ⁷⁸⁰| *MS:* Race at
once!—we § corrected in pencil to § once! We   *1835:* race   ⁷⁸¹| *MS:* But to
put forth our   *1849:* To put forth just our   ⁷⁸²| *MS:*—All < > equipped
§ corrected in pencil to § equipp'd alike § corrected in pencil to § alike,   *1835:* All
1849: equipped   ⁷⁸³| *MS:* alike and § corrected in pencil to § alike, and eagle-
eyed, true-hearted . . . § corrected in pencil to § true-hearted.   *1849:* alike, all eagle-
eyed, true-hearted—   ⁷⁸⁴| *MS:* beat thy angels yet!— § corrected in pencil to §
yet!   *1863:* beat the angels   *1868:* beat thine angels   ⁷⁸⁵| *MS:*—Such < >
task— —I § corrected in pencil to § task. I   *1835:* Such   ⁷⁸⁶| *MS:* Mysterious
knowledge   *1849:* The sacred knowledge   ⁷⁸⁷| *MS:* or ever-
hidden—§ corrected in pencil to § ever-hidden,   *1835:* ever-hidden;   *1849:* or never
found.   ⁷⁸⁸| *MS:* sad, or   *1868:* sad or   ⁷⁸⁹| *MS:* Man's < > God's?
1835: man's   *1868:* God's,   ⁷⁹⁰| *MS:* why have mistrust?   *1849:* why dare
mistrust?

Apart from his, like those who set themselves
To find the nature of the spirit they bore,
795 And, taught betimes that all their gorgeous dreams
Were only born to vanish in this life,
Refused to fit them to its narrow sphere,
But chose to figure forth another world
And other frames meet for their vast desires,—
800 And all a dream! Thus was life scorned; but life
Shall yet be crowned: twine amaranth! I am priest!
And all for yielding with a lively spirit
A poor existence, parting with a youth
Like those who squander every energy
805 Convertible to good, on painted toys,
Breath-bubbles, gilded dust! And though I spurn
All adventitious aims, from empty praise
To love's award, yet whoso deems such helps
Important, and concerns himself for me,
810 May know even these will follow with the rest—
As in the steady rolling Mayne, asleep
Yonder, is mixed its mass of schistous ore.
My own affections laid to rest awhile,
Will waken purified, subdued alone
815 By all I have achieved. Till then—till then . . .
Ah, the time-wiling loitering of a page

793| *1849:* His   *1868:* his   795–796| *MS:* dreams / And beauteous fancies,
hopes and aspirations / Were born only to wither in   *1835:* hopes, and aspirations,
1849: dreams / Were only born to vanish in   797| *MS:* to curb or moderate
their longings, / Or fit them to this narrow sphere, but chose / To figure and
conceive another   *1849:* to fit < > sphere, / But chose to figure forth another
1863: to its narrow   799| *MS:* desires,   *1849:* desires,—   800| *MS:*
dream!—thus   *1835:* dream! Thus < > scorn'd   *1849:* Still, all < > scorned
1863: And all   801| *MS:* crowned . . twine < > Priest!   *1835:* crown'd: twine
< > priest!   *1849:* crowned   803| *MS:* existence—parting   *1863:* existence,
parting   804| *MS:* Like theirs who   *1868:* Like those who   805| *MS:*
good on   *1849:* good, on   806| *MS:* and tho'   *1835:* And though
809| *MS:* Important and   *1835:* me   *1849:* Important, and < > me,
812–813| *MS:* is mingled and involved a mass / Of schistous particles of ore . . and
even / My own affections, laid   *1835:* ore. And < > / < > awhile—   *1849:* is
mixed its mass of schistous ore. / My < > awhile,   *1888:* affections laid
815| *MS:* achieved, . . till then—till then — — —   *1835:* achieved; till then—till then
. . .   *1863:* achieved. Till then—till   816| *MS:* time-wiling . . loitering   *1835:*
time-wiling loitering

106

Through bower and over lawn, till eve shall bring
The stately lady's presence whom he loves—
The broken sleep of the fisher whose rough coat
820 Enwraps the queenly pearl—these are faint types!
See, see, they look on me: I triumph now!
But one thing, Festus, Michal! I have told
All I shall e'er disclose to mortal: say—
Do you believe I shall accomplish this?
825 FESTUS I do believe!

MICHAL   I ever did believe!

PARACELSUS Those words shall never fade from out my brain!
This earnest of the end shall never fade!
Are there not, Festus, are there not, dear Michal,
Two points in the adventure of the diver,
830 One—when, a beggar, he prepares to plunge,
One—when, a prince, he rises with his pearl?
Festus, I plunge!

FESTUS   We wait you when you rise!

817| *MS:* Thro' < > over § illegible word cancelled by § lawn, 'till   *1835:*
Through   *1849:* till   818| *MS:* loves . . . .   *1835:* loves—   820| *MS:*
pearl——these   *1835:* pearl—these   821| *MS:* me—I   *1849:* See how they
1863: See, see they   *1888:* See, see, they   822| *MS:* Tell me, Festus, Michal,
but one thing—I   *1849:* But one thing, Festus, Michal!—I   *1863:* Michal! I
823| *MS:* mortal: . . . how,   *1835:* mortal . . . now,   *1849:* mortal: say—
825| *MS:* believe! MICHAL And I, dear Aureole!   *1849:* believe! MICHAL I ever did
believe!   826| *MS:* brain: — —   *1849:* brain!   827| *MS:* 'Tis earnest
< > end: — —shall   *1835:* "Tis < > end—shall   *1849:* This earnest < > end
shall   828| *MS:* not dear Michal   *1835:* Michal,   *1849:* not, Festus, are < >
not, dear   829| *MS:* diver— —   *1835:* diver: *1868:* diver,   830| *MS:*
beggar he < > plunge   *1835:* when a < > plunge?   *1849:* when, a beggar, he
1863: plunge,   831| *MS:* when a prince he < > pearl,?   *1835:* pearl?   *1849:*
when, a prince, he   832| *MS:* plunge!   *1849:* plunge! FESTUS I wait you when
you rise!   *1863:* plunge! FESTUS We wait

SCENE—*Constantinople; the house of a Greek Conjurer.* 1521.

PARACELSUS.

Over the waters in the vaporous West
The sun goes down as in a sphere of gold
Behind the arm of the city, which between,
With all that length of domes and minarets,
5   Athwart the splendour, black and crooked runs
Like a Turk verse along a scimitar.
There lie, sullen memorial, and no more
Possess my aching sight! 'Tis done at last.
Strange—and the juggles of a sallow cheat
10 Have won me to this act! 'Tis as yon cloud
Should voyage unwrecked o'er many a mountain-top
And break upon a molehill. I have dared
Come to a pause with knowledge; scan for once
The heights already reached, without regard
15 To the extent above; fairly compute

SCENE| *MS: "The House of the Greek."* 1849: *"The House of the Greek-conjuror."* 1863: *the House of a Greek conjurer.* 1888: *the house of a Greek Conjurer.* 1| 1835: *west* 1863: *West* 2| 1849: *gold,* 1863: gold 3–5| *MS: between / Athwart the splendour black* 1835: *between, / splendour, black* 1849: *the outstretched city < > between, / With all that length of domes and minarets, / Athwart* 1863: *the arm of the city* 6| *MS: scimetar— — —* 1835: *scimetar.* 1863: *scimitar.* 7| 1849: *lie, thou saddest writing, and while* 1863: *lie, sullen memorial, and no more* 8| *MS: sight:—'tis < > last!* 1835: *sight. 'Tis* 1849: *Relieve my* 1863: *Possess my* 1868: *last.* 9| *MS: Strange— —and § written over by § !—* 1835: *Strange—and* 10| *MS: act—'tis* 1835: *act: 'tis* 1849: *Could win < > act! 'Tis* 1863: *Have won* 11| 1835: *unwreck'd* 1868: *unwrecked* 12| *MS: molehille;—I* 1835: *molehill. I* 13| *MS: pause at last—and scan* 1835: *last, and* 1849: *pause with knowledge; scan* 14| 1835: *reach'd* 1863: *reached* 15| *MS: above—fairly* 1835: *above; fairly*

All I have clearly gained; for once excluding
A brilliant future to supply and perfect
All half-gains and conjectures and crude hopes:
And all because a fortune-teller wills
His credulous seekers should inscribe thus much
Their previous life's attainment, in his roll,
Before his promised secret, as he vaunts,
Make up the sum: and here amid the scrawled
Uncouth recordings of the dupes of this
Old arch-genethliac, lie my life's results!

A few blurred characters suffice to note
A stranger wandered long through many lands
And reaped the fruit he coveted in a few
Discoveries, as appended here and there,
The fragmentary produce of much toil,
In a dim heap, fact and surmise together
Confusedly massed as when acquired; he was
Intent on gain to come too much to stay
And scrutinize the little gained: the whole

---

¹⁶| *MS:* gained, for   *1835:* gained; for   *1849:* What I   *1863:* All I
¹⁷| *1849:* My future which should finish and fulfil   *1863:* A brilliant future to
supply and perfect   ¹⁸| *MS:* half-gains, and conjectures, and < > hopes—
1849: conjectures, and mere hopes—   *1863:* half-gains and conjectures and crude
hopes—   *1868:* hopes: ¹⁹| *MS:*—And   *1835:* And   *1849:* And this, because
a fortune-teller bids   *1863:* And all, because a fortune-teller wills   *1868:* all
because   ²⁰⁻²³| *MS:* much / Within this roll——and   *1835:* roll: and here,
amid the scrawl'd   *1849:* credulous enquirers write thus much, / Their previous life's
attainment, in his book, / Before his promised secret, as he vaunts, / Make that life
perfect: here, accordingly   *1863:* credulous seekers should inscribe thus much, / < >
his roll, // Make up the sum: and here, amid the scrawled   *1888:* much /// < >
here amid   ²⁴| *1849:* 'Mid the uncouth recordings of such dupes,   *1863:*
Uncouth recordings of the dupes of this   ²⁵| *1849:*—Scrawled in like fashion,
lie   *1863:* Old arch-genethliac, lie   ²⁶| *1849:* These few   *1863:* A few
²⁷| *MS:* long in many   *1835:* wander'd   *1849:* wandered long through
many   ²⁸| *1835:* reap'd   *1849:* reaped   ²⁹| *MS:* Discoveries—
§ above §, as < > there,—   *1835:* Discoveries, as < > there,   ³⁰| *MS:* of
those toils   *1835:* toils,   *1849:* of much toil   ³¹| *MS:* to-gether   *1835:*
together   ³²| *MS:* acquired—he was   *1835:* mass'd, as < > acquired; he
1849: massed < > acquired; himself   *1863:* massed as < > acquired; he was
³³| *1849:* Too bent on gaining more to calmly stay   *1863:* Intent on gain to come
too much to stay   ³⁴| *MS:* scrutinize whate'er was gained—the   *1835:* gain'd:
the   *1849:* scrutinize the little which he gained: *1863:* little gained: the whole

35 Slipt in the blank space 'twixt an idiot's gibber
And a mad lover's ditty—there it lies.

And yet those blottings chronicle a life—
A whole life, and my life! Nothing to do,
No problem for the fancy, but a life
40 Spent and decided, wasted past retrieve
Or worthy beyond peer. Stay, what does this
Remembrancer set down concerning "life"?
" 'Time fleets, youth fades, life is an empty dream,'
It is the echo of time; and he whose heart
45 Beat first beneath a human heart, whose speech
Was copied from a human tongue, can never
Recall when he was living yet knew not this.
Nevertheless long seasons pass o'er him
Till some one hour's experience shows what nothing,
50 It seemed, could clearer show; and ever after,
An altered brow and eye and gait and speech
Attest that now he knows the adage true
'Time fleets, youth fades, life is an empty dream.' "

Ay, my brave chronicler, and this same hour

35| *MS:* twixt an ideot's   *1835:* 'twixt   *1849:* idiot's   36| *MS:* ditty—
—there   *1835:* ditty—there   *1849:* ditty—lies the whole!   *1863:* ditty—there it
lies.   37| *MS:* life   *1835:* life—   38| *MS:*——A < > life! no thing to do,
1835: A < > nothing   *1849:* life,—mine! No thought to turn to act   *1863:* life,—and
my life! Nothing to do,   *1868:* life, and   40| *MS:* decided,—wasted   *1835:*
decided, wasted < > retrieve—   *1849:* past recall,   *1863:* past retrieve
41-42| *MS:* beyond a peer——stay < > / < > "life"? § above § — — — —   *1835:*
peer. Stay < > / < > "life?"   *1849:* beyond peer. Stay, turn the page / And take its
chance,—thus: what, concerning "life" / Does this remembrancer set down?—"We
say   *1863:* peer. Stay, what does this / Remembrancer set down concerning
"life"?   43| *MS:* dream'   *1835:* dream,'   *1849:* dream.'   *1888:*
dream,'   44| *MS:* time—he whose heart beat   *1835:* time: he   *1849:* 'Tis the
mere echo of time; and he < > heart   *1863:* It is the echo   45| *MS:* First
underneath a   *1849:* Beat first beneath a   46| *MS:* tongue—can   *1835:* tongue,
can   47| *MS:* knew it not: *1849:* knew not this.   48| *1835:* him,
1849: seasons come and go,   *1863:* seasons pass o'er him   49| *MS:* Until, one
hour's < > nothing   *1835:* Until one   *1849:* Till some one < > what nought,
1863: what nothing,   50| *MS:* show—and < > after   *1835:* seem'd < > show,
and   *1849:* He deemed, could < > show; and   *1863:* It seemed, could < >
after,   51| *1835:* alter'd brow, and eye, and gait, and   *1849:* altered   *1863:*
brow and eye and gait and   52| *MS: now* he *knows* this adage   *1849:* now he
knows the adage   53| *MS:* dream' "   *1835:* dream.' "   54| *1849:* same
time   *1863:* same hour

55   As well as any: now, let my time be!

Now! I can go no farther; well or ill,
'Tis done. I must desist and take my chance.
I cannot keep on the stretch: 'tis no back-shrinking—
For let but some assurance beam, some close
60   To my toil grow visible, and I proceed
At any price, though closing it, I die.
Else, here I pause. The old Greek's prophecy
Is like to turn out true: "I shall not quit
His chamber till I know what I desire!"
65   Was it the light wind sang it o'er the sea?

An end, a rest! strange how the notion, once
Encountered, gathers strength by moments! Rest!
Where has it kept so long? this throbbing brow
To cease, this beating heart to cease, all cruel
70   And gnawing thoughts to cease! To dare let down
My strung, so high-strung brain, to dare unnerve
My harassed o'ertasked frame, to know my place,

55| MS: any:—now   1835: any: now   1849: any: let my hour speak now!   1863:
any: now, let my time be!   56| MS: Now!—I < > farther——well or ill
1835: Now! I < > farther; well or ill—   1849: Now! I   1863: ill,   57| MS:
'Tis done——I < > chance—   1835: 'Tis done. I < > chance;   1863:
chance.   58| MS: keep at this—'tis no back-shrinking,—   1835: this; 'tis no
back shrinking—   1849: keep on the stretch; 'tis no back-shrinking—
59| 1849: let the least assurance dawn, some end   1863: let but some assurance
beam, some close   60| MS: To this my toil appear, and   1849: To my toil
seem possible, and   1863: toil grow visible, and   61| MS: tho' < > die: . . . .
1835: though < > die . . .   1849: price, by any sacrifice: 1863: price, though
closing it, I die.   62| MS: But here I pause:—the   1835: pause: the   1849:
Else, here I pause: the   1863: pause. The   63| MS: true—I   1849: true—"I
1863: true: "I   64-66| MS: desire. / § space § / An end,—a   1835: 'till < > /
§ space § / An end, a < > notion, once   1849: till < > desire!" / Was it the light
wind sung it, o'er the sea? / § space § / An   1863: sang it o'er   67| MS:
moments—rest!   1835: Encounter'd < > moments. Rest!   1849: Admitted, gains
strength every moment! Rest!   1863: Encountered, gathers strength by
moments   68| MS: long?——this   1835: long? this   1849: Where kept that
thought so   1863: Where has it kept so   69| MS: cease—this < > cease—all
1849: heart to cease—its crowd   1863: cease, this < > cease, all cruel
70| MS: cease! to   1835: cease!—to   1849: of gnawing < > cease!—To
1863: And gnawing < > cease! To   71| MS: brain—to   1863: brain, to
72| MS: frame——to § written over by § frame—to   1835: harass'd o'er task'd
1849: harassed o'ertasked   1863: frame, to < > place!   1868: place,

My portion, my reward, even my failure,
Assigned, made sure for ever! To lose myself
75 Among the common creatures of the world,
To draw some gain from having been a man,
Neither to hope nor fear, to live at length!
Even in failure, rest! But rest in truth
And power and recompense . . . I hoped that once!

80 What, sunk insensibly so deep? Has all
Been undergone for this? This the request
My labour qualified me to present
With no fear of refusal? Had I gone
Slightingly through my task, and so judged fit
85 To moderate my hopes; nay, were it now
My sole concern to exculpate myself,
End things or mend them,—why, I could not choose
A humbler mood to wait for the event!
No, no, there needs not this; no, after all,
90 At worst I have performed my share of the task:

73| *MS:* reward—even   *1835:* reward, even   *1849:*—My portion, my reward, my
failure even,   *1863:* My portion, my reward, even my failure   74| *MS:*
Assigned—made < > forever!—to   *1835:* Assign'd, made < > for ever   *1849:*
Assigned < > ever!—To   *1863:* ever! To   75| *MS:* world,—   *1835:* world—
1863: world,   76| *MS:* Man,—   *1835:* man—   *1863:* man,   77| *MS:*
fear— — —to   *1835:* fear—to   *1863:* fear, to   78-80| *MS:* rest! . . . . but
§ written over by § rest!—but rest, in Truth / < > recompense— — —/ § space § / 'Tis
little wonder truly—things go on / And at their worst they end or mend—'tis time / To
look about with matters at this pass:— / Have I insensibly sunk as deep . . . has
1835: power, and recompense . . . / § space § / 'Tis < > truly; things < > // < >
about, with < > pass: / < > deep—has   *1849:* Oh, were it but in failure, to have rest!
/ What, sunk insensibly so deep? has   *1863:* Even in failure, rest! But rest in truth
/ And power and recompense . . . I hoped that once! / § space § / What
81| *MS:* this? *this,* the   *1835:* this? *this* the   *1849:* this? Was this the prayer
1863: this? This the request   83| *MS:* refusal— —had § written over by §
refusal?—had   *1835:* refusal? Had   84| *MS:* thro' my task and therefore
judged   *1835:* through my task, and   *1849:* Carelessly through < > and so judged
fit   *1863:* Slightingly through   85| *MS:* It fit to < > hopes,—nay, were it
1835: hopes; nay   *1849:* To moderate < > it now   86| *MS:* myself— — —
1835: myself—   *1849:* myself,   87| *MS:*—To flounder thro' the scrape— —I
§ written over by § scrape— I < > chuse   *1835:* To   *1849:* And lessen
punishment,—I   *1863:* End things or mend them,—why, I   88| *MS:* An
1849: the decree!   *1863:* A < > the event!   89| *MS:*—No, no < > this—no
1835: No, no < > this; no   90| *MS: my*   *1835:* perform'd < > task.   *1849:*
performed my < > task: *1863:* task;   *1888:* task § only upper half of ; or :
printed §   *1889:* task:

The rest is God's concern; mine, merely this,
To know that I have obstinately held
By my own work. The mortal whose brave foot
Has trod, unscathed, the temple-court so far
95 That he descries at length the shrine of shrines,
Must let no sneering of the demons' eyes,
Whom he could pass unquailing, fasten now
Upon him, fairly past their power; no, no—
He must not stagger, faint, fall down at last,
100 Having a charm to battle them; behold,
He bares his front: a mortal ventures thus
Serene amid the echoes, beams and glooms!
If he be priest henceforth, if he wake up
The god of the place to ban and blast him there,
105 Both well! What's failure or success to me?
I have subdued my life to the one purpose
Whereto I ordained it; there alone I spy,
No doubt, that way I may be satisfied.
Yes, well have I subdued my life! beyond
110 The obligation of my strictest vow,

91| *MS:*—The < > concern— —mine, merely, this— *1835:* The < > concern—mine
< > this, *1863:* concern; mine 93| *MS:* work— —the § written over by §
work:—the *1835:* work: the *1849:* work. The 94| *MS:* trod so far the Temple-
courts unscathed *1835:* temple-courts unscathed, *1849:* trod, unscathed, the temple-
courts so far 96| *MS:* daemons' eyes *1835:* demon's eyes, 97–98| *MS:*
Which he < > now / Upon < > power—no—no *1835:* power; no, no, *1849:*
Whose wrath he met unquailing, follow sly / And fasten on him, fairly past their
power, / If where he stands he dares but stay; no, no— *1863:* Whom he could pass
unquailing, fasten now / Upon him, fairly past their power; no, no— 99| *MS:*
stagger and fall down *1849:* stagger, faint and fall at *1863:* faint, fall down
at 100| *MS:* behold *1835:* behold, *1849:*—Knowing a *1863:* Having
a 101| *MS:* front—a *1835:* front: a *1849:* front—a *1863:* front; a
102| *MS:* glooms!— *1835:* beams, and glooms! *1863:* beams and 103| *MS:*
Priest henceforth—if *1835:* priest henceforth, if he *1849:* henceforth, or if he
wake *1863:* henceforth, if he wake up 104| *MS:* God < > there,— *1835:*
god < > there. *1849:* there,— *1863:* there, 105| *MS:* well!. .what's
1835: well! What's 106| *MS:* one end *1863:* one purpose 107| *MS:* it
. . . there *1835:* ordain'd it; there *1849:* Ordained life; there alone I cannot
doubt, *1863:* Whereto I ordained it; there < > I spy, 108| *MS:* doubt—
—that < > satisfied: / § no space § / *1835:* doubt; that < > satisfied. *1849:*
That only way < > satisfied. *1863:* No doubt, that way *1888:* satisfied. /
§ space § / 109| *MS:* life— —beyond § written over by § life!—beyond *1835:*
life! beyond 110| *MS:* vows, *1868:* vow,

The contemplation of my wildest bond,
Which gave my nature freely up, in truth,
But in its actual state, consenting fully
All passionate impulses its soil was formed
115 To rear, should wither; but foreseeing not
The tract, doomed to perpetual barrenness,
Would seem one day, remembered as it was,
Beside the parched sand-waste which now it is,
Already strewn with faint blooms, viewless then.
120 I ne'er engaged to root up loves so frail
I felt them not; yet now, 'tis very plain
Some soft spots had their birth in me at first,
If not love, say, like love: there was a time
When yet this wolfish hunger after knowledge
125 Set not remorselessly love's claims aside.
This heart was human once, or why recall
Einsiedeln, now, and Würzburg which the Mayne
Forsakes her course to fold as with an arm?

And Festus—my poor Festus, with his praise
130 And counsel and grave fears—where is he now

112| *MS:* gave, in truth, my nature freely up, *1863:* gave my nature freely up, in truth, 113-115| *MS:* state— —consenting fully / All < > formed / To < > wither—but foreseing *1835:* state—consenting < > / < > form'd / < > wither; but *1849:* In what it should be, more than what it was— / Consenting that whatever passions slept, / Whatever impulses lay unmatured, / Should wither in the germ,—but scarce foreseeing *1863:* But in its actual state, consenting fully / All passionate impulses its soil was formed / To rear, should wither; but foreseeing not 116| *MS:* tract doomed < > barrenness *1835:* tract doom'd *1849:* That the soil, doomed thus to perpetual waste, *1863:* The tract, doomed to perpetual barrenness, 117| *MS:* was *1849:* remembered in its youth *1863:* remembered as it was, 118| *MS:* Beside the § *the* inserted above the line § parched sand-tract which *1835:* parch'd *1849:* parched *1863:* sand-waste which 119| *MS:* then ... *1835:* then. 121| *MS:* not .. yet § written over by § not—yet < > tis *1835:* not, yet < > 'tis *1849:* not; yet 122| *1835:* first— *1863:* first, 123| *MS:* love:—there *1835:* love: there 125| *MS:* remorselessly its claims aside .... *1835:* remorselessly its < > aside; *1849:* remorselessly love's claims *1863:* aside. 127| *MS:* Einsiedeln, even now—and Würzburg whom the *1835:* now, and Würzburg, whom *1849:* Einsiedeln, now, and Würzburg, which the *1868:* Würzburg which 128| *MS:* The Mayne § cancelled § Forsakes < > arm— — — § written over by § arm? — — *1835:* arm? ... *1849:* arm? 129| *MS:* Festus— —my < > Festus—with his praise, *1835:* Festus—my < > Festus, with *1863:* praise 130| *MS:* fears— —where < > now? *1835:* counsel, and < > fears—where *1863:* counsel and < > now

With the sweet maiden, long ago his bride?
I surely loved them—that last night, at least,
When we . . . gone! gone! the better. I am saved
The sad review of an ambitious youth
135 Choked by vile lusts, unnoticed in their birth,
But let grow up and wind around a will
Till action was destroyed. No, I have gone
Purging my path successively of aught
Wearing the distant likeness of such lusts.
140 I have made life consist of one idea:
Ere that was master, up till that was born,
I bear a memory of a pleasant life
Whose small events I treasure; till one morn
I ran o'er the seven little grassy fields,
145 Startling the flocks of nameless birds, to tell
Poor Festus, leaping all the while for joy,
To leave all trouble for my future plans,
Since I had just determined to become
The greatest and most glorious man on earth.
150 And since that morn all life has been forgotten;
All is one day, one only step between
The outset and the end: one tyrant all-
Absorbing aim fills up the interspace,

131| MS: long ago § *ago* inserted above the line § his bride,— — — 1835: bride?
1849: bride 1863: bride? 133| MS: we— —gone! gone! the better:—I 1835:
we . . . gone! gone! the better: I 1863: better. I 134| 1835: youth, 1863:
youth 135| MS: lusts unnoticed < > birth 1835: lusts, unnoticed < >
birth, 136| MS: Which have grown up and wound < > Will 1835: will
1849: But let grow up and wind 137| MS: destroyed:—No 1835: destroy'd.
No 1849: destroyed 139| MS: such loves: 1835: loves. 1849: such
lusts. 1889: lusts 140| MS: idea: . . 1835: idea: 141| MS: Ere *that*
was master . . up 'till < > born 1835: E're < > master—up 'till *that* 1849: Ere
that was master—up till that was born— 1863: master, up < > born,
143| MS: I can recall even to 1835: recall, even 1849: I treasure; till one
morn 144| MS: The morn I ran § *I ran* inserted above the line § over the
grassy fields 1849: I ran o'er the seven little grassy fields, 147| MS: plans
1835: plans, 1849: for futurity 1863: for my future plans 148| MS: For I
1835: determin'd 1849: Since I < > determined 149| MS: glorious being on
earth; 1835: earth. 1849: glorious man on 150| MS: But since that hour,
all < > forgotten:— 1835: hour all < > forgotten. 1849: And since that morn all
< > forgot; 1863: forgotten; 151| MS: 'Tis as one day— —one 1835: 'Tis
< > day—one 1849: All is one 1863: day, one 152| MS: all 1835:
all— 1849: tyrant aim, 1863: tyrant all— 153| 'MS: the interval: 1835:
interval— 1849: Absorbing all, fills 1863: Absorbing aim fills up the interspace,

One vast unbroken chain of thought, kept up
155 Through a career apparently adverse
To its existence: life, death, light and shadow,
The shows of the world, were bare receptacles
Or indices of truth to be wrung thence,
Not ministers of sorrow or delight:
160 A wondrous natural robe in which she went.
For some one truth would dimly beacon me
From mountains rough with pines, and flit and wink
O'er dazzling wastes of frozen snow, and tremble
Into assured light in some branching mine
165 Where ripens, swathed in fire, the liquid gold—
And all the beauty, all the wonder fell
On either side the truth, as its mere robe;
I see the robe now—then I saw the form.
So far, then, I have voyaged with success,
170 So much is good, then, in this working sea
Which parts me from that happy strip of land:
But o'er that happy strip a sun shone, too!
And fainter gleams it as the waves grow rough,
And still more faint as the sea widens; last
175 I sicken on a dead gulf streaked with light
From its own putrefying depths alone.

154| *MS:* thought kept   *1835:* thought, kept   155| *MS:* Throughout a course
apparently   *1849:* Through a career or friendly or opposed   *1863:* career apparently
adverse   156| *MS:* existence—life   *1835:* existence: life < > light, and
1849: light and shade   *1863:* light and shadow,   157| *MS:* shews < > world
. . were   *1835:* shows < > world, were   158| *MS:* thence   *1835:*
thence,   159–161| *MS:* delight— — / < > which I went: / For   *1835:*
delight—   *1849:* Not instruments of < > delight: / For   *1863:* Not ministers of
< > / A wondrous natural robe in which she went. / For   163| *MS:* Oer < >
snow—and tremble   *1835:* O'er < > snow, and   164| *MS:* mine,   *1863:*
mine   165–170| *MS:* ripens swathed in fire the < > gold, Yet all was then
o'erlooked, tho' noted now:— / So < > good then, in   *1835:* ripens swathed in fire,
the < > gold— / < > o'erlook'd < > now. / < > good, then   *1849:* gold— / And
all the beauty, all the wonder fell / On either side the truth, as its mere robe; / Men
saw the robe—I saw the august form. / So far, then, I have voyaged with success, / So
much   *1863:* robe; / I see the robe now—then I saw the form. / So far
171| *MS:* land;   *1835:* land.   *1849:* land—   *1863:* land;   172| *MS:* shone
too!   *1849:* shone, too!   174| *MS:* widens . . last,   *1835:* widens. Last,
1849: widens; last   175| *1835:* gulf, streak'd   *1849:* gulph, streaked   *1863:*
gulf streaked   176| *MS:* putrifying < > alone!—   *1835:* alone!   *1863:*
putrefying

Then, God was pledged to take me by the hand;
Now, any miserable juggle can bid
My pride depart. All is alike at length:
180 God may take pleasure in confounding pride
By hiding secrets with the scorned and base—
I am here, in short: so little have I paused
Throughout! I never glanced behind to know
If I had kept my primal light from wane,
185 And thus insensibly am—what I am!

Oh, bitter; very bitter!
                And more bitter,
To fear a deeper curse, an inner ruin,
Plague beneath plague, the last turning the first
To light beside its darkness. Let me weep
190 My youth and its brave hopes, all dead and gone,
In tears which burn! Would I were sure to win
Some startling secret in their stead, a tincture
Of force to flush old age with youth, or breed
Gold, or imprison moonbeams till they change
195 To opal shafts!—only that, hurling it
Indignant back, I might convince myself

177| *MS: Then*—God < > hand,— *1835:* hand; *1849:* Then *1863:* Then,
God   178| *MS: Now*—any *1849:* Now < > juggler bends *1863:* Now,
any < > juggle can bid   179–180| *MS:* depart—all < > length, God < >
confounding us *1835:* depart. All *1849:* pride to him. All seems alike at length: /
Who knows which are the wise and which the fools? / God < > confounding pride
1863: pride depart. All is alike at length: / God   181–182| *MS:* secrets in the
< > base— — — / I *1835:* scorn'd and base . . . *1849:* secrets with the scorned
and base— / He who stoops lowest may find most—in short, / I am here; and all
seems natural; I start not: *1863:* base— / I am here, in short: so little have I
paused   183| *MS:* Throughout— —I *1835:* Throughout. I *1849:* And never
having glanced *1863:* Throughout. I never glanced *1868:* Throughout! I
185| *MS: 1849:* insensibly grown—what *1863:* insensibly am—what
186| *MS:* bitter, very bitter! / And < > bitter *1835:* bitter; very *1849:* more
bitter,   187| *MS: 1835:* ruin— *1863:* ruin,   ·   188| *MS:* plague— —the
1835: plague—the *1863:* plague, the   189| *MS:* darkness: let *1835:*
darkness. Let *1849:* darkness. Better weep *1863:* darkness. Let me weep
190| *MS:* hopes all dead and gone, *1835:* hopes, all   191| *MS:* burn—
—would *1835:* burn. Would *1849:* burn! Would   192| *MS:* stead—a
1835: stead! a *1849:* stead!—a *1863:* stead, a   195| *MS:* opal-shafts— —
—only *1835:* opal shafts! only *1849:* shafts!—only

My aims remained supreme and pure as ever!
Even now, why not desire, for mankind's sake,
That if I fail, some fault may be the cause,
200 That, though I sink, another may succeed?
O God, the despicable heart of us!
Shut out this hideous mockery from my heart!

'Twas politic in you, Aureole, to reject
Single rewards, and ask them in the lump;
205 At all events, once launched, to hold straight on:
For now 'tis all or nothing. Mighty profit
Your gains will bring if they stop short of such
Full consummation! As a man, you had
A certain share of strength; and that is gone
210 Already in the getting these you boast.
Do not they seem to laugh, as who should say—
"Great master, we are here indeed, dragged forth
To light; this hast thou done: be glad! Now, seek
The strength to use which thou hast spent in getting!"

215 And yet 'tis much, surely 'tis very much,
Thus to have emptied youth of all its gifts,
To feed a fire meant to hold out till morn
Arrived with inexhaustible light; and lo,

197| *MS:* Aim's   *1835:* aims remain'd   *1849:* remained as ever supreme and
pure!   *1863:* remained supreme and pure as ever!   198| *MS:* Mankind's sake
1835: mankind's sake,   199| *MS:* fail, it may be for some fault,—   *1835:*
fault;   *1849:* fail, some fault may be the cause,—   *1863:* cause,   200| *MS:*
That tho' < > succeed?—   *1835:* That, though < > succeed?   201| *MS:*—I
cannot! O God I am despicable!   *1835:* God, I   *1849:* O God, the despicable heart
of us!   202| *1835:* heart! . . .   *1849:* heart!   204| *MS:* rewards— —to ask
< > lump . . .   1835| *MS:* rewards, to < > lump;   *1849:* rewards, and ask
205| *MS:* on;   *1835:* launch'd < > on: *1849:* launched   206| *MS:*
nothing—mighty   *1835:* nothing. Mighty   208| *MS:* as   *1835:* As
209| *MS:* strength, and   *1863:* strength; and   210| *MS:* boast . . .   *1835:*
boast.   211| *MS:* laugh as < > say   *1835:* laugh, as < > say—
212| *MS:* Master < > here, indeed,—dragged   *1835:* master < > indeed; dragg'd
1849: dragged   *1863:* indeed, dragged   213| *MS:* light—this < > done—be
< > now   *1835:* light: this < > done; be   *1863:* Now   214| *MS:* use,
which   *1835:* use which   215| *MS:* very much   *1835:* surely, 'tis very much,
1849: 'tis surely much, 'tis   *1863:* 'tis much, surely 'tis   216| *MS:* gifts   *1835:*
gifts,   217| *MS:* Morn   *1835:* morn   218| *MS:* light—and   *1835:* light;
and   *1849:* Arrive   *1863:* Arrived

I have heaped up my last, and day dawns not!
220 And I am left with grey hair, faded hands,
And furrowed brow. Ha, have I, after all,
Mistaken the wild nursling of my breast?
Knowledge it seemed, and power, and recompense!
Was she who glided through my room of nights,
225 Who laid my head on her soft knees and smoothed
The damp locks,—whose sly soothings just began
When my sick spirit craved repose awhile—
God! was I fighting sleep off for death's sake?

God! Thou art mind! Unto the master-mind
230 Mind should be precious. Spare my mind alone!
All else I will endure; if, as I stand
Here, with my gains, thy thunder smite me down,
I bow me; 'tis thy will, thy righteous will;
I o'erpass life's restrictions, and I die;
235 And if no trace of my career remain
Save a thin corpse at pleasure of the wind
In these bright chambers level with the air,
See thou to it! But if my spirit fail,
My once proud spirit forsake me at the last,
240 Has thou done well by me? So do not thou!
Crush not my mind, dear God, though I be crushed!

219| *MS:* last——and Day   *1835:* heap'd < > last, and day   *1849:* heaped
220| *MS:* hands   *1835:* hands,   *1849:* While I   *1863:* And I   221| *MS:*
brow—ha, have I after all   *1835:* furrow'd brow. Ha, have I, after all,   *1849:*
furrowed   222–224| *MS:* breast . . . / Was < > nights—   *1835:* breast? / < >
through < > nights;   *1849:* breast? / Knowledge it seemed, and Power, and
Recompense! / Was < > nights,—   *1868:* power < > recompense!   225| *MS:*
knees, and   *1835:* smooth'd   *1849:* smoothed   *1863:* knees and   226| *MS:*
locks——whose   *1835:* locks; whose   *1849:* locks,—whose   227| *MS:* awhile
. . .   *1849:* awhile—   228| *MS:* Sleep off, for Death's   *1835:* off for   *1849:*
sake? / § no space § /   *1863:* sake? / § space § /   *1868:* sleep < > death's
229| *MS:* Mind!—unto the Master-Mind,   *1835:* Mind! Unto the Master-Mind   *1868:*
mind < > master-mind   230| *MS:* precious . . . spare   *1835:* precious.
Spare   231| *MS:* endure: if,   *1863:* endure; if   232| *MS:* down   *1835:*
down,   *1863:* Thy   *1868:* thy   233| *MS:* me—'tis thy will—thy < > will—
—   *1835:* me; 'tis thy will, thy < > will;   *1863:* Thy < > Thy   *1868:* thy < >
thy   234| *MS:* restrictions and I die . . .   *1835:* restrictions, and I die: *1863:*
die;   235| *1835:* remain,   *1863:* remain   237| *1835:* chambers, level
1863: chambers level   238| *MS:* it: but < > fail—   *1835:* fail,   *1849:* it!
But   *1863:* Thou   *1868:* thou   240| *1863:* Thou < > Thou!   *1868:* thou
< > thou   241| *MS:* tho' < > crushed . . .   *1835:* though < > crush'd:
1849: crushed!

Hold me before the frequence of thy seraphs
And say—"I crushed him, lest he should disturb
My law. Men must not know their strength: behold
245 Weak and alone, how he had raised himself!"

But if delusions trouble me, and thou,
Not seldom felt with rapture in thy help
Throughout my toils and wanderings, dost intend
To work man's welfare through my weak endeavour,
250 To crown my mortal forehead with a beam
From thine own blinding crown, to smile, and guide
This puny hand and let the work so wrought
Be styled my work,—hear me! I covet not
An influx of new power, an angel's soul:
255 It were no marvel then—but I have reached
Thus far, a man; let me conclude, a man!
Give but one hour of my first energy,
Of that invincible faith, but only one!
That I may cover with an eagle-glance
260 The truths I have, and spy some certain way
To mould them, and completing them, possess!

Yet God is good: I started sure of that,

242| MS: Seraphs 1835: seraphs, 1863: Thy seraphs 1868: thy
243| MS: say "I < > him lest 1835: say—"I crush'd him, lest 1849:
crushed 244| MS: Law——Men < > behold, 1835: law, men 1888: behold
§ , after behold probably dropped in error § 245| 1849: how near he raised
1863: how he had raised 246| MS: Thou,— 1835: me—and Thou, 1863:
me, and 1868: thou 247| MS:—Not 1835: Not 1863: Thy 1868:
thy 248| MS: And stay, throughout my wanderings — § above § , dost 1835:
wanderings, dost 1849: Throughout my toil and wanderings 249| MS: Man's
< > thro' < > Endeavour . . . 1835: man's < > through < > endeavour— 1863:
endeavour, 251| MS: crown——to 1835: crown—to 1863: Thine < >
crown, to 1868: thine 252| MS: hand, and < > so framed 1863: so
wrought 1868: hand and 253| MS: styled his § cancelled by § my work—
§ above § , hear 1835: work—hear 1849: work,—hear 254| MS: soul——
1835: soul: 255| MS: have gone 1849: have reached 256| MS: Man—
—let § written over by § Man—let < > Man! 1835: man; let me conclude a man!
1849: far, a man; let me conclude, a 257| MS: energy 1835: energy,
258| MS:—Of 1835: Of < > faith—but 1849: faith—one only hour! 1863: faith,
but only one! 259| MS:——I should go over with 1835: I 1849: That I
may cover with 261–262| MS: them and complete them and pursue them . . . /
§ space § / (After a pause) / Yet 1835: them, and < > them, and < > them! ///
Yet < > good: I < > that, 1849: completing them, possess! / § space § Yet

And why dispute it now? I'll not believe
But some undoubted warning long ere this
265 Had reached me: a fire-labarum was not deemed
Too much for the old founder of these walls.
Then, if my life has not been natural,
It has been monstrous: yet, till late, my course
So ardently engrossed me, that delight,
270 A pausing and reflecting joy, 'tis plain,
Could find no place in it. True, I am worn;
But who clothes summer, who is life itself?
God, that created all things, can renew!
And then, though after-life to please me now
275 Must have no likeness to the past, what hinders
Reward from springing out of toil, as changed
As bursts the flower from earth and root and stalk?
What use were punishment, unless some sin
Be first detected? let me know that first!
280 No man could ever offend as I have done . . .

[*A voice from within.*]

I hear a voice, perchance I heard
Long ago, but all too low,
So that scarce a care it stirred
If the voice were real or no:

263| *MS:* now——I'll § written over by § now?—I'll   *1835:* now? I'll
265–266| *MS:* me . . a labarum < > / Too < > walls:—   *1835:* reach'd me: a < >
deem'd / < > walls.   *1849:* reached me: stars would write his will in heaven, / As
once when a labarum was not deemed / Too   *1863:* reached me: a fire-labarum was
not deemed / Too   267| *MS:*—Then, if my § *my* inserted above the line § life
have < > natural   *1835:* then < > has < > natural,   268| *MS:* monstruous . .
yet till   *1835:* monstrous: yet, till   269| *MS:* delight,—   *1835:* engross'd < >
delight,   *1849:* engrossed   270–271| *MS:* joy—'tis plain, / Could < > it: 'tis
true, I am worn,   *1835:* joy, 'tis < > / < > it. "Tis < > worn;   *1849:* plain, /
Though such were meant to follow as its fruit, / Could < > it. True, I   *1863:* plain, /
Could   272–274| *MS:* Life itself? / —And then tho'   *1835:* And then, though
1849: itself? / God, that created all things, can renew! / And   *1868:* Who < >
Who   *1868:* who < > who   276| *MS:* toil § written over by § toil   *1835:*
toil   277| *1835:* earth, and root, and   *1863:* earth and root and
278| *MS:*—What   *1835:* What   279–297| *MS:* Were first detected?—let < >
first! / No < > done . . . . . . / [*A* < > *within.*] / Lost, Lost!—yet   *1835:* detected?
let < > first: / < > done . . . / § space § / [*A* < > *within.*] / Lost, lost! yet   *1849:*
Be first < > first! § space § [*Aprile, from within.*] I hear a voice, perchance I heard
/ Long ago, but all too low, / So that scarce a thought was stirred / If really spoke
the voice or no: /

121

I heard it in my youth when first
The waters of my life outburst:
But, now their stream ebbs faint, I hear
That voice, still low, but fatal-clear—
As if all poets, God ever meant
Should save the world, and therefore lent
Great gifts to, but who, proud, refused
To do his work, or lightly used
Those gifts, or failed through weak endeavour,
So, mourn cast off by him for ever,—
As if these leaned in airy ring
To take me; this the song they sing.

"Lost, lost! yet come,
With our wan troop make thy home.
Come, come! for we
Will not breathe, so much as breathe
Reproach to thee,
Knowing what you sink'st beneath.
So sank we in those old years,
We who bid thee, come! thou last
Who, living yet, hast life o'erpast.

I heard it in my youth, when first / The waters of my life outburst: / But now their stream ebbs faint, I hear / The voice, still low, but fatal-clear— / As if all Poets, that God meant / Should save the world, and therefore lent / Great gifts to, but who, proud, refused / To do his work, or lightly used / Those gifts, or failed through weak endeavour, / And mourn, cast off by him forever,— / As if these leaned in airy ring / To call me; this the song they sing. / "Lost, lost § 297–339 § indented farther than 281–296 §   279-281| *1863:* first! / No man could ever offend as I have done . . . / § space § / [A voice from within.] / § space § / I hear a   283| *1863:* a care it stirred   284| *1863:* If the voice was real or   *1868:* voice were real   285| *1863:* youth when   287| *1868:* But, now   288| *1863:* That voice, still low but   289| *1863:* Poets, God ever meant   *1868:* poets   292| *1863:* His   *1868:* his   294| *1863:* So, mourn cast < > Him for ever,—   *1868:* him   296| *1863:* To take me   297-339| *1888:* § indentation aligned with 281–296 §   298| *MS:* home   *1835:* home: *1863:* home.   299| *MS:* Come, come,—for   *1835:* Come, come! for   301-304| *MS:* thee! / Lost one, come! the last   *1849:* thee! / Knowing what thou sink'st beneath; / So we sank in those old years, / We who bid thee, come! thou last   *1863:* beneath.   *1868:* Reproach to thee,   305| *MS:* living, hast < > o'erpast   *1835:* o'erpast,   *1849:* Who, a living man, hast   *1863:* Who, living yet, hast   *1868:* o'erpast.

And altogether we, thy peers,
Will pardon crave for thee, the last
Whose trial is done, whose lot is cast
With those who watch but work no more,
310 Who gaze on life but live no more.
Yet we trusted thou shouldst speak
The message which our lips, too weak,
Refused to utter,—shouldst redeem
Our fault: such trust, and all a dream!
315 Yet we chose thee a birthplace
Where the richness ran to flowers:
Couldst not sing one song for grace?
Not make one blossom man's and ours?
Must one more recreant to his race
320 Die with unexerted powers,
And join us, leaving as he found
The world, he was to loosen, bound?
Anguish! ever and for ever;
Still beginning, ending never.
325 Yet, lost and last one, come!
How couldst understand, alas,
What our pale ghosts strove to say,
As their shades did glance and pass

306| *MS:* And, all together we   *1835:* And all   *1849:* And all together we, thy
peers,   **307|** *MS:* Will ask for us and ask for thee   *1835:* thee,   *1849:* Will
pardon ask for thee, the last   *1888:* pardon crave for   **308|** *MS:* is past
whose   *1835:* past, whose   *1849:* trial is done, whose   **309|** *MS:* more,
1835: more—   *1849:* watch, but   *1863:* watch but   **310-315|** *MS:* Life, but
< > more: . . / Yet < > birth-place   *1835:* life < > more: *1849:* more: / And yet
we trusted thou shouldst speak / God's message which our lips, too weak, / Refused to
utter,—shouldst redeem / Our fault: such trust, and all, a dream! / So we < > a
bright birth-place   *1863:* life but < > more. / Yet we < > / The message // < >
all a < > / Yet we < > a birthplace   **316|** *MS:* flowers . . .   *1849:* flowers—
1863: flowers;   *1888:* flowers: **317|** *MS:* Could'st < > for us?   *1849:*
Couldst < > for grace?   **318|** *MS:* blossom ours,   *1835:* ours—   *1849:*
blossom man's and ours?   **319-323|** *MS:* Not one of the sweet race? / Anguish
< > for ever,   *1835:* for ever;   *1849:* Must one more recreant to his race / Die
with unexerted powers, / And join us, leaving as he found / The world, he was to
loosen, bound? / Anguish   **324|** *MS:* never!   *1888:* never.   **326|** *MS:*
could'st   *1849:* couldst   **327|** *MS:* say   *1835:* say,

Before thee night and day?
330 Thou wast blind as we were dumb:
Once more, therefore, come, O come!
How should we clothe, how arm the spirit
Shall next thy post of life inherit—
How guard him from thy speedy ruin?
335 Tell us of thy sad undoing
Here, where we sit, ever pursuing
Our weary task, ever renewing
Sharp sorrow, far from God who gave
Our powers, and man they could not save!"

APRILE *enters.*

340 Ha, ha! our king that wouldst be, here at last?
Art thou the poet who shall save the world?
Thy hand to mine! Stay, fix thine eyes on mine!
Thou wouldst be king? Still fix thine eyes on mine!
PARACELSUS Ha, ha! why crouchest not? Am I not king?
345 So torture is not wholly unavailing!
Have my fierce spasms compelled thee from thy lair?
Art thou the sage I only seemed to be,
Myself of after-time, my very self
With sight a little clearer, strength more firm,

329-331| *MS:* thee, night and day— / O come, come! *1835:* day . . . *1849:* day? /
Thou wert blind, as we were dumb: / Once more, therefore, come, O come! *1863:*
Thou wast blind as *1888:* thee night 332| *MS:* How shall we *1849:* we
better arm *1863:* we clothe, how arm *1888:* How should we 333| *MS:*
Who next shall thy post inherit— — *1835:* inherit— *1849:* post of life inherit—
1868: Shall next thy 334| *1849:* thy ruin? *1863:* thy speedy ruin?
338-342| *MS:* from— — —/ § space § / APRILE *enters* / § space § / Ha, ha, our King
< > last? /. . . Thy < > mine . . . stay—fix < > mine, *1835:* from . . . //// < >
king < > / Thy < > mine. Stay, fix < > mine. *1849:* from God who gave Our
powers, and man they could not save!" // APRILE *enters* / § no space § / A spirit
better armed, succeeding me? / Ha, ha < > last? / Art thou the Poet who shall save
the world? / Thy *1863: enters.* / Ha, ha *1868: enters* / § space § // < > poet
< > / < > mine! Stay 343| *MS:* King?— still < > mine— — — *1835:*
king? Still < > mine. 344| *MS:* Ha, ha, why < > not?—am < > King?
1835: Ha, Ha! why < > not? am < > king? *1849:* Am 346-352| *MS:* lair? /
Ay, look on me!—shall I be king or no? / I *1835:* compell'd < > / < > me! shall
1849: compelled < > lair? / Art thou the Sage I only seemed to be, / Myself of after-
time, my very self / With sight a little clearer, strength more firm, / Who robs me of
my prize and takes my place / For just a fault, a weakness, a neglect? / I *1863:*
sage < > // < > firm, / Who robes him in my robe and grasps my crown / For

124

350 Who robes him in my robe and grasps my crown
  For just a fault, a weakness, a neglect?
  I scarcely trusted God with the surmise
  That such might come, and thou didst hear the while!
  APRILE Thine eyes are lustreless to mine; my hair
355 Is soft, nay silken soft: to talk with thee
  Flushes my cheek, and thou art ashy-pale.
  Truly, thou hast laboured, hast withstood her lips,
  The siren's! Yes, 'tis like thou hast attained!
  Tell me, dear master, wherefore now thou comest?
360 I thought thy solemn songs would have their meed
  In after-time; that I should hear the earth
  Exult in thee and echo with thy praise,
  While I was laid forgotten in my grave.
  PARACELSUS Ah fiend, I know thee, I am not thy dupe!
365 Thou art ordained to follow in my track,
  Reaping my sowing, as I scorned to reap
  The harvest sown by sages passed away.
  Thou art the sober searcher, cautious striver,
  As if, except through me, thou hast searched or striven!
370 Ay, tell the world! Degrade me after all,
  To an aspirant after fame, not truth—
  To all but envy of thy fate, be sure!

353| *MS:* That thou would'st come——and thou did'st   *1835:* wouldst come, and
thou didst   *1849:* That such might come   354| *MS:* mine,—my   *1835:* mine:
my   355| *MS:* silkensoft—to   *1835:* silken soft: to   356| *MS:* cheek . .
and < > ashy-pale . . .   *1835:* cheek, and < > ashy-pale.   *1849:* ashy-pale,   *1863:*
ashy-pale.   357| *MS:* Truly thou < > withstood their lips   *1835:* labour'd
< > lips,   *1849:* True, thou < > laboured < > withstood her lips,   *1863:* Truly,
thou   358| *MS:*—Their kisses . . . yes   *1835:* Their kisses. Yes < > attain'd.
1849: The siren's! Yes < > attained!   359| *MS:* Master   *1835:*
master   361| *MS:* after-time—that   *1835:* after-time: that   362| *MS:* thee,
and < > praise   *1835:* praise,   *1888:* thee and   364| *MS:* Ah, fiend   *1849:*
Not so! I know   *1863:* Ah, fiend, I know   *1868:* Ah fiend   365–366| *MS:*
track——— § above § track, ——/ To reap < > I disdained to   *1835:* ordain'd
track, / < > sowing—as I disdain'd   *1849:* ordained < > track, / Even as thou
sayest, succeeding to my place, / Reaping my sowing—as I scorned to   *1863:* track, /
Reaping my sowing, as   367–370| *MS:* harvest left by sages long since gone . . . .
/ I am to be degraded, after all,   *1835:* gone.   *1849:* harvest sown by sages passed
away. / Thou art the sober searcher, cautious striver, / As if, except through me, thou
had'st searched or striven! / Ay, tell the world! Degrade me, after all,   *1863:* thou
hadst searched   *1888:* me after   371| *MS:* Fame, not Truth . . .   *1835:* fame,
not truth—   372| *MS:* . . . To   *1835:* To

APRILE Nay, sing them to me; I shall envy not:
Thou shalt be king! Sing thou, and I will sit
375 Beside, and call deep silence for thy songs,
And worship thee, as I had ne'er been meant
To fill thy throne: but none shall ever know!
Sing to me; for already thy wild eyes
Unlock my heart-strings, as some crystal-shaft
380 Reveals by some chance blaze its parent fount
After long time: so thou reveal'st my soul.
All will flash forth at last, with thee to hear!
PARACELSUS (His secret! I shall get his secret—fool!)
I am he that aspired to KNOW: and thou?
385 APRILE I would LOVE infinitely, and be loved!
PARACELSUS Poor slave! I am thy king indeed.
APRILE   Thou deem'st
That—born a spirit, dowered even as thou,
Born for thy fate—because I could not curb
My yearnings to possess at once the full
390 Enjoyment, but neglected all the means
Of realizing even the frailest joy,
Gathering no fragments to appease my want,
Yet nursing up that want till thus I die—
Thou deem'st I cannot trace thy safe sure march

374| *MS:* king—sing thou and   *1835:* king. Sing thou, and   *1849:* will stand
1863: will sit   **375|** *MS:* Beside and   *1835:* Beside, and   **377|** *MS:*
throne . . . but < > know: *1835:* throne. But < > know!   *1849:* throne—but
1863: throne: but   **378|** *1835:* me: for   *1863:* me; for   **379|** *MS:*
heartsprings < > chrystal-shaft   *1835:* heart-springs < > crystal-shaft
381| *MS:* time— —so < > revealest my soul!   *1835:* time—so < > reveal'st   *1863:*
time: so < > soul.   **382|** *MS:* . . All   *1835:* All   **383|** *MS:* secret . . .
fool!)—I am   *1835:* secret—fool!) I   *1849:* secret! my succesor's secret—fool!)   *1863:*
secret! I shall get his secret   **384|** *MS:* The mortal who aspired to KNOW . . . and
Thou?   *1835:* KNOW—and thou?   *1849:* I am he that aspired to KNOW   *1863:*
KNOW: and   **385|** *MS:* LOVE   *1835:* LOVE   **386|** *MS:* King indeed:
APRILE < > deemest   *1835:* king indeed APRILE < > deem'st   **387|** *MS:*
That,—born a spirit dowered   *1835:* That—born a spirit, dower'd   *1849:*
dowered   **388|** *MS:* fate,—because   *1835:* fate—because   **390|** *MS:*
Enjoyment— —but   *1835:* Enjoyment: but   *1849:* Enjoyment: yet neglected   *1863:*
Enjoyment, but neglected   **391|** *MS:* joy,—   *1835:* joy;   *1863:* joy,
392| *MS:* want   *1835:* want,   **393|** *MS:* die . . . .   *1835:* die—
394| *MS:* That I cannot conceive thy < > March,   *1835:* safe, sure march,   *1849:*
Thou deem'st I cannot trace thy   *1888:* safe sure

126

395 O'er perils that o'erwhelm me, triumphing,
Neglecting nought below for aught above,
Despising nothing and ensuring all—
Nor that I could (my time to come again)
Lead thus my spirit securely as thine own.
400 Listen, and thou shalt see I know thee well.
I would love infinitely . . . Ah, lost! lost!
Oh ye who armed me at such cost,
How shall I look on all of ye
With your gifts even yet on me?
405 PARACELSUS (Ah, 'tis some moonstruck creature after all!
Such fond fools as are like to haunt this den:
They spread contagion, doubtless: yet he seemed
To echo one foreboding of my heart
So truly, that . . . no matter! How he stands
410 With eve's last sunbeam staying on his hair
Which turns to it as if they were akin:
And those clear smiling eyes of saddest blue
Nearly set free, so far they rise above
The painful fruitless striving of the brow
415 And enforced knowledge of the lips, firm-set
In slow despondency's eternal sigh!
Has he, too, missed life's end, and learned the cause?)
I charge thee, by thy fealty, be calm!

395| _MS:_ Triumphing o'er the perils that o'erwhelm me, _1849:_ O'er perils that
o'erwhelm me, triumphing, **397|** _MS:_ all . . . _1835:_ all— **398|** _MS:_ . .
That I could not, my < > again, _1835:_ That _1849:_ Nor that I could (my < >
again) **399|** _MS:_ Lead my own spirit < > own; _1835:_ Lead this my spirit
_1849:_ Lead thus my _1849:_ own: _1863:_ own. **400|** _MS:_ well: _1849:_
well. **401–403|** _MS:_ love § written over by § Love < > Ah— § above § , lost,
lost, / How _1835:_ love < > Ah, lost! lost! _1849:_ lost! lost! / O ye who armed me
at such cost, / Your faces shall I bear to see _1863:_ cost, / How shall I look on all of
ye **404|** _MS:_ me . . . . _1835:_ me . . . _1849:_ me?— _1863:_ me?
405| _MS:_ (Ah,—tis _1835:_ (Ah, 'tis **406–418|** _MS:_ den:— —) _1849:_ den: / They
spread contagion, doubtless: yet he seemed / To echo one foreboding of my heart / So
truly, that . . . no matter! How he stands / With eve's last sunbeam staying on his hair
/ Which turns to it, as if they were akin: / And those clear smiling eyes of saddest
blue / Nearly set free, so far they rise above / The painful fruitless striving of that
brow / And enforced knowledge of those lips, firm-set / In slow despondency's eternal
sigh! / Has he, too, missed life's end, and learned the cause?) / Be calm, I charge
thee, by thy fealty! **411|** _1868:_ it as **414|** _1863:_ of the brow
415| _1863:_ of the lips **418|** _1863:_ I charge thee, by thy fealty, be calm!

Tell me what thou wouldst be, and what I am.
420 APRILE I would love infinitely, and be loved.
First: I would carve in stone, or cast in brass,
The forms of earth. No ancient hunter lifted
Up to the gods by his renown, no nymph
Supposed the sweet soul of a woodland tree
425 Or sapphirine spirit of a twilight star,
Should be too hard for me; no shepherd-king
Regal for his white locks; no youth who stands
Silent and very calm amid the throng,
His right hand ever hid beneath his robe
430 Until the tyrant pass; no lawgiver,
No swan-soft woman rubbed with lucid oils
Given by a god for love of her—too hard!
Every passion sprung from man, conceived by man,
Would I express and clothe it in its right form,
435 Or blend with others struggling in one form,
Or show repressed by an ungainly form.
Oh, if you marvelled at some mighty spirit
With a fit frame to execute its will—
Even unconsciously to work its will—
440 You should be moved no less beside some strong

419| *MS:* be and < > am!   *1835:* be, and < > am.   420| *MS:* Love
infinitely and be loved!   *1835:* love infinitely, and be loved.   421| *MS:* First,
I < > stone or < > brass   *1835:* First: I < > stone, or < > brass,
422| *MS:* Earth:—no   *1835:* earth. No   *1849:* hunter, raised   *1863:* hunter
lifted   423| *MS:* Gods by his renown,—no nymph § written over by § Nymph
1835: gods < > renown; no nymph   *1863:* renown, no   424| *MS:* tree,
1863: tree   425| *MS:* star   *1835:* star,   426| *1835:* shepherd-king,
1863: shepherd-king   427| *MS:* locks . . no   *1835:* locks; no   *1849:* Regal
with his   *1863:* Regal for his   429| *MS:* right-hand < > robe,   *1835:* right
hand < > robe   430| *MS:* pass,—no law-giver,   *1835:* pass; no law-giver;
1863: lawgiver,   431| *1835:* woman, rubb'd < > oils,   *1849:* rubbed   *1863:*
woman rubbed   *1868:* oils   432| *MS:* God < > her,—too hard.   *1835:* god
< > her—too   *1849:* hard!   433| *MS:* Man < > Man   *1835:* man < >
man,   *1849:* Each passion   *1863:* Every passion   434–436| *MS:* clothe in its
fit form,— / Or show, repressed < > ungainly form,— / Or blend < > one form,—
1835: clothe in its fit form, / Or show repress'd < > ungainly form, / < > one
form.   *1849:* clothe it in its right form, / Or blend < > one form, / Or show
repressed < > ungainly form.   437| *MS:*—O if you marveled < > Spirit
1835: Oh, if you marvell'd < > spirit   *1849:* For, if you marvelled   *1863:* Oh,
if   438| *MS:* execute his will,   *1835:* will—   *1863:* execute its will—
439| *MS:*—Even < > work his will, . . .   *1835:* Even < > will—   *1849:* Ay,
even   *1863:* Even < > work its will—   440| *1835:* strong,   *1888:* strong

Rare spirit, fettered to a stubborn body,
Endeavouring to subdue it and inform it
With its own splendour! All this I would do:
And I would say, this done, "His sprites created,
445 God grants to each a sphere to be its world,
Appointed with the various objects needed
To satisfy its own peculiar want;
So, I create a world for these my shapes
Fit to sustain their beauty and their strength!"
450 And, at the word, I would contrive and paint
Woods, valleys, rocks and plains, dells, sands and wastes,
Lakes which, when morn breaks on their quivering bed,
Blaze like a wyvern flying round the sun,
And ocean isles so small, the dog-fish tracking
455 A dead whale, who should find them, would swim thrice
Around them, and fare onward—all to hold
The offspring of my brain. Nor these alone:
Bronze labyrinth, palace, pyramid and crypt,
Baths, galleries, courts, temples and terraces,
460 Marts, theatres and wharfs—all filled with men,
Men everywhere! And this performed in turn,
When those who looked on, pined to hear the hopes
And fears and hates and loves which moved the crowd,

441| *MS: 1835:* fetter'd *1849:* fettered 442| *1835:* it, and *1863:* it
and 443| *MS:* splendour!—All < > do, *1835:* splendour! All *1863:*
do: 444| *1849:* done, "God's sprites being made, *1863:* done, "His sprites
created, 445| *MS:* be his world, *1849:* He grants < > be its world, *1863:*
God grants 447| *MS:* satisfy his own < > wants; *1849:* satisfy its spiritual
desires; *1863:* satisfy its own peculiar wants; *1868:* want; 450| *MS:*—And
at *1835:* And, at 451| *MS:* wastes *1835:* rocks, and plains < > sands, and
wastes, *1863:* rocks and plains < > sands and 452| *MS:* which when < >
bed *1849:* which, when < > bed, 453| *MS:* sun,— *1849:* sun; *1863:*
sun, 454| *MS:*—And ocean-isles *1835:* And *1888:* ocean isles
456| *MS:* onward— — —all *1835:* onward—all 457| *MS:* brain—nor < >
alone . . . *1835:* brain. Nor < > alone— *1863:* alone: 458| *MS:* labyrinths
< > pyramid and crypt *1835:* pyramid, and crypt, *1863:* labyrinth < > pyramid
and 459| *MS:* temples, and terraces *1835:* terraces, *1863:* temples
and 460| *MS:* wharfs— —all < > men! § written over by § Men! *1835:*
theatres, and wharfs—all fill'd < > men! *1849:* filled *1863:* theatres and *1868:*
men, 461| *MS:* every where:—and < > performed, in *1835:* everywhere! And
< > perform'd *1849:* performed *1863:* performed in 462| *MS:* on pined
1835: look'd < > hopes, *1849:* looked on, pined *1863:* hopes 463| *1835:*
fears, and hates, and *1849:* crowd,— *1863:* fears and hates and < > crowd,

I would throw down the pencil as the chisel,
465 And I would speak; no thought which ever stirred
A human breast should be untold; all passions,
All soft emotions, from the turbulent stir
Within a heart fed with desires like mine,
To the last comfort shutting the tired lids
470 Of him who sleeps the sultry noon away
Beneath the tent-tree by the wayside well:
And this in language as the need should be,
Now poured at once forth in a burning flow,
Now piled up in a grand array of words.
475 This done, to perfect and consummate all,
Even as a luminous haze links star to star,
I would supply all chasms with music, breathing
Mysterious motions of the soul, no way
To be defined save in strange melodies.
480 Last, having thus revealed all I could love,
Having received all love bestowed on it,
I would die: preserving so throughout my course
God full on me, as I was full on men:
He would approve my prayer, "I have gone through
485 The loveliness of life; create for me
If not for men, or take me to thyself,

464| *MS:* chisel   *1835:* chisel,   465| *MS:* Speak,—no   *1835:* speak: no < >
stirr'd   *1849:* stirred   *1863:* speak; no   466| *MS:* passions   *1835:* passions,
1849: untold; no passions,   *1863:* untold; all passions,   467| *MS:*
emotions,—from   *1835:* emotions, from   *1849:* No soft   *1863:* All soft
468| *MS:* mine . . .   *1835:* mine—   *1863:* mine,   469| *1835:* comfort,
shutting   *1863:* comfort shutting   471| *MS:* wayside-well: . . . § written over
by § well:—   *1835:* way-side well: *1863:* wayside   472| *MS:* this, in < >
be,—   *1835:* this in < > be,   473| *MS:* Now,—poured   *1835:* Now pour'd
1849: poured   474| *MS:* Now,—piled < > words:—   *1835:* Now piled < >
words.   475| *MS:* done— § above § , to   *1835:* done, to   476| *MS:* to
star   *1835:* to star,   477| *MS:* music § written over by § Music,—breathing
1835: music, breathing   479| *MS:* melodies: *1835:* melodies.
480| —Last   *1835:* Last < > reveal'd   *1849:* revealed   481| *MS:* on
them,—   *1835:* bestow'd on it,   *1849:* And having < > bestowed   *1863:*
Having   482| *MS:* die: having preserved throughout   *1849:* die: so preserving
through my   *1863:* die: preserving so throughout my   483| *MS:* Men: *1835:*
men.   *1849:* men: 484| *MS:* prayer—"I < > thro'   *1835:* through   *1849:*
And he would grant my   *1863:* He would approve my prayer, "I   485| *MS:*
Life,—create   *1835:* life, create   *1849:* All loveliness of life; make more for me,
1863: The loveliness of life; create for me   486| *MS:* Men,—or take   *1835:*
men—or   *1863:* men, or < > Thyself,   *1868:* thyself,

Eternal, infinite love!"

                             If thou has ne'er
Conceived this mighty aim, this full desire,
Thou hast not passed my trial, and thou art
490 No king of mine.

PARACELSUS   Ah me!

APRILE   But thou art here!
Thou didst not gaze like me upon that end
Till thine own powers for compassing the bliss
Were blind with glory; nor grow mad to grasp
At once the prize long patient toil should claim,
495 Nor spurn all granted short of that. And I
Would do as thou, a second time: nay, listen!
Knowing ourselves, our world, our task so great,
Our time so brief, 'tis clear if we refuse
The means so limited, the tools so rude
500 To execute our purpose, life will fleet,
And we shall fade, and leave our task undone.
We will be wise in time: what though our work
Be fashioned in despite of their ill-service,
Be crippled every way? 'Twere little praise
505 Did full resources wait on our goodwill
At every turn. Let all be as it is.
Some say the earth is even so contrived
That tree and flower, a vesture gay, conceal
A bare and skeleton framework. Had we means

487| *MS:* Love   *1868:* love   488| *MS:* Aim < > Desire   *1835:* aim < >
desire,   489| *1835:* pass'd   *1849:* passed   490| *MS:* mine! PARACELSUS
1835: mine. PARACELSUS   491| *MS:* did'st < > End   *1835:* didst < >
end   493| *MS:* glory:—nor   *1835:* glory; nor   494| *MS:* claim: *1863:*
claim,   495| *MS:* that—and   *1835:* that. And   496| *MS:* thou, if that
might be; Nay, listen:—   *1835:* be; nay, listen—   *1849:* thou, a second time: nay
1863: listen!   497| *MS:* world,—our   *1835:* world, our   498| *MS:*
brief—'tis   *1835:* brief; 'tis   *1849:* brief,—'tis   *1863:* brief, 'tis   500| *MS:*
fleet   *1835:* fleet,   501| *MS:* fade and nothing will be done—   *1835:* fade, and
< > done.   *1849:* and leave our task undone.   502| *MS:* tho'   *1835:*
though   *1849:* Rather, grow wise   *1863:* We will be wise   503| *MS:* ill
service,   *1835:* fashion'd < > ill-service,   *1849:* fashioned   505| *MS:* good
will   *1863:* goodwill   506| *MS:* turn: . . let < > is:—   *1835:* turn. Let < >
is.   507| *MS:* contrived—   *1835:* contrived   508| *1835:* tree, and
1863: tree and   509| *MS:* framework——had § written over by § framework:—
1835: framework: had   *1863:* framework. Had

510 Answering to our mind! But now I seem
　　Wrecked on a savage isle: how rear thereon
　　My palace? Branching palms the props shall be,
　　Fruit glossy mingling; gems are for the East;
　　Who heeds them? I can pass them. Serpents' scales,
515 And painted birds' down, furs and fishes' skins
　　Must help me; and a little here and there
　　Is all I can aspire to: still my art
　　Shall show its birth was in a gentler clime.
　　"Had I green jars of malachite, this way
520 I'd range them: where those sea-shells glisten above,
　　Cressets should hang, by right: this way we set
　　The purple carpets, as these mats are laid,
　　Woven of fern and rush and blossoming flag."
　　Or if, by fortune, some completer grace
525 Be spared to me, some fragment, some slight sample
　　Of the prouder workmanship my own home boasts,
　　Some trifle little heeded there, but here
　　The place's one perfection—with what joy
　　Would I enshrine the relic, cheerfully
530 Foregoing all the marvels out of reach!
　　Could I retain one strain of all the psalm
　　Of the angels, one word of the fiat of God,
　　To let my followers know what such things are!
　　I would adventure nobly for their sakes:

510| _MS:_ mind! . . but   _1835:_ mind! But   _1849:_ That answered   _1863:_
Answering   511| _MS:_ isle—how   _1835:_ Wreck'd < > isle. How   _1849:_
Wrecked < > isle: how   512| _MS:_ palace?—branching   _1835:_ palace?
Branching   513| _MS:_ East,—   _1835:_ east;   _1863:_ East;   514| _MS:_
them: serpent scales   _1835:_ them. Serpent's scales,   _1849:_ can waive them   _1863:_
can pass them. Serpents'   515| _1835:_ furs, and   _1849:_ Birds' feathers, down
furs   _1863:_ And painted birds' down, furs and   517| _MS:_ Art   _1835:_
art   518| _MS:_ clime: _1835:_ clime.   522| _MS:_ laid   _1835:_ laid,
523| _MS:_ blossoming-flag."   _1835:_ blossoming flag."   _1849:_ of mere fern   _1863:_ of
fern   526| _MS:_ Home   _1835:_ home   _1849:_ Of my own land's completer
workmanship,   _1863:_ Of the prouder workmanship my own home boasts,
527| _MS: here_   _1849:_ here   528| _MS:_ The one perfection of the place,—how
gladly   _1835:_ place, how   _1849:_ The place's one perfection—with what joy
529| _MS:_ relic—cheerfully   _1863:_ relic, cheerfully   530| _1835:_ reach—
_1849:_ reach!   531| _MS:_ Psalm   _1835:_ psalm   532| _MS:_ Angels— —
—one   _1835:_ angels—one < > God—   _1863:_ angels, one < > God,
533| _MS:_ are! . . .   _1835:_ are!   534| _MS:_—I < > sakes;   _1835:_ I < > sakes:

132

535 When nights were still, and still the moaning sea,
And far away I could descry the land
Whence I departed, whither I return,
I would dispart the waves, and stand once more
At home, and load my bark, and hasten back,
540 And fling my gains to them, worthless or true.
"Friends," I would say, "I went far, far for them,
Past the high rocks the haunt of doves, the mounds
Of red earth from whose sides strange trees grow out,
Past tracts of milk-white minute blinding sand,
545 Till, by a mighty moon, I tremblingly
Gathered these magic herbs, berry and bud,
In haste, not pausing to reject the weeds,
But happy plucking them at any price.
To me, who have seen them bloom in their own soil,
550 They are scarce lovely: plait and wear them, you!
And guess, from what they are, the springs that fed them,
The stars that sparkled o'er them, night by night,
The snakes that travelled far to sip their dew!"
Thus for my higher loves; and thus even weakness
555 Would win me honour. But not these alone
Should claim my care; for common life, its wants
And ways, would I set forth in beauteous hues:
The lowest hind should not possess a hope,
A fear, but I'd be by him, saying better
560 Than he his own heart's language. I would live

535| *MS:* still and still < > sea   *1835:* still, and   *1849:* and still, the   *1868:* and
still the   *1888:* sea   *1889:* sea,   536| *MS:* Land   *1835:* land
537| *MS:* return, . .   *1835:* return,   538| *MS:* waves and   *1835:* waves,
and   539| *MS:* bark and < > back   *1835:* bark, and < > back,   540| *MS:*
true,   *1835:* true.   *1849:* gains before them, rich or poor—   *1863:* gains to them,
worthless or true—   *1888:* true.   541| *MS:* them   *1835:* them,
542| *MS:* doves—the   *1835:* doves, the   546| *1835:* Gather'd   *1849:*
Gathered   547| *MS:* haste— —not < > weeds   *1835:* haste—not < > weeds,
1863: haste, not   548| *MS:* happy, plucking < > price: *1835:* happy plucking
< > price.   549| *MS:* soil   *1835:* soil,   550| *MS:* lovely:—plait   *1835:*
lovely: plait < > them you!   *1849:* them, you!   551| *MS:* guess from   *1835:*
are the < > them,   *1849:* guess, from < > are, the < > fed—   *1863:* fed them,
553| *1835:* travell'd   *1849:* travelled   554| *MS:* loves— —and   *1835:* loves; and
555| *MS:* honour:—but   *1835:* honour. But   556| *MS:* care,—for   *1835:* care;
for   557| *MS:* ways would < > hues,— —   *1835:* ways, would < >
hues: 558| *MS:* hope   *1835:* hope,   560| *MS:* he, his < >
Language—I   *1835:* he his < > language. I

133

For ever in the thoughts I thus explored,
As a discoverer's memory is attached
To all he finds; they should be mine henceforth,
Imbued with me, though free to all before:
565 For clay, once cast into my soul's rich mine,
Should come up crusted o'er with gems. Nor this
Would need a meaner spirit, than the first;
Nay, 'twould be but the selfsame spirit, clothed
In humbler guise, but still the selfsame spirit:
570 As one spring wind unbinds the mountain snow
And comforts violets in their hermitage.

But, master, poet, who hast done all this,
How didst thou 'scape the ruin whelming me?
Didst thou, when nerving thee to this attempt,
575 Ne'er range thy mind's extent, as some wide hall,
Dazzled by shapes that filled its length with light,
Shapes clustered there to rule thee, not obey,
That will not wait thy summons, will not rise
Singly, nor when thy practised eye and hand
580 Can well transfer their loveliness, but crowd
By thee for ever, bright to thy despair?
Didst thou ne'er gaze on each by turns, and ne'er
Resolve to single out one, though the rest
Should vanish, and to give that one, entire

562| 1835: attach'd 1849: attached 563| MS: finds—they < > be mine
henceforth § mine inserted above the line § 1835: finds: they 1863: finds;
they 564| MS: before,— 1835: before; 1863: before: 565| MS:
mine 1868: mine, 566| MS: oer < > gems: nor 1835: o'er 1863: gems.
Nor 567| MS: first: 1863: first; 568| MS:—Nay 1835: Nay
569| MS: guise,—but 1835: guise, but < > spirit— 1863: spirit:
570| 1835: snow, 1863: snow 571| 1863: hermitage. / § no space § /
1888: hermitage. / § space § / 572| MS: . . . But, Master, Poet 1835: But
master, poet 1849: But, master 573| MS: did'st < > ruin I have met?
1835: didst 1863: ruin whelming me? 574| MS: Did'st 1835: Didst
575| MS: Hall, 1835: hall, 576| 1835: fill'd 1849: filled
577| MS: there, to < > obey,— 1835: cluster'd there to < > obey— 1849:
clustered 1863: obey, 578| MS: summons—will 1835: summons, will
579| MS: Singly— § above § , nor 1835: Singly, nor 580| MS: loveliness—
§ above § , but are 1835: loveliness, but 1849: but crowd 581| MS:
despair! 1835: despair? 582| MS: turns,—and 1835: turns, and
583| MS: One,—tho' 1835: one, though 1863: one 584| MS: One 1835:
one

585 In beauty, to the world; forgetting, so,
Its peers, whose number baffles mortal power?
And, this determined, wast thou ne'er seduced
By memories and regrets and passionate love,
To glance once more farewell? and did their eyes
590 Fasten thee, brighter and more bright, until
Thou couldst but stagger back unto their feet,
And laugh that man's applause or welfare ever
Could tempt thee to forsake them? Or when years
Had passed and still their love possessed thee wholly,
595 When from without some murmur startled thee
Of darkling mortals famished for one ray
Of thy so-hoarded luxury of light,
Didst thou ne'er strive even yet to break those spells
And prove thou couldst recover and fulfil
600 Thy early mission, long ago renounced,
And to that end, select some shape once more?
And did not mist-like influences, thick films,
Faint memories of the rest that charmed so long
Thine eyes, float fast, confuse thee, bear thee off,
605 As whirling snow-drifts blind a man who treads

585| *MS:* world—and to forget   *1835:* world; and   *1849:* world; forgetting, so,
586| *MS:* peers whose < > power;—   *1835:* peers, whose < >
power?   587| *MS:*—And < > wert   *1835:* And   *1863:* wast   588| *MS:*
love   *1835:* memories and regrets, and < > love,   *1863:* memories and regrets
and   589| *MS:* farewel— — —and   *1835:* farewell? and   591| *MS:*
could'st < > feet   *1835:* couldst < > feet,   592| *MS:* Man's   *1835:* man's
1849: welfare once   *1863:* welfare ever   593| *MS:* them: . . or   *1835:* them?
Or   594| *MS:* passed, and   *1835:* pass'd, and < > possess'd < > wholly;
1849: passed < > possessed   *1863:* passed and < > wholly,   596| *1835:*
mortals, famish'd   *1849:* famished   *1863:* mortals famished   597| *MS:* so
hoarded   *1835:* so-hoarded   598| *MS:* Did'st < > break their spells . . .
1835: Didst < > spells,   *1849:* break those spells,   *1863:* spells   599| *MS:* . . .
To prove that even yet thou could'st fulfil   *1835:* To < > couldst   *1849:* And
prove thou couldst recover and fulfil   600| *MS:* renounced,—   *1835:*
renounced,   601| *MS:* And, to < > more   *1835:* more?   *1868:* And to
602| *MS:* — — —And   *1835:* And   603| *MS:* rest, so long before   *1849:* rest,
that charmed so long   *1863:* rest that   604| *MS:* eyes, fast float, confuse < >
off   *1835:* off,   *1849:* eyes, float fast, confuse   605| *MS:* snowdrifts   *1835:*
snow-drifts

A mountain ridge, with guiding spear, through storm?
Say, though I fell, I had excuse to fall;
Say, I was tempted sorely: say but this,
Dear lord, Aprile's lord!

PARACELSUS   Clasp me not thus,
610   Aprile! That the truth should reach me thus!
We are weak dust. Nay, clasp not or I faint!

APRILE My king! and envious thoughts could outrage thee?
Lo, I forget my ruin, and rejoice
In thy success, as thou! Let our God's praise
615   Go bravely through the world at last! What care
Through me or thee? I feel thy breath. Why, tears?
Tears in the darkness, and from thee to me?

PARACELSUS Love me henceforth, Aprile, while I learn
To love; and, merciful God, forgive us both!
620   We wake at length from weary dreams; but both
Have slept in fairy-land: though dark and drear
Appears the world before us, we no less
Wake with our wrists and ankles jewelled still.
I too have sought to KNOW as thou to LOVE—

606-607| *MS:* mountain-ridge < > thro' storm:— / Did'st not perceive, spoiled by the
subtle ways / Of intricate but instantaneous thought, / That common speech was
useless to its ends, / That language, wedded from the first to Thought / Will
strengthen as it strengthens——but, divorced, / Will dwindle while Thought widens
more and more?.. / Say < > fell I < > fall,—   *1835:* mountain ridge < > through
storm? / Didst < > // < > ends—/ < > thought, / < > strengthens; but < > /
< > thought < > and more?... / < > fell, I < > fall;   *1849:* storm? / Say
608| *MS:* Say I < > sorely,—say but this   *1835:* sorely. Say but this,   *1849:* Say, I
< > sorely: say   609| *MS:* lord § written over by § Lord < > Lord!
PARACELSUS < > thus   *1835:* lord < > lord! PARACELSUS < > thus,
610| *MS:* Aprile!—that   *1835:* Aprile!... That   *1863:* Aprile! That
611| *MS:* dust . . . nay   *1835:* dust. Nay < > not, or   *1863:* not or
612| *MS:* King < > thee!   *1835:* king   *1868:* thee?   613| *MS:*—Lo < > ruin
and   *1835:* Lo < > ruin, and   614| *MS:* thou: let   *1835:* thou! Let
615| *MS:* thro' < > last!—what   *1835:* through < > last! What   616| *MS:*
Thro' < > breath . . . why,—tears   *1835:* Through < > breath . . . why tears?
1849: why, tears?   *1863:* breath. Why   617| *MS:* darkness— —and   *1835:*
darkness—and   *1863:* darkness, and   618| *MS:* henceforth Aprile < > I
1835: henceforth, Aprile   *1849:* I   619| *MS:* love—and merciful God forgive
1835: love; and, merciful God, forgive   620| *MS:* dreams . . but   *1835:*
dreams; but   621| *MS:* fairy-land—tho'   *1835:* fairy-land. Though   *1849:* fairy-
land: though   623| *MS:* ancles < > still: .   *1835:* jewell'd still.   *1849:*
jewelled   *1863:* ankles   624| *MS:* I, too, have < > KNOW < > LOVE   *1835:*
KNOW < > LOVE—   *1868:* I too have

₆₂₅ Excluding love as thou refusedst knowledge.
Still thou hast beauty and I, power. We wake:
What penance canst devise for both of us?
APRILE I hear thee faintly. The thick darkness! Even
Thine eyes are hid. 'Tis as I knew: I speak,
₆₃₀ And now I die. But I have seen thy face!
O poet, think of me, and sing of me!
But to have seen thee and to die so soon!
PARACELSUS Die not, Aprile! We must never part.
Are we not halves of one dissevered world,
₆₃₅ Whom this strange chance unites once more? Part? never!
Till thou the lover, know; and I, the knower,
Love—until both are saved. Aprile, hear!
We will accept our gains, and use them—now!
God, he will die upon my breast! Aprile!
₆₄₀ APRILE To speak but once, and die! yet by his side.
Hush! hush!

Ha! go you ever girt about
With phantoms, powers? I have created such,
But these seem real as I.
PARACELSUS   Whom can you see
Through the accursed darkness?
APRILE   Stay; I know,

₆₂₅| *MS:* refused'st knowledge: . .   *1835:* knowledge.   *1849:* refusedst
₆₂₆| *MS:* I power: we   *1835:* power. We wake: *1849:* I, power   ₆₂₈| *MS:*
faintly . . the < > even   *1835:* faintly . . . the < > Even   *1863:* faintly. The
₆₂₉| *MS:* hid: 'tis < > knew . . I speak   *1835:* hid. 'Tis < > knew: I speak,
₆₃₀| *MS:* die— —but   *1835:* die. But   ₆₃₁| *MS:* O dear soul, think of me,—
—and < > me . . .   *1835:* O, dear < > me, and < > me . . .   *1849:* O, poet, think
of me, and < > me!   ₆₃₂| *MS:*— —But < > thee, and   *1835:* But
₆₃₃| *MS:* Aprile . . . we < > part . . .   *1835:* Aprile: we < > part.   *1863:* Aprile!
We   ₆₃₄| *MS:* world   *1835:* dissever'd world,   *1849:* dissevered
₆₃₅| *MS:* part   *1835:* Part   ₆₃₆| *MS:* thou, the Lover, know,—and I, the
Knower,   *1835:* lover, know; and < > knower,   *1868:* thou the lover
_{637–639}| *MS:* Love— —until < > saved—Aprile § written over by § saved! Aprile,
hear! / God! he < > breast: Aprile!   *1835:* Love—until < > saved. Aprile, hear! /
God, he < > breast! Aprile!   *1849:* hear! / We will accept our gains, and use
them—now! / God   ₆₄₀| *MS:* once and die! yet < > side: *1835:* once, and
< > side,   ₆₄₁| *MS:* Hush, hush— / Ha, go < > girt   *1835:* Hush! hush /
Ha! go   *1849:* girt about   ₆₄₂| *MS:* Phantoms, Powers? . . . I   *1835:*
phantoms, powers? I   ₆₄₃| *MS:* I:— — PARACELSUS   *1835:* I . . . PARACELSUS
1849: I! PARACELSUS   *1863:* I? PARACELSUS   *1868:* I. PARACELSUS   ₆₄₄| *MS:*
Thro' < > darkness? . . . APRILE—Stay, I know   *1835:* Through < > darkness? APRILE
Stay; I know,

137

645 I know them: who should know them well as I?
White brows, lit up with glory; poets all!
PARACELSUS Let him but live, and I have my reward!
APRILE Yes; I see now. God is the perfect poet,
Who in his person acts his own creations.
650 Had you but told me this at first! Hush! hush!
PARACELSUS Live! for my sake, because of my great sin,
To help my brain, oppressed by these wild words
And their deep import. Live! 'tis not too late.
I have a quiet home for us, and friends.
655 Michal shall smile on you. Hear you? Lean thus,
And breathe my breath. I shall not lose one word
Of all your speech, one little word, Aprile!
APRILE No, no. Crown me? I am not one of you!
'Tis he, the king, you seek. I am not one.
660 PARACELSUS Thy spirit, at least, Aprile! Let me love!

I have attained, and now I may depart.

645| *1835:* as I?— *1863:* as I? 646| *MS:* brows—lit < > glory—Poets
1835: brows, lit < > glory; poets 648| *MS:* Yes, I see now—God < >
PERFECT POET: *1835:* Yes; I see now—God < > PERFECT POET, *1863:* now. God
1868: perfect poet, 649–650| *MS:* person, acts < > / < > first! . . hush, hush
. . . . *1835:* person acts < > / < > first! . . . Hush! hush! *1849:* Who in creation
acts his own conceptions. / Shall man refuse to be aught less than God? / Man's
weakness is his glory—for the strength / Which raises him to heaven and near God's
self, / Came spite of it: God's strength his glory is, / For thence came with our
weakness sympathy / Which brought God down to earth, a man like us. / Had
1863: Who in His person acts His own creations. / Had < > first! Hush! hush!
1868: his < > his 651| *MS:* sake— —because < > sin *1835:* sake, because
< > sin, 652| *MS:* brain oppressed by your § probably, cancelled by § these
wild *1835:* brain, oppress'd *1849:* oppressed 653| *MS:* import— —Live
< > late,— *1835:* import. Live < > late: *1863:* late. 654| *MS:* home far
§ probably, cancelled by § for us—and friends,— *1835:* us, and friends.
655| *MS:* you— —hear you? lean thus *1835:* you . . . Hear < > Lean thus, *1863:*
you. Hear 656| *MS:* breath— —I *1835:* breath: I *1863:* breath. I
657| *MS:* speech—one *1835:* speech—one < > Aprile. *1849:* speech—no little < >
Aprile! *1863:* speech, one little 658| *MS:* No, no—crown *me*? I *1835:* No,
no . . . Crown *1849:* me *1863:* No, no. Crown 659| *MS:* Tis < > King you
seek . . I < > one . . . *1835:* 'Tis < > king, you seek. I *1863:* one.
669| *MS:* Aprile!—Let *me* love! . . . *1835:* Aprile, let *1849:* Give me thy < > least!
Let me love, too! *1863:* Thy < > least, Aprile! Let me love! 661| *MS:* I HAVE
ATTAIN'D, AND NOW I MAY DEPART § small capitals probably a printer's misinterpretation;
MS has two lines at end of Parts I and II § *1849:* I have attained, and now I may depart.

PART III. PARACELSUS.

S C E N E—*Basil; a chamber in the house of* PARACELSUS. 1526.

PARACELSUS, FESTUS.

PARACELSUS Heap logs and let the blaze laugh out!
FESTUS   True, true!
'Tis very fit all, time and chance and change
Have wrought since last we sat thus, face to face
And soul to soul—all cares, far-looking fears,
5   Vague apprehensions, all vain fancies bred
By your long absence, should be cast away,
Forgotten in this glad unhoped renewal
Of our affections.
PARACELSUS   Oh, omit not aught
Which witnesses your own and Michal's own
10   Affection: spare not that! Only forget
The honours and the glories and what not,
It pleases you to tell profusely out.

SCENE| MS: A < > *Paracelsus at Basil.* 1526.   1863: *Basil; a* < > *Paracelsus.*
1526.   1| MS: out: FESTUS True, true,—   1835: logs, and < > out. FESTUS
True, true;   1849: out! FESTUS True, true!   1863: true, true   1868: logs and < >
True, true!   2| MS: all Time and Chance   1835: time, and chance, and
1849: fit that all, time, chance   1863: fit all, time and chance and   3| MS:
sate   1849: to face,   1863: sat < > to face   4| MS: soul——all cares,—far-
looking fears   1835: soul—all cares, far-looking fears,   5| MS:
apprehensions—all   1835: apprehensions, all   6| MS: absence— — —should
1835: absence, should   8| MS: affection: PARACELSUS   1835: affections.
PARACELSUS   9| MS: Michals   1835: Michal's   1849: Michal's love!   1863:
Michal's own   10| MS: Affection—spare not that! forget alone   1835: Affection;
spare   1849: I bade you not spare that! Forget   1863: Affection: spare not that!
Only forget   11| MS: not   1835: glories, and what not,   1849: glories, and
the rest,   1863: glories and what not,   12| MS: That you § *you* inserted above
the line § are pleased to   1849: You seemed disposed to   1863: It pleases you to

FESTUS Nay, even your honours, in a sense, I waive:
The wondrous Paracelsus, life's dispenser,
15 Fate's commissary, idol of the schools
And courts, shall be no more than Aureole still,
Still Aureole and my friend as when we parted
Some twenty years ago, and I restrained
As best I could the promptings of my spirit
20 Which secretly advanced you, from the first,
To the pre-eminent rank which, since, your own
Adventurous ardour, nobly triumphing,
Has won for you.
PARACELSUS   Yes, yes. And Michal's face
Still wears that quiet and peculiar light
25 Like the dim circlet floating round a pearl?
FESTUS Just so.
PARACELSUS   And yet her calm sweet countenance,
Though saintly, was not sad; for she would sing
Alone. Does she still sing alone, bird-like,
Not dreaming you are near? Her carols dropt
30 In flakes through that old leafy bower built under
The sunny wall at Würzburg, from her lattice
Among the trees above, while I, unseen,
Sat conning some rare scroll from Tritheim's shelves,
Much wondering notes so simple could divert

---

¹³| MS: honours in a certain sense: . . 1835: sense. 1849: honours, in a sense, I
waive: ¹⁴| MS: Paracelsus—the dispenser 1849: Paracelsus—Life's
dispenser, 1863: Paracelsus, Life's 1868: life's   ¹⁵| MS: Of life—the
commissary of fate—the idol 1835: life, the < > Fate, the 1849: Fate's
commissary, idol of the schools, 1863: schools   ¹⁶| MS: Of Princes— —is no
< > still,— 1835: princes, is < > still— 1849: And Courts, shall be no 1863:
courts < > still,   ¹⁷| MS: friend, as 1868: friend as   ¹⁸| MS: ago,
when I 1835: ago, when I restrain'd 1849: ago, and I restrained   ¹⁹| MS:
As I best could 1835: spirit, 1863: As best I could < > spirit   ²⁰| 1835:
you from the first 1849: you, from the first,   ²¹| MS: which since 1835:
since your 1849: which, since, your   ²³| MS: PARACELSUS — —Yes, yes . . .
and 1835: PARACELSUS Yes, Yes; and 1849: Yes, Yes; and 1863: Yes, yes.
And   ²⁴| 1835: light, 1863: light   ²⁶| MS: so: PARACELSUS < >
countenance 1835: so. PARACELSUS < > countenance,   ²⁷| MS: saintly was
not sad—for 1835: saintly, was not sad; for   ²⁸| MS: Alone . . does < >
alone? bird-like, 1835: Alone . . . Does < > alone, bird-like, 1863: Alone.
Does   ²⁹| MS: near: her 1835: near? Her   ³⁰| MS: thro' 1835:
through   ³²| MS: above . . while I unseen 1835: above, while I,
unseen,   ³³| MS: Sate < > rare roll from < > shelves, 1849: rare scroll
from 1863: Sat 1888: shelves

35 My mind from study. Those were happy days.
Respect all such as sing when all alone!
FESTUS Scarcely alone: her children, you may guess,
Are wild beside her.
PARACELSUS   Ah, those children quite
Unsettle the pure picture in my mind:
40 A girl, she was so perfect, so distinct:
No change, no change! Not but this added grace
May blend and harmonize with its compeers,
And Michal may become her motherhood;
But 'tis a change, and I detest all change,
45 And most a change in aught I loved long since.
So, Michal—you have said she thinks of me?
FESTUS O very proud will Michal be of you!
Imagine how we sat, long winter-nights,
Scheming and wondering, shaping your presumed
50 Adventure, or devising its reward;
Shutting out fear with all the strength of hope.
For it was strange how, even when most secure
In our domestic peace, a certain dim
And flitting shade could sadden all; it seemed
55 A restlessness of heart, a silent yearning,
A sense of something wanting, incomplete—

35| MS: study . . . those § corrected in pencil to § study. Those < > days!   1835:
study. Those   1863: days.   36| MS: alone.   1863: alone!   37| MS:
alone—her < > guess § corrected in pencil to § guess,   1863: alone: her
38| MS: her . . . PARACELSUS   1863: her. PARACELSUS   39| MS: mind:–
§ corrected in pencil to § mind.   1835: mind: 1868: Unsettled   1888:
Unsettle   40| MS: girl—she < > distinct, . . § corrected in pencil to § distinct
. . .   1863: girl, she < > distinct.   1888: distinct: 41| MS: No change, no
change!—not § corrected in pencil to § No change, no change! Not   43| MS:
mother-hood;   1849: motherhood;   44| MS: tis § corrected in pencil to § 'tis a
change—and   1863: change, and   45| MS: since: 1849: since!   1863:
since.   46| MS: But Michal . . . you   1849: So, Michal . . . you   1863:
Michal—you   48| MS: sate   1863: sat   49| MS: wondering—shaping
1863: wondering, shaping   50| MS: devising your reward;   1835: Adventure,
or   1849: Adventures, or devising their reward;   1863: Adventure, or devising its
reward;   51| MS: fear as long as hopes might be— § —in pencil §   1849: fear
with all the strength of hope.   52| MS: . . . § deleted in pencil § For   1849:
Though it   1863: For it   54| MS: all—it seemed § altered in pencil to § all; it
seem'd   1849: seemed   55| MS: heart—a § altered in pencil to § heart, a < >
yearning, § , added in pencil §   56| MS: incomplete,—   1835: incomplete—

Not to be put in words, perhaps avoided
By mute consent—but, said or unsaid, felt
To point to one so loved and so long lost.
60 And then the hopes rose and shut out the fears—
How you would laugh should I recount them now
I still predicted your return at last
With gifts beyond the greatest of them all,
All Tritheim's wondrous troop; did one of which
65 Attain renown by any chance, I smiled,
As well aware of who would prove his peer.
Michal was sure some woman, long ere this,
As beautiful as you were sage, had loved . . .
PARACELSUS Far-seeing, truly, to discern so much
70 In the fantastic projects and day-dreams
Of a raw restless boy!
FESTUS   Oh, no: the sunrise
Well warranted our faith in this full noon!
Can I forget the anxious voice which said
"Festus, have thoughts like these ere shaped themselves
75 In other brains than mine? have their possessors
Existed in like circumstance? were they weak

58| *MS:* consent— § above § , § , cancelled in pencil § but felt no less, §, added in
pencil § when traced, §, added in pencil §   *1849:* but, said or unsaid, felt
59| *MS:* lost. § altered in pencil to § lost—   *1835:* lost;   *1849:* lost.
60| *MS:* — § cancelled in pencil § Not but, to balance fears, were glowing hopes— —
— § altered in pencil to § hopes.   *1849:* And then the hopes rose and shut out the
fears—   61| *MS:* now!   *1888:* now   62| *MS:*— § cancelled in pencil § I
< > last, § , added in pencil §   *1868:* last   63| *MS:* greatest of them all,
1849: greatest vaunt of all,   *1863:* greatest of them all,   64| *MS:* troop—did
1835: troop; did   65| *MS:* smiled— § —added in pencil §   *1863:*
smiled,   66| *MS:* peer: *1835:* peer.   67| *MS:* sure that long ere this
some being, § , added in pencil §   *1849:* sure some woman, long ere this,
68| *MS:* were brave, had loved . . . . . § altered in pencil to § loved . . .   *1849:* were
sage, had   69| *MS:* Far-seeing, § , added in pencil § truly, § , added in pencil §
to discern as much   *1849:* discern so much   71| *MS:* raw, restless boy. FESTUS
— —Oh no, the   *1835:* FESTUS Oh   *1849:* boy! FESTUS Say, one whose sunrise
1863: FESTUS Oh, no: the sunrise   *1868:* raw restless   72| *MS:* Noon;   *1835:*
noon: *1849:* noon!   73| *MS:* Have I forgotten < > voice that said   *1849:*
Can I forget < > voice which said,   *1868:* said   74| *MS:* e'er   *1888:*
ere   75| *MS:* mine— —have § altered in pencil to § mine—have § cancelled in
pencil to § mine—have   *1863:* mine? have   76| *MS:* circumstance— —were
§ altered in pencil to § circumstance?—were § cancelled in pencil to §
circumstance—were   *1863:* circumstance? were

As I, or ever constant from the first,
Despising youth's allurements and rejecting
As spider-films the shackles I endure?
80 Is there hope for me?"—and I answered gravely
As an acknowledged elder, calmer, wiser,
More gifted mortal. O you must remember,
For all your glorious . . .
PARACELSUS   Glorious? ay, this hair,
These hands—nay, touch them, they are mine! Recall
85 With all the said recallings, times when thus
To lay them by your own ne'er turned you pale
As now. Most glorious, are they not?
FESTUS   Why—why—
Something must be subtracted from success
So wide, no doubt. He would be scrupulous, truly,
90 Who should object such drawbacks. Still, still, Aureole,
You are changed, very changed! 'Twere losing nothing
To look well to it: you must not be stolen
From the enjoyment of your well-won meed.
PARACELSUS My friend! you seek my pleasure, past a doubt:
95 You will best gain your point, by talking, not
Of me, but of yourself.
FESTUS   Have I not said

77| MS: I—or § altered in pencil to § I?—or § cancelled in pencil to § I—or   1863: I,
or   78| MS: allurements and § altered in pencil to § allurements, and   1863:
allurements and   80| MS: me?"——and I answered § altered in pencil to §
me?"—and I answer'd   1849: answered grave   1863: gravely   81| MS:
wiser   1835: wiser,   82| MS: mortal . . . O § altered in pencil to § mortal.
O   82| MS: glorious . . . . . PARACELSUS § altered in pencil to § glorious . . .
PARACELSUS < > ay,   to wit this § altered in pencil to § wit, this   1849: ay, this
hair,   86| 1835: turn'd you pale,   1849: turned   1863: pale   87| MS:
now:—most glorious are § altered in pencil to § now. Most glorious, are < > Why . . .
Why . . .   1835: Why . . . why . . .   1863: Why—why—   89| MS: doubt:—he
< > scrupulous truly § altered in pencil to § doubt. He < > scrupulous, truly,
90| MS: drawbacks: . . still . . still § altered in pencil to § drawbacks. Still—still
1835: Still, still Aureole   1849: Still, still, Aureole,   91| MS: are
changed—very changed . . . 'twere § altered in pencil to § very changed. 'Twere
1863: changed, very   93| MS: well won § altered in pencil to § well-
won   94| MS: My Friend!—you < > doubt; § altered in pencil to § My Friend!
you < > doubt. § altered in pencil to § doubt: 1863: friend   95| MS: point
by   1849: By talking, not of me, but of yourself,   1863: You will best
gain your point, by talking, not   96| 1849: You will best gain your point.
FESTUS   1863: Of me, but of yourself. FESTUS

All touching Michal and my children? Sure
You know, by this, full well how Aennchen looks
Gravely, while one disparts her thick brown hair;
100 And Aureole's glee when some stray gannet builds
Amid the birch-trees by the lake. Small hope
Have I that he will honour (the wild imp)
His namesake. Sigh not! 'tis too much to ask
That all we love should reach the same proud fate.
105 But you are very kind to humour me
By showing interest in my quiet life;
You, who of old could never tame yourself
To tranquil pleasures, must at heart despise . . .
PARACELSUS Festus, strange secrets are let out by death
110 Who blabs so oft the follies of this world:
And I am death's familiar, as you know.
I helped a man to die, some few weeks since,
Warped even from his go-cart to one end—
The living on princes' smiles, reflected from
115 A mighty herd of favourites. No mean trick
He left untried, and truly well-nigh wormed
All traces of God's finger out of him:
Then died, grown old. And just an hour before,
Having lain long with blank and soulless eyes,

97| *MS:* sure   *1835:* Sure   98| *MS:* Annchen   *1849:* Aennchen
99| *MS:* hair,— § altered in pencil to § hair;   101| *MS:* lake— —small § altered
in pencil to § lake.— —Small   *1835:* lake. Small   102| *MS:* honour,—the wild
imp!—   *1835:* honour, the wild imp!   *1849:* imp,   *1863:* honour (the wild
imp)   103| *MS:* namesake;— —sigh not!—'tis § altered in pencil to § namesake.—
—Sigh not! 'tis   *1835:* namesake. Sigh   *1849:* namesake! Sigh   *1868:* namesake.
Sigh   104| *MS:* fate: § altered in pencil to § fate.   108| *MS:* despise
. . . . . § altered in pencil to § despise . . .   109| *MS:* Death, § , added in
pencil §   *1868:* death   110| *MS:* world: § altered in pencil to § world.   *1835:*
world: 111| *MS:* I, as you know, am Death's familiar oft: § altered in pencil
to § oft.   *1849:* And I am Death's familiar, as you know.   *1868:* death's
112| *MS:* helped § altered in pencil to § help'd   *1849:* helped   113| *MS:*
Warped § altered in pencil to § Warp'd   *1849:* Warped   114| *MS:* To live on
Princes' smiles—reflected § altered in pencil to § smiles, reflected   *1835:* prince's
1849: The living on princes'   115| *MS:* favourites:—no § altered in pencil to §
favourites. No   116| *MS:* untried, and < > well nigh wormed § altered in
pencil to § worm'd   *1849:* untried; and < > wormed   *1863:* untried, and < > well-
nigh   117| *MS:* him.   *1863:* him: 118| *MS:* He died < > old;—and
< > before,— § altered in pencil to § old; and < > before—   *1849:* Then died
1863: old. And < > before,   119| *MS:* eyes, § altered in pencil to § eyes—
1863: eyes,

144

120 He sat up suddenly, and with natural voice
Said that in spite of thick air and closed doors
God told him it was June; and he knew well,
Without such telling, harebells grew in June;
And all that kings could ever give or take
125 Would not be precious as those blooms to him.
Just so, allowing I am passing sage,
It seems to me much worthier argument
Why pansies,* eyes that laugh, bear beauty's prize
From violets, eyes that dream—(your Michal's choice)—
130 Than all fools find to wonder at in me
Or in my fortunes. And be very sure
I say this from no prurient restlessness,
No self-complacency, itching to turn,
Vary and view its pleasure from all points,
135 And, in this instance, willing other men
May be at pains, demonstrate to itself
The realness of the very joy it tastes.
What should delight me like the news of friends
Whose memories were a solace to me oft,
140 As mountain-baths to wild fowls in their flight?
Ofter than you had wasted thought on me

°Citrinula (flammula) herba Paracelso multum familiaris.—DORN

120| MS: sate   1863: sat   121| MS: Said, that   1863: Said that
122| MS: well § altered in pencil to § well,   123| 1835: hare-bells   1863:
harebells   124| MS: And that all kings   1835: And all that kings
125| MS: him: .... § altered in pencil to § him.   126| MS: passing wise,
1863: passing sage,   128| MS: pansies °—eyes < > laugh—are lovelier   1835:
pansies, ° eyes < > laugh, are   1849: laugh, bear beauty's prize   129| MS:
Than violets—eyes   1835: violets, eyes   1849: From violets   130| 1835:
me,   1868: me   131| MS: fortunes: and   1863: fortunes. And
132| MS: restlessness—   1863: restlessness,   133| MS:—No self-complacency
itching to vary § altered in pencil to § self-complacency—itching to vary,   1835: No
1849: to turn,   1863: self-complacency, itching   134| MS: And turn and
§ altered in pencil to § turn, and   1849: Vary, and   1868: Vary and
135| MS: Men   1835: men   1849: this matter, willing   1863: this instance,
willing   136| MS: Should be at pains to demonstrate to it   1849: Should argue
and demonstrate to itself   1863: Should be at pains, demonstrate   1888: May
be   137| MS: joy it lives on .... § altered in pencil to § on.   1849: it
tastes.   138| MS: What joy is better than the   1863: What should delight me
like the   141| MS: Oftener that you   1849: Yes, ofter than you wasted   1863:
Ofter than you had wasted

145

Had you been wise, and rightly valued bliss.
But there's no taming nor repressing hearts:
God knows I need such!—So, you heard me speak?
145 FESTUS Speak? when?
PARACELSUS　　　　　When but this morning at my class?
There was noise and crowd enough. I saw you not.
Surely you know I am engaged to fill
The chair here?—that 'tis part of my proud fate
To lecture to as many thick-skulled youths
150 As please, each day, to throng the theatre,
To my great reputation, and no small
Danger of Basil's benches long unused
To crack beneath such honour?
FESTUS　　　　　　　　　I was there;
I mingled with the throng: shall I avow
155 Small care was mine to listen?—too intent
On gathering from the murmurs of the crowd
A full corroboration of my hopes!
What can I learn about your powers? but they
Know, care for nought beyond your actual state,
160 Your actual value; yet they worship you,
Those various natures whom you sway as one!
But ere I go, be sure I shall attend . . .

142| *MS:* been sage, and < > bliss,— § altered in pencil to § bliss;　*1849:* If you
were sage < > bliss!　*1863:* Had you been wise, and　*1868:* bliss.　144| *MS:*
such! . . . so you　*1835:* So　*1849:* such!—So　*1863:* So, you　146| *MS:*
enough—I § altered in pencil to § enough. I < > not:　*1849:* not.　148| *MS:*
here? that　*1849:* here?—that　149| *MS:* thick-sculled § altered in pencil to §
thick-scull'd　*1849:* thick-sculled　*1863:* thick-skulled　150| *MS:* please to
throng the theatre § written over by § Theatre each day § altered in pencil to § day,
1849: please, each day, to throng the theatre,　152| *MS:* Peril of benches, long
unused to crack　*1849:* Danger of Basil's benches, long unused　*1868:* benches
long　153| *MS:* Beneath < > there, indeed:— § altered in pencil to § indeed.
1849: To crack beneath < > there;　155| *MS:* to listen?—I § altered in pencil
to § listen? I was intent　*1849:* I had small care to listen?—too intent　*1863:* Small
care was mine to　157| *MS:* hopes: § altered in pencil to § hopes.　*1849:*
hopes!　158| *MS:* I < > powers?—but § altered in pencil to § powers? but
they　*1849:* I < > they　159| *MS:* state, § altered in pencil to § state—
1863: state,　160| *MS:* value— —yet § altered in pencil to § value. Yet < >
you!　*1849:* value; and yet worship　*1863:* value; yet they worship you,
161| *MS:* one:— § altered in pencil to § one.　*1849:* one!　162| *MS:* attend
. . . .　*1835:* attend . . .

PARACELSUS Stop, o' God's name: the thing's by no means yet
Past remedy! Shall I read this morning's labour
165 —At least in substance? Nought so worth the gaining
As an apt scholar! Thus then, with all due
Precision and emphasis—you, beside, are clearly
Guiltless of understanding more, a whit,
The subject than your stool—allowed to be
170 A notable advantage.
FESTUS   Surely, Aureole,
You laugh at me!
PARACELSUS   I laugh? Ha, ha! thank heaven,
I charge you, if't be so! for I forget
Much, and what laughter should be like. No less,
However, I forego that luxury
175 Since it alarms the friend who brings it back.
True, laughter like my own must echo strangely
To thinking men; a smile were better far;
So, make me smile! If the exulting look
You wore but now be smiling, 'tis so long
180 Since I have smiled! Alas, such smiles are born
Alone of hearts like yours, or herdsmen's souls
Of ancient time, whose eyes, calm as their flocks,
Saw in the stars mere garnishry of heaven,

164| MS: remedy,—shall § altered in pencil to § remedy. Shall < > labour?   1849:
remedy! Shall < > morning's work   1863: morning's labour   165| MS: At
least, in < > nought § altered in pencil to § Nought   1835: least in
1849:—At   166| MS: scholar: thus   1849: scholar! Thus   167| MS:
emphasis;—(you § altered in pencil to § emphasis—(you, besides, are   1863:
emphasis—you   1868: beside   168| MS: more a whit   1849: understanding a
whit more   1863: understanding more, a whit,   169| MS: subject, than < >
stool,—allowed § altered in pencil to § stool—allowed   1835: subject than < >
allow'd   1849: allowed   170| MS: advantage:) § altered in pencil to §
advantage) ... FESTUS   1863: advantage. FESTUS   171| MS: I   1849: I
173| MS: Much—and < > like: no less, § , added in pencil §   1849: like! No   1863:
Much, and   1868: like. No   174| MS: luxury, § , added in pencil §   1863:
luxury   175| MS: it offends the   1849: it alarms the   176| 1849:
strange   1863: strangely   177| MS: men;—a § altered in pencil to § men; a < >
far,— § altered in pencil to § far,   1835: far—   1863: far;   178| MS: So make
me smile!—if § altered in pencil to § smile, if   1849: smile! If   179| MS: now,
be smiling, 'tis § altered in pencil to § smiling. 'Tis   1835: now be   1849: smiling,
'tis   180| MS: alas   1849: Alas   181| MS: yours,—and § altered in pencil
to § yours, and those old Herds'   1835: herds,   1849: yours, or shepherds old   1863:
or herdsmen's souls   182| MS: eyes—calm < > flocks— § altered in pencil to §
eyes, calm < > flocks,

And in the earth a stage for altars only.
185 Never change, Festus: I say, never change!
FESTUS My God, if he be wretched after all!
PARACELSUS When last we parted, Festus, you declared,
—Or Michal, yes, her soft lips whispered words
I have preserved. She told me she believed
190 I should succeed (meaning, that in the search
I then engaged in, I should meet success)
And yet be wretched: now, she augured false.
FESTUS Thank heaven! but you spoke strangely: could I venture
To think bare apprehension lest your friend,
195 Dazzled by your resplendent course, might find
Henceforth less sweetness in his own, could move
Such earnest mood in you? Fear not, dear friend,
That I shall leave you, inwardly repining
Your lot was not my own!
PARACELSUS   And this for ever!
200 For ever! gull who may, they will be gulled!
They will not look nor think; 'tis nothing new
In them: but surely he is not of them!
My Festus, do you know, I reckoned, you—
Though all beside were sand-blind—you, my friend,

184| *MS:* only:— § altered in pencil to § only.   *1849:* In earth < > altars, nothing
more.   *1868:* And in the earth < > altars only.   185| *MS:* Festus: I say, never
§ altered in pencil to § Festus, I say: never   *1835:* Festus: I say, never
186| *1888:* all   *1889:* all!   187| *MS:* declared— — § altered in pencil to §
declared—   *1835:* declared,   188| *MS:* Or Michal— —yes § altered in pencil
to § Michal—yes *her* < > whispered § altered in pencil to § whisper'd what   *1835:*
yes, *her*   *1849:*—Or did your Michal's soft lips whisper words   *1863:*—Or Michal, yes,
her soft lips whispered words   189| *MS:* preserved: the   *1849:* preserved?
She   *1863:* preserved. She   190| *MS:* succeed, (meaning   *1835:* succeed
(meaning   191| *1835:* in I < > success),   *1849:* in, I   *1868:* success)
192| *1835:* augur'd   *1849:* augured   193| *MS:* strangely! could   *1863:*
strangely: could   195| *MS:* course, should find   *1849:* course, might
find   196| *1849:* own, awakes   *1868:* own, could move   197| *MS:* you?
fear § altered in pencil to § you? Fear < > Friend,   *1835:* friend,   199| *MS:*
Such lot < > own . . . . PARACELSUS < > forever! § altered in pencil to § for ever!
1849: Your lot < > own! PARACELSUS And this, for   *1868:* this for   200| *MS:*
Forever § altered in pencil to § For ever < > be blind!   *1863:* be gulled!
201| *MS:* think—'tis   *1863:* think; 'tis   202| *MS:* them— —but § altered in
pencil to § *them;* but < > *he*   *1835: them:* but   *1849:* them; but < > he   *1863:*
them: but   203| *MS:* know I reckoned § altered in pencil to § reckon'd *you*—
1849: know, I reckoned, you—   204| *MS:* Tho' § altered in pencil to § Though

148

205 Would look at me, once close, with piercing eye
Untroubled by the false glare that confounds
A weaker vision: would remain serene,
Though singular amid a gaping throng.
I feared you, or I had come, sure, long ere this,
210 To Einsiedeln. Well, error has no end,
And Rhasis is a sage, and Basil boasts
A tribe of wits, and I am wise and blest
Past all dispute! 'Tis vain to fret at it.
I have vowed long ago my worshippers
215 Shall owe to their own deep sagacity
All further information, good or bad.
Small risk indeed my reputation runs,
Unless perchance the glance now searching me
Be fixed much longer; for it seems to spell
220 Dimly the characters a simpler man
Might read distinct enough. Old Eastern books
Say, the fallen prince of morning some short space
Remained unchanged in semblance; nay, his brow
Was hued with triumph: every spirit then
225 Praising, *his* heart on flame the while:—a tale!
Well, Festus, what discover you, I pray?

FESTUS Some foul deed sullies then a life which else

205| *MS:* eye, § , added in pencil § *1863:* eye   206| *MS:* by false glare that
well confounds   *1849:* by the false glare that confounds   207| *MS:* vision;
would   *1888:* vision: would   208| *MS:* Tho' singular, amid < > throng:
§ altered in pencil to § Though < > throng.   *1868:* singular amid   209| *MS:*
this,   *1835:* fear'd   *1849:* feared < > or had   *1863:* or I had   210| *MS:*
Einsiedeln: . . . well,—error § altered in pencil to § Einsiedeln. Well, error
213| *MS:* 'tis § altered in pencil to § 'Tis   214| *1835:* vow'd   *1849:* vowed
long since that my   *1863:* long ago my   216| *MS:* bad: *1835:* bad.   *1849:*
bad: *1863:* bad.   217| *MS:* risk, indeed, my < > runs   *1835:* risk indeed my
< > runs,   *1849:* And little risk my   *1863:* Small risk indeed my   219| *MS:*
longer . . . for § altered in pencil to § longer—for   *1835:* fix'd   *1849:* fixed   *1863:*
longer; for   220| *1849:* Dimly, the   *1863:* Dimly the   221| *MS:* enough:
old § altered in pencil to § enough. Old   *1835:* eastern   *1888:* Eastern
222| *MS:* Say the < > Prince of Morning   *1835:* prince of morning   *1849:* Say,
the   223| *MS:* Remained unchanged in seeming— —nay his § altered in pencil
to § Remain'd unchang'd in seeming—nay, his   *1835:* unchanged   *1849:* Remained
< > in feature—nay   *1863:* in semblance; nay   224| *1849:* Seemed hued
1863: Was hued   225| *MS:* Praising; *his* < > while: a tale!   *1835:* while . . . a
tale!   *1849:* while:—a tale!   *1863:* Praising, *his*

149

Were raised supreme?

PARACELSUS   Good: I do well, most well
Why strive to make men hear, feel, fret themselves
230 With what is past their power to comprehend?
I should not strive now: only, having nursed
The faint surmise that one yet walked the earth,
One, at least, not the utter fool of show,
Not absolutely formed to be the dupe
235 Of shallow plausibilities alone:
One who, in youth, found wise enough to choose
The happiness his riper years approve,
Was yet so anxious for another's sake,
That, ere his friend could rush upon a mad
240 And ruinous course, the converse of his own,
His gentle spirit essayed, prejudged for him
The perilous path, foresaw its destiny,
And warned the weak one in such tender words,
Such accents—his whole heart in every tone—
245 That oft their memory comforted that friend
When it by right should have increased despair:

228| *MS:* raised above— — — PARACELSUS < > well—most well! *1835:* above . . .
PARACELSUS *1849:* raised supreme? PARACELSUS *1863:* well, most *1888:* most
well   **229|** *MS:* make them know and § altered in pencil to § know, and feel,
and fret *1849:* make men hear, feel, fret themselves **230|** *MS:* Themselves
with what 'tis < > to know, *1849:* With what 'tis past their power to
comprehend? *1888:* what is past **231|** *MS:* Or feel, or comprehend?
still,—having § altered in pencil to § still, having *1835:* Still *1849:* I would not
strive now: only, having *1863:* I should not **232|** *1835:* walk'd *1849:*
walked **233|** *MS: One* < > shew, *1835:* show, *1849:* One
234| *1835:* form'd *1849:* formed **235|** *MS:* alone;— § altered in pencil to §
alone; *1888:* alone: **236|** *MS:* youth found *1888:* youth, found
237| *MS:* That happiness *1849:* The happiness **238|** *MS:* sake *1849:*
sake, **239|** *MS:* That ere his Friend *1835:* friend *1849:* That, ere < > a
course *1863:* a mad **240|** *1849:* Mad, ruinous, the *1863:* And ruinous
course, the **241|** *MS:* spirit had already tried *1849:* gentler spirit essayed,
prejudged for him *1863:* gentle **242|** *MS:* foreseen *1849:* foresaw
243| *MS:* words— § added in pencil § *1849:* words, **244|** *MS:*—Such accents
. . . his § written over by § accents—his < > every one . . . § written over by § one—
1835: Such *1849:* every tone— **245|** *MS:* That they oft served § altered in
pencil to § serv'd to comfort him, in hours *1835:* served *1849:* That oft their
memory comforted that friend **246|** *MS:* When they, by right, should—
—despair;— — § altered in pencil to § despair; *1835:* despair: *1849:* When rather
it should *1863:* When it by right should

—Having believed, I say, that this one man
Could never lose the light thus from the first
His portion—how should I refuse to grieve
250 At even my gain if it disturb our old
Relation, if it make me out more wise?
Therefore, once more reminding him how well
He prophesied, I note the single flaw
That spoils his prophet's title. In plain words,
255 You were deceived, and thus were you deceived—
I have not been successful, and yet am
Most miserable; 'tis said at last; nor you
Give credit, lest you force me to concede
That common sense yet lives upon the world!
260 FESTUS You surely do not mean to banter me?
PARACELSUS You know, or—if you have been wise enough
To cleanse your memory of such matters—knew,
As far as words of mine could make it clear,
That 'twas my purpose to find joy or grief
265 Solely in the fulfilment of my plan
Or plot or whatsoe'er it was; rejoicing
Alone as it proceeded prosperously,
Sorrowing then only when mischance retarded

247| _MS:_ Having < > say, such happy One   _1835:_ one   _1849:_—Having < > say,
that this one man   248| _1849:_ the wisdom from   _1863:_ the light thus
from   249| _MS:_ portion,—I § altered in pencil to § portion—I can not refuse
_1835:_ cannot   _1849:_ portion—how should I refuse   250-251| _MS:_ Even at my
< > / Relation,—if < > _me_ out the wiser .... § altered in pencil to § Relation; < >
wiser.   _1849:_ At even my < > it attest his loss, / At triumph which so signally
disturbs / Our old relations, proving me more wise?   _1863:_ it disturb our old /
Relation, if it make me out more   254| _MS:_ That seems to cross his title: in
< > words   _1849:_ That spoils his prophet's title   _1863:_ title. In   255| _MS:_
thus were you deceived:— § altered in pencil to § deceived—   257| _1849:_ Most wretched; there—'tis < > last; but give   _1863:_
Most miserable; 'tis < > last; nor you   258| _MS:_ to believe   _1849:_ No credit
< > to concede   _1863:_ Give credit   259| _MS:_ world.   _1849:_ the earth.
_1863:_ the world.   _1868:_ world!   261| _MS:_ know,—or,—if § written over by § or,
(if § altered in pencil to § or (if   _1835:_ know, or   _1863:_ or—if   262| _MS:_
matters,—knew, § written over by § matters,) knew, § altered in pencil to § matters)
knew,   _1863:_ matters—knew,   265| _MS:_ Alone in < > plan,   _1849:_ Solely
in   _1863:_ plan   266| _MS:_ plot, or < > was:—rejoicing   _1835:_ was:
rejoicing   _1849:_ was; rejoicing   _1863:_ plot or   267| _MS:_ prosperously;—
§ altered in pencil to § prosperously;   _1849:_ prosperously,   268| _MS:_ only,
when   _1849:_ Sorrowing alone when any chance retarded   _1863:_ Sorrowing then
only when mischance retarded

Its progress. That was in those Würzburg days!

270 Not to prolong a theme I thoroughly hate,
I have pursued this plan with all my strength;
And having failed therein most signally,
Cannot object to ruin utter and drear
As all-excelling would have been the prize

275 Had fortune favoured me. I scarce have right
To vex your frank good spirit late so glad
In my supposed prosperity, I know,
And, were I lucky in a glut of friends,
Would well agree to let your error live,

280 Nay, strengthen it with fables of success.
But mine is no condition to refuse
The transient solace of so rare a godsend,
My solitary luxury, my one friend:
Accordingly I venture to put off

285 The wearisome vest of falsehood galling me,
Secure when he is by. I lay me bare,
Prone at his mercy—but he is my friend!

269–270| *MS:* progress: nor § altered in pencil to § progress. Nor was this the scheme of
one / Enamoured § altered in pencil to § Enamour'd of a lot unlike the world's, / And
thus far sure from common casualty— § —added in pencil § / (Folly of follies!) in
§ altered in pencil to § follies!)—in that, thus, the Mind / Became the only arbiter of
fate:— § altered in pencil to § fate. / No: what § altered in pencil to § No; what I
termed, and § altered in pencil to § termed and might conceive my choice, § , added in
pencil § / Already had been rooted in my soul— — § altered in pencil to § soul— /
Had long been part and portion of my self: § altered in pencil to § self. / Not < >
hate,— § altered in pencil to § hate,   *1835:* (Folly of follies!) in < > mind // < >
term'd < > // < > myself.   *1849:* progress. That was in those Würzburg days! /
Not   271| *MS:* I have since followed § altered in pencil to § follow'd it with
1849: have pursued this plan with   272| *MS:* failed § altered in pencil to §
fail'd   *1849:* failed   273| *MS:* ruin utter § altered in pencil to § ruin, utter
1863: ruin utter   275| *MS:* favoured me: I § altered in pencil to § favour'd me.
I   *1849:* favoured < > scarce do right   *1863:* scarce have right   276| *1835:*
spirit, late   *1849:* late rejoiced   *1863:* late so glad   *1868:* spirit late
277| *MS:* prosperity I know;— § altered in pencil to § prosperity, I know;   *1849:* By
my < > know,   *1863:* In my   278| *MS:* And were < > friends   *1849:* And,
were < > friends,   280| *MS:* And strengthen < > success;— § altered in pencil
to § success: *1835:* success.   *1849:* Nay, strengthen < > success: *1863:*
success.   281| *MS:* But I'm in no   *1849:* But mine is no   282| *MS:*
Godsend,   *1849:* a chance,   *1863:* a godsend,   283| *MS:* friend;   *1835:*
luxury—my   *1849:* luxury, my Festus—   *1863:* my one friend: 286| *MS:* by:
I § altered in pencil to § by. I < > bare   *1849:* bare,   287| *MS:* And at his
mercy— — —but § altered in pencil to § mercy—but   *1849:* Prone at

Not that he needs retain his aspect grave;
That answers not my purpose; for 'tis like,
290 Some sunny morning—Basil being drained
Of its wise population, every corner
Of the amphitheatre crammed with learned clerks,
Here Œcolampadius, looking worlds of wit,
Here Castellanus, as profound as he,
295 Munsterus here, Frobenius there, all squeezed
And staring,—that the zany of the show,
Even Paracelsus, shall put off before them
His trappings with a grace but seldom judged
Expedient in such cases:—the grim smile
300 That will go round! Is it not therefore best
To venture a rehearsal like the present
In a small way? Where are the signs I seek,
The first-fruits and fair sample of the scorn
Due to all quacks? Why, this will never do!
305 FESTUS These are foul vapours, Aureole; nought beside!
The effect of watching, study, weariness.
Were there a spark of truth in the confusion
Of these wild words, you would not outrage thus
Your youth's companion. I shall ne'er regard
310 These wanderings, bred of faintness and much study.

288| *M S*: his grave respect— *1849*: his aspect grave; 290| *M S*: morning,—Basil *1835*: morning—Basil < > drain'd *1849*: drained 291| *M S*: population,—every § altered in pencil to § population, every 292| *M S*: Amphitheatre crammed < > clerks— § altered in pencil to § cramm'd < > clerks, *1835*: amphitheatre *1849*: crammed 293| *M S*: Œcolampadius looking < > wit, § altered in pencil to § Œcolampadius, looking < > wit; *1849*: wit, 294| *M S*: Castellanus as < > he, § altered in pencil to § Castellanus, as < > he; *1849*: he, 295| *M S*: there . . all § altered in pencil to § there; all *1849*: there,—all squeezed, *1863*: there, all *1868*: squeezed 296–298|. *M S*: staring;—that < > shew § altered in pencil to § staring—that < > shew, // < > grace not seldom *1835*: show, *1849*: staring, and expectant,—then, I say, / 'Tis like that the poor zany of the show, / Your friend, will choose to put his trappings off / Before them, bid adieu to cap and bells / And motley with a grace but seldom *1863*: staring,—that the zany of the show, / Even Paracelsus, shall put off before them / His trappings with 299| *M S*: cases;—the § altered in pencil to § cases. The *1849*: cases:— 300| *M S*: round!—Is *1835*: round! Is 302| *M S*: way?—where *1835*: way? Where 304| *M S*: Quacks? why § altered in pencil to § Quacks? Why *1835*: quacks 306| *M S*: weariness,— — § altered in pencil to § weariness. 309| *M S*: companion: . . I § altered in pencil to § companion. I 310| *M S*: study— — — — § altered in pencil to § study.

'Tis not thus you would trust a trouble to me,
To Michal's friend.
PARACELSUS   I have said it, dearest Festus!
For the manner, 'tis ungracious probably;
You may have it told in broken sobs, one day,
315 And scalding tears, ere long: but I thought best
To keep that off as long as possible.
Do you wonder still?
FESTUS   No; it must oft fall out
That one whose labour perfects any work,
Shall rise from it with eye so worn that he
320 Of all men least can measure the extent
Of what he has accomplished. He alone
Who, nothing tasked, is nothing weary too,
May clearly scan the little he effects:
But we, the bystanders, untouched by toil,
325 Estimate each aright.
PARACELSUS   This worthy Festus
Is one of them, at last! 'Tis so with all!
First, they set down all progress as a dream;
And next, when he whose quick discomfiture

311| *MS:* Tis   *1835:* 'Tis   *1849:* You would not trust a trouble thus to   *1863:* 'Tis not thus you would trust a trouble to   **312|** *MS:* friend: PARACELSUS § altered in pencil to § friend. PARACELSUS < > Festus;   *1849:* Festus!   **313|** *MS:* manner—'tis ungracious, probably— § altered in pencil to § manner—'tis < > probably;   *1849:* The manner is   *1863:* For the manner, 'tis   *1868:* ungracious probably;   **314|** *MS:*—You   *1835:* You   *1849:* More may be told   *1863:* You may have it told   **315|** *MS:* long,—I § altered in pencil to § long, I thought it best   *1835:* long. I   *1849:* long: but I thought best   **316|** *MS:* possible: . . . . § altered in pencil to § possible.   **317|** *MS:* No: it § altered in pencil to § No; it   **318|** *MS:* That he whose < > work   *1849:* That one whose < > work,   **319|** *MS:* worn, that he,   *1835:* he   *1868:* worn that   **320|** *MS:* Least of all men, can   *1835:* men can   *1849:* Of all men least can   **321|** *MS:* Of that he has accomplished;—he alone, § altered in pencil to § accomplish'd. He alone,   *1849:* Of what he has accomplished   *1868:* alone   **322|** *MS:* weary, he   *1835:* task'd   *1849:* tasked < > weary too,   **323|** *MS:* Can clearly < > he has done:— § altered in pencil to § done: *1849:* he effects: *1863:* May clearly   **324|** *MS:* we,—the § altered in pencil to § we, the   *1835:* untouch'd   *1849:* untouched   **325** | *MS:* We estimate aright . . . . . PARACELSUS This worthy Festus, § altered in pencil to § aright. PARACELSUS This, worthy   *1849:* Estimate each aright. PARACELSUS This worthy Festus   **326|** *MS:* Tis < > all: *1835:* 'Tis   *1849:* all!   **327|** *MS:* First they < > dream,   *1849:* First, they   *1863:* dream;   **328|** *MS:* he, whose   *1868:* he whose

Was counted on, accomplishes some few
330 And doubtful steps in his career,—behold,
They look for every inch of ground to vanish
Beneath his tread, so sure they spy success!
FESTUS Few doubtful steps? when death retires before
Your presence—when the noblest of mankind,
335 Broken in body or subdued in soul,
May through your skill renew their vigour, raise
The shattered frame to pristine stateliness?
When men in racking pain may purchase dreams
Of what delights them most, swooning at once
340 Into a sea of bliss or rapt along
As in a flying sphere of turbulent light?
When we may look to you as one ordained
To free the flesh from fell disease, as frees
Our Luther's burning tongue the fettered soul?
345 When . . .
PARACELSUS When and where, the devil, did you get
This notable news?
FESTUS   Even from the common voice;
From those whose envy, daring not dispute
The wonders it decries, attributes them

329| MS: on— —accomplishes § altered in pencil to § on,   **330|** MS:
career,—behold § altered in pencil to § career, behold   1849: career,—behold,
332| 1835: tread—so   1849: tread, so < > they judge success!   1863: they spy
success!   **333|** MS: Few, doubtful steps / . . . when § altered in pencil to §
steps? when   1835: Few doubtful   **334|** MS: presence,— § altered in pencil
to § presence—when   **335|** MS: body, yet untired in spirit,   1849: body, or
subdued in mind,   1863: body or subdued in soul,   **336|** MS: thro' § altered in
pencil to § through   **337|** MS: shattered § altered in pencil to § shatter'd < >
stateliness . . . .   1835: stateliness: 1849: shattered < > stateliness?
338| MS: That men   1835: When men   **339|** MS: most—swooning   1863:
most, swooning   **340|** MS: bliss—or   1835: bliss; or   1868: bliss or
341| MS: light—   1835: light: 1849: light?   **342|** 1835: ordain'd   1849:
ordained   **344|** MS: fettered § altered in pencil to § fetter'd soul,—   1835:
soul: 1849: fettered soul?   **345|** MS: When . . . . . PARACELSUS And when and
§ altered in pencil to § When . . . PARACELSUS And when, and where the devil did
1835: And when and   1849: PARACELSUS Rather, when and where, friend, did
1863: PARACELSUS When and where, the devil, did   **346|** MS: FESTUS—Even
1835: FESTUS Even   **348|** MS: it descries, attributes   1835: it decries,
attributes

155

To magic and such folly.

PARACELSUS   Folly? Why not

350 To magic, pray? You find a comfort doubtless
In holding, God ne'er troubles him about
Us or our doings: once we were judged worth
The devil's tempting . . . I offend: forgive me,
And rest content. Your prophecy on the whole

355 Was fair enough as prophesyings go;
At fault a little in detail, but quite
Precise enough in the main; and hereupon
I pay due homage: you guessed long ago
(The prophet!) I should fail—and I have failed.

360 FESTUS You mean to tell me, then, the hopes which fed
Your youth have not been realized as yet?
Some obstacle has barred them hitherto?
Or that their innate . . .

PARACELSUS   As I said but now,
You have a very decent prophet's fame,

365 So you but shun details here. Little matter
Whether those hopes were mad,—the aims they sought,
Safe and secure from all ambitious fools;
Or whether my weak wits are overcome
By what a better spirit would scorn: I fail.

370 And now methinks 'twere best to change a theme

349| MS: folly;— PARACELSUS Folly?——Why § altered in pencil to § folly.
PARACELSUS Folly? Why   350| MS: pray—you § altered in pencil to § pray?
You   351| MS: holding God   1849: holding, God   352| MS:
doings:—once § altered in pencil to § doings: once   1863: Him   1868: him
353| MS: tempting———I   1835: tempting . . . I   354| MS: content: your
§ altered in pencil to § content. Your   355| MS: go,— § altered in pencil to §
go;   356| MS:—At   1835: At   357| 1849: main; accordingly   1863:
main; and hereupon   358| 1835: guess'd   1849: guessed   359| MS:
prophet) I < > fail . . . . and § written over by § fail—and   1835: have fail'd.   1849:
prophet!) I < > have failed.   360| MS: then,—the § altered in pencil to § then,
the   362| MS:—Some < > hitherto,— § altered in pencil to § hitherto,   1835:
Some < > barr'd   1849: barred < > hitherto?   363| MS: now   1835:
now,   364| MS: fame   1849: fame,   365| MS: shun these details;—little
§ altered in pencil to § details. Little matters   1849: shun details here. Little   1863:
matter   366| MS: mad and § altered in pencil to § mad, and what they sought
1849: mad,—the aims they sought,   367| MS: fools,— § altered in pencil to §
fools,   1849: fools;   369| MS: scorn:—I § altered in pencil to § scorn—I
1849: scorn: I   370| MS: change the theme.   1849: change a theme,   1868:
theme

I am a sad fool to have stumbled on.
I say confusedly what comes uppermost;
But there are times when patience proves at fault,
As now: this morning's strange encounter—you
375 Beside me once again! you, whom I guessed
Alive, since hitherto (with Luther's leave)
No friend have I among the saints at peace,
To judge by any good their prayers effect.
I knew you would have helped me—why not he,
380 My strange competitor in enterprise,
Bound for the same end by another path,
Arrived, or ill or well, before the time,
At our disastrous journey's doubtful close?
How goes it with Aprile? Ah, they miss
385 Your lone sad sunny idleness of heaven,
Our martyrs for the world's sake; heaven shuts fast:
The poor mad poet is howling by this time!
Since you are my sole friend then, here or there,
I could not quite repress the varied feelings
390 This meeting wakens; they have had their vent,
And now forget them. Do the rear-mice still
Hang like a fretwork on the gate (or what

371| *MS:* on it— — § altered in pencil to § on it. *1849:* on.   372| *MS:*
uppermost . . . . § altered in pencil to § uppermost— *1835:* uppermost;
373| *MS:* fault,— § altered in pencil to § fault,   374| *MS:* now;—this § altered
in pencil to § now; this   *1835:* now: this   375| *MS:* guessed *1835:* guess'd
1849: guessed   376| *MS:* hitherto, (with § altered in pencil to § hitherto (with
1835: Alive—since *1849:* Alive, since   377–389| *MS:* saints above; § altered in
pencil to § above / (The poor < > time:) § altered in pencil to § time.) / I   *1835:*
above— / < > time)—   *1849:* saints at rest, / To judge by any good their prayers
effect— / I knew you would have helped me!—So would He, / My strange competitor
in enterprise, / Bound for the same end by another path, / Arrived, or ill or well,
before the time, / At our disastrous journey's doubtful close— / How goes it with
Aprile? Ah, your heaven / Receives not into its beatitudes / Mere martyrs for the
world's sake; heaven shuts fast: / The poor < > time! / Since you are my sole friend
then, here or there, / I   377| *1863:* saints at peace,   378| *1868:*
effect: *1888:* effect.   379| *1863:* me!—Why not He,   *1868:* me—why not
he,   382| *1888:* time,   384–386| *1863:* Ah, they miss / Your lone, sad,
sunny idleness of Heaven, / Our martyrs < > Heaven   385| *1868:*
heaven   386| *1868:* heaven   390| *MS:* wakens,—they § altered in pencil
to § wakens; they < > their way,   *1849:* their vent,   391| *MS:* them:—do
§altered in pencil to § them. Do   392| *MS:* fret-work < > gate, (or § altered in
pencil to § gate (or   *1888:* fretwork

In my time was a gate) fronting the road
From Einsiedeln to Lachen?
FESTUS   Trifle not:
395 Answer me, for my sake alone! You smiled
Just now, when I supposed some deed, unworthy
Yourself, might blot the else so bright result;
Yet if your motives have continued pure,
Your will unfaltering, and in spite of this,
400 You have experienced a defeat, why then
I say not you would cheerfully withdraw
From contest—mortal hearts are not so fashioned—
But surely you would ne'ertheless withdraw.
You sought not fame nor gain nor even love,
405 No end distinct from knowledge,—I repeat
Your very words: once satisfied that knowledge
Is a mere dream, you would announce as much,
Yourself the first. But how is the event?
You are defeated—and I find you here!

393| *MS:* time, was § altered in pencil to § time was ╻ 394| *MS:* FESTUS—Trifle
§ altered in pencil to § FESTUS Trifle   *1849:* not!   *1863:* not: 395| *MS:* me—
for < > alone:—you § altered in pencil to § alone. You   *1863:* me, for   *1868:* alone! For
396| · *MS:* deed § written over by § Deed unworthy   *1835:* deed   *1849:* deed,
unworthy   397| *MS:* Yourself, might < > result . . . . § written over by § result—
§ altered in pencil to § yourself might < > result;   *1863:* Yourself, might
398-401| *MS:* But if < > pure, / Your earnest will, unfaultering— —if § altered in
pencil to § will unfaultering; if you still / Remain unchanged, and if in spite of all /
You have experienced the defeat you tell . . . § altered in pencil to § tell— / I say not,
you < > cheerfully resign   *1835:* unfaltering: if < > / < > if, in < > all,   *1849:*
Yet if < > / < > of this, / < > experienced a defeat that proves / Your aims for
ever unattainable—I   *1863:* pure, / Your will unfaltering, and in spite of this, / You
have < > defeat, why, then / I < > cheerfully withdraw   *1868:* why then / I say
not you   402| *MS:* The contest— —mortal < > fashioned . . . . § altered in
pencil to § The contest—mortal < > fashioned—   *1835:* fashion'd—   *1849:*
fashioned—   *1863:* From contest   403| *MS:* ne'ertheless resign; § altered in
pencil to § resign.   *1849:* But sure you would resign it, ne'ertheless.   *1863:* But
surely you would, ne'ertheless, withdraw.   *1868:* would ne'ertheless withdraw.
404| *MS:* fame, nor Gain, nor < > Love— § altered in pencil to § fame, nor gain, nor
< > love;   *1868:* fame nor gain nor < > love,   405| *MS:* Knowledge:—I
§ altered in pencil to § Knowledge.—I   *1835:* knowledge. I   *1849:*
knowledge,—I   406| *MS:* words:— once § altered in pencil to § words: once
< > Knowledge   *1835:* knowledge   407| *1835:* much   *1849:* much,
408| *MS:* the first:— —but § altered in pencil to § first. But   409| *MS:*
defeated . . . and < > *here!— —* § altered in pencil to § defeated—and < > *here!*
1849: here!

410 PARACELSUS As though "here" did not signify defeat!
     I spoke not of my little labours here,
     But of the break-down of my general aims:
     For you, aware of their extent and scope,
     To look on these sage lecturings, approved
415 By beardless boys, and bearded dotards worse,
     As a fit consummation of such aims,
     Is worthy notice. A professorship
     At Basil! Since you see much much in it,
     And think my life was reasonably drained
420 Of life's delights to render me a match
     For duties arduous as such post demands,—
     Be it far from me to deny my power
     To fill the petty circle lotted out
     Of infinite space, or justify the host
425 Of honours thence accruing. So, take notice,
     This jewel dangling from my neck preserves
     The features of a prince, my skill restored
     To plague his people some few years to come:
     And all through a pure whim. He had eased the earth
430 For me, but that the droll despair which seized

410| *MS:* tho' *"here"* did § altered in pencil to § though "here" did   *1849:* though
"here" did   411-412| *MS:* my labours *here:*—§ altered in pencil to § here: past
doubt / I am quite competent to answer all / Demands, in any such capacity,—
§ altered in pencil to § capacity, / But   *1835:* here—past < > // < > capacity—
1849: my little labours here— / But   *1863:* here,   *1868:* here   *1888:* here,
413| *MS:* you—aware < > scope— § altered in pencil to § you, aware < > scope,
1849: That you   *1863:* For you   414| *MS:* lecturings, commended   *1849:*
Should look < > lecturings, approved   *1863:* To look   415| *MS:* By silly
beardless boys, and < > dotards,   *1849:* By beardless < > dotards worse,   *1863:*
dotards worse,   416| *MS:* of those aims   *1835:* aims,   *1849:* of such
aims,   417| *MS:* notice:—a § altered in pencil to § notice—a   *1849:* notice! A
1868: notice. A   418| *MS:* Basil! . . . since § altered in pencil to § Basil! Since
< > it,—   *1835:* it;   *1849:* it,   419| *MS:* Since 'tis but just my life should have
been drained   *1835:* drain'd   *1849:* And think my life was reasonably drained
420| *MS:* Of its delights   *1849:* Of life's delights   421| *MS:* Post demands; . . . .
§ altered in pencil to § demands;   *1835:* post   *1849:* demands,—   422| *MS:* Far
be it from   *1868:* Be it far from   424| *MS:* or to the   *1849:* or justify
the   425| *MS:* accruing: so take notice: § altered in pencil to § notice.   *1849:* so,
take notice,   *1863:* accruing. So   427| *MS:* Prince my   *1835:* prince   *1849:*
prince, my   428| *MS:* come: § : added in pencil §   429| *MS:*— —And all
thro' < > whim—he § altered in pencil to § And all through < > whim. He

159

The vermin of his household, tickled me.
I came to see. Here, drivelled the physician,
Whose most infallible nostrum was at fault;
There quaked the astrologer, whose horoscope
435 Had promised him interminable years;
Here a monk fumbled at the sick man's mouth
With some undoubted relic—a sudary
Of the Virgin; while another piebald knave
Of the same brotherhood (he loved them ever)
440 Was actively preparing 'neath his nose
Such a suffumigation as, once fired,
Had stunk the patient dead ere he could groan,
I cursed the doctor and upset the brother,
Brushed past the conjurer, vowed that the first gust
445 Of stench from the ingredients just alight
Would raise a cross-grained devil in my sword,
Not easily laid: and ere an hour the prince
Slept as he never slept since prince he was.
A day—and I was posting for my life,
450 Placarded through the town as one whose spite
Had near availed to stop the blessed effects

431| *MS:* me:— § altered in pencil to § me.   **432|** *MS:* —I < > see:—here,
drivelled the Physician § altered in pencil to § see: here, drivell'd the physician
1835: I < > physician,   *1849:* drivelled   *1863:* see. Here   **433|** *MS:* fault; —
— § altered in pencil to § fault;   **434|** *MS:* There shook the Astrologer § altered
in pencil to § astrologer in his shoes, whose grand   *1849:* There quaked the
astrologer, whose horoscope   **435|** *MS:* Horoscope promise further score of
years;— — § altered in pencil to § years;   *1849:* Had promised him interminable
years;   **436|** *MS:* at the sick § *the* inserted above the line § man's nose   *1849:*
man's mouth   **437|** *MS:* relic . . . a § altered in pencil to § relic—a
438| *MS:* Virgin;— —while some half-a-dozen § altered in pencil to § Virgin; while
some half-dozen knaves   *1849:* some other dozen knaves   *1863:* while another
piebald knave   **440|** *MS:* Were making active preparations for   *1849:* Were
actively preparing 'neath his nose   *1863:* Was   **443|** *MS:*—I < > Doctor, and
upset the Wiper;   *1835:* I < > doctor < > wiper;   *1849:* upset the brother;
1868: brother,   **444|** *MS:* Brushed < > conjurer—vowed § altered in pencil to §
Brush'd < > conjurer;—vow'd   *1835:* conjurer; vow'd   *1849:* Brushed < >
vowed   *1868:* conjurer, vowed   **446|** *MS:* cross-grained § altered in pencil to §
cross-grain'd   *1849:* cross-grained   **447|** *MS:* laid:—and < > Prince § altered
in pencil to § laid; and < > prince   *1849:* hour, the   *1863:* laid: *1868:* hour the
448| *MS:* Prince § altered in pencil to § prince   **449|** *MS:* life   *1835:*
life,   **450|** *MS:* thro' the Town § altered in pencil to § through the town
451| *MS:* blessed § altered in pencil to § bless'd   *1835:* avail'd   *1849:* availed < >
blessed

Of the doctor's nostrum which, well seconded
By the sudary, and most by the costly smoke—
Not leaving out the strenuous prayers sent up
455 Hard by in the abbey—raised the prince to life:
To the great reputation of the seer
Who, confident, expected all along
The glad event—the doctor's recompense—
Much largess from his highness to the monks—
460 And the vast solace of his loving people,
Whose general satisfaction to increase,
The prince was pleased no longer to defer
The burning of some dozen heretics
Remanded till God's mercy should be shown
465 Touching his sickness: last of all were joined
Ample directions to all loyal folk
To swell the complement by seizing me
Who—doubtless some rank sorcerer—endeavoured
To thwart these pious offices, obstruct
470 The prince's cure, and frustrate heaven by help
Of certain devils dwelling in his sword.
By luck, the prince in his first fit of thanks
Had forced this bauble on me as an earnest

452| *MS:* Doctor's § altered in pencil to § doctor's nostrum, which *1868:*
nostrum which   453| *MS:* smoke; . . § altered in pencil to § smoke—
454| *MS:*—Not § altered in pencil to § Not   455| *MS:* by, in the Abbey,—raised
§ altered in pencil to § Abbey—raised the Prince to life . . . . § altered in pencil to §
life— *1835:* abbey < > prince to life; *1888:* life: 456| *MS:* of the Sage
1835: sage, *1849:* of the seer, *1863:* seer   458| *MS:* Doctor's recompense
. . . § altered in pencil to § recompense— *1835:* doctor's   459| *MS:* Highness
< > Monks,— — § altered in pencil to § Monks— *1835:* highness < >
monks—   461| *MS:* increase, § , added in pencil §   462| *MS:* Prince
1835: prince   463| *MS:* heretics, § , added in pencil § *1868:* heretics
464| *MS:* 'till *1868:* till   465–466| *MS:* all, were joined § altered in pencil
to § join'd / Ample *1849:* sickness, as a prudent pledge / To make it surer: last of
all were joined / Ample *1863:* sickness: last < > joined / Ample   467| *MS:*
To seize myself, to swell the complement, *1849:* To swell the complement, by
seizing me *1868:* complement by   468| *MS:* doubless < > sorcerer—had
endeavoured § altered in pencil to § endeavour'd *1835:* doubtless *1849:*
endeavoured *1868:* sorcerer—endeavoured   469| *MS:* offices— — —obstruct
§ altered in pencil to § offices, obstruct   470| *MS:* Prince's < > frustrate all
by *1835:* prince's *1849:* frustrate Heaven, by *1863:* Heaven by *1868:*
heaven   471| *MS:* in his sword: § *my* written in pencil below *his* §
sword.   472| *MS:* Prince § altered in pencil to § prince

161

Of further favours. This one case may serve
475 To give sufficient taste of many such,
So, let them pass. Those shelves support a pile
Of patents, licences, diplomas, titles
From Germany, France, Spain, and Italy;
They authorize some honour; ne'ertheless,
480 I set more store by this Erasmus sent;
He trusts me; our Frobenius is his friend,
And him "I raised" (nay, read it) "from the dead."
I weary you, I see. I merely sought
To show, there's no great wonder after all
485 That, while I fill the class-room and attract
A crowd to Basil, I get leave to stay,
And therefore need not scruple to accept
The utmost they can offer, if I please:
For 'tis but right the world should be prepared
490 To treat with favour e'en fantastic wants
Of one like me, used up in serving her.
Just as the mortal, whom the gods in part
Devoured, received in place of his lost limb

474| *MS:* favours; this § altered in pencil to § favours. This **476|** *MS:* So let
< > pass:— — —those § altered in pencil to § pass. Those *1835:* pass: those *1863:*
pass. Those *1868:* So, let **477–479|** *MS:* Of Patents, Licenses, Diplomas, got
§ altered in pencil to § Of patents, licenses, diplomas, got / In France and Spain and
Italy, as well / As Germany;—they § altered in pencil to § Germany; they authorize my
claims / To honour from the world—nevertheless § altered in pencil to § world.
Nevertheless *1835:* France, and Spain, and *1849:* diplomas, titles, / From
Germany, France, Spain, and Italy: / They authorise some honour: ne'ertheless,
1863: Italy; / < > authorize < > honour; ne'ertheless, *1868:* Spain and *1888:*
Spain, and **480|** *MS:* sends— —§ altered in pencil to § sends. *1835:* sends; *1849:*
sent; **481|** *MS:* me—our < > friend *1835:* me: our < > friend, *1849:* me; our
482| *MS:* him I raised (nay < > it) from the dead;— — — § altered in pencil to §
dead. *1835:* dead . . . *1849:* him "I raised" (nay, read it) "from the dead" . . .
1863: dead." **483|** *MS:* see— —I *1835:* see; I *1863:* see. I
484| *MS:* show there's *1849:* show, there's **485|** *MS:* That while < > class-
room, and attract *1868:* That, while < > class-room and **486|** *MS:* I have
leave to stay; *1849:* I get leave *1888:* stay, **487|** *MS:* And that I need
1849: And therefore need **488|** *MS:* offer . . if § written over by § offer—if I
love it: *1849:* I please: *1868:* offer, if **490|** *MS:* To treat especially the
several wants *1849:* To treat with favour e'en fantastic wants **491|** *MS:*
her;— § altered in pencil to § her; *1849:* her. **492|** *MS:* Gods *1863:*
gods **493|** *MS:* Devoured § altered in pencil to § Devour'd *1849:* Devoured

Some virtue or other—cured disease, I think;
495 You mind the fables we have read together.
FESTUS You do not think I comprehend a word.
The time was, Aureole, you were apt enough
To clothe the airiest thoughts in specious breath;
But surely you must feel how vague and strange
500 These speeches sound.
PARACELSUS   Well, then: you know my hopes;
I am assured, at length, those hopes were vain;
That truth is just as far from me as ever;
That I have thrown my life away; that sorrow
On that account is idle, and further effort
505 To mend and patch what's marred beyond repairing,
As useless: and all this was taught your friend
By the convincing good old-fashioned method
Of force—by sheer compulsion. Is that plain?
FESTUS Dear Aureole, can it be my fears were just?
510 God wills not . . .
PARACELSUS   Now, 'tis this I most admire—
The constant talk men of your stamp keep up
Of God's will, as they style it; one would swear
Man had but merely to uplift his eye,
And see the will in question charactered
515 On the heaven's vault. 'Tis hardly wise to moot

494| *MS:* think;— § altered in pencil to § think;   496| *MS:* word: *1863:*
word.   497| *MS:* Aureole, when you were not slow   *1849:* Aureole, you
were apt enough   498| *MS:* specious words;— § altered in pencil to § words;
1849: specious breath;   501| *MS:* length, they may not be: § altered in pencil
to § be;   *1849:* length, those hopes were vain;   502| *MS:* Truth < > ever:
§ altered in pencil to § ever;   *1835:* truth   503| *MS:* away——that § altered in
pencil to § away; that   504| *MS:* is vain and § altered in pencil to § vain, and
1863: is idle, and   505| *MS:* repairing   *1835:* marr'd   *1849:* marred < >
repairing,   506| *MS:* taught to me   *1868:* taught your friend   507| *MS:*
convincing, good oldfashioned § altered in pencil to § oldfashion'd   *1835:* old-
fashion'd   *1849:* old-fashioned   *1868:* convincing good   508| *MS:*
compulsion:— Is § altered in pencil to § compulsion. Is   509| *MS:* Aureole! can
< > just!   *1849:* Aureole! you confess my < > just?   *1863:* Aureole! can it be
my   *1868:* Aureole, can   510| *MS:* Now 'tis   *1835:* Now, 'tis
512| *MS:* will,—as < > it . . . one § altered in pencil to § will, as < > it—one
1835: it; one   514| *MS:* To see < > charactered § altered in pencil to §
character'd   *1849:* charactered   *1863:* And see   515| *MS:* vault: . . . . 'tis
§ altered in pencil to § vault. 'Tis

163

Such topics: doubts are many and faith is weak.
I know as much of any will of God
As knows some dumb and tortured brute what Man,
His stern lord, wills from the perplexing blows
520 That plague him every way; but there, of course,
Where least he suffers, longest he remains—
My case; and for such reasons I plod on,
Subdued but not convinced. I know as little
Why I deserve to fail, as why I hoped
525 Better things in my youth. I simply know
I am no master here, but trained and beaten
Into the path I tread; and here I stay,
Until some further intimation reach me,
Like an obedient drudge. Though I prefer
530 To view the whole thing as a task imposed
Which, whether dull or pleasant, must be done—
Yet, I deny not, there is made provision
Of joys which tastes less jaded might affect;
Nay, some which please me too, for all my pride—
535 Pleasures that once were pains: the iron ring
Festering about a slave's neck grows at length
Into the flesh it eats. I hate no longer
A host of petty vile delights, undreamed of

516| *MS:* topics:—doubts <> weak:— § altered in pencil to § topics: doubts <>
weak.   517| *MS:* will of His   *1849:* will of God's,   *1868:* God
518| *MS:* tortured § altered to § tortur'd brute of what   *1849:* tortured brute what
Man,   519| *MS:* lord will <> the bewildering blows   *1849:* lord, wills <>
the perplexing blows   520| *MS:* way,—and there   *1835:* way, and   *1863:*
way; but there   521| *MS:* he will stay— § altered in pencil to § stay: *1849:* he
remains—   522| *MS:* on . . . § altered in pencil to § on—   *1849:* on,
523| *MS:* Subdued, but not convinced: I § altered in pencil to § convinced. I   *1868:*
Subdued but   525| *MS:* youth . . . . I § altered in pencil to § youth. I
526| *MS:* trained § altered in pencil to § train'd   *1849:* trained   527| *MS:*
tread;—and § altered in pencil to § tread; and   528| *MS:* me, § , added in
pencil §   529| *MS:* drudge;—and though I like   *1835:* drudge: and   *1849:*
drudge: though I prefer   *1863:* drudge. Though   530| *MS:* The best to <> task
1849: To view <> task imposed,   *1868:* imposed   531| *MS:* Imposed—which,
dull <> done; . . . . . § altered in pencil to § done—   *1849:* Which, whether
dull   533| *MS:* affect;— § altered in pencil to § affect;   534| *MS:* pride
. . . § altered in pencil to § pride—   535| *MS:* pains; the iron-ring   *1835:* pains:
the iron ring   536| *MS:* neck, grows   *1835:* neck grows   537| *MS:*
eats— — —I § altered in pencil to § eats. I   *1849:* no more   *1863:* no longer
538| *MS:* petty, vile delights—undreamed § altered in pencil to § undream'd   *1835:*
delights, undream'd   *1849:* undreamed   *1868:* petty vile

Or spurned before; such now supply the place
540 Of my dead aims: as in the autumn woods
Where tall trees used to flourish, from their roots
Springs up a fungous brood sickly and pale,
Chill mushrooms coloured like a corpse's cheek.
FESTUS If I interpret well your words, I own
545 It troubles me but little that your aims,
Vast in their dawning and most likely grown
Extravagantly since, have baffled you.
Perchance I am glad; you merit greater praise;
Because they are too glorious to be gained,
550 You do not blindly cling to them and die;
You fell, but have not sullenly refused
To rise, because an angel worsted you
In wrestling, though the world holds not your peer;
And though too harsh and sudden is the change
555 To yield content as yet, still you pursue
The ungracious path as though 'twere rosy-strewn.
'Tis well: and your reward, or soon or late,
Will come from him whom no man serves in vain.

539| *MS:* spurned, before:—such § altered in pencil to § spurn'd, before: such   *1835:*
before; such   *1849:* spurned   **540|** *MS:* Aims; as < > Autumn   *1835:* aims:
as < > autumn   **541|** *MS:* trees flourished § altered in pencil to §
flourish'd—from their very roots   *1849:* trees used to flourish, from their roots
542| *MS:* brood, sickly   *1868:* brood sickly   **543|** *MS:* mushrooms, coloured
§ altered in pencil to § colour'd < > cheek.... *1835:* cheek... *1849:* coloured
< > cheek.   *1868:* mushrooms coloured   **544|** *MS:*—If   *1835:* If   *1849:*
well what words I seize,   *1863:* well your words, I own   **545|** *MS:* Aims,
1835: aims,   **546|** *1835:* dawning, and   *1868:* dawning and   **547|** *MS:*
have proved abortive:— § altered in pencil to § abortive: *1849:* have baffled
you.   **548|** *MS:* glad—you have the greater   *1835:* glad; you < > praise,
1849: you merit greater praise;   **549|** *MS:* gained, § altered in pencil to §
gain'd,   *1835:* gain'd—   *1849:* gained,   **550|** *MS:* You have not < > clung
< > and died   *1849:* You do not < > cling < > and die;   **551|** *MS:* With
them: you § written over by § them; you have   *1835:* them—you   *1849:* You fell,
but have   **553|** *MS:* tho' § altered in pencil to § peer;   *1849:* world holds not < >
peer: § altered in pencil to § peer;   *1849:* world holds not < > peer   *1863:* peer;
554| *MS:* tho' § inserted above the line; altered in pencil to § though   **555|** *MS:*
To yield your pleasure, as yet,—still, you § altered in pencil to § yet—still   *1849:* To
yield content as   *1863:* yet, still you   **556|** *MS:* rosy-strewn: § altered in pencil
to § rosy-strewn.   **557|** *MS:* Tis < > reward, sooner or later, § , added in
pencil §   *1835:* 'Tis   *1849:* reward, or soon or late,   **558|** *MS:* Him whom none
e'er served   *1849:* whom no man serves   *1868:* him

PARACELSUS Ah, very fine! For my part, I conceive
560 The very pausing from all further toil,
Which you find heinous, would become a seal
To the sincerity of all my deeds.
To be consistent I should die at once;
I calculated on no after-life;
565 Yet (how crept in, how fostered, I know not)
Here am I with as passionate regret
For youth and health and love so vainly lavished,
As if their preservation had been first
And foremost in my thoughts; and this strange fact
570 Humbled me wondrously, and had due force
In rendering me the less averse to follow
A certain counsel, a mysterious warning—
You will not understand—but 'twas a man
With aims not mine and yet pursued like mine,
575 With the same fervour and no more success,
Perishing in my sight; who summoned me
As I would shun the ghastly fate I saw,
To serve my race at once; to wait no longer

559| *MS:* Ah! very fine:—for § altered in pencil to § fine: for my part   *1849:* Ah,
very fine! For my part   561| *MS:* heinous . . would § altered in pencil to §
heinous, would be as a   *1868:* would become a   562| *MS:* deeds: *1849:*
deeds.   563| *MS:* once;— § altered in pencil to § once;   564–565| *MS:*
after-life, . . . § altered in pencil to § after-life, / Nay, was assured no such could be for
me, / Yet . . . (how § written over by § Yet—(how < > not— § written over by § not)
1835: after-life; // < > foster'd   *1849:* after-life; / Yet (how < > fostered < >
not)   567| *MS:* youth, and health, and love < > lavished, § altered in pencil
to § lavish'd   *1849:* vainly lost,   *1863:* youth and health and < > vainly
lavished,   569| *MS:* thoughts . . . and § altered in pencil to § thoughts;
and   571| *1849:* the more disposed to   *1863:* the less averse to
572| *MS:* counsel— — —a § altered in pencil to § counsel, a < > warning,   *1835:*
warning—   573–576| *MS:* — —You < > understand— —but § altered in pencil
to § You < > understand—but < > Man / Perishing < > sight, who summoned
§ altered in pencil to § summon'd me, § , added in pencil §   *1835:* man   *1849:* man
/ With aims not mine, but yet pursued like mine, / With the same fervor and no more
success, / Who perished < > sight; but summoned me   *1863:* mine and < > / < >
fervour < > / Perishing < > sight; who summoned   577| *MS:* saw, § , added
in pencil §   578| *MS:* Race at once— —to § altered in pencil to § once—to
1835: race at once; to

That God should interfere in my behalf,
580 But to distrust myself, put pride away,
And give my gains, imperfect as they were,
To men. I have not leisure to explain
How, since, a singular series of events
Has raised me to the station you behold,
585 Wherein I seem to turn to most account
The mere wreck of the past,—perhaps receive
Some feeble glimmering token that God views
And may approve my penance: therefore here
You find me, doing most good or least harm.
590 And if folks wonder much and profit little
'Tis not my fault; only, I shall rejoice
When my part in the farce is shuffled through,
And the curtain falls: I must hold out till then.
FESTUS Till when, dear Aureole?
PARACELSUS   Till I'm fairly thrust
595 From my proud eminence. Fortune is fickle
And even professors fall: should that arrive,
I see no sin in ceding to my bent.
You little fancy what rude shocks apprise us
We sin; God's intimations rather fail

579–580| *MS:* behalf, § , added in pencil § / Nor trust to Time——but § altered in
pencil to § Time—but to distrust myself, *1835:* behalf— / < > time; but *1849:*
'Till God < > behalf, / And let the next world's knowledge dawn on this; / But to
distrust myself, put pride away, *1863:* That God < > behalf, / But
581| *MS:* gains imperfect < > were *1835:* gains, imperfect < > were,
582| *MS:* Men:——I § altered in pencil to § Men. I *1835:* men **583|** *MS:*
How since *1849:* a strange succession of *1863:* a singular series of *1868:* How,
since **586|** *MS:* The sad wreck < > past, and to receive *1849:* The mere
wreck < > past,—perhaps receive *1863:* Past *1868:* past **588|** *MS:*
penance—therefore § altered in pencil to § penance; therefore *1835:* penance:
therefore **589|** *MS:* me——doing § altered in pencil to § me—doing good as
best I may, *1835:* may; *1849:* doing most good or least harm: *1863:* me, doing
< > harm. **591|** *MS:* Tis < > fault——only I § altered in pencil to § 'Tis < >
fault; only *1849:* only, I **592|** *MS:* thro', § altered in pencil to §
through, **593|** *MS:* falls;——I § altered in pencil to § falls. I < > 'till *1835:*
falls; I *1863:* falls: I < > till **594|** *1835:* 'Till < > 'Till *1849:* Till
when *1868:* PARACELSUS Till **595|** *MS:* eminence:——fortune § altered in
pencil to § eminence. Fortune **596|** *MS:* Professors < > arrive *1835:*
professors < > arrive, **597–598|** *MS:* bent / Whatever that may be——but not
till then: § altered in pencil to § be—but < > then. / You < > apprize *1835:* bent,
1849: bent. / You *1863:* apprise **599|** *MS:* sin—God's *1835:* sin: God's
1868: sin; God's

600 In clearness than in energy: 'twere well
Did they but indicate the course to take
Like that to be forsaken. I would fain
Be spared a further sample. Here I stand,
And here I stay, be sure, till forced to flit.
605 FESTUS Be you but firm on that head! long ere then
All I expect will come to pass, I trust:
The cloud that wraps you will have disappeared.
Meantime, I see small chance of such event:
They praise you here as one whose lore, already
610 Divulged, eclipses all the past can show,
But whose achievements, marvellous as they be,
Are faint anticipations of a glory
About to be revealed. When Basil's crowds
Dismiss their teacher, I shall be content
615 That he depart.
PARACELSUS   This favour at their hands
I look for earlier than your view of things
Would warrant. Of the crowd you saw to-day,
Remove the full half sheer amazement draws,
Mere novelty, nought else; and next, the tribe
620 Whose innate blockish dulness just perceives
That unless miracles (as seem my works)
Be wrought in their behalf, their chance is slight

600| *MS:* energy——'twere § altered in pencil to § energy: 'twere   602| *MS:*
forsaken: I § altered in pencil to § forsaken. I   603| *MS:* sample . . . here I am
1835: Here   *1849:* sample! Here I stand,   *1868:* sample. Here   605| *MS:*
head—long   *1835:* head; long   *1849:* Remain but   *1863:* Be you but   *1888:*
head! long   607| *MS:* disappeared. § altered in pencil to § disappear'd.   *1849:*
disappeared.   608| *MS:* At present, I   *1835:* present I   *1849:* Meantime,
I   609| *MS:* Lore § altered to § lore already   *1849:* lore, divulged   *1863:*
lore, already   610| *MS:* Divulged eclipses < > Past can show § altered in
pencil to § past can show,   *1849:* Already, eclipses   *1863:* Divulged, eclipses < >
Past   *1868:* past   612| *MS:* a light   *1849:* a glory   613| *MS:* Which
shall hereafter be revealed . . . when They § altered in pencil to § reveal'd. When
they   *1849:* About to be revealed. When Basil's crowds   615| *MS:*
depart—PARACELSUS   *1835:* depart. PARACELSUS   617| *MS:* warrant;—of
§ altered in pencil to § warrant. Of < > to-day   *1863:* to-day,   618| *MS:*
the herd whom sheer amazement brings,   *1849:* the full half sheer amazement
draws,   619| *MS:*—The novelty < > else;—and § altered in pencil to § else;
and   *1835:* The   *1863:* Mere novelty   622| *MS:* behalf, they are not like
1849: behalf, their chance is slight

168

To puzzle the devil; next, the numerous set
Who bitterly hate established schools, and help
625 The teacher that oppugns them, till he once
Have planted his own doctrine, when the teacher
May reckon on their rancour in his turn;
Take, too, the sprinkling of sagacious knaves
Whose cunning runs not counter to the vogue
630 But seeks, by flattery and crafty nursing,
To force my system to a premature
Short-lived development. Why swell the list?
Each has his end to serve, and his best way
Of serving it: remove all these, remains
635 A scantling, a poor dozen at the best,
Worthy to look for sympathy and service,
And likely to draw profit from my pains.
FESTUS 'Tis no encouraging picture: still these few
Redeem their fellows. Once the germ implanted,
640 Its growth, if slow, is sure.
PARCELSUS   God grant it so!
I would make some amends: but if I fail,
The luckless rogues have this excuse to urge,

623| *MS:* devil: and § altered in pencil to § devil; and a numerous   *1849:* devil;
next, the numerous   **624|** *MS:* established § altered in pencil to § establish'd
schools and   *1835:* schools, and   *1849:* established schools, so help   *1863:* schools,
and help   **625|** *MS:* A Teacher § altered in pencil to § teacher < > 'till
1849: The teacher < > them, and o'erthrows,   *1863:* them, till he once
626| *MS:* Teacher § altered in pencil to § teacher   *1849:* 'Till having < > doctrine,
he   *1863:* Have < > doctrine, when the teacher   **628|** *MS:* With a good
sprinkling   *1849:* Take, too, the sprinkling   **629|** *1835:* vogue,   *1868:*
vogue   **630|** *MS:* seeks by § altered in pencil to § seeks, by   *1849:* and nursing
craft   *1863:* and crafty nursing   *1868:* nursing,   **632|** *MS:* development:—
—why § altered in pencil to § development—why   *1835:* developement . . . Why
1849: development   *1863:* development. Why   **634|** *MS:* Of pushing it
1849: Of serving it   **635-636|** *MS:* scantling—a < > best, § altered in pencil to §
best— / Worthy   *1849:* best— / That really come to learn for learning's sake; /
Worthy   *1863:* scantling, a < > best, / Worthy   **637|** *MS:* pains   *1835:*
pains.   **638|** *MS:* Tis   *1835:* 'Tis   **639|** *MS:* fellows—once < >
implanted   *1835:* fellows. Once   *1849:* Once implant the germ   *1863:* Once the
germ implanted,   **640|** *MS:* The rest will fail not to succeed: § altered in pencil
to § succeed. PARCELSUS God < > it!   *1849:* Its growth, if slow, is sure. PARCELSUS
God < > it so!   **641-642|** *MS:* amends . . . the § altered in pencil to §
amends—the hate between us / Is of one side: should it prove otherwise, / The
1835: amends: the < > / Is on one side. Should   *1849:* amends: but if I fail, / The

That much is in my method and my manner,
My uncouth habits, my impatient spirit,
645 Which hinders of reception and result
My doctrine: much to say, small skill to speak!
These old aims suffered not a looking-off
Though for an instant; therefore, only when
I thus renounced them and resolved to reap
650 Some present fruit—to teach mankind some truth
So dearly purchased—only then I found
Such teaching was an art requiring cares
And qualities peculiar to itself:
That to possess was one thing—to display
655 Another. With renown first in my thoughts,
Or popular praise, I had soon discovered it:
One grows but little apt to learn these things.
FESTUS If it be so, which nowise I believe,
There needs no waiting fuller dispensation
660 To leave a labour of so little use.
Why not throw up the irksome charge at once?
PARACELSUS A task, a task!

But wherefore hide the whole

645| *MS:* of its influence and reception   *1849:* of reception and result
646-647| *MS:* speak: / ——It is, I fancy, some slight proof my old / Devotion suffered
§ altered in pencil to § suffer'd   *1835:* speak . . . / It < > / < > looking-off,   *1849:*
speak! / Those old aims suffered   *1868:* These old < > looking-off   648| *MS:*
Tho' § altered in pencil to § Though < > instant, seeing that then alone   *1849:*
instant; therefore, only when   649| *MS:* When I renounced it, and   *1835:* it
and   *1849:* I thus renounced them and   650| *MS:* fruit——to § altered in pencil
to § fruit—to < > Mankind the truth   *1835:* mankind   *1849:* mankind some
truth   651| *MS:* purchased—then I first discovered § altered in pencil to §
discover'd   *1849:* purchased—only then I found   653| *MS:* itself;— § altered in
pencil to § itself: *1849:* itself;   *1888:* itself: 654| *MS:* thing . . . to § altered in
pencil to § thing—to   *1849:* display,   *1868:* display   655-656| *MS:* Another—I
had never dreamed § altered in pencil to § Another. I < > dream'd of this; / Had but
renown been present in my thoughts / Or < > soon found it out:— § altered in pencil
to § out: *1835:* this: / < > thoughts, / < > out.   *1849:* Another. / Had renown
been in my thoughts, Or < > soon discovered it!   *1868:* Another. With renown first in
< > / < > it: 658| *MS:* so,—which < > believe— § altered in pencil to § so,
which < > believe,   660| *MS:* labour to so < > use: *1863:* use.   *1868:*
labour of so   662| *MS:* A task, a task! . . . / . . . but   *1835:* A task, a task! . . . /
But   *1849:* hide from you   *1863:* A task, a task! / But < > hide the whole

Extent of degradation, once engaged
In the confessing vein? Despite of all
665 My fine talk of obedience and repugnance,
Docility and what not, 'tis yet to learn
If when the task shall really be performed,
My inclination free to choose once more,
I shall do aught but slightly modify
670 The nature of the hated task I quit.
In plain words, I am spoiled; my life still tends
As first it tended; I am broken and trained
To my old habits: they are part of me.
I know, and none so well, my darling ends
675 Are proved impossible: no less, no less,
Even now what humours me, fond fool, as when
Their faint ghosts sit with me and flatter me
And send me back content to my dull round?
How can I change this soul?—this apparatus
680 Constructed solely for their purposes,
So well adapted to their every want,
To search out and discover, prove and perfect;

663| *1849:* The whole extent of degradation, once   *1863:* Extent of degradation,
once engaged   664| *MS:* vein? In spite   *1849:* Engaged in the confession?
Spite   *1863:* In the confessing vein? Despite   665| *MS:* obedience, and
1868: obedience and   666| *1835:* Docility, and   *1868:* Docility and
667| *MS:* performed, § altered in pencil to § perform'd,   *1849:* the old task really is
performed,   *1863:* the task shall really be performed,   668| *MS:* inclinations
< > more . . . § altered in pencil to § more—   *1835:* more,   *1849:* And my will free
once more, to choose a new,   *1863:* My inclinations free to choose once more,
1868: inclination   670| *MS:* Its nature in the next career they try: § altered in
pencil to § try.   *1849:* The nature of the hated one I quit.   *1863:* hated task
I   671| *MS:* spoiled:—my § altered in pencil to § spoil'd: my   *1849:* spoiled
1868: spoiled; my   672| *MS:* tended . . . I < > trained § altered in pencil to §
tended. I < > train'd   *1849:* trained   *1868:* tended; I   673| *MS:* habits—they
§ altered in pencil to § habits; they < > me: *1849:* me.   *1868:* habits: they
674| *MS:* know— —and § altered in pencil to § know, and < > Ends § altered to §
ends   675| *MS:* impossible— —no less— —no less § altered in pencil to §
impossible—no less—no less   *1835:* impossible: no less, no less,   677| *MS:* me,
and   *1835:* flatter me,   *1868:* with me < > me   678| *MS:* round? . . § altered
in pencil to § round?   679| *MS:* soul . . . this § written over by § soul—this
§ altered in pencil to § soul?—this   *1835:* soul? this   *1849:* soul?—this
680| *MS:* purposes— — § altered in pencil to § purposes—   *1835:* purposes?   *1868:*
purposes,   681| *MS:* their wants and uses,   *1835:* uses—   *1849:* their every
want,   682| *MS:* To search, discover, and dissect, and prove . . . § altered in
pencil to § prove—   *1835:* prove: *1849:* search out and discover, prove and perfect;

171

This intricate machine whose most minute
And meanest motions have their charm to me
685 Though to none else—an aptitude I seize,
An object I perceive, a use, a meaning,
A property, a fitness, I explain
And I alone:—how can I change my soul?
And this wronged body, worthless save when tasked
690 Under that soul's dominion—used to care
For its bright master's cares and quite subdue
Its proper cravings—not to ail nor pine
So he but prosper—whither drag this poor
Tried patient body? God! how I essayed
695 To live like that mad poet, for a while,
To love alone; and how I felt too warped
And twisted and deformed! What should I do,
Even tho' released from drudgery, but return
Faint, as you see, and halting, blind and sore,
700 To my old life and die as I began?
I cannot feed on beauty for the sake

683| *MS:* machine whose   *1849:* minute,   *1863:* machine whose < >
minute   **684|** *1835:* charms   *1849:* Least obvious motions < > charm   *1863:*
And meanest motions   **685|** *MS:* Tho' § altered in pencil to § Though < >
else——an < > I see—— § written over by § else—an < > I see—   *1849:* I
seize,   **686|** *MS:* perceive—   *1849:* perceive, a   **687|** *1835:* explain,
1868: explain   **688|** *MS:* alone . . . how < > soul?—   *1835:* soul?   *1849:*
alone:—how   **689|** *MS:* wronged § altered in pencil to § wrong'd   *1835:*
task'd   *1849:* wronged < > tasked   **691|** *MS:* Masters § altered in pencil to §
masters care, and to subdue   *1835:* master's   *1849:* and quite subdue   *1868:* cares
and   **692|** *MS:* cravings . . not § altered in pencil to § cravings—not to ail nor
pine § altered in pencil to § ail, nor pine,   *1863:* ail nor   *1868:* pine
693| *MS:* He § altered in pencil to § he but prosper———whither < > poor,   *1835:*
prosper—whither   *1849:* So the soul prosper   *1863:* So he but prosper   *1868:*
poor   **694|** *MS:* Tried, patient body? God! how I essayed § altered in pencil
to § essay'd   *1835:* essay'd   *1849:* essayed,   *1868:* Tried patient < > essayed
695-696| *MS:* while!——§ altered in pencil to § while! / To Love alone ——and
§ written over by § alone!—and § altered in pencil to § alone! and < > warped § altered
in pencil to § warp'd   *1835:* love   *1849:* while, / To catch Aprile's spirit, as I hoped,
/ And love < > warped   *1863:* while, / To love   *1868:* alone; and   **697|** *MS:*
deformed § altered in pencil to § deform'd   *1849:* deformed   **698|** *MS:* Released
from this sad drudgery but   *1835:* drudgery, but   *1849:* Even tho' released from
drudgery   **699|** *MS:* Faint as I am and halting——blind § altered in pencil to §
halting, blind   *1835:* halting, blind   *1849:* Faint, as you see, and halting
700| *MS:* begun!   *1835:* life—and   *1863:* began!   *1868:* life and   *1888:*
began?   **701|** *MS:* beauty, for   *1868:* beauty for

Of beauty only, nor can drink in balm
From lovely objects for their loveliness;
My nature cannot lose her first imprint;
705 I still must hoard and heap and class all truths
With one ulterior purpose: I must know!
Would God translate me to his throne, believe
That I should only listen to his word
To further my own aim! For other men,
710 Beauty is prodigally strewn around,
And I were happy could I quench as they
This mad and thriveless longing, and content me
With beauty for itself alone: alas,
I have addressed a frock of heavy mail
715 Yet may not join the troop of sacred knights;
And now the forest-creatures fly from me,
The grass-banks cool, the sunbeams warm no more.
Best follow, dreaming that ere night arrive,
I shall o'ertake the company and ride
720 Glittering as they!
        FESTUS   I think I apprehend
What you would say: if you, in truth, design
To enter once more on the life thus left,
Seek not to hide that all this consciousness

702| MS: only— —not § altered in pencil to § only—nor   1835: only; nor   1868: only,
nor   703| MS: loveliness . . . . § altered in pencil to § loveliness.   1835:
loveliness;   704| MS: impress: § altered in pencil to § impress;   1849: first
intent;   1863: first imprint;   705| MS: hoard, and heap, and < > Truths
§ altered in pencil to § truths   1863: hoard and heap and   706| MS: One
§ altered in pencil to § one < > purpose—one intent— — § altered in pencil to §
intent.   1849: purpose: I must know!   707| 1863: His   1868: his
708| MS: Words   1835: words   1863: His   1868: his word   709| MS: Aims
§ altered in pencil to § aims! full well I know   1835: Full   1849: aims! For other
men,   1868: aim   710| MS: strown   1835: strewn   711| MS: I trample
under   1849: I quench as they   712| MS: longing, be content   1863: longing,
and content me   713| MS: alone;— —alas! § altered in pencil to § alone; alas!
1835: alone: alas!   1868: alas,   714| MS: addressed § altered in pencil to §
address'd   1835: mail,   1849: addressed   1868: mail   715| MS: knights;—
§ altered in pencil to § knights;   717| MS: more!   1863: more.
718| MS:—Best § altered in pencil to § Best < > arrive   1849: arrives   1863:
arrive,   719| MS: company, and   1868: company and   720| MS:
FESTUS—I think I   1835: FESTUS I think I   722| MS: enter on such life again,
seek not   1849: enter once more on the life thus left,   723| MS: To hide that
much of all the § altered in pencil to § this   1849: Seek not to hide that all

Of failure is assumed!

PARACELSUS   My friend, my friend,
725 I toil, you listen; I explain, perhaps
You understand: there our communion ends.
Have you learnt nothing from to-day's discourse?
When we would thoroughly know the sick man's state
We feel awhile the fluttering pulse, press soft
730 The hot brow, look upon the languid eye,
And thence divine the rest. Must I lay bare
My heart, hideous and beating, or tear up
My vitals for your gaze, ere you will deem
Enough made known? You! who are you, forsooth?
735 That is the crowning operation claimed
By the arch-demonstrator—heaven the hall,
And earth the audience. Let Aprile and you
Secure good places: 'twill be worth the while.

FESTUS Are you mad, Aureole? What can I have said
740 To call for this? I judged from your own words.

PARACELSUS Oh, doubtless! A sick wretch describes the ape
That mocks him from the bed-foot, and all gravely
You thither turn at once: or he recounts
The perilous journey he has late performed,

724| *MS:* assumed——PARACELSUS *1835:* assumed. PARACELSUS *1868:* assumed!
PARACELSUS   **725|** *MS:* I tell . . . you listen;—I explain——perhaps § altered in
pencil to § I tell—you listen; I explain—perhaps *1849:* I speak, you < > explain,
perhaps *1863:* I tell, you *1888:* I toil, you   **726|** *MS:* understand:——there
§ altered in pencil to § understand: there   **728|** *MS:*—When *1835:*
When   **729|** *MS:* pulse—press § altered in pencil to § pulse, press
730| *MS:* brow—look § altered in pencil to § brow, look   **731|** *MS:* rest—
—must § altered in pencil to § rest. Must   **732|** *MS:* heart—hideous and
beating—or § altered in pencil to § heart, hideous and beating, or   **734|** *MS:*
known?—You *1835:* known? You   **735|** *MS:—That* < > claimed § altered in
pencil to § claim'd *1835: That 1849:* That < > claimed   **736|** *MS:* Arch-
demonstrator *1835:* arch-demonstrator   **737|** *MS:* audience.——Let § altered
in pencil to § audience. Let   **738|** *MS:* places—'twill < > while . . . § altered in
pencil to § while. *1863:* places: 'twill be worth the while.   **739|** *MS:* what
1835: What   **740|** *MS:* this . . I < > words.— § altered in pencil to § this? I
< > words.   **741|** *MS:* a *1835:* A *1849:* Oh, true! A fevered wretch
1863: Oh, doubtless! A sick wretch   **742|** *MS:* bed-foot . . . and § altered in
pencil to § bed-foot, and *1849:* and you turn *1863:* and all gravely
743| *1849:* All gravely thither at *1863:* You thither turn at   **744|** How sweet
the gardens where he slept last night, § cancelled by § The perilous journey he has late
performed, § altered in pencil to § perform'd *1849:* performed,

745 And you are puzzled much how that could be!
You find me here, half stupid and half mad;
It makes no part of my delight to search
Into these matters, much less undergo
Another's scrutiny; but so it chances
750 That I am led to trust my state to you:
And the event is, you combine, contrast
And ponder on my foolish words as though
They thoroughly conveyed all hidden here—
Here, loathsome with despair and hate and rage!
755 Is there no fear, no shrinking and no shame?
Will you guess nothing? will you spare me nothing?
Must I go deeper? Ay or no?

FESTUS   Dear friend . . .

PARACELSUS True: I am brutal—'tis a part of it;
The plague's sign—you are not a lazar-haunter,
760 How should you know? Well then, you think it strange
I should profess to have failed utterly,
And yet propose an ultimate return
To courses void of hope: and this, because
You know not what temptation is, nor how
765 'Tis like to ply men in the sickliest part.

746| *MS:* here—half-stupid § written over by § here; half-stupid § altered in pencil
to § here, half-stupid and half mad:— § altered in pencil to § mad: *1835:* half stupid
1863: mad;   747| *MS:*——It   *1835:* it   748| *MS:* things—much § written
over by § things; much less to undergo   *1835:* things, much   *1868:* these matters,
much less undergo   749| *MS:* scrutiny;—but   *1835:* scrutiny; but
750-751| *MS:* you / As calm, as sincerely as I may,— § altered in pencil to § may; /
And   *1835:* sincerely, as < > / < > contrast,   *1849:* you: / And   *1868:*
contrast   752| *MS:* tho' § altered in pencil to § though   *1835:* words, as
1868: words as   753| *MS:* conveyed < > here, § altered in pencil to § convey'd
< > here—   *1849:* conveyed < > here—   754| *MS: Here*— —loathsome
§ altered in pencil to § *Here*—loathsome   *1835: Here,* loathsome < > despair, and
hate, and   *1849: Here*   *1868:* despair and hate and   755| *MS:* shrinking, or
no   *1863:* shrinking or   *1868:* shrinking and no   757| *MS:* Aye or No?
FESTUS — — —Dear Friend, ... § altered in pencil to § FESTUS Dear Friend . . .
1835: no < > friend . . .   *1863:* Ay   758| *MS:* True:—I § altered in pencil to §
True: I am brutal—'tis < > it;—   *1835:* it;   759| *MS:* A plague fit:—you
§ altered in pencil to § plague fit: you   *1849:* The plague's sign—you   761| *MS:*
failed § altered in pencil to § fail'd   *1849:* failed   764| *MS:* temptation § written
over by § Temptation   *1835:* temptation   765| *MS:* Tis < > to ply me in my
sickliest part   *1835:* 'Tis < > in the sickliest   *1849:* ply men in

175

You are to understand that we who make
Sport for the gods, are hunted to the end:
There is not one sharp volley shot at us,
Which 'scaped with life, though hurt, we slacken pace
770 And gather by the wayside herbs and roots
To staunch our wounds, secure from further harm:
We are assailed to life's extremest verge.
It will be well indeed if I return,
A harmless busy fool, to my old ways!
775 I would forget hints of another fate,
Significant enough, which silent hours
Have lately scared me with.
FESTUS   Another! and what?
PARACELSUS After all, Festus, you say well: I am
A man yet: I need never humble me.
780 I would have been—something, I know not what;
But though I cannot soar, I do not crawl.
There are worse portions than this one of mine.
You say well!
FESTUS   Ah!
PARACELSUS   And deeper degradation!
If the mean stimulants of vulgar praise,

766| *MS:* .. You § altered in pencil to § You < > understand, that we, who   *1835:*
we who   *1868:* understand that   **767|** *MS:* Gods   *1835:* gods
768| *MS:* us   *1835:* us,   **768-770|** *MS:* 'tho § altered in pencil to § though
< > pace / And gather   *1835:* way-side   *1849:* Which if we manage to escape with
life, / Though touched and hurt, we straight may slacken pace / And gather   *1863:*
Which 'scaped with life, though hurt, we slacken pace / And gather < >
wayside   **771|** *MS:* harm: . . . § altered to § harm . . .   *1849:* harm—   *1863:*
stanch < > harm: *1868:* staunch   **772|** *MS:* assailed § altered in pencil to §
assail'd < > verge: § altered to § verge.   *1849:* No; we are chased to   *1863:* We are
assailed to   **774|** *MS:* ways! . . . § altered in pencil to § ways!   **775|** *MS:*
fate   *1849:* fate,   **777|** *MS:* with;—FESTUS § altered to § with; FESTUS § altered
in pencil to § with. FESTUS   **778|** *MS:* . . . After § altered to § After   *1849:* I
stand   *1863:* I am   **779|** *MS:* A Man yet—I need < > me;— — § altered in pencil
to § me;   *1835:* A man   *1849:* me.   *1863:* yet: I   **780|** been— —something I
< > what,— § altered in pencil to § been—something I < > what;   *1835:* something,
I   **781|** *MS:* tho' § altered in pencil to § though < > crawl: *1863:*
crawl.   **782|** *MS:* mine,— § altered in pencil to § mine;   *1863:* mine.
783| *MS:* well . . . FESTUS Ah! . . PARACELSUS . . . And § & altered in pencil to And §
< > degradation: *1849:* well! FESTUS < > degradation!   *1863:* Ah!
PARACELSUS   **784|** *MS:* praise, § , added in pencil §

785 If vanity should become the chosen food
Of a sunk mind, should stifle even the wish
To find its early aspirations true,
Should teach it to breathe falsehood like life-breath—
An atmosphere of craft and trick and lies;
790 Should make it proud to emulate, surpass
Base natures in the practices which woke
Its most indignant loathing once . . . No, no!
Utter damnation is reserved for hell!
I had immortal feelings; such shall never
795 Be wholly quenched: no, no!
                         My friend, you wear
A melancholy face, and certain 'tis
There's little cheer in all this dismal work.
But was it my desire to set abroach
Such memories and forebodings? I foresaw
800 Where they would drive. 'Twere better we discuss
News from Lucerne or Zurich; ask and tell
Of Egypt's flaring sky or Spain's cork-groves.
FESTUS I have thought: trust me, this mood will pass away!

785| MS: And vanity—should § altered in pencil to § vanity,—should 1835: vanity,
should 1868: If vanity should 786| MS: mind,—should § altered in pencil to §
mind; should 1868: mind, should 787| MS: true— — § altered in pencil to §
true; 1868: true, 788| MS: life-breath;— § altered in pencil to § life-
breath— 789| MS: lies;— § altered in pencil to § lies— 1835: craft, and trick,
and 1849: lies; 1863: craft and trick and 790| MS: emulate or surpass
1868: emulate, surpass 792| MS: once . . . . No, No. 1835: once . . . No, no:
1849: No, no! 793| MS: Hell!— § altered in pencil to § Hell! 1868:
hell! 794| MS: had < > feelings—such 1849: had 1863: feelings: such
1868: feelings; such 795| MS: quenched . . No—No— — § altered in pencil to §
quench'd—No,—No. 1835: no, no. 1849: quenched—no, no! 1863: quenched: no,
no! 796| MS: 'tis, 1849: and truth to speak, 1863: and, certain 'tis 1868:
and certain 797| MS: work; 1863: work. 798| MS: But 'twas not
my 1868: But was it my 799| MS: forbodings . . I § altered in pencil to §
forbodings. I 1835: forebodings 1863: forebodings: I 1868: forebodings?
I 800| MS: drive— —'twere § altered in pencil to § drive; 'twere better to
discuss 1849: better you detailed 1863: drive. 'Twere better to discuss 1868:
better we discuss 801| MS: News of Lucerne or Zurich; or to tell 1849: or I
described 1863: or to tell 1868: News from Lucerne or Zurich; ask and tell
802| MS: sky, or < > cork-groves: . . § written over by § cork-groves:— § altered in
pencil to § cork-groves: 1835: cork-groves. 1849: Great Egypt's 1863: Of
Egypt's < > sky or 803| MS: away: § altered in pencil to § away. 1849:
thought now: yes, this 1863: thought: trust me, this 1868: away!

177

I know you and the lofty spirit you bear,
805 And easily ravel out a clue to all.
These are the trials meet for such as you,
Nor must you hope exemption: to be mortal
Is to be plied with trials manifold.
Look round! The obstacles which kept the rest
810 From your ambition, have been spurned by you;
Their fears, their doubts, the chains that bind them all,
Were flax before your resolute soul, which nought
Avails to awe save these delusions bred
From its own strength, its selfsame strength disguised,
815 Mocking itself. Be brave, dear Aureole! Since
The rabbit has his shade to frighten him,
The fawn a rustling bough, mortals their cares,
And higher natures yet would slight and laugh
At these entangling fantasies, as you
820 At trammels of a weaker intellect,—
Measure your mind's height by the shade it casts!
I know you.
PARACELSUS And I know you, dearest Festus!
And how you love unworthily; and how
All admiration renders blind.
FESTUS   You hold

804| *MS:*—I § altered in pencil to § I < > you, and   *1868:* you and
805| *MS:* all: *1849:* all.   806| *MS:* you . . . § altered in pencil to § you—
1835: you,   807| *MS:*—Nor § altered in pencil to § Nor   809| *1835:*
round! the obstacles   *1849:* round! The obstacles   810| *MS:* ambition have
< > spurned by you § altered in pencil to § spurn'd by you: *1849:* Of men from
< > ambition, you have spurned;   *1863:* From < > ambition, have been spurned by
you;   811| *MS:* doubts . . the § altered in pencil to § doubts—the < > them
best   *1835:* doubts, the < > best,   *1863:* them all,   813| *MS:* awe, save
1835: delusions, bred   *1863:* delusions bred   *1868:* awe save   814| *MS:*
strength—its selfsame   *1835:* strength, its < > strength, disguised—   *1863:* strength
disguised—   *1868:* disguised,   815| *MS:* itself—be § altered in pencil to § itself.
be < > since   *1835:* itself. Be   *1849:* Since   817| *MS:* bough,—mortals
§ altered in pencil to § bough, mortals   *1835:* bough; mortals   *1849:* bough,
mortals   818| *MS:* Natures   *1835:* natures   *1849:* yet their power to laugh
1863: yet would slight and laugh   820| *MS:* weaker mind;—but judge   *1835:*
mind; but   *1849:* weaker intellect.   *1863:* intellect,—   821| *MS: Your* mind's
dimensions by   *1849:* Measure your mind's height by   822| *MS:* you:
PARACELSUS § altered in pencil to § you. PARACELSUS   823| *MS:* unworthily . . and
§ altered in pencil to § unworthily; and

825 That admiration blinds?

PARACELSUS   Ay and alas!

FESTUS Nought blinds you less than admiration, friend!
Whether it be that all love renders wise
In its degree; from love which blends with love—
Heart answering heart—to love which spends itself
830 In silent mad idolatry of some
Pre-eminent mortal, some great soul of souls,
Which ne'er will know how well it is adored.
I say, such love is never blind; but rather
Alive to every the minutest spot
835 Which mars its object, and which hate (supposed
So vigilant and searching) dreams not of.
Love broods on such: what then? When first perceived
Is there no sweet strife to forget, to change,
To overflush those blemishes with all
840 The glow of general goodness they disturb?
—To make those very defects an endless source
Of new affection grown from hopes and fears?
And, when all fails, is there no gallant stand
Made even for much proved weak? no shrinking-back
845 Lest, since all love assimilates the soul
To what it loves, it should at length become
Almost a rival of its idol? Trust me,

825| *MS:* Aye, and   *1863:* Ay and   826| *MS:* admiration: *1849:* admiration
will.   *1868:* admiration, friend!   828| *MS:* degree . . . from Love < > Love
§ altered in pencil to § degree; from Love < > Love—   *1835:* love < >
love—   829| *MS:*——Heart < > heart———to that which § altered in pencil
to § Heart < > heart—to   *1849:* to love which   831| *MS:* mortal—some < >
Soul of Souls—   *1835:* soul of souls—   *1849:* mortal, some < > of souls,
832| *MS:* adored: . . . . § altered in pencil to § adored: *1849:* adored:—   *1863:*
adored.   833| *MS:* . . I < > blind,—but § altered in pencil to § I < > blind; but
835| *MS:* That mars < > Hate   *1835:* hate   *1849:* Which mars   836| *MS:*
of: *1863:* of.   837| *MS:* then? in § altered in pencil to § then? In the first
case   *1849:* then? When first perceived   *1863:* perceived,   *1888:* perceived
840| *MS:* of goodness they disturb?   *1849:* of general goodness they
disturb?   841| *MS:* To   *1849:*—To   843| *MS:*—And § altered in pencil
to § And in the last,—is   *1835:* last, is   *1849:* And, when all fails, is
845| *MS:* Lest, since § written over by § Lest (since   *1849:* Lest, rising even as its
idol sinks,   *1863:* Lest, since all love assimilates the soul   846| *MS:* loves, it
§ written over by § loves) it   *1849:* It nearly reach the sacred place, and stand
1863: To what it loves, it should at length become   847| *1849:* of that idol
1863: of its idol

If there be fiends who seek to work our hurt,
To ruin and drag down earth's mightiest spirits
850 Even at God's foot, 'twill be from such as love,
Their zeal will gather most to serve their cause;
And least from those who hate, who most essay
By contumely and scorn to blot the light
Which forces entrance even to their hearts:
855 For thence will our defender tear the veil
And show within each heart, as in a shrine,
The giant image of perfection, grown
In hate's despite, whose calumnies were spawned
In the untroubled presence of its eyes.
860 True admiration blinds not; nor am I
So blind. I call your sin exceptional;
It springs from one whose life has passed the bounds
Prescribed to life. Compound that fault with God!
I speak of men; to common men like me
865 The weakness you reveal endears you more,
Like the far traces of decay in suns.
I bid you have good cheer!

PARACELSUS   *Præclare! Optime!*

848| *MS:* Fiends <> hurt,— § altered in pencil to § hurt,   *1835:* fiends
849| *MS:* Earth's   *1835:* earth's <> spirits,   *1863:* spirits   850| *MS:* foot—
§ above § , twill <> love— § written over by § Love—§ — added in pencil §   *1835:*
foot, 'twill <> love—   *1849:* love,   853| *MS:* Light   *1835:* light
854| *MS:* Which will have entrance <> *their* hearts;   *1849:* their   *1863:* Which
forces entrance <> hearts: 855| *MS:* . . For § altered in pencil to § For <>
Defender   *1835:* defender   *1849:* Defender   *1863:* defender   856| *MS:* And
show within the heart § *show* inserted above the line §   *1849:* within each
heart   857| *MS:* Perfection   *1868:* perfection   858| *MS:* In their despite
<> spawned § altered in pencil to § spawn'd   *1849:* In hate's despite <>
spawned   859| *MS:* eyes!   *1868:* eyes.   860| *MS:* not: nor   *1835:* not;
nor   861–862| *MS:* blind: I know your unexampled sins, / But I know too, what
sort of soul is prone / To errors of that stamp;—sins like to spring / From one alone,
whose <> passed § altered in pencil to § pass'd   *1835:* too what <> / <>
stamp—sins <> / <> alone whose   *1849:* blind: I call your sin exceptional; / It
springs from one whose <> passed   *1863:* blind. I   863| *MS:* life . . .
compound § altered in pencil to § life—compound *that*   *1835:* life. Compound
1849: that   864| *MS:* Men . . to § altered in pencil to § Men; to <> Men
1835: men <> men   865| *MS:* you confess endears you more, § altered in
pencil to § more—   *1863:* more,   866| *MS:* suns:— § altered in pencil to §
suns: *1863:* suns.   867| *MS: Præclarè! Optimè!*   *1868: Præclare! Optime!*

Think of a quiet mountain-cloistered priest
Instructing Paracelsus! yet 'tis so.
870 Come, I will show you where my merit lies.
'Tis in the advance of individual minds
That the slow crowd should ground their expectation
Eventually to follow; as the sea
Waits ages in its bed till some one wave
875 Out of the multitudinous mass, extends
The empire of the whole, some feet perhaps,
Over the strip of sand which could confine
Its fellows so long time: thenceforth the rest,
Even to the meanest, hurry in at once,
880 And so much is clear gained. I shall be glad
If all my labours, failing of aught else,
Suffice to make such inroad and procure
A wider range for thought: nay, they do this;
For, whatsoe'er my notions of true knowledge
885 And a legitimate success, may be,
I am not blind to my undoubted rank
When classed with others: I precede my age:

868| *MS:* mountain-cloistered Priest § altered in pencil to § mountain-cloister'd
Priest   *1835:* priest   *1863:* mountain-cloistered   869-870| *MS:* so: And that
his flittering words should soothe me better § : added in pencil § / Than fulsome
tributes . . . not § altered in pencil to § tributes—not that 'tis so § *'tis so* cancelled by
that § that strange:— / Come   *1835:* yet, 'tis so: / < > better / < > tributes: not
that that is strange: / Come   *1849:* so. / Come   *1868:* yet 'tis   870-871| *MS:*
lies: / I ne'er supposed that since *I* failed no other / Needs hope success . . . I
§ altered in pencil to § success. I act as though each one / Who hears me, may aspire;
now mark me well:— § altered in pencil to § well: / Tis   *1835:* lies. / < > fail'd
< > / < > success: I < > / < > me may < > / 'Tis   *1849:* lies. / 'Tis
873| *MS:* follow,— —as § written over by § follow,—as   *1835:* follow—as   *1863:*
follow; as   874| *MS:* bed, 'till   *1868:* bed 'till   *1888:* till   875| *MS:* Of
all the < > mass extends   *1849:* Out of the multitude aspires, extends   *1863:*
multitudinous mass, extends   878| *MS:* fellows, so long time:—thenceforth
§ altered in pencil to § time: thenceforth   879| *MS:* once,—
§ altered in pencil to § once,   880| *MS:* gained: . . . I § altered in pencil
to § gained. I   882| *MS:* inroad— —to § altered in pencil to § in road—to
procure   *1849:* inroad, and procure   *1863:* inroad and   883| *MS:* Thought
< > *do* this,— § altered in pencil to § this;   *1835:* thought   *1849:* do
884| *MS:* For whatsoe'er   *1849:* For, whatsoe'er   885| *MS:* success . . . no
§ altered in pencil to § success—no less   *1835:* success may be,   *1849:* success,
may   887| classed < > others:—I § altered in pencil to § class'd < > others.
I   *1849:* others: I

181

And whoso wills is very free to mount
These labours as a platform whence his own
890 May have a prosperous outset. But, alas!
My followers—they are noisy as you heard;
But, for intelligence, the best of them
So clumsily wield the weapons I supply
And they extol, that I begin to doubt
895 Whether their own rude clubs and pebble-stones
Would not do better service than my arms
Thus vilely swayed—if error will not fall
Sooner before the old awkward batterings
Than my more subtle warfare, not half learned.
900 FESTUS I would supply that art, then, or withhold
New arms until you teach their mystery.
PARACELSUS Content you, 'tis my wish; I have recourse
To the simplest training. Day by day I seek
To wake the mood, the spirit which alone
905 Can make those arms of any use to men.
Of course they are for swaggering forth at once

888-889| *MS:* wills, is < > to make / That use of me which I disdained § altered in
pencil to § disdain'd to make / Of my forerunners—(vanity, perchance: But had I
deemed § altered in pencil to § deem'd their learning wonder-worth, / I had been
other than I am)— —to § altered in pencil to § am)—to mount / Those labours, as < >
whence their own   *1835:* labours as a platform, whence   *1849:* to mount / These
labours   *1868:* will is < > / < > platform whence his own   890| *MS:*
outset;—but § altered in pencil to § outset; but   *1863:* outset. But   891| *MS:*
followers . . . they § altered in pencil to § followers—they < > heard,   *1868:*
heard;   892| *MS:* But for intelligence;— —the § altered in pencil to §
intelligence; the   *1835:* intelligence—the   *1868:* But, for intelligence, the
893| *MS:* supply,   *1835:* supply   894| *MS:* extol,—that § altered in pencil to §
extol, that   897| *MS:* swayed,—if § altered in pencil to § swayed—if   *1835:*
sway'd   *1849:* swayed   898| *MS:* before their aukward   *1835:* awkward
1849: the old awkward   899-900| *MS:* warfare! FESTUS In that case, / I < > art
and would withold   *1835:* art, and < > withhold   *1849:* warfare, not half learned.
/ FESTUS I < > art, then, and withhold   *1868:* then, or withhold   901| *MS:*
The arms until their mystery was made known.   *1849:* Its arms until you have taught
their mystery.   *1868:* New arms < > you teach their   902| *MS:* you; 'tis
§ altered in pencil to § you, 'tis   903| *MS:* training: day by   *1835:* training.
Day by   905| *MS:* to them.   *1849:* to men.   906| *MS:*— —Of § altered
in pencil to § Of   *1849:* course, they   *1868:* course they

182

Graced with Ulysses' bow, Achilles' shield—
Flash on us, all in armour,' thou Achilles!
Make our hearts dance to thy resounding step!
910 A proper sight to scare the crows away!
FESTUS Pity you choose not then some other method
Of coming at your point. The marvellous art
At length established in the world bids fair
To remedy all hindrances like these:
915 Trust to Frobenius' press the precious lore
Obscured by uncouth manner, or unfit
For raw beginners; let his types secure
A deathless monument to after-time;
Meanwhile wait confidently and enjoy
920 The ultimate effect: sooner or later
You shall be all-revealed.
PARACELSUS   The old dull question
In a new form; no more. Thus: I possess
Two sorts of knowledge; one,—vast, shadowy,
Hints of the unbounded aim I once pursued:
925 The other consists of many secrets, caught
While bent on nobler prize,—perhaps a few
Prime principles which may conduct to much:
These last I offer to my followers here.

907–910| MS: With Hercules' club, Achilles' shield, Ulysses' / Bow—a choice sight
1849: Graced with Ulysses' club, Achilles' shield— / Flash on us, all in armour, thou
Achilles! / Make our hearts dance to thy resounding step! / A proper sight   1863:
Ulysses' bow, Achilles'   911| MS: no, then, some   1888: not then some
912| MS: point:—the § altered in pencil to § point. The   913| 1835:
establish'd   1849: established   915| MS: Press   1835: press   917| MS:
beginners—let   1849: beginners; let   918| MS: after-times;   1868: after-
time;   919| MS: Meanwhile enjoy and confidently wait   1849: Meanwhile
wait confidently and enjoy   920| 1849: later,   1868: later   921| MS:
An ancient question   1835: all-reveal'd   1849: all-revealed. PARACELSUS The old dull
question   922| MS: more: thus § altered in pencil to § more. Thus
923| MS: Knowledge,—one § altered in pencil to § Knowledge—one, vast, shadowy
hints   1835: knowledge   1849: knowledge; one,—vast, shadowy,   924| MS:
Of < > Aim < > pursued;— § altered in pencil to § pursued—   1835: aim   1849:
Hints of < > pursued: 925| MS: other, many secrets, made my own   1849:
other consists of many secrets, learned   1863: secrets, caught   926| MS: prize,
and not a   1849: prize,—perhaps a   927| MS: First principles < > much;
§ altered in pencil to § much: 1863: Prime principles   928| MS: here:—
§ altered in pencil to § here: 1835: here.

183

Now, bid me chronicle the first of these,
930 My ancient study, and in effect you bid
Revert to the wild courses just abjured:
I must go find them scattered through the world.
Then, for the principles, they are so simple
(Being chiefly of the overturning sort),
935 That one time is as proper to propound them
As any other—to-morrow at my class,
Or half a century hence embalmed in print.
For if mankind intend to learn at all,
They must begin by giving faith to them
940 And acting on them: and I do not see
But that my lectures serve indifferent well:
No doubt these dogmas fall not to the earth,
For all their novelty and rugged setting.
I think my class will not forget the day
945 I let them know the gods of Israel,
Aetius, Oribasius, Galen, Rhasis,
Serapion, Avicenna, Averröes,
Were blocks!
FESTUS   And that reminds me, I heard something
About your waywardness: you burned their books,
950 It seems, instead of answering those sages.
PARACELSUS And who said that?
FESTUS   Some I met yesternight

929| *MS:* Now bid < > these,— § altered in pencil to § these,   *1868:* Now,
bid   930| *MS:* study— § above § , and < > bid me   *1835:* effect you   *1868:*
bid   931-933| *MS:* course I have abjured:— § altered in pencil to § abjured. /
And, for   *1849:* courses just abjured: / I must go find them scattered through the
world. / Then, for   934| *MS:*—(Being < > sort), § , added in pencil §   *1835:*
(Being   936| *MS:* other—tomorrow < > class, § , added in pencil §   *1835:* to-
morrow   937| *MS:* print—   *1835:* embalm'd in print;   *1849:* embalmed in
print: *1863:* print.   938| *MS:* Mankind < > all   *1835:* mankind < >
all,   939| *1835:* them,   *1868:* them   940| *1835:* them; and   *1888:*
them: and   942| *MS:* earth   *1835:* earth,   943| *MS:* setting; § altered in
pencil to § setting.   945| *MS:* Gods   *1835:* gods   947| *MS:* And
Avicenna, and Averröes,   *1849:* Serapion, Avicenna, Averröes,—   *1868:*
Averröes,   948| *MS:* blocks!—FESTUS — —And < > me,—they § altered in pencil
to § me, they said something   *1835:* blocks! FESTUS And   *1849:* me, I heard
something   949| *MS:* books   *1835:* burn'd < > books,   *1849:* burned
950| *MS:* It seems instead < > sages . . . .   *1835:* seems, instead < > sages . . .
1849: sages.

184

With Œcolampadius. As you know, the purpose
Of this short stay at Basil was to learn
His pleasure touching certain missives sent
955 For our Zuinglius and himself. 'Twas he
Apprised me that the famous teacher here
Was my old friend.
PARACELSUS   Ah, I forgot: you went . . .
FESTUS From Zurich with advices for the ear
Of Luther, now at Wittenberg—(you know,
960 I make no doubt, the differences of late
With Carolostadius)—and returning sought
Basil and . . .
PARACELSUS   I remember. Here's a case, now,
Will teach you why I answer not, but burn
The books you mention. Pray, does Luther dream
965 His arguments convince by their own force
The crowds that own his doctrine? No, indeed!
His plain denial of established points
Ages had sanctified and men supposed
Could never be oppugned while earth was under
970 And heaven above them—points which chance or time
Affected not—did more than the array
Of argument which followed. Boldly deny!
There is much breath-stopping, hair-stiffening

952| MS: Œcolampadius: as   1835: Œcolampadius. As   953| MS: Basil,
was   1835: Basil was   955| MS: himself:—'twas § altered in pencil to §
himself. 'Twas   956| MS: Apprized   1863: Apprised   957| MS: friend—
— PARACELSUS < > went . . . .   1835: friend. PARACELSUS < > went . . .
959| MS: Luther now at Wittemburg——(you   1835: Luther, now at
Wittemburg—(you   1888: Wittenberg   961| MS: Carolostadius-),- and   1835:
Carolostadius)—and   962| MS: and Œcolempadius. PARACELSUS Here's a case
now,   1835: now   1849: and . . . PARACELSUS I remember. Here's a case, now,
964| MS: mention: Pray   1835: pray   1888: mention. Pray   966| MS:
indeed: 1888: indeed!   967| MS: established § altered in pencil to §
establish'd   1849: established   968| MS: sanctified, and none supposed
1835: sanctified and   1849: and men supposed   969| MS: Could be oppugned
< > under him   1835: oppugn'd   1849: Could never be oppugned < >
under   970| MS: heaven above——which § written over by § above—which
chance or change or § altered in pencil to § change, or time   1849: above
them—points which chance, or time   1863: chance or time   971| MS: not . . .
did § altered in pencil to § not—did   972| MS: followed: boldly § altered in
pencil to § followed. Boldly deny!—   1835: follow'd < > deny!   1849: followed

185

Awhile; then, amazed glances, mute awaiting
975 The thunderbolt which does not come: and next,
Reproachful wonder and inquiry: those
Who else had never stirred, are able now
To find the rest out for themselves, perhaps
To outstrip him who set the whole at work,
980 —As never will my wise class its instructor.
And you saw Luther?

FESTUS   'Tis a wondrous soul!

PARACELSUS True: the so-heavy chain which galled mankind
Is shattered, and the noblest of us all
Must bow to the deliverer—nay, the worker
985 Of our own project—we who long before
Had burst our trammels, but forgot the crowd,
We should have taught, still groaned beneath their load:
This he has done and nobly. Speed that may!
Whatever be my chance or my mischance,
990 What benefits mankind must glad me too;
And men seem made, though not as I believed,
For something better than the times produce.
Witness these gangs of peasants your new lights

974| MS: Awhile,—amazed glances—mute   1835: Awhile, amazed glances, mute
1849: Awhile; then, amazed   975| MS: thunder-bolt < > come,— —and next
§ altered in pencil to § come—and next   1835: thunderbolt   1849: come; and next,
1868: come: and   976| MS: inquiry—those § altered in pencil to § inquiry;
those   1849: inquiry: those   977| MS: stirred § altered in pencil to § stirr'd
1835: stirr'd are   1849: stirred, are   978| MS: themselves . . perhaps § altered
in pencil to § themselves—perhaps   1868: find rest for themselves, perhaps   1888:
find the rest out for   979| MS: work; . . . § altered in pencil to § work:,   1835:
work,   980| MS: . . . As < > instructor:— § altered in pencil to § As < >
instructor: 1835: instructor . . .   1849:—As < > instructor.   981| MS:—And
< > Soul!   1835: And < > soul!   982| MS: so heavy < > galled § altered in
pencil to § gall'd Mankind   1835: so-heavy < > mankind   983| MS:
shattered—and § altered in pencil to § shatter'd, and   1849: shattered   984| MS:
Deliverer— —, nay § altered in pencil to § deliverer—nay   985| MS: projects
1863: project   986| MS: burst its trammels < > crowd   1849: crowd,   1863:
burst our trammels   1868: trammels but   1888: trammels, but   987| MS: We
would have < > beneath the load:— § altered in pencil to § load: 1835: groan'd
1849: should < > taught, still groaned   1889: beneath their load: 988| MS:
nobly; speed § altered in pencil to § nobly. Speed   989| MS: or my despair,
1835: despair   1849: despair,   1863: or my mischance,   990| MS: too: 1888:
too;   991| MS: Men < > tho'   1835: men < > though   992| MS: times
can show;— § altered in pencil to § show: 1849: times produce: 1863:
produce.   993| MS: Peasants   1835: peasants

186

From Suabia have possessed, whom Münzer leads,
995 And whom the duke, the landgrave and the elector
Will calm in blood! Well, well; 'tis not my world!
FESTUS Hark!
PARACELSUS 'Tis the melancholy wind astir
Within the trees; the embers too are grey:
Morn must be near.
FESTUS   Best ope the casement: see,
1000 The night, late strewn with clouds and flying stars,
Is blank and motionless: how peaceful sleep
The tree-tops altogether! Like an asp,
The wind slips whispering from bough to bough.
PARACELSUS Ay; you would gaze on a wind-shaken tree
1005 By the hour, nor count time lost.
FESTUS   So you shall gaze:
Those happy times will come again.
PARACELSUS   Gone, gone,
Those pleasant times! Does not the moaning wind
Seem to bewail that we have gained such gains
And bartered sleep for them?
FESTUS   It is our trust
1010 That there is yet another world to mend
All error and mischance.
PARACELSUS   Another world!
And why this world, this common world, to be
A make-shift, a mere foil, how fair soever,

994| MS: Munzer 1835: possess'd 1849: possessed 1863: Münzer
995| MS: Duke, the Landgrave, and the Elector 1835: duke < > landgrave < >
elector 1868: landgrave and 996| MS: blood——well, well § altered in
pencil to § blood—well, well—'tis 1835: blood! Well, well < > world. 1849:
world! 1868: Well, well; 'tis 997| MS: PARACELSUS——Tis 1835:
PARACELSUS 'Tis 998| MS: trees——the § altered in pencil to § trees; the < >
grey, 1863: grey: 999| MS:—Morn < > near: FESTUS < > see 1835:
Morn < > near. FESTUS 1849: see, 1001| MS: motionless;—how § altered in
pencil to § motionless; how 1835: motionless: how 1002| MS: all together!
like an asp 1849: Like an asp, 1868: altogether 1004| MS:—Ay: you
1835: Ay; you 1005| MS: lost? FESTUS 1835: lost FESTUS 1006| MS:
again ... PARACELSUS Gone! Gone! 1863: again. PARACELSUS Gone, gone,
1007| MS: times! ... does § altered in pencil to § times! Does 1008| MS:
gained § altered in pencil to § gain'd 1849: gained 1009| 1835: barter'd
1849: bartered 1011| MS: mischance.——— PARACELSUS 1835: mischance
.... PARACELSUS 1849: mischance. PARACELSUS 1012| MS: world to 1849:
world, to 1013| MS: make-shift— § above § , a 1835: make-shift, a

187

To some fine life to come? Man must be fed
1015 With angels' food, forsooth; and some few traces
Of a diviner nature which look out
Through his corporeal baseness, warrant him
In a supreme contempt of all provision
For his inferior tastes—some straggling marks
1020 Which constitute his essence, just as truly
As here and there a gem would constitute
The rock, their barren bed, one diamond.
But were it so—were man all mind—he gains
A station little enviable. From God
1025 Down to the lowest spirit ministrant,
Intelligence exists which casts our mind
Into immeasurable shade. No, no:
Love, hope, fear, faith—these make humanity;
These are its sign and note and character,
1030 And these I have lost!—gone, shut from me for ever,
Like a dead friend safe from unkindness more!
See, morn at length. The heavy darkness seems
Diluted, grey and clear without the stars;
The shrubs bestir and rouse themselves as if
1035 Some snake, that weighed them down all night, let go

1014| *MS:* to-come   *1849:* to come   1015| *MS:* Angels'   *1835:* angel's
1868: angels'   1017| *MS:* Thro' § altered to § Through < > baseness warrant
1849: baseness, warrant   1018| *MS:* contempt for all   *1863:* contempt of
all   1019| *MS:* tastes . . . some   *1835:* tastes—some   1021| *MS:* gem,
would   *1835:* gem would   1022| *MS:* bed, a diamond.   *1863:* bed, one
diamond.   1023| *MS:*—But < > so, . . were § written over by and altered to §
so—were Man all mind . . the § written over by § Mind—the station   *1835:* But < >
man all mind   *1849:* mind—he gains   1024| *MS:* he gains is little enviable: . .
from § written over by and altered to § enviable. From   *1849:* A station little
1025| *MS:* ministrant   *1849:* ministrant,   1026| *MS: our* Mind   *1835:* mind
1849: our   1027| *MS:* shade . . No, No:— § altered to § shade. No, No: *1835:*
No, no: 1028| *MS:* Love, Hope, Fear, Faith . . . . these § written over by §
Faith—These < > Humanity: *1835:* Love, hope, fear, faith—these < >
humanity;   1029| *MS:* sign, and note, and character . . . . § altered to §
character;   *1863:* sign and note and character,   1030| *MS:*— —And § altered
to § And < > lost! gone—shut < > for ever   *1835:* gone; shut < > for ever,   *1849:*
lost!—gone, shut   1031| *MS:* friend, safe   *1868:* friend safe   1032| *MS:*
length— —the § altered to § length. The   *1835:* See morn   *1863:* See, morn
1033| *MS:* Diluted,—grey < > stars,   *1835:* Diluted; grey < > stars;   *1888:*
Diluted, grey   1034| *MS:*—The < > themselves, as though   *1835:* The
1849: as if   *1888:* themselves as   1035| *MS:* snake, that < > night, let
§ altered to § snake that < > night let   *1835:* weigh'd   *1849:* snake, that weighed
< > night, let

188

His hold; and from the East, fuller and fuller,
Day, like a mighty river, flowing in;
But clouded, wintry, desolate and cold.
Yet see how that broad prickly star-shaped plant,
1040 Half-down in the crevice, spreads its woolly leaves
All thick and glistering with diamond dew.
And you depart for Einsiedeln this day,
And we have spent all night in talk like this!
If you would have me better for your love,
1045 Revert no more to these sad themes.
FESTUS   One favour,
And I have done. I leave you, deeply moved;
Unwilling to have fared so well, the while
My friend has changed so sorely. If this mood
Shall pass away, if light once more arise
1050 Where all is darkness now, if you see fit
To hope and trust again, and strive again,
You will remember—not our love alone—
But that my faith in God's desire that man
Should trust on his support, (as I must think
1055 You trusted) is obscured and dim through you:
For you are thus, and this is no reward.
Will you not call me to your side, dear Aureole?

1036| MS: East § altered to § east, fuller and fuller   1863: East   1889:
fuller,   1037| 1849: river, is flowing   1868: river, flowing   1038| MS:
desolate, and cold: 1863: desolate and cold.   1039| MS: plant   1835: broad,
prickly, star-shaped plant,   1863: broad prickly star-shaped   1040| MS: Half
down   1835: leaves,   1868: half-down < > leaves   1041| MS: dew:—
§ altered to § dew.   1042| 1835: day: 1868: day,   1043| MS: this!— —
§ altered to § this!   1044| MS: love   1849: love,   1045| MS:
themes;—FESTUS § altered to § themes. FESTUS   1046| MS: done:—I < >
moved: 1835: done. I < > moved;   1048| MS: Friend < > sorely: if   1835:
friend   1863: sorely. If   1049| MS: away— —if   1835: away—if   1863: away,
if   1050| MS: now— —if   1835: now—if   1863: now, if   1051| MS:
hope, and < > again,—   1835: again;   1863: again,   1868: hope and
1053| MS: Man   1835: man   1849: desire for man   1863: desire that man
1054| MS: support . . . as   1835: support, as   1849: support, (as   1863: Should
trust on His   1868: his   1055| MS: trusted . . . . is < > thro' you,—   1835:
trusted, is < > through you;   1849: trusted,) is   1868: trusted) is   1888:
you: 1056| MS: reward;—   1835: reward: 1849: reward.   1057| 1849:
dear friend?   1863: dear Aureole?

PART IV. PARACELSUS ASPIRES.
SCENE—*Colmar in Alsatia: an Inn.* 1528.

PARACELSUS, FESTUS.

PARACELSUS [*to* JOHANNES OPORINUS, *his Secretary*]. *Sic itur ad astra!* Dear
Von Visenburg
Is scandalized, and poor Torinus paralysed,
And every honest soul that Basil holds
Aghast; and yet we live, as one may say,
5 Just as though Liechtenfels had never set
So true a value on his sorry carcass,
And learned Pütter had not frowned us dumb.
We live; and shall as surely start to morrow
For Nuremberg, as we drink speedy scathe
10 To Basil in this mantling wine, suffused
A delicate blush, no fainter tinge is born
I' the shut heart of a bud. Pledge me, good John—
"Basil; a hot plague ravage it, and Pütter
Oppose the plague!" Even so? Do you too share

SCENE| *MS: A House at Colmar in Alsatia.* 1528.   *1863: Colmar in Alsatia: an Inn.*
1528.   ¹| *MS:* PARACELSUS [to JOHN OPORINUS < > astra! . . . . dear   *1835:*
astra! Dear   *1863:* PARACELSUS [to JOHANNES OPORINUS   ⁴| *MS:* Aghast . . .
and < > live—as < > say— § altered in pencil to § Aghast; and < > live, as < >
say,   ⁵| *MS:* tho   *1835:* though   ⁶| *MS:* carcass . . . § written over
by § carcass— § altered in pencil to § carcass,   ⁷| *MS:* dumb; . . . § altered in
pencil to § dumb.   *1835:* frown'd   *1849:* frowned   ⁸| *MS:* live, and § altered
in pencil to § live; and < > to-morrow   *1888:* to morrow   ⁹| *MS:*
Nuremburg, as § altered in pencil to § Nuremburg as   *1849:* Nuremburg, as   *1888:*
Nuremberg   ¹¹| *MS:* blush; no   *1835:* blush—no   *1849:* With a   *1863:* A < >
blush, no   ¹²| *MS:* th' < > bud;——pledge < > John,—§ altered in pencil to §
John—   *1835:* bud: pledge   *1863:* bud. Pledge   *1868:* the   ¹³| *MS:*
"Basil—a § altered in pencil to § "Basil; a   *1849:* it, with Pütter   ¹⁴| *MS:*
plague!"—even so! do § altered in pencil to § so? Do   *1835:* plague!" Even   *1849:*
To stop the   *1863:* Oppose the

190

Their panic, the reptiles? Ha, ha; faint through these,
Desist for these! They manage matters so
At Basil, 'tis like: but others may find means
To bring the stoutest braggart of the tribe
Once more to crouch in silence—means to breed
20 A stupid wonder in each fool again,
Now big with admiration at the skill
Which stript a vain pretender of his plumes:
And, that done,—means to brand each slavish brow
So deeply, surely, ineffaceably,
25 That henceforth flattery shall not pucker it
Out of the furrow; there that stamp shall stay
To show the next they fawn on, what they are,
This Basil with its magnates,—fill my cup,—
Whom I curse soul and limb. And now despatch,
30 Despatch, my trusty John; and what remains
To do, whate'er arrangements for our trip
Are yet to be completed, see you hasten
This night; we'll weather the storm at least: to-morrow
For Nuremberg! Now leave us; this grave clerk

15| MS: panic . . . the reptiles! Ha § altered in pencil to § panic—the reptiles? Ha, ha, faint thro' *them,* *1835:* Ha, ha; faint through *1863:* panic, the *1868:* through these, **16–18|** MS: for *them!* . . . they § altered in pencil to § They < > / < > like— —but § altered in pencil to § like; but *1835: them!* They < > / < > like; but *1849: them!*—while means enough exist / To bow the stoutest *1863: them!* They manage matters so / At Basil 'tis like: but others may find means / To bring the stoutest *1868:* for these! They **19|** *1849:* more in crouching silence *1863:* more to crouch in silence **20|** MS: again *1835:* again, **22|** MS: stripped < > plumes,—§ altered in pencil to § plumes;— *1835:* stript < > plumes; *1888:* plumes: **23|** MS: done, means *1863:* done,—means **24|** MS: deeply-sure—so § altered in pencil to § deeply-sure, so ineffaceably, *1849:* deeply, surely, ineffaceably, **25|** MS: That, thenceforth, flattery § altered in pencil to § That thenceforth flattery *1868:* that henceforth flattery **26|** MS: So well but there the hideous stamp *1835:* stay, *1849:* Out of the furrow of that hideous stamp *1863:* furrow; there that stamp shall stay **27–29|** MS: To teach the man they < > on, who § altered in pencil to § on who they are / Whom < > limb: and § altered in pencil to § limb. And now dispatch, § , added in pencil § *1849:* Which shows the next they fawn on, what they are, / This Basil with its magnates one and all, / Whom *1863:* To show < > / < > magnates,—fill my cup,— *1888:* despatch, **30|** MS: Dispatch < > John, and *1835:* John; and *1888:* Despatch **31|** MS: do—whate'er § altered in pencil to § do; whate'er *1835:* do, whate'er **33|** MS: night—we'll < > least—to-morrow § altered in pencil to § night: we'll < > least: to-morrow *1835:* night; we'll **34|** MS: Nuremburg!—Now < > us—this § altered in pencil to § us; this *1835:* Nuremburg! Now *1888:* Nuremberg

35   Has divers weighty matters for my ear: [OPORINUS *goes out.*
     And spare my lungs. At last, my gallant Festus,
     I am rid of this arch-knave that dogs my heels
     As a gaunt crow a gasping sheep; at last
     May give a loose to my delight. How kind,
40   How very kind, my first best only friend!
     Why, this looks like fidelity. Embrace me!
     Not a hair silvered yet? Right! you shall live
     Till I am worth your love; you shall be proud,
     And I—but let time show! Did you not wonder?
45   I sent to you because our compact weighed
     Upon my conscience—(you recall the night
     At Basil, which the gods confound!)—because
     Once more I aspire. I call you to my side:
     You come. You thought my message strange?
     FESTUS   So strange
50   That I must hope, indeed, your messenger
     Has mingled his own fancies with the words
     Purporting to be yours.
     PARACELSUS   He said no more,

35| *MS:* ear——. *1835:* ear, *1863:* ear: **36|** *MS:* lungs—at § altered in pencil to § lungs. At *1849:* Festus *1863:* Festus,   **37|** *MS:* I have got rid < > dogs me *1849:* I am rid < > that follows me *1863:* that dogs my heels   **38|** *MS:* sheep,—and § altered in pencil to § sheep;—and now *1835:* sheep; and *1849:* sheep; at last   **39|** *MS:* delight; how § altered in pencil to § delight. How   **40|** *MS:* kind!—my first, best, only Friend! *1835:* kind, my < > friend! *1868:* first best only friend!   **41|** *MS:*—Why this < > fidelity:—embrace § altered in pencil to § fidelity. Embrace me,— *1835:* Why < > me: *1863:* Why, this < > me!   **42|** *MS:*—Not < > Right: you *1835:* Not < > silver'd yet! Right *1849:* silvered *1863:* yet? Right! you   **43|** *MS:* love—you < > proud § altered in pencil to § love; you < > proud; *1835:* love; you < > proud,   **44|** *MS:* I——but time will show: did § altered in pencil to § I—but < > show. Did *1849:* but let time show. *1888:* show! Did   **45|** *MS:* weigh'd *1849:* weighed   **46|** *MS:* conscience, (you § altered in pencil to § conscience—(you *1849:* recal *1863:* recall   **47|** *MS:* Gods confound)—because *1835:* gods *1863:* confound!)—because   **48|** *MS:* more, I aspire!——and you are here! all this § altered in pencil to § more I aspire! And you are here! All this *1849:* aspire! I call you to my side; *1863:* aspire. I *1888:* side: **49|** *MS:* Is strange;—and § altered in pencil to § strange, and strange my message? FESTUS I confess *1835:* message. FESTUS I confess, *1849:* You come. You thought my message strange? FESTUS So strange   **50|** *MS:* So strange that I must think your *1849:* That I must hope, indeed, your   **52|** *MS:* yours . . . . . PARACELSUS *1835:* yours. PARACELSUS

'Tis probable, than the precious folk I leave
Said fiftyfold more roughly. Well-a-day,
55 'Tis true! poor Paracelsus is exposed
At last; a most egregious quack he proves:
And those he overreached must spit their hate
On one who, utterly beneath contempt,
Could yet deceive their topping wits. You heard
60 Bare truth; and at my bidding you come here
To speed me on my enterprise, as once
Your lavish wishes sped me, my own friend!
FESTUS What is your purpose, Aureole?
PARACELSUS   Oh, for purpose,
There is no lack of precedents in a case
65 Like mine; at least, if not precisely mine,
The case of men cast off by those they sought
To benefit.
FESTUS   They really cast you off?
I only heard a vague tale of some priest,
Cured by your skill, who wrangled at your claim,
70 Knowing his life's worth best; and how the judge
The matter was referred to, saw no cause
To interfere, nor you to hide your full

53| *MS:* Tis < > folks   *1835:* 'Tis   *1888:* folk   **54|** *MS:* Have said more
roughly fifty-fold—alack § altered in pencil to § fifty-fold: Alack,   *1835:* fifty-fold.
Alack,   *1849:* Said fifty-fold more roughly. Well-a-day,   *1863:* fiftyfold
55| *MS:* Tis true: poor   *1835:* 'Tis   *1849:* true; poor   *1863:* true! poor
56| *MS:* last—a § altered in pencil to § last; a < > quack is he,   *1835:* last: a < >
he;   *1849:* last; a < > quack he proves,   *1863:* proves: **57|** *1835:*
overreach'd   *1849:* overreached   **58|** *MS:* who— § above § , utterly < >
contempt,—   *1835:* who, utterly < > contempt,   **59|** *MS:* wits—He said
§ altered in pencil to § wits. He said   *1849:* wits. You heard   **60|** *MS:* you are
here   *1849:* you come here   **62|** *MS:* me; my § altered in pencil to § me,
my   *1835:* friend?   *1863:* friend!   **63-64|** *MS:* And now, what < > Aureole?
/ PARACELSUS There   *1849:* What < > Aureole? PARACELSUS Oh, for purpose, /
There   **65|** *MS:* mine . . . . at § altered to § mine; at   *1835:* mine,
at   *1849:* mine; at   **67|** *MS:* benefit— — — FESTUS < > off? . . .   *1835:*
benefit . . . FESTUS   *1849:* off?   *1863:* benefit. FESTUS   **68|** *MS:* I merely heard
< > priest, § , added in pencil §   *1849:* I only heard   **69|** *MS:* wrangled at
the just   *1849:* at your claim,   **70|** *MS:* Reward you claimed . . . and § altered
in pencil to § claimed; and that the Magistrate   *1835:* claim'd < > magistrate
1849: Knowing his life's worth best; and how the judge   **71|** *MS:* to saw
1835: referr'd   *1849:* referred to, saw   **72|** *MS:* interfere— —nor § altered in
pencil to § interfere, nor

Contempt of him; nor he, again, to smother
His wrath thereat, which raised so fierce a flame
75 That Basil soon was made no place for you.
PARACELSUS The affair of Liechtenfels? the shallowest fable,
The last and silliest outrage—mere pretence!
I knew it, I foretold it from the first,
How soon the stupid wonder you mistook
80 For genuine loyalty—a cheering promise
Of better things to come—would pall and pass;
And every word comes true. Saul is among
The prophets! Just so long as I was pleased
To play off the mere antics of my art,
85 Fantastic gambols leading to no end,
I got huge praise: but one can ne'er keep down
Our foolish nature's weakness. There they flocked,
Poor devils, jostling, swearing and perspiring,
Till the walls rang again; and all for me!
90 I had a kindness for them, which was right;
But then I stopped not till I tacked to that
A trust in them and a respect—a sort

73| *MS:* him——nor § altered in pencil to § him, nor   *1835:* him; nor
74| *MS:* wrath which § altered in pencil to § wrath, which raised so hot an
opposition   *1849:* wrath thereat, which < > so fierce a flame   75| soon
became no   *1849:* soon was made no   76| *MS:* Liechtenfels? The § altered in
pencil to § Liechtenfels! The shallowest pretext,   *1835:* Liechtenfels? the   *1849:*
shallowest cause,   *1863:* shallowest fable,   77| *MS:* outrage!——mere § altered
in pencil to § outrage—mere   *1835:* pretence.   *1849:* pretence!   78| *MS:*—I
< > it—I first— § altered in pencil to § it, I < > first: *1835:* I knew < >
first,   80| *MS:* loyalty, a   *1835:* loyalty—a   81| *MS:* come, would < >
pass . . .   *1835:* come—would < > pass;   82| *MS:* true—Saul   *1835:* true.
Saul   83| *MS:* just   *1835:* Just   84| *MS:* off all the marvels of my
art—   *1849:* off the mere marvels   *1863:* mere antics of my art,   85| *MS:*
end,—   *1835:* end—   *1863:* end,   86-87| *MS:* I had huge praise, and
doubtless might have grown / Grey in the exposition of such antics / Had my stock
lasted long enough;—but such / Was not my purpose—one can ne'er keep down / Our
< > weakness——there < > flocked   *1835:* enough; but such / < > purpose: one
< > / < > weakness . . . There < > flock'd,   *1849:* I got huge praise; but one can
ne'er keep down / Our < > weakness: there < > flocked,   *1863:* praise: but < > /
< > weakness. There   88| *MS:* perspiring   *1835:* swearing, and perspiring,
1863: swearing and perspiring,   89| *MS:* again——. . . and   *1835:* again;
and   90| *MS:* for them— § above § , which was right—   *1835:* them, which
was right;   91| *MS:* 'till I   *1835:* stopp'd not till I tack'd   *1849:* stopped
< > tacked   92| *MS:* respect——a   *1835:* respect—a

194

Of sympathy for them; I must needs begin
To teach them, not amaze them, "to impart
95 The spirit which should instigate the search
Of truth," just what you bade me! I spoke out.
Forthwith a mighty squadron, in disgust,
Filed off—"the sifted chaff of the sack," I said,
Redoubling my endeavours to secure
100 The rest. When lo! one man had tarried so long
Only to ascertain if I supported
This tenet of his, or that; another loved
To hear impartially before he judged,
And having heard, now judged; this bland disciple
105 Passed for my dupe, but all along, it seems,
Spied error where his neighbours marvelled most;
That fiery doctor who had hailed me friend,
Did it because my by-paths, once proved wrong
And beaconed properly, would commend again
110 The good old ways our sires jogged safely o'er,
Though not their squeamish sons; the other worthy
Discovered divers verses of St. John,
Which, read successively, refreshed the soul,
But, muttered backwards, cured the gout, the stone,

93| MS: them— —I, in short, began   1835: them: I   1849: I must needs begin
1868: them; I   94| MS: them; to   1849: them: "to   1863: them, "to
96-98| MS: Of truth— —forthwith a mighty squadron straight / Filed off:—"the sifted
< > said,—   1835: truth. Forthwith < > / < > off—"the sifted < > sack," I said,
1849: Of truth:" just what you bade me! I spoke out. / Forthwith < > squadron, in
disgust, / Filed   1863: Of truth," just   100| MS: rest; when   1849: had
stayed thus long   1863: rest. When < > had tarried so long   102| MS: tenet
or the other;—another   1835: other; another   1849: tenet of his, or that;
another   103-105| MS: judged, / And now was satisfied;—one had all along
1835: satisfied; one   1849: judged, / And having heard, now judged; this bland
disciple / Passed for my dupe, but all along, it seems,   106-110| MS: marveled
most:— / —This doctor set a school up to revive / The good old ways which could
content our sires   1835: marvell'd most: // < > sires,   1849: marvelled most: /
That fiery doctor who had hailed me friend, / Did it because my bye-paths, once
proved wrong / And beaconed properly, would commend again / The good old ways
our sires jogged safely o'er,   1863: most; // < > by-paths   111| MS: Tho
< > sons;—the   1835: Though < > sons; the   112| MS: St. John   1835: St.
John,   113| MS: Which read successively refreshed the soul   1835: refresh'd
1849: Which, read successively, refreshed   114| MS: But muttered backwards
cured the gout, the stone   1835: mutter'd < > stone,   1849: But, muttered
backwards, cured

115 The colic and what not. *Quid multa?* The end
Was a clear class-room, and a quiet leer
From grave folk, and a sour reproachful glance
From those in chief who, cap in hand, installed
The new professor scarce a year before;
120 And a vast flourish about patient merit
Obscured awhile by flashy tricks, but sure
Sooner or later to emerge in splendour—
Of which the example was some luckless wight
Whom my arrival had discomfited,
125 But now, it seems, the general voice recalled
To fill my chair and so efface the stain
Basil had long incurred. I sought no better,
Only a quiet dismissal from my post,
And from my heart I wished them better suited
130 And better served. Good night to Basil, then!
But fast as I proposed to rid the tribe
Of my obnoxious back, I could not spare them
The pleasure of a parting kick.
FESTUS   You smile:
Despise them as they merit!
PARACELSUS   If I smile,
135 'Tis with as very contempt as ever turned
Flesh into stone. This courteous recompense,
This grateful . . . Festus, were your nature fit

115| *MS:* cholic < > not—*quid multa?*—the   *1835:* cholic, and < > *multa?* The
1849: not:—*quid*   *1863:* colic < > not. *Quid*   *1868:* colic and   116| *MS:*
class-room and   *1835:* class-room, and   *1849:* class-room, with a   *1863:* class-room,
and a   117| *MS:* reproachful look   *1849:* reproachful glance
118| *1835:* chief, who < > install'd   *1849:* installed   *1863:* chief who
119| *MS:* Professor < > before,—   *1835:* professor < > before;   120| *MS:*—
—And   *1835:* And   122| *MS:* splendour,—   *1835:* splendour—
124| *MS:* discomfited   *1835:* discomfited,   125| *1835:* recall'd   *1849:*
recalled   126| *1835:* chair, and   *1863:* chair and   127| *MS:* incurred;—
——I < > better: *1835:* incurr'd. I < > better—   *1849:* incurred   *1863:*
better,   128| *MS:*—Nought but a < > Post—   *1835:* Nought < > post;
1863: Only a < > post,   129| *1835:* wish'd < > suited,   *1849:* While from
< > wished   *1863:* And from < > suited   130| *MS:* served:—goodnight
1835: served. Good night   132| *MS:* obnoxious self, I   *1849:* obnoxious back,
I   133| *MS:* kick: . . . FESTUS You smile:——   *1835:* kick. FESTUS You
smile: 134| *MS:* smile   *1835:* smile: *1863:* smile,   135| *MS:* Tis
1835: 'Tis < > turn'd   *1849:* turned   136| *MS:* stone: this   *1849:*
recompense! *1863:* stone. This   *1868:* recompense,

To be defiled, your eyes the eyes to ache
At gangrene-blotches, eating poison-blains,
140 The ulcerous barky scurf of leprosy
Which finds—a man, and leaves—a hideous thing
That cannot but be mended by hell fire,
—I would lay bare to you the human heart
Which God cursed long ago, and devils make since
145 Their pet nest and their never-tiring home.
Oh, sages have discovered we are born
For various ends—to love, to know: has ever
One stumbled, in his search, on any signs
Of a nature in us formed to hate? To hate?
150 If that be our true object which evokes
Our powers in fullest strength, be sure 'tis hate!
Yet men have doubted if the best and bravest
Of spirits can nourish him with hate alone.
I had not the monopoly of fools,
155 It seems, at Basil.
FESTUS   But your plans, your plans!
I have yet to learn your purpose, Aureole!
PARACELSUS Whether to sink beneath such ponderous shame,

138| _MS:_ defiled——your eyes, the   _1835:_ defiled, your eyes the   139| _MS:_
At festering blotches—eating poisoning   _1835:_ blotches, eating   _1849:_ At gangrened
blotches, eating poisonous   _1863:_ gangrene-blotches, eating poison-blains,
140| _1849:_ ulcered   _1863:_ ulcerous   141| _MS:_ finds a Man, and leaves a
< > Thing   _1835:_ man and < > thing   _1849:_ finds—a man, and leaves—a
142-143| _MS:_ hell-fire——— / I < > bare the heart of man to you;—   _1835:_ hell
fire, / < > you,   _1849:_ fire, / —I say that, could you see as I could show, / I would
lay bare to you these human hearts   _1863:_ fire, / —I would < > you the human
heart   144| _MS:_ ago,—which devils have made   _1835:_ ago—which   _1849:_
ago, and devils make since   145| _MS:_ pet-nest < > home, ...   _1835:_ pet
nest < > home.   146| _MS:_———O, sages have found out that Man is born
_1835:_ O < > man   _1849:_ have discovered we are born   _1888:_ Oh   147| _MS:_
ends,—to love, to know;—has   _1835:_ ends—to < > know. Has   _1849:_ know:
has   148| _MS:_ stumbled in his search on   _1849:_ stumbled, in his search,
on   149| _MS:_ in him formed to _Hate?_ . . to _Hate?_   _1835:_ form'd to _hate?_ To
hate?   _1849:_ formed to hate? To hate?   _1863:_ in us formed   150| _MS:_ . . . If
< > be Man's true   _1835:_ If < > man's   _1849:_ be our true   151-157| _MS:_
His powers < > Hate;— / Yet Men < > bravest / Of < > Hate alone! . . . / I < >
fools, / It < > Basil;—FESTUS < > plans—your / I have yet < > Aureole! / Whether
< > shame—   151| _1835:_ hate: 152| _1835:_ men   153| _1835:_ hate
alone.   155| _1835:_ Basil. FESTUS < > plans, your plans: 156| _1835:_
Aureole.   151-157| _1849:_ Our powers < > hate! / But I have yet < > Aureole!
/ PARACELSUS What purpose were the fittest now for me? / Decide! To

To shrink up like a crushed snail, undergo
In silence and desist from further toil,
160 And so subside into a monument
Of one their censure blasted? or to bow
Cheerfully as submissively, to lower
My old pretensions even as Basil dictates,
To drop into the rank her wits assign me
165 And live as they prescribe, and make that use
Of my poor knowledge which their rules allow,
Proud to be patted now and then, and careful
To practise the true posture for receiving
The amplest benefit from their hoofs' appliance
170 When they shall condescend to tutor me?
Then, one may feel resentment like a flame
Within, and deck false systems in truth's garb,
And tangle and entwine mankind with error,
And give them darkness for a dower and falsehood
175 For a possession, ages: or one may mope
Into a shade through thinking, or else drowse
Into a dreamless sleep and so die off.

151-157| *1863:* hate! / Yet men have doubted if the best and bravest / Of spirits can nourish him with hate alone. / I had not the monopoly of fools. / It seems at Basil. FESTUS But your plans, your plans! / I have yet < > Aureole! / PARACELSUS Whether to < > shame, 155| *1868:* seems, at 158| *MS:* shrink in like < > shame— *1835:* crush'd *1849:* shrink up like a crushed snail—undergo *1863:* snail—to endure *1835:* crush'd *1849:* shrink up like a crushed snail—undergo *1863:* snail, undergo 159| *MS:* toil *1835:* toil, *1863:* toil *1888:* toil, 161| *MS:* Or *1835:* blasted; or *1863:* blasted? or 162| *MS:* submissively,—to *1835:* submissively—to *1863:* submissively, to 163| *MS:* as they dictate, *1835:* dictate— *1849:* as Basil dictates— *1863:* dictates, 164| *MS:* rank their wit assigns me, *1849:* rank her wits assign *1863:* me 165| *1863:* prescribe and *1868:* prescribe, and 166| *MS:* Of all my knowledge < > allow— *1849:* Of my poor knowledge *1863:* allow, 168| *MS:* the fit posture *1849:* the true posture 169| *MS:* hoofs *1835:* hoofs' appliance, *1863:* appliance 170| *MS:* me?— — *1835:* me. *1863:* me? 171| *MS:—* —Then one *1835:* Then *1849:* flame, *1863:* flame *1868:* Then, one 172| *MS:* Within—and < > garb *1835:* Within, and < > Truth's garb, *1849:* Prompting to deck *1863:* Within, and deck < > truth's 173| *MS:* error *1835:* error; *1849:* error, 174| *MS:* dower, and *1863:* dower and 175| *1849:* possession: or < > mope away *1863:* possession, ages: or < > mope 176| *MS:* shade, for thinking: or may drowse *1835:* shade for thinking; or *1849:* shade through thinking; or else drowse *1863:* thinking, or 177| *MS:* off:— *1835:* sleep, and < > off: *1863:* sleep and < > off.

But I,—now Festus shall divine!—but I
Am merely setting out once more, embracing
180 My earliest aims again! What thinks he now?
FESTUS Your aims? the aims?—to Know? and where is found
The early trust . . .
PARACELSUS   Nay, not so fast; I say,
The aims—not the old means. You know they made me
A laughing-stock; I was a fool; you know
185 The when and the how: hardly those means again!
Not but they had their beauty; who should know
Their passing beauty, if not I? Still, dreams
They were, so let them vanish, yet in beauty
If that may be. Stay: thus they pass in song!   [*He sings.*

190   Heap cassia, sandal-buds and stripes
        Of labdanum, and aloe-balls,
        Smeared with dull nard an Indian wipes
        From out her hair: such balsam falls
        Down sea-side mountain pedestals,
195   From tree-tops where tired winds are fain,

178| *MS:* But I . . . now < > divine— — but I   *1835:* But I—now < > divine—but
I   *1849:* But I, but I—now < > divine!   *1863:* But I,—now < > divine!—but
I   **179|** *MS:* more-embracing   *1835:* more, embracing   *1849:*—Am < > out
in life once more,   *1863:* Am < > out once more, embracing   **180|** *MS:*
what   *1835:* What   *1849:* Embracing my old aims! What   *1863:* My earliest aims
again! What   **181|** *MS: The Aims?—to know* § written over by § *Know?*—and
1835: the aims?—to know?—and   *1849:* the aims?—to know? and   *1863:*
Know   **182|** *MS:* The trust, the sure belief . . . . PARACELSUS < > fast;—   *1835:*
belief . . . PARACELSUS < > fast;   *1849:* The early trust . . . PARACELSUS < > fast; I
say,   **183|** *MS: The Aims,* . . . but not the Means—you   *1835:* The aims—but
< > means. You   *1849:* The aims—not the old means. You know what made   *1863:*
know they made   **184|** *MS:* laughing stock— —I < > fool—you   *1835:*
laughing-stock: I < > fool; you   *1849:* laughing-stock; I   **185|** *MS:*
how—hardly < > Means again! . . .   *1835:* how: hardly < > means again;   *1849:*
again!   **186|** *MS:* beauty— —who   *1835:* beauty—who   *1863:* beauty;
who   **187|** *MS:* beauty if not I?—but still   *1835:* I? But   *1849:* beauty, if
1868: I? Still, dreams   **188|** *MS:* They were dreams, so < > vanish!—yet
1835: vanish: yet in beauty,   *1863:* vanish, yet   *1868:* They were, so   *1888:*
beauty   **189|** *MS:* may be,— —stay—   *1835:* be. Stay . . .   *1849:* Stay—thus
they pass in song!   *1863:* Stay: thus   **190|** *MS:* sandal-buds, and   *1863:*
sandal-buds and   **191|** *MS:* aloe-balls   *1863:* aloe-balls,   **192|** *1835:*
Smear'd   *1849:* Smeared   **193-195|** *MS:* hair . . . such < > falls / From tall
trees where   *1835:* hair: such   *1849:* hair: (such < > falls / Down sea-side
mountain pedestals, / From summits where   *1863:* hair: such < > / < > seaside
< > / From tree-tops where   *1868:* sea-side

Spent with the vast and howling main,
To treasure half their island-gain.

And strew faint sweetness from some old
 Egyptian's fine worm-eaten shroud
200 Which breaks to dust when once unrolled;
 Or shredded perfume, like a cloud
 From closet long to quiet vowed,
 With mothed and dropping arras hung,
 Mouldering her lute and books among,
205 As when a queen, long dead, was young.

Mine, every word! And on such pile shall die
My lovely fancies, with fair perished things,
Themselves fair and forgotten; yes, forgotten,
Or why abjure them? So, I made this rhyme
210 That fitting dignity might be preserved;
No little proud was I; though the list of drugs
Smacks of my old vocation, and the verse
Halts like the best of Luther's psalms.
FESTUS   But, Aureole,
Talk not thus wildly and madly. I am here—
215 Did you know all! I have travelled far, indeed,

197| MS: island-gain; . . . / § end of page § / And 1835: island-gain; / § no space §
/ And 1849: island-gain.) / § space § / And 1863: island-gain. 199| MS:
Egyptians 1835: Egyptian's < > shroud, 1863: shroud 200| MS:
unrolled;— — 1835: unroll'd; 1849: unrolled; 201| MS: perfume like
1835: perfume, like 1849: And shred dim perfume 1863: Or shredded perfume,
like 202| MS: closet, long < > vowed 1835: closet long < > vow'd,
1849: From chamber long < > vowed, 1863: From closet long 203| 1835:
moth'd 1849: mothed 204| MS: among 1835: among, 1849: Mouldering
the lute < > among 1863: Mouldering her lute < > among, 205| MS:
Queen 1835: queen 1849: Of queen, long dead, who lived there young. 1863:
As when a queen, long dead, was young. 206| MS: word!—and 1835: word;
and 1849: word!—and 1863: word! And 207| MS: fancies—with 1835:
fancies with < > perish'd 1849: fancies, with < > perished 208| MS:
forgotten—yes, forgotten 1835: forgotten; yes 209| MS: them?—so I 1835:
them? So 1863: So, I 210| MS: preserved: . . . 1835: preserved: 1863:
preserved; 211| MS: was I— —tho' 1835: I; though 213| MS:
psalms— — —FESTUS 1835: psalms . . . FESTUS 1849: psalms! FESTUS 1863:
psalms. FESTUS 214| MS: madly; I 1835: madly. I 215| MS: all!—but
I have travelled far 1835: all! But < > travell'd 1849: all, indeed! I < >
travelled 1863: all! I < > far, indeed,

To learn your wishes. Be yourself again!
For in this mood I recognize you less
Than in the horrible despondency
I witnessed last. You may account this, joy;
220 But rather let me gaze on that despair
Than hear these incoherent words and see
This flushed cheek and intensely-sparkling eye.
PARACELSUS Why, man, I was light-hearted in my prime,
I am light-hearted now; what would you have?
225 Aprile was a poet, I make songs—
'Tis the very augury of success I want!
Why should I not be joyous now as then?
FESTUS Joyous! and how? and what remains for joy?
You have declared the ends (which I am sick
230 Of naming) are impracticable.
PARACELSUS   Ay,
Pursued as I pursued them—the arch-fool!
Listen: my plan will please you not, 'tis like,
But you are little versed in the world's ways.
This is my plan—(first drinking its good luck)—
235 I will accept all helps; all I despised
So rashly at the outset, equally
With early impulses, late years have quenched:

216| MS: wishes .. Be   1835: wishes. Be <> again;   1849: again!
219| MS: last: you <> joy, . . .   1835: witness'd last. You <> this joy;   1849:
witnessed <> this, joy;   220| MS: on your despair   1849: on that
despair   221| MS: hear your incoherent words, and   1849: hear these
incoherent   1863: words and   222| MS: That flushed cheek, and intensely
sparkling eye . . .   1835: flush'd <> intensely-sparkling eye.   1849: This flushed
<> eye!   1863: eye.   223| MS: lighthearted <> prime,—   1835: light-
hearted <> prime,   1888: prime   224–226| MS: lighthearted now——what
<> have? / ——Tis   1835: light-hearted now; what <> / 'Tis   1849: have? /
Aprile was a poet, I make songs— / 'Tis   227| MS: joyous even as   1849:
joyous now as   228| MS: Joyous? and   1835: Joyous! and   229| MS:
Ends   1835: ends   230| MS: impracticable . . . PARACELSUS Aye,   1835:
impracticable. PARACELSUS   1863: Ay,   231| MS: them——the   1835:
them—the   232| MS:—Listen—my   1835: Listen: my <> like;   1863:
like,   233| MS: ways:—   1835: ways . . .   1849: ways.   234| MS: plan,
(first <> luck!)—   1835: plan—(first <> luck)—   235| MS: all helps!—all
1835: helps; all   1849: accept all helps   237| MS: impulses which lately
seemed   1835: impulses, which <> seem'd   1849: impulses, late years have
quenched:

I have tried each way singly: now for both!
All helps! no one sort shall exclude the rest.
240 I seek to know and to enjoy at once,
Not one without the other as before.
Suppose my labour should seem God's own cause
Once more, as first I dreamed,—it shall not baulk me
Of the meanest earthliest sensualest delight
245 That may be snatched; for every joy is gain,
And gain is gain, however small. My soul
Can die then, nor be taunted—"what was gained?"
Nor, on the other hand, should pleasure follow
As though I had not spurned her hitherto,
250 Shall she o'ercloud my spirit's rapt communion
With the tumultuous past, the teeming future,
Glorious with visions of a full success.
FESTUS Success!
PARACELSUS   And wherefore not? Why not prefer
Results obtained in my best state of being,
255 To those derived alone from seasons dark
As the thoughts they bred? When I was best, my youth

238| *MS:* The mere persuasion of fantastic dreams;—   *1835:* dreams;   *1849:* I have
tried each way singly—now for both: *1863:* singly: now   **239|** *MS:* helps . . .
no < > rest:—   *1835:* helps—no < > rest: *1849:* rest.   *1863:* helps! no
240-242| *MS:* Know < > Enjoy:—well then,—§ *know* and *enjoy* in print § / For all
my cause should seem the cause of God   *1835:* KNOW < > ENJOY   *1849:* ENJOY at
once, / Not one without the other as before. / Suppose my labour should seem God's
own cause   *1863:* know < > enjoy   **243|** *1835:* dream'd, it   *1849:*
dreamed   *1863:* dreamed,—it   **244|** *MS:* meanest, earthliest, sensualest   *1868:*
meanest earthliest sensualest   **245|** *MS:* be realized;—for joy   *1835:* realized;
for   *1849:* be snatched; for every joy   **246-248|** *MS:* is gain however small: nor,
should / On < > hand those honeyed pleasures   *1835:* is gain, however < > nor
should, / < > hand, those honey'd   *1849:* And why spurn gain, however small? My
soul / Can die then, nor be taunted "what was gained?" / Nor, on < > hand, if
pleasure meets me   *1863:* And gain is gain, however small. My soul / < >
taunted—"what < > / < > hand, should pleasure follow   **249|** *MS:* tho' < >
spurned them hitherto,   *1835:* though < > spurn'd   *1849:* spurned her
hitherto,   **250|** *MS:* Shall they o'ercloud my spirits   *1835:* spirit's   *1849:*
Shall she o'ercloud   **251|** *MS:* Past < > Future   *1835:* past < > future,
1863: Past < > Future,   *1868:* past < > future   **252|** *MS:* success . . . .
1835: success . . .   *1849:* success!   *1868:* success.   **254|** *MS:* The grand results
< > state   *1835:* obtain'd   *1849:* Results obtained in < > state of being,
255| *MS:* Of being, to < > derived from   *1835:* being to   *1849:* To those derived
alone from   **256|** *MS:* best—my   *1863:* best, my

Unwasted, seemed success not surest too?
It is the nature of darkness to obscure.
I am a wanderer: I remember well
260 One journey, how I feared the track was missed,
So long the city I desired to reach
Lay hid; when suddenly its spires afar
Flashed through the circling clouds; you may conceive
My transport. Soon the vapours closed again,
265 But I had seen the city, and one such glance
No darkness could obscure: nor shall the present—
A few dull hours, a passing shame or two,
Destroy the vivid memories of the past.
I will fight the battle out; a little spent
270 Perhaps, but still an able combatant.
You look at my grey hair and furrowed brow?
But I can turn even weakness to account:
Of many tricks I know, 'tis not the least
To push the ruins of my frame, whereon
275 The fire of vigour trembles scarce alive,
Into a heap, and send the flame aloft.
What should I do with age? So, sickness lends
An aid; it being, I fear, the source of all
We boast of: mind is nothing but disease,

257| MS: Unwasted—seemed   1835: seem'd   1849: seemed   1863: Unwasted, seemed   258| MS: Is it not Darkness' nature to obscure   1835: darkness'   1849: It is the nature of darkness to obscure.   259| MS:——I am   1835: I am   260| MS: missed,—   1835: fear'd < > miss'd—   1849: feared < > missed,   262| MS: hid—when   1835: hid, when   1849: hid; when   263| MS: thro' < > clouds——you   1835: Flash'd through < > clouds; you   1849: Flashed < > clouds; conceive my joy!   1863: clouds; you may conceive   264| MS: transport:—soon   1835: transport: soon   1849: Too soon the vapours closed o'er it again,   1863: My transport. Soon the vapours closed again,   266–268| MS: obscure:——nor shall sad days / Destroy < > past: 1835: obscure: nor < > / < > past: 1849: shall the present / A few dull hours, a passing shame or two, / Destroy < > past.   1863: Present— // < > Past.   1868: present— // < > past.   269| MS: out!——a § written over by § out!—a   1849: little tired,   1863: little spent   1868: out; a   270| MS: Perhaps—but < > combatant: 1835: combatant.   1863: Perhaps, but   271| 1835: furrow'd brow;   1849: furrowed brow?   272| MS: account—— § altered in pencil to § account—   1835: account: 274| MS: frame whereon   1835: frame, whereon   275| MS: alive   1835: alive,   276| MS: aloft!   1868: aloft.   277| MS:—What < > Age?—so sickness   1835: What < > age? so   1863: age? So, sickness   278| MS: aid;—it   1835: aid; it   279| MS: disease   1835: disease,   1863: disease   1868: disease,

280 And natural health is ignorance.
FESTUS   I see
But one good symptom in this notable scheme.
I feared your sudden journey had in view
To wreak immediate vengeance on your foes;
'Tis not so: I am glad.
PARACELSUS   And if I please
285 To spit on them, to trample them, what then?
'Tis sorry warfare truly, but the fools
Provoke it. I would spare their self-conceit,
But if they must provoke me, cannot suffer
Forbearance on my part, if I may keep
290 No quality in the shade, must needs put forth
Power to match power, my strength against their strength,
And teach them their own game with their own arms—
Why, be it so and let them take their chance!
I am above them like a god, there's no
295 Hiding the fact: what idle scruples, then,
Were those that ever bade me soften it,
Communicate it gently to the world,
Instead of proving my supremacy,
Taking my natural station o'er their head,
300 Then owning all the glory was a man's!

---

²⁸⁰| *MS:* ignorance:—FESTUS There is   *1835:* ignorance. FESTUS   *1849:* FESTUS I
see   ²⁸¹| *MS:* scheme: *1849:* notable plan: *1863:* notable scheme.
²⁸²| *MS:* sudden project had   *1835:* fear'd   *1849:* feared < > sudden journey
had   ²⁸³| *MS:* foes,—   *1835:* foes;   *1888:* foes   ²⁸⁴| *MS:* Tis   *1835:*
'Tis   *1849:* pleased   *1863:* please   ²⁸⁵| *MS:* them—to < > them,—what
1835: them, to < > them, what   ²⁸⁷⁻²⁸⁸| *MS:* it: I ne'er sought to domineer,—
/ The mere asserting my supremacy / Has little mortified their self-conceit / —I took
my natural station and no more; / But if they *will* provoke me,—will not suffer   *1835:*
domineer; // < > self-conceit; / < > more: / < > more-will   *1849:* I had spared
their self-conceit, / But if they must provoke me—cannot suffer   *1863:* it. I would
spare < > / < > provoke me, cannot   *1888:* self-conceit   ²⁸⁹| *MS:* part,—if I
can have   *1835:* part—if   *1849:* may keep   *1863:* part, if   ²⁹⁰| *MS:* shade,
but must put   *1849:* shade, must needs put forth   ²⁹¹| *MS:* Power for
power—my < > against theirs—   *1835:* for power; my   *1849:* Power to match
power, my < > against their strength,   ²⁹²| *MS:* Must teach < > arms . . .
1835: arms—   *1849:* And teach   ²⁹³| *MS:* Why be it so, and   *1863:* Why, be
it so and   ²⁹⁴| *MS:* God—there's   *1849:* God—in vain   *1863:* God, there's no
1868: god   ²⁹⁵⁻³⁰⁰| *MS:* fact—and, had I been but wise, / Had ne'er concerned
myself with scruples, nor / Communicated ought to such a race;—But been content to
own myself a Man,

—And in my elevation man's would be.
But live and learn, though life's short, learning, hard!
And therefore, though the wreck of my past self,
I fear, dear Pütter, that your lecture-room
305 Must wait awhile for its best ornament,
The penitent empiric, who set up
For somebody, but soon was taught his place;
Now, but too happy to be let confess
His error, snuff the candles, and illustrate
310 *(Fiat experientia corpore vili)*
Your medicine's soundness in his person. Wait,
Good Pütter!
FESTUS   He who sneers thus, is a god!
PARACELSUS Ay, ay, laugh at me! I am very glad
You are not gulled by all this swaggering; you
315 Can see the root of the matter!—how I strive
To put a good face on the overthrow
I have experienced, and to bury and hide
My degradation in its length and breadth;
How the mean motives I would make you think
320 Just mingle as is due with nobler aims,
The appetites I modestly allow

295–300| *1835:* concern'd < > / < > race; / < > man, *1849:* To hide the
fact—what idle scruples, then, / Were those that ever bade me soften it, /
Communicate it gently to the world, / Instead of proving my supremacy, / Taking my
natural station o'er their heads, / Then owning all the glory was a man's
295| *1863:* Hiding the fact: what   299| *1868:* head,   300| *1863:*
man's!   301| *MS:* And < > elevation, Man's < > be . . . *1835:* man's *1849:*
be! *1863:*—And < > be.   302–303| *MS:* tho' life's so short: as 'tis,— / —
—Tho' no more than the wreck < > self, . . *1835:* Though < > short! as 'tis— /
Though < > self— *1849:* life's short; learning, hard! / Still, one thing I have
learned—not to despair: / And therefore, though the < > self, *1863:* short, learning,
hard! / And   305| *MS:* ornament,— *1835:* ornament,   306| *MS:*
Empiric who *1835:* empiric, who   307| *MS:* place . . *1835:* place— *1863:*
place;   309–311| *MS:* illustrate / Your tenets' soundness < > person . . . wait,
1835: person. Wait, *1849:* illustrate / *(Fiat experientia corpore vili)* / Your
medicine's soundness   312| *MS:* God! *1868:* god!   313| *MS:* Ay, Ay
1835: Ay, ay   314| *MS:* swaggering— —*you* *1835:* gull'd < > swaggering;
you *1849:* gulled < > you   317| *MS:* experienced—and to hide and bury
1835: experienced, and *1849:* to bury and hide   318| *MS:* breadth *1835:*
breadth;   319| *MS:*—And how the motives *1835:* And *1849:* How the mean
motives   320| *MS:* nobler passions,— *1835:* passions, *1849:* nobler
aims,   321| *MS:* The cursed lusts I *1849:* The appetites I

May influence me as being mortal still—
Do goad me, drive me on, and fast supplant
My youth's desires. You are no stupid dupe:
325 You find me out! Yes, I had sent for you
To palm these childish lies upon you, Festus!
Laugh—you shall laugh at me!
FESTUS   The past, then, Aureole,
Proves nothing? Is our interchange of love
Yet to begin? Have I to swear I mean
330 No flattery in this speech or that? For you,
Whate'er you say, there is no degradation;
These low thoughts are no inmates of your mind,
Or wherefore this disorder? You are vexed
As much by the intrusion of base views,
335 Familiar to your adversaries, as they
Were troubled should your qualities alight
Amid their murky souls; not otherwise,
A stray wolf which the winter forces down
From our bleak hills, suffices to affright
340 A village in the vales—while foresters
Sleep calm, though all night long the famished troop
Snuff round and scratch against their crazy huts.

322| *MS:* as I am mortal still,—   *1835:* me—as < > still—   *1863:* me as being
mortal   323| *MS:* Are goading me, and fast supplanting all   *1849:* Do goad
me, drive me on, and fast supplant   324| *MS:* desires:——*you* < > dupe,
1835: desires: you < > dupe;   *1849:* you   *1863:* desires. You < > dupe:
325| *MS:* out——yes   *1835:* out. Yes   *1849:* out! Yes   327| *MS:* Laugh,—*you*
< > FESTUS—Dear Aureole, then   *1835:* Laugh—*you* < > FESTUS Dear   *1849:* you
< > FESTUS The past, then, Aureole,   *1863:* Past   *1868:* past   328| *MS:* The
Past is nothing? is our intercourse   *1835:* past < > Is   *1849:* Proves nothing? Is
our interchange of love   329| *MS:* begin—have   *1835:* begin? Have
330| *MS:* this or that? Whatever   *1849:* this speech or that? For you,
331| *MS:* You be, this is no degradation . . these   *1835:* degradation—these   *1849:*
Whate'er you say, there is no degradation,   *1863:* degradation;   332| *MS:*
Unworthy thoughts no < > mind;   *1849:* These low thoughts are no   *1863:*
mind,   333| *MS:* you are troubled   *1835:* You   *1849:* are vexed
334| *MS:* views   *1835:* views,   336| *MS:* Would be should your high
qualities   *1849:* Were troubled should your qualities   337| *MS:* souls: and
even so   *1849:* souls: not otherwise,   *1888:* souls; not   339| *MS:* From the
bleak hills suffices   *1849:* From our bleak hills, suffices   340| *MS:* vales—
—while   *1835:* vales—while   341| *MS:* Sleep sound tho' < > troops   *1835:*
though < > famish'd   *1849:* Sleep calm though < > famished   *1868:* calm,
though   *1888:* troop   342| *MS:* huts:— — —   *1835:* huts: *1863:* huts.

206

These evil thoughts are monsters, and will flee.
PARACELSUS May you be happy, Festus, my own friend!
345 FESTUS Nay, further; the delights you fain would think
The superseders of your nobler aims,
Though ordinary and harmless stimulants,
Will ne'er content you. . . .
PARACELSUS   Hush! I once despised them,
But that soon passes. We are high at first
350 In our demand, nor will abate a jot
Of toil's strict value; but time passes o'er,
And humbler spirits accept what we refuse:
In short, when some such comfort is doled out
As these delights, we cannot long retain
355 Bitter contempt which urges us at first
To hurl it back, but hug it to our breast
And thankfully retire. This life of mine
Must be lived out and a grave thoroughly earned:
I am just fit for that and nought beside.
360 I told you once, I cannot now enjoy,
Unless I deem my knowledge gains through joy;
Nor can I know, but straight warm tears reveal
My need of linking also joy to knowledge:

343| *MS:* evil things are monsters and   *1849:* evil thoughts are monsters, and
345| *MS:* further . . . the § altered to § further—the   *1835:* further; the
346| *MS:* Have superseded nobler aims,— — §written over by § aims,—the harmless
1835: aims, the   *1849:* The superseders of your nobler aims,   347| *MS:* And
ordinary stimulants, will never   *1849:* Though ordinary and harmless
stimulants,   348| *MS:* Content you— — — PARACELSUS Ah, forbear!—I once
despised— — —   *1835:* you . . . PARACELSUS Oh, forbear! I < > despised . . .   *1849:*
Will ne'er content you . . . PARACELSUS Hush! I < > despised them,   349| *MS:*
passes: we   *1863:* passes. We   350| *MS:* demands   *1868:* demand
351| *MS:* Of their strict value . . . but < > o'er   *1835:* value; but   *1849:* Of toil's
strict < > o'er,   352| *MS:* refuse—   *1835:* refuse;   *1863:* refuse:
353| *MS:* short when   *1835:* short, when   354| *MS:* delights— —we   *1853:*
delights—we   *1849:* delights, we   355| *MS:* The bitter   *1868:* Bitter
356| *MS:* back— —but   *1835:* back—but   *1849:* back, but
357| retire:—this   *1835:* retire. This   358| *MS:* earned;—   *1835:* earn'd:
1849: out, and < > earned: *1863:* out and   360| *MS:— —*I told < >
Enjoy   *1835:* I told < > Enjoy,   *1863:* enjoy,   361| *MS:* Knowledge gains
thereby,—   *1835:* knowledge < > thereby;   *1849:* gains through joy;
362| *MS:* Know without warm tears revealing   *1835:* know, without   *1849:* Know,
but straight warm < > reveal   *1863:* know   363| *MS:* The need of linking
some Delight to Knowledge,—   *1835:* delight to knowledge: *1849:* My need of
linking also joy to

So, on I drive, enjoying all I can,
365 And knowing all I can. I speak, of course,
Confusedly; this will better explain—feel here!
Quick beating, is it not?—a fire of the heart
To work off some way, this as well as any.
So, Festus sees me fairly launched; his calm
370 Compassionate look might have disturbed me once,
But now, far from rejecting, I invite
What bids me press the closer, lay myself
Open before him, and be soothed with pity;
I hope, if he command hope, and believe
375 As he directs me—satiating myself
With his enduring love. And Festus quits me
To give place to some credulous disciple
Who holds that God is wise, but Paracelsus
Has his peculiar merits: I suck in
380 That homage, chuckle o'er that admiration,
And then dismiss the fool; for night is come,
And I betake myself to study again,
Till patient searchings after hidden lore
Half wring some bright truth from its prison; my frame

364| *MS:* So on I drive . . . Enjoying < > can   *1835:* drive—enjoying   *1849:*
can,   *1863:* So, on I drive, enjoying   365| *MS:* Knowing < > can:—I   *1835:*
knowing < > can. I   366| *MS:* Confusedly—*this* < > explain . . feel   *1835:*
Confusedly; *this* < > explain—feel   *1849:* this   367| *MS:* not? a fire which
must   *1849:* not?—a fire of the heart   368| *MS:* Be worked off someway < >
any: *1835:* work'd   *1849:* To work < > any!   *1863:* any.   369| *MS:* So
Festus < > launched;—his   *1835:* launch'd; his   *1849:* So, Festus < >
launched   370| *1835:* disturb'd   *1849:* disturbed   371| *MS:* invite it—
—   *1835:* it.   *1849:* invite   372| *MS:* I can lament with him, and lay   *1849:*
What bids me press the closer, lay   373| *MS:* and receive his pity,   *1849:* and
be soothed with pity;   374| *MS:* And hope < > hope—and believe   *1835:*
command hope; and   *1863:* I hope, if   *1868:* command hope, and   375| *MS:*
What he would have me;—satiating   *1835:* me—satiating   *1849:* As he directs
me—satiating   376| *MS:* love:—and he shall leave me   *1835:* love: and
1849: and Festus quits me   *1863:* love. And   379| *MS:* merits——I   *1835:*
merits. I   *1863:* merits: I   380| *MS:* His homage—chuckle o'er his
admiration   *1835:* homage, chuckle < > admiration,   *1849:* That homage < > o'er
that admiration,   381| *MS:* dismiss him in his turn:—night comes,   *1835:* turn:
night   *1849:* dismiss the fool; for night is come,   *1863:* come.   *1889:* come,
382| *MS:* And I shall give myself to painful study   *1835:* study;   *1849:* And I
betake myself to study again,   383| *MS:* And patient searchings < > lore,
1835: lore   *1849:* Till patient searchings   384| *MS:*—Shall wring   *1835:*
Shall   *1849:* Half wring

385 Trembles, my forehead's veins swell out, my hair
Tingles for triumph. Slow and sure the morn
Shall break on my pent room and dwindling lamp
And furnace dead, and scattered earths and ores,
When, with a failing heart and throbbing brow,
390 I must review my captured truth, sum up
Its value, trace what ends to what begins,
Its present power with its eventual bearings,
Latent affinities, the views it opens,
And its full length in perfecting my scheme.
395 I view it sternly circumscribed, cast down
From the high place my fond hopes yielded it,
Proved worthless—which, in getting, yet had cost
Another wrench to this fast-falling frame.
Then, quick, the cup to quaff, that chases sorrow!
400 I lapse back into youth, and take again
My fluttering pulse for evidence that God
Means good to me, will make my cause his own.
See! I have cast off this remorseless care
Which clogged a spirit born to soar so free,

385| *MS:* Shall tremble, and my thin lips swell—my   *1835:* swell, my   *1849:*
Trembles, my forehead's veins swell out, my   **386|**   *MS:* Tingle—and all for
triumph: and the   *1835:* Tingle, and   *1849:* Tingles for triumph! Slow and sure
the   *1868:* triumph. Slow   **387|**   *1835:* room, and   *1863:* room and
388| *MS:* And scattered papers and unfinished scrawls,   *1835:* scatter'd papers, and
unfinish'd scrawls;   *1849:* And furnace dead, and scattered earths and ores,   *1863:*
ores;   *1889:* ores,   **389|**   *MS:* And with < > brow   *1849:* When, with < >
brow,   **390–393|**   I shall review < > truth—and trace / Its end and consequence,
its further bearings, / Its true affinities   *1835:* captur'd truth, and   *1849:* I must
review my captured truth, sum up / Its value, trace what ends to what begins, / Its
present power with its eventual bearings, / Latent affinities   **394|**   *MS:* The
length it goes in < > Scheme,   *1835:* scheme,   *1849:* And its full length in < >
scheme;   *1863:* scheme.   **395|**   *MS:* And view it < > circumscribed—cast
1849: I view < > circumscribed, cast   **396|**   *MS:* it,—   *1835:* it,
397| *MS:* worthless— § above § which in getting yet   *1835:* worthless—which
1849: which, in getting, yet   **398|**   *MS:* frame;—   *1863:* frame.
399| *MS:* And I shall quaff the cup that < > sorrow   *1849:* The, quick, the cup to
quaff, that < > sorrow!   *1868:* chaces   *1888:* chases   **400–401|**   *MS:* And lapse
< > youth again—and take / My   *1835:* again, and   *1849:* I lapse < > youth, and
take again / Mere hopes of bliss for proofs that bliss will be, / —My < > pulse, for
1863: again / My   *1868:* pulse for   **402|**   *MS:* me, and see my hopes come
true,   *1849:* me, will make my cause his own;   *1863:* His own.   *1868:* his
403| *MS:* And flee away from this   *1849:* See! I have cast off this   **404|**   *MS:*
clogs < > free   *1835:* free,   *1849:* clogged

405 And my dim chamber has become a tent,
Festus is sitting by me, and his Michal . . .
Why do you start? I say, she listening here,
(For yonder—Würzburg through the orchard-bough!)
Motions as though such ardent words should find
410 No echo in a maiden's quiet soul,
But her pure bosom heaves, her eyes fill fast
With tears, her sweet lips tremble all the while!
Ha, ha!
FESTUS It seems, then, you expect to reap
No unreal joy from this your present course,
415 But rather , . .
PARACELSUS Death! To die! I owe that much
To what, at least, I was. I should be sad
To live contented after such a fall,
To thrive and fatten after such reverse!
The whole plan is a makeshift, but will last
420 My time.
FESTUS   And you have never mused and said,
"I had a noble purpose, and the strength
To compass it; but I have stopped half-way,
And wrongly given the first-fruits of my toil
To objects little worthy of the gift.
425 Why linger round them still? why clench my fault?

405| *MS:* chamber shall become   *1849:* chamber has become   **406–409**| *MS:*
And Festus shall sit by me, and sweet Michal / Shall make as tho' my ardent   *1835:*
though   *1849:* Festus is sitting by me, and his Michal . . . / Why do you start? I say,
she listening here, / (For yonder's Würzburg through the orchard-boughs) Motions as
though such ardent   *1868:* yonder—Würzburg < > orchard-bough!)   **410**| *MS:*
soul—   *1849:* soul,   **411**| *MS:* bosom shall heave   *1849:* bosom heaves,
her   **412**| *MS:* her lips shall tremble, all   *1835:* tremble all   *1849:* her sweet
lips tremble   **413**| *MS:* FESTUS—It seems then   *1835:* FESTUS It < > then you
1849: seems, then, you   **414**| *MS:* course;   *1849:* course,   **415**| *MS:* That
you expect . . . PARACELSUS To   *1849:* But rather . . . PARACELSUS Death! To
416| *MS:* what I *was*, at least——I   *1835: was* at least. I   *1849:* what, at least, I
was. I   **417**| *MS:* fall——   *1835:* fall—   *1863:* fall,   **420**| *MS:* time:
FESTUS   *1835:* time . . . FESTUS   *1849:* time. FESTUS   **421**| *MS:* purpose—and
1835: purpose, and   *1849:* purpose, and full strength   *1863:* and the strength
422| *MS:* halfway   *1835:* stopp'd half-way,   *1849:* stopped   **423**| *MS:* And
have bestowed the first fruits   *1835:* bestow'd   *1849:* And wrongly give the   *1863:*
given the firstfruits   *1888:* first-fruits   **424**| *MS:* On objects < > worthy to
receive them: *1849:* To objects < > worthy of the gift: *1863:* gift.

Why seek for consolation in defeat,
In vain endeavours to derive a beauty
From ugliness? why seek to make the most
Of what no power can change, nor strive instead
430 With mighty effort to redeem the past
And, gathering up the treasures thus cast down,
To hold a steadfast course till I arrive
At their fit destination and my own?"
You have never pondered thus?
PARACELSUS   Have I, you ask?
435 Often at midnight, when most fancies come,
Would some such airy project visit me:
But ever at the end . . . or will you hear
The same thing in a tale, a parable?
You and I, wandering over the world wide,
440 Chance to set foot upon a desert coast.
Just as we cry, "No human voice before
Broke the inveterate silence of these rocks!"
—Their querulous echo startles us; we turn:
What ravaged structure still looks o'er the sea?
445 Some characters remain, too! While we read,
The sharp salt wind, impatient for the last
Of even this record, wistfully comes and goes,
Or sings what we recover, mocking it.
This is the record; and my voice, the wind's.   [*He sings.*

450   Over the sea our galleys went,
        With cleaving prows in order brave

426| MS: defeat   *1835:* defeat—   *1863:* defeat,   **429|**   MS: change, in place
of striving   *1849:* change, nor strive instead   **430|**   MS: past,   *1863:* Past
1868: past   **431|**   MS: To gather < > treasures I cast   *1849:* And, gathering
< > treasures thus cast   **432|**   MS: And hold < > 'till   *1849:* To hold   *1863:*
till   **433|**   MS: own:"   *1835:* destination—and my own."   *1849:* destination,
and my own?"   *1863:* destination and   **434–450|**   MS: this? / § space § /
PARACELSUS (sings) Over < > went,—   *1835:* ponder'd thus?   **434|**   *1849:*
pondered thus? PARACELSUS Have I, you ask?   **435–449|**   § added in 1849;
variants from 1889 §   **438–439|**   *1849:* parable? / It cannot prove more tedious;
listen then! / You   *1863:* parable? / You   **440|**   *1849:* coast: *1863:*
coast.   **446|**   *1849:* sharp, salt   *1863:* sharp salt   **449–450|**   *1849:* wind's /
§ space § / (He sings.) / Over   *1863:* wind's. [He sings. § space § / Over
451| MS:—Cleaving < > brave,   *1835:* Cleaving   *1849:* With cleaving   *1888:*
brave

211

To a speeding wind and a bounding wave,
    A gallant armament:
    Each bark built out of a forest-tree
455   Left leafy and rough as first it grew,
    And nailed all over the gaping sides,
    Within and without, with black bull-hides,
    Seethed in fat and suppled in flame,
    To bear the playful billows' game:
460   So, each good ship was rude to see,
    Rude and bare to the outward view,
        But each upbore a stately tent
    Where cedar pales in scented row
    Kept out the flakes of the dancing brine,
465   And an awning drooped the mast below,
    In fold on fold of the purple fine,
    That neither noontide nor starshine
    Nor moonlight cold which maketh mad,
        Might pierce the regal tenement.
470   When the sun dawned, oh, gay and glad
    We set the sail and plied the oar;
    But when the night-wind blew like breath,
    For joy of one day's voyage more,
    We sang together on the wide sea,
475   Like men at peace on a peaceful shore;
    Each sail was loosed to the wind so free,
    Each helm made sure by the twilight star,

452| MS: With speeding < > wave—   1849: To a speeding   1863: wave,
453| MS:—A < > Armament   1835: armament: 454| 1835: forest-tree,
1888: forest-tree   455| MS: grew   1835: grew,   456| MS: sides   1835:
nail'd < > sides,   1849: nailed   457| MS: without with black-bull hides
1835: without, with < > hides,   1863: black bull-hides,   458–460| MS: flame,—
/ So each   1835: Seeth'd < > flame;   1849: Seethed < > flame, / To bear the
playful billows' game; / So   1863: game: / So, each   461| MS: to outward
view,—   1835: view,   1849: to the outward   462| MS: tent:—   1835: tent:
1849: tent;   1863: tent   463| MS: Cedar-pales   1849: Where cedar-
pales   1868: cedarpales   464| MS: flakes of dancing brine;—   1835: brine:
1849: of the dancing   1863: brine,   465–467| MS: An < > below, / That < >
noon-tide, nor star-shine,   1835: droop'd < > / < > noon-tide nor   1849: And an
< > drooped < >· below, / In fold on fold of the purple fine, That < > noon-tide,
nor   1863: noontide nor star-shine   1868: starshine   470| MS: dawned, gay
1835: dawn'd   1849: dawned, oh, gay   473| MS: more   1835: more,
474| MS: sea   1835: sea,   475| MS: show;—   1835: shore;   477| MS:
twilight-star,   1835: twilight star,

And in a sleep as calm as death,
We, the voyagers from afar,
480   Lay stretched along, each weary crew
In a circle round its wondrous tent
Whence gleamed soft light and curled rich scent,
And with light and perfume, music too:
So the stars wheeled round, and the darkness past,
485   And at morn we started beside the mast,
And still each ship was sailing fast.

Now, one morn, land appeared—a speck
Dim trembling betwixt sea and sky:
"Avoid it," cried our pilot, "check
490   The shout, restrain the eager eye!"
But the heaving sea was black behind
For many a night and many a day,
And land, though but a rock, drew nigh;
So, we broke the cedar pales away,
495   Let the purple awning flap in the wind,
And a statue bright was on every deck!
We shouted, every man of us,
And steered right into the harbour thus,
With pomp and pæan glorious.

478| *MS:* death   *1835:* death,   **479|**   *1849:* the strangers from   *1863:* the
voyagers from   **480|** *MS:* stretched—each   *1835:* stretch'd   *1849:* stretched
along, each   **481|** *MS:* round their § cancelled by § its wondrous tent   *1835:*
tent,   *1863:* tent   **482|** *MS:* scent   *1835:* gleam'd < > curl'd < > scent,
1849: gleamed < > curled   **483–485|** *MS:* too— — — / At morn, they
§ cancelled by § we   *1835:* too: / At morn we   *1849:* too: / So the stars wheeled
round, and the darkness past, / And at   **486|** *MS:* fast!   *1835:* fast! / § no
space §   *1849:* fast! / § space §   *1868:* fast.   **487|** *MS:* Now one more land
appeared!— —a   *1835:* appeared!—a   *1849:* One morn, the land   *1863:* Now, one
morn, land   **488|** *MS:* § indented § sky:—   *1835:* sky—   *1849:* § not
indented §   *1849:* sky: **489|** *MS:*—Not so the Isles our voyage must find
1835: Not < > isles   *1849:* Avoid it, cried our pilot, check   *1863:* "Avoid it," cried
< > pilot, "check   **490|** *MS:* Should meet our longing eye: *1835:* eye;   *1849:*
The shout, restrain the longing eye!   *1863:* the eager eye!"   **492|** *MS:* Many
1849: For many   **493|** *MS:* tho' < > rock, was nigh,   *1835:* though < >
nigh;   *1849:* rock, drew nigh;   **494|** *MS:* So we < > cedar-pales   *1835:* cedar
pales   *1863:* So, we   **495|** *MS:* And let the purple flap   *1835:* wind: *1849:*
Let the purple awning flap < > wind,   **498|**   *1835:* steer'd   *1849:* steered

A hundred shapes of lucid stone!
All day we built its shrine for each,
A shrine of rock for every one,
Nor paused till in the westering sun
We sat together on the beach
To sing because our task was done.
When lo! what shouts and merry songs!
What laughter all the distance stirs!
A loaded raft with happy throngs
Of gentle islanders!
"Our isles are just at hand," they cried,
"Like cloudlets faint in even sleeping;
Our temple-gates are opened wide,
Our olive-groves thick shade are keeping
For these majestic forms"—they cried.
Oh, then we awoke with sudden start
From our deep dream, and knew, too late,
How bare the rock, how desolate,
Which had received our precious freight:
Yet we called out—"Depart!
Our gifts, once given, must here abide.
Our work is done; we have no heart

500| *MS:* An < > shapes § written over by § Shapes   *1835:* shapes   *1863:*
A   **501|** *MS:* each—   *1863:* each,   **502|** *MS:*—A < > one,—   *1835:* A
< > one—   *1863:* one,   **503|** *MS:* 'till   *1835:* till   *1849:* paused we till
1868: paused till   **504|** *MS:* sate   *1863:* sat   **505|** *MS:* done . . .   *1835:*
sing, because < > done;   *1863:* sing because < > done.   **508|** *MS:* raft and
happy   *1835:* raft, and   *1849:* What raft comes loaded with its throngs   *1863:* A
loaded raft with happy throngs   **509|** *MS:* Islanders!   *1835:* islanders!   *1849:*
islanders?   *1863:* islanders!   **510|** *1835:* cried;   *1849:* The isles   *1863:* Our
isles < > cried,   **511|** *MS:* sleeping,   *1849:* faint at even   *1863:* faint in
even sleeping;   *1888:* sleeping; § ; probable; upper half only printed §   *1889:*
sleeping   **512|** *1835:* open'd   *1849:* opened   **513|** *MS:* olive groves
1835: olive-groves   **514|** *MS:* Forms," they cried: *1835:* forms < > cried.
1849: For the lucid shapes you bring"—they   *1863:* For these majestic
forms"—they   **515|** *MS:* Then we   *1849:* Oh, then   **516|** *MS:* knew too
late   *1835:* knew, too late,   *1849:* dream; we knew   *1863:* dream, and knew
518| *MS:* freight   *1835:* freight: *1849:* To which we had flung our   *1863:* Which
had received our   **519|** *MS:*—Yet < > out "Depart!   *1835:* Yet we call'd
out—"Depart!   *1849:* called   **520|** *MS:* abide!   *1835:* abide: *1863:*
abide.   **521|** *MS:* § not indented § done—we   *1835:* § indented § done; we

To mar our work,"—we cried.

FESTUS In truth?

PARACELSUS   Nay, wait: all this in tracings faint
On rugged stones strewn here and there, but piled
525 In order once: then follows—mark what follows!
"The sad rhyme of the men who proudly clung
To their first fault, and withered in their pride."
FESTUS Come back then, Aureole; as you fear God, come!
This is foul sin; come back! Renounce the past,
530 Forswear the future; look for joy no more,
But wait death's summons amid holy sights,
And trust me for the event—peace, if not joy.
Return with me to Einsiedeln, dear Aureole!
PARACELSUS No way, no way! it would not turn to good.
535 A spotless child sleeps on the flowering moss—
'Tis well for him; but when a sinful man,
Envying such slumber, may desire to put
His guilt away, shall he return at once
To rest by lying there? Our sires knew well
540 (Spite of the grave discoveries of their sons)
The fitting course for such: dark cells, dim lamps,

---

⁵²²| MS: § indented § work;" we cried! 1835: § not indented § work," we cried.
1849: work, though vain"—we 1863: work,"—we ^{523–524}| MS: truth?..
PARACELSUS nay wait,—all < > faint / On < > stones,—strewn < > there—but
piled 1835: truth? PARACELSUS Nay, wait: all < > / < > stones, strewn < > there,
but 1849: faint / May still be read on that deserted rock, / On 1863: stones
strewn 1868: faint / On ⁵²⁵| MS: what follows; — — — 1835: once; then
< > what follows— 1863: once: then < > what follows: 1868: what
follows! ⁵²⁶| MS: § in italics § Men 1835: men 1849: § in roman §
⁵²⁷| MS: § in italics § pride!" 1835: wither'd 1849: § in roman § withered
1868: pride." ⁵²⁸| 1835: back, then 1868: back then ⁵²⁹| MS:
sin—come back—renounce 1835: sin; come back: renounce 1863: back. Renounce
the Past, 1868: back! Renounce the past. ⁵³⁰| MS: future . . . look 1835:
future; look 1863: Future < > more 1868: future 1888: more, ⁵³¹| MS:
wait for death amid all peaceful sights 1835: sights, 1849: wait death's summons
amid holy sights, ⁵³²| MS: went——peace if not joy!— 1835: event—peace, if
not joy! 1863: joy. ⁵³³| 1835: Aureole. 1863: Aureole! ⁵³⁴| MS: No
way, no way!——it < > good— — 1835: good. 1863: No way, no way! it
⁵³⁶| MS: Tis < > him; and one deformed by sin, 1835: 'Tis < > deform'd 1849:
him; but when a sinful man, ⁵³⁷| MS: slumber may 1835: slumber,
may ⁵³⁸| MS: away . . . shall 1835: away: shall 1849: away, shall
⁵³⁹| MS: To boyhood's carelessness? our 1835: Our 1849: To rest by lying there?
Our ⁵⁴¹| MS: such——dark 1835: such—dark 1849: such; dark 1888:
such: dark

215

A stone floor one may writhe on like a worm:
No mossy pillow blue with violets!
FESTUS I see no symptom of these absolute
545 And tyrannous passions. You are calmer now.
This verse-making can purge you well enough
Without the terrible penance you describe.
You love me still: the lusts you fear will never
Outrage your friend. To Einsiedeln, once more!
550 Say but the word!
PARACELSUS   No, no; those lusts forbid:
They crouch, I know, cowering with half-shut eye
Beside,you; 'tis their nature. Thrust yourself
Between them and their prey; let some fool style me
Or king or quack, it matters not—then try
555 Your wisdom, urge them to forego their treat!
No, no; learn better and look deeper, Festus!
If you knew how a devil sneers within me
While you are talking now of this, now that,
As though we differed scarcely save in trifles!
560 FESTUS Do we so differ? True, change must proceed,
Whether for good or ill; keep from me, which!
Do not confide all secrets: I was born

542| MS: stone-floor < > worm . . . 1835: stone floor < > worm; 1863:
worm: 543| MS: pillow, blue 1835: violets. 1849: violets! 1863: pillow
blue 544| MS: these overbearing 1849: these absolute 545| MS:
passions:—you < > now:— 1835: passions. You < > now. 546| 1835:
enough, 1863: enough 547| MS: describe;— 1835: describe.
548| MS: still——the § written over by § still—the 1835: still: the 1849: fear,
will 1888: fear will 549| MS: friend: to 1835: friend. To 550| MS:
No, No: those < > forbid; 1835: No, no; those < > forbid: 551| MS:
know,—cowering 1835: know, cowering 552| MS: you—'tis 1835: you;
'tis 553| MS: prey . . . let 1835: prey; let 554| MS: King or Quack
< > not—§ above § , and let 1835: king or quack < > not, and 1849: and try
1888: not—then try 555| MS: wisdom urge 1849: wisdom then, at urging
their retreat! 1863: wisdom, urge them to forego their treat! 556| MS: No,
no: learn < > Festus: 1835: no, no; learn < > Festus. 1849: Festus!
558| MS: that 1835: that, 559| MS: tho' 1835: though we differ'd 1849:
differed 560| MS: I know what you would say:—all change proceeds, 1835:
say: all 1849: Do we so differ? True, change must proceed, 561-562| MS:
keep that from me! Do not confide those secrets 1849: keep from me, which! / God
made you and knows what you may become— / Do not confide all secrets 1863:
which! / Do

To hope, and you . . .

PARACELSUS   To trust: you know the fruits!

FESTUS Listen: I do believe, what you call trust

565 Was self-delusion at the best: for, see!

So long as God would kindly pioneer

A path for you, and screen you from the world,

Procure you full exemption from man's lot,

Man's common hopes and fears, on the mere pretext

570 Of your engagement in his service—yield you

A limitless licence, make you God, in fact,

And turn your slave—you were content to say

Most courtly praises! What is it, at last,

But selfishness without example? None

575 Could trace God's will so plain as you, while yours

Remained implied in it; but now you fail,

And we, who prate about that will, are fools!

In short, God's service is established here

As he determines fit, and not your way,

580 And this you cannot brook. Such discontent

Is weak. Renounce all creatureship at once!

Affirm an absolute right to have and use

Your energies; as though the rivers should say—

563| *MS:* hope,—and < > trust: you § altered in pencil to § trust:—you < > the
rest. *1835:* hope, and < > trust: you   *1849:* the fruits!   **564|** *MS:* believe
the trust you boast,   *1835:* boast   *1849:* believe, what you call trust
565| *MS:* best; so long   *1835:* best. So   *1849:* Was self-reliance at the best: for,
see!   *1863:* Was self-delusion at   **566|** *MS:* As < > pioneer your path,—
1835: path—   *1849:* So long as < > pioneer   **567|** *MS:* Would undertake to
screen   *1835:* world—   *1849:* A path for you, and screen < > world,
568| *MS:* from their lot   *1835:* lot,   *1849:* from man's lot,   **569|** *MS:* The
common   *1849:* Man's common   **570|** *MS:* service,—yield   *1835:*
service—yield   *1863:* His   *1868:* his   **571|** *MS:* license . . . make you God
in   *1835:* license—make you God, in   *1849:* license, make   *1863:* license
572| *MS:* slave— § above § , you   *1835:* slave—you   **573|** *MS:* praises: what is
it at last   *1849:* praises! What is it, at last,   **574|** *MS:* example?—None
1835: example? None   **576|** *MS:* it—but *now,* you   *1835:* Remain'd < > it;
but *now* you   *1849:* Remained < > now   **577|** *MS:* we who < > will are
fools;—   *1835:* fools.   *1849:* we, who < > will, are fools!   **578|** *MS:* service
must be ordered here   *1835:* order'd   *1849:* service is established here
579| *1849:* He   *1868:* he   **580|** *MS:* brook: such   *1849:* brook! Such   *1863:*
brook. Such   **581|** *MS:* weak:—renounce all creatureship—affirm   *1835:* weak.
Renounce   *1849:* creatureship at once!   **582|** *MS:* An < > and to dispose
1849: Affirm an < > and use   **583|** *MS:* energies—as tho' < > say   *1835:*
energies; as though < > say—

217

"We rush to the ocean; what have we to do
585 With feeding streamlets, lingering in the vales,
Sleeping in lazy pools?" Set up that plea,
That will be bold at least!
PARACELSUS   'Tis like enough.
The serviceable spirits are those, no doubt,
The East produces: lo, the master bids,—
590 They wake, raise terraces and garden-grounds
In one night's space; and, this done, straight begin
Another century's sleep, to the great praise
Of him that framed them wise and beautiful,
Till a lamp's rubbing, or some chance akin,
595 Wake them again. I am of different mould.
I would have soothed my lord, and slaved for him
And done him service past my narrow bond,
And thus I get rewarded for my pains!
Beside, 'tis vain to talk of forwarding
600 God's glory otherwise; this is alone
The sphere of its increase, as far as men
Increase it; why, then, look beyond this sphere?
We are his glory; and if we be glorious,

584| *MS:* ocean—what   *1835:* ocean; what   585| *MS:* vales   *1835:* vales,
1849: the marshes,   *1863:* the vales,   586| *MS:* plea.   *1835:* plea,
587| *MS:* least. PARACELSUS Tis   *1835:* 'Tis   *1849:* least! PARACELSUS Perhaps,
perhaps!   *1863:* PARACELSUS 'Tis like enough!   *1868:* enough.   588| *1849:*
Your only servicable spirits are those   *1863:* The serviceable < > those, no
doubt,   589| *MS:* produces;—lo, the Master nods—   *1835:* east produces. Lo,
the master nods,   *1849:* produces:—lo   *1863:* The East produces: lo   *1888:* master
bids,—   590| *MS:* And they raise   *1849:* terraces, spread garden-grounds
1863: terraces and garden-grounds   *1888:* They wake, raise   591| *MS:*
space,—and this done, straight relapse   *1835:* space; and, this   *1849:* straight
begin   592| *MS:* Into a century's sleep— — —to the great honour   *1835:* sleep,
to   *1849:* Another century's < > great praise   593| *MS:* beautiful;   *1835:*
beautiful,   594| *MS:* akin   *1835:* akin,   595| *MS:* Release their limbs:—
—I   *1835:* limbs. I   *1849:* Wake them again. I   596| *MS:* Lord and   *1835:*
Lord, and < > him,   *1849:* lord   *1888:* him   599| *MS:* Beside 'tis   *1835:*
Beside, 'tis   600| *MS:* His glory otherwise—*this* is the sphere   *1835:* otherwise;
this   *1849:* God's glory < > this is alone   601| *MS:* Alone of < > far as we
1849: The sphere of < > far as men   602| *MS:* Can be concerned, or I am
much deceived;— —   *1835:* concern'd < > deceived: *1849:* Increase it; why, then,
look beyond this sphere?   603| *MS:* glory, and if *we* be glorious   *1835:* glory;
and < > glorious,   *1849:* We are His < > we   *1868:* his

Is not the thing achieved?

FESTUS   Shall one like me
605 Judge hearts like yours? Though years have changed you much,
And you have left your first love, and retain
Its empty shade to veil your crooked ways,
Yet I still hold that you have honoured God.
And who shall call your course without reward?
610 For, wherefore this repining at defeat
Had triumph ne'er inured you to high hopes?
I urge you to forsake the life you curse,
And what success attends me?—simply talk
Of passion, weakness and remorse; in short,
615 Anything but the naked truth—you choose
This so-despised career, and cheaply hold
My happiness, or rather other men's.
Once more, return!

PARACELSUS   And quickly. John the thief
Has pilfered half my secrets by this time:
620 And we depart by daybreak. I am weary,
I know not how; not even the wine-cup soothes
My brain to-night . . .
Do you not thoroughly despise me, Festus?
No flattery! One like you needs not be told
625 We live and breathe deceiving and deceived.

605| *MS:* your's?——tho   *1835:* yours? Though   **607|**   *MS:* to gild your
1849: to veil your   **608|**   *MS: have* < > God—   *1835:* honour'd God;   *1849:*
have honoured   *1863:* God.   **609|**   *MS:* And has your course been all without
1849: And who shall call your course without   **610|** *MS:* For wherefore < >
defeat,   *1849:* For, wherefore   *1868:* defeat   **612|**   *MS:*——I < > curse
1835: I < > curse,   **613|**   *1835:* me? simply   *1849:* me?—simply
614| *MS:* weakness, and remorse——in short   *1835:* remorse; in short,   *1863:*
weakness and   **615|**   *MS:* Any thing   *1835:* truth: you   *1863:* Anything < >
truth—you   **616|**   *MS:* so despised   *1835:* so-despised   *1849:* and rather
praise   *1863:* and cheaply hold   **617|**   *MS:* Men's:——   *1835:* men's.   *1849:*
Than take my happiness   *1863:* My happiness, or rather other   **618|**   *MS:* more
return! PARACELSUS—And quickly—Oporinus   *1835:* PARACELSUS And quickly.
Oporinus   *1849:* And soon. Oporinus   *1863:* And quickly. Oporinus   *1888:* quickly.
John the thief   **619|**   *MS:* time—   *1835:* pilfer'd   *1849:* pilfered < >
time: **620|**   *MS:* day-break:—I am weary   *1835:* day-break. I am weary,
621| *MS:* how——not   *1835:* how; not   **622|**   *MS:* to-night———   *1835:* to-
night . . .   **624|**   *MS:*——No flattery! . . one   *1835:* No flattery! One   *1849:*
you, needs   *1863:* you needs   **625|** *MS:* and deceived———   *1835:* deceived.

Do you not scorn me from your heart of hearts,
Me and my cant, each petty subterfuge,
My rhymes and all this frothy shower of words,
My glozing self-deceit, my outward crust
630 Of lies which wrap, as tetter, morphew, furfair
Wrapt the sound flesh?—so, see you flatter not!
Even God flatters: but my friend, at least,
Is true. I would depart, secure henceforth
Against all further insult, hate and wrong
635 From puny foes; my one friend's scorn shall brand me:
No fear of sinking deeper!
FESTUS   No, dear Aureole!
No, no; I came to counsel faithfully.
There are old rules, made long ere we were born,
By which I judge you. I, so fallible,
640 So infinitely low beside your mighty
Majestic spirit!—even I can see
You own some higher law than ours which call
Sin, what is no sin—weakness, what is strength.
But I have only these, such as they are,
645 To guide me; and I blame you where they bid,

626| *MS:* of hearts? *1863:* of hearts, **627|** *MS:* Me—and my cant—my petty subterfuges— *1835:* Me and *1863:* cant, my < > subterfuges, *1868:* cant, each petty subterfuge, **628|** *MS:* These rhymes *1835:* rhymes, and < > words— *1849:* My rhymes *1863:* rhymes and < > words, **629|** *1835:* self-deceit—my *1863:* self-deceit, my **630|** *MS:* tetter morphew furfair *1835:* lies; which wrap, as tetter, morphew, furfair *1863:* lies which **631|** *MS:* Wrap < > flesh . . so see < > not!— *1835:* flesh?—so < > not! *1849:* so, see *1888:* Wrapt **632|** *MS:* flatters— —but § written over by § flatters!—but *1835:* flatters! but *1849:* Why, even *1863:* Even *1868:* flatters: but **633|** *MS:* true: I < > depart secure *1835:* true. I < > depart, secure **634|** *1835:* hate, and *1863:* hate and **635|** *MS:* foes: my < > me! *1835:* me— *1863:* foes; my **636|** *MS:* deeper!—FESTUS *1835:* deeper. FESTUS *1849:* deeper! FESTUS **637|** *MS:* No, No—I < > faithfully:— — *1835:* No, no; I < > faithfully: *1863:* faithfully. **638|** *MS:* rules made < > born *1835:* rules, made < > born, **639|** *MS:* you—I, so fallible *1835:* you. I, so fallible, **640|** *1849:* your spirit *1863:* beside your mighty, *1868:* mighty **641|** *MS:* spirit:— — —even *1835:* spirit—even *1849:* Mighty, majestic!—even *1863:* Majestic spirit!—even **642|** *MS:* law— —they make that out *1835:* law. They *1849:* law than ours which call *1863:* calls *1868:* call **643|** *MS:* Sin—which is no sin— —weakness—which is strength, *1835:* Sin which < > sin—weakness which is strength; *1849:* Sin, what is < > weakness, what is strength; *1863:* strength. **644|** *MS:* are *1835:* are, **645|** *MS:* me—§ above §, and < > bid *1835:* me; and < > bid, *1849:* they blame, *1863:* they bid,

Only so long as blaming promises
To win peace for your soul: the more, that sorrow
Has fallen on me of late, and they have helped me
So that I faint not under my distress.
650 But wherefore should I scruple to avow
In spite of all, as brother judging brother,
Your fate is most inexplicable to me?
And should you perish without recompense
And satisfaction yet—too hastily
655 I have relied on love: you may have sinned,
But you have loved. As a mere human matter—
As I would have God deal with fragile men
In the end—I say that you will triumph yet!
PARACELSUS Have you felt sorrow, Festus?—'tis because
660 You love me. Sorrow, and sweet Michal yours!
Well thought on: never let her know this last
Dull winding-up of all: these miscreants dared
Insult me—me she loved:—so, grieve her not!
FESTUS Your ill success can little grieve her now.
665 PARACELSUS Michal is dead! pray Christ we do not craze!
FESTUS Aureole, dear Aureole, look not on me thus!
Fool, fool! this is the heart grown sorrow-proof—

646| *MS:* As long as any chance remains of winning   *1849:* Only so long as blaming
promises   **647|** *MS:* Your troubled soul to peace . . the more that   *1835:* peace;
the   *1849:* To win peace for your soul; the more, that   *1863:* soul: the
648| *1835:* help'd   *1849:* helped   **649|** *MS:* distress: *1835:* distress.
650| *MS:* to confess   *1849:* to avow   **651|** *MS:* That spite   *1835:* That,
spite   *1849:* In spite   **652|** *MS:* me: *1835:* fate to me is most inexplicable:
1863: inexplicable?   *1888:* fate is most inexplicable to me?   **653|** *MS:* perish
yet without reward   *1835:* reward—   *1849:* perish without recompense
654| *MS:*—Some great reward—I have too   *1835:* Some   *1849:* And satisfaction
yet—too   **655|** *MS:* Relied on love's effect . . you < > sinned   *1835:* effect.
You < > sinn'd,   *1849:* I have relied on love: you < > sinned,   **656|** *MS:*
loved: as < > matter,   *1849:* loved. As < > matter—   **657|** *MS:*—As < >
Men   *1835:* As < > men   **658|** *MS:* end . . I   *1835:* end—I   **659|** *MS:*
You have felt < > Festus? 'tis   *1835:* Have you felt < > Festus? 'tis   *1849:*
Festus?—'tis   **660|** *MS:* me——sorrow < > your's?   *1835:* me. Sorrow < >
yours!   **661|** *MS:* on . . never   *1835:* on; never   *1868:* on: never
662| *MS:* winding up of all—these   *1835:* winding-up of all: these   **663|** *MS:*
loved;—so grieve   *1835:* loved; so < > not.   *1863:* loved: so, grieve   *1868:*
loved:—so   **664|** *MS:* now— — —   *1835:* now.   **665|** *MS:* dead!——pray
§ written over by § dead!—pray   *1835:* dead! pray   **666|** *MS:* Aureole——dear
Aureole— § above §. look < > thus!— —   *1835:* Aureole, dear Aureole, look < >
thus!   **667|** *MS:* Fool,—fool < > sorrow-proof!—   *1835:* Fool, fool < > sorrow-
proof—

I cannot bear those eyes.

PARACELSUS   Nay, really dead?

FESTUS 'Tis scarce a month.

PARACELSUS   Stone dead!—then you have laid her

670 Among the flowers ere this. Now, do you know,
I can reveal a secret which shall comfort
Even you. I have no julep, as men think,
To cheat the grave; but a far better secret.
Know, then, you did not ill to trust your love

675 To the cold earth: I have thought much of it:
For I believe we do not wholly die.

FESTUS Aureole!

PARACELSUS   Nay, do not laugh; there is a reason
For what I say: I think the soul can never
Taste death. I am, just now, as you may see,

680 Very unfit to put so strange a thought
In an intelligible dress of words;
But take it as my trust, she is not dead.

FESTUS But not on this account alone? you surely,
—Aureole, you have believed this all along?

685 PARACELSUS And Michal sleeps among the roots and dews,
While I am moved at Basil, and full of schemes
For Nuremberg, and hoping and despairing,
As though it mattered how the farce plays out,
So it be quickly played. Away, away!

668| *MS:* eyes;—— PARACELSUS   *1835:* eyes. PARACELSUS   **669|** *MS:* a year—
— PARACELSUS Stone-dead? then   *1835:* year . . . PARACELSUS Stone dead! then
1849: a month . . . PARACELSUS dead!—then   *1863:* month. PARACELSUS
670| *MS:* this——now   *1835:* this . . . Now   *1849:* this. Now   **672|** *MS:* you
. . I < > julep as they think   *1835:* you. I < > julep, as < > think,   *1849:* as men
think,   **673|** *MS:* grave—but < > secret;——   *1835:* grave; < > secret.
674| *MS:* Know then   *1863:* Know, then   **675|** *MS:* earth——I < > it—
1835: earth: *1849:* it: **676|** *MS:* die:—   *1835:* die.   **677|** *MS:*
Aureole . . . PARACELSUS Nay < > laugh—there   *1835:* laugh; there   *1863:* Aureole!
PARACELSUS   **678|** *MS:* say—I   *1835:* say: I   **679|** *MS:* death——I am
just < > see   *1835:* death. I am, just < > see,   **681|** *MS:* words———
1835: words;   **682|** *MS:* dead!   *1835:* dead.   **683|** *MS:* alone? O you
surely . .   *1835:* alone? you surely,   **684|** *MS:* . . . Aureole   *1835:* Aureole
1849:—Aureole   **685|** *MS:*——And   *1835:* And   **686|** *MS:* and
wondering   *1849:* and full of schemes   **687|** *MS:* With Nuremburg < >
despairing   *1835:* Nuremberg < > despairing,   *1849:* For Nuremberg
688| *MS:* tho' < > out   *1835:* though it matter'd < > out,   *1849:* mattered
689| *MS:* played——Away, Away!   *1835:* play'd. Away, away!   *1849:* played

690 Have your will, rabble! while we fight the prize,
Troop you in safety to the snug back-seats
And leave a clear arena for the brave
About to perish for your sport!—Behold!

690| *MS:* prize   *1835:* prize,   691| *MS:* back-seats,   *1868:* back-seats
692| *MS:* Brave   *1835:* brave   693| *MS:* sport:—Behold!   *1835:* sport . . .
Behold!   *1849:* sport!—Behold!

PART V. PARACELSUS ATTAINS.

SCENE—*Salzburg; a cell in the Hospital of St. Sebastian.* 1541.

FESTUS, PARACELSUS.

FESTUS No change! The weary night is well-nigh spent,
The lamp burns low, and through the casement-bars
Grey morning glimmers feebly: yet no change!
Another night, and still no sigh has stirred
5 That fallen discoloured mouth, no pang relit
Those fixed eyes, quenched by the decaying body,
Like torch-flame choked in dust. While all beside
Was breaking, to the last they held out bright,
As a stronghold where life intrenched itself;
10 But they are dead now—very blind and dead:
He will drowse into death without a groan.

My Aureole—my forgotten, ruined Aureole!
The days are gone, are gone! How grand thou wast!
And now not one of those who struck thee down—

SCENE| *MS: A <> Sebastian at Salzburg.* 1541. *1863: Salzburg; a <> Sebastian.*
1541. 1| *MS: change!—the <> well nigh 1835: change! The 1863: well-
nigh 3| MS: The grey morn <> feebly——yet 1835: feebly—yet 1849:
Grey morning 1863: feebly: yet 4| 1835: stirr'd 1849: stirred
5| MS: fall'n 1835: discolour'd 1849: fallen discoloured 6| MS: body
1835: quench'd <> body, 1849: quenched 7| MS: dust;—while 1835:
dust: while 1863: dust. While 8| MS: bright 1835: bright, 9| MS:
strong-hold <> itself... 1835: intrench'd itself; 1849: intrenched 1863:
stronghold 10| MS: now—very <> dead:—— 1835: now—very <>
dead. 1863: and dead: 11| MS:——He <> groan! 1835: He 1868:
groan. 12| MS: Aureole, my 1835: Aureole; my <> ruin'd 1849:
Aureole—my <> ruined 13| MS: how <> thou wert,—— 1835: How
<> wert: 1863: thou wast! 14| MS: down 1835: down—

15 Poor glorious spirit—concerns him even to stay
And satisfy himself his little hand
Could turn God's image to a livid thing.

Another night, and yet no change! 'Tis much
That I should sit by him, and bathe his brow,
20 And chafe his hands; 'tis much: but he will sure
Know me, and look on me, and speak to me
Once more—but only once! His hollow cheek
Looked all night long as though a creeping laugh
At his own state were just about to break
25 From the dying man: my brain swam, my throat swelled,
And yet I could not turn away. In truth,
They told me how, when first brought here, he seemed
Resolved to live, to lose no faculty;
Thus striving to keep up his shattered strength,
30 Until they bore him to this stifling cell:
When straight his features fell, an hour made white
The flushed face, and relaxed the quivering limb,
Only the eye remained intense awhile
As though it recognized the tomb-like place,

15| MS: Poor, glorious Spirit! concerns   1835: spirit—concerns   1868: Poor
glorious   17| MS: thing!   1835: thing.   1849: thing. § end of page §   1863:
thing. § no space §   1868: thing. / § space §   18| MS: change!—'tis   1835:
change! 'Tis   19| MS: should look on § cancelled by § sit by him and < >
brow   1835: him, and < > brow,   20| MS: hands——'tis much—but   1835:
hands—'tis much; but   1863: hands; 'tis much: but   21| MS: me and   1835:
me, and   22| MS: once!—his § written over by § His   1835: once! His
23| MS: Looked, all < > tho'   1835: Look'd all < > though   1849:
Looked   25| MS: man . . . my < > swam and my throat   1835: man: my
1849: swam, my throat swelled,   26| MS: Swelled thick, and yet I § cancelled
by § Swelled yet for all I < > away!   1835: Swell'd, yet   1849: And yet I < >
away. In truth,   27| MS: In truth they < > how he seemed at first   1835:
truth, they < > seem'd   1849: They < > how, when first brought here, he
seemed   28| MS: live—to let no power forsake him;—   1835: him;   1849:
live—to lose no faculty;   1863: live, to   29| MS: strength   1835: shatter'd
strength,   1849: shattered   30| MS: they brought him < > cell   1835:
cell: 1849: they bore him   31| MS:——At once his features fell——an
1835: At < > fell—an   1849: When straight his   1863: fell, an   32| MS:
limb—   1835: flush'd face and relax'd < > limb;   1849: flushed < > relaxed   1863:
limb,   33| 1835: remain'd < > while,   1849: remained   1863: awhile
34| MS: tho'   1835: though < > place;   1863: place,

And then he lay as here he lies.

Ay, here!
Here is earth's noblest, nobly garlanded—
Her bravest champion with his well-won prize—
Her best achievement, her sublime amends
For countless generations fleeting fast
40 And followed by no trace;—the creature-god
She instances when angels would dispute
The title of her brood to rank with them.
Angels, this is our angel! Those bright forms
We clothe with purple, crown and call to thrones,
45 Are human, but not his; those are but men
Whom other men press round and kneel before;
Those palaces are dwelt in by mankind;
Higher provision is for him you seek
Amid our pomps and glories: see it here!
50 Behold earth's paragon! Now, raise thee, clay!

God! Thou art love! I build my faith on that.
Even as I watch beside thy tortured child
Unconscious whose hot tears fall fast by him,
So doth thy right hand guide us through the world

35| *MS:* lay, as < > lies:— / Ay   *1835:* lay as < > lies . . . / Ay, here: *1849:*
lies. / Ay, here!   **36|**   *MS:* garlanded!   *1835:* noblest nobly garlanded—
1849: noblest, nobly   **37|**   *MS:* well-won meed!   *1835:* champion, with < >
meed—   *1863:* champion with   *1868:* well-won prize—   **38|**   *MS:* best
production—all that makes amends   *1849:* best achievement, her sublime
amends   **39|**   *1835:* generations, fleeting   *1863:* generations fleeting
40| *MS:* trace—the all-surpassing   *1835:* follow'd   *1849:* followed < > trace:—the
creature-god   **41|**   *MS:* Creature she cites when Angels   *1835:* angels   *1849:*
She instances when   **42|**   *MS:* them . .   *1835:* them . . .   *1849:* them—
1863: them.   **43-45|**   *MS:* Angel!   those < > forms / Are the man— —but not
his,—those < > Men   *1835:* angel!—those < > / Are human, but not his: those < >
men   *1849:* forms / We clothe with purple, crown and call to thrones, / Are   *1863:*
angel! Those < > // Are human; but   *1868:* human, but not his; those
46| *MS:* the rest press around < > before—   *1849:* Whom other men press round
and   *1863:* before;   **47|**   *MS:* Mankind—   *1835:* mankind;
48-50| *MS:*— —Other provision < > seek— — / Behold < > paragon!—Now < >
Clay!   *1835:* Other < > seek. / < > paragon! Now < > clay!   *1849:* Higher
provision < > seek / Amid our pomps and glories: see it here! / Behold   *1863:* clay!
§ end of page §   *1868:* clay! § no space §   *1888:* clay! / § space §   **51|**   *MS:*
Love < > that: *1849:* that!   *1868:* love   *1888:* that   *1889:* that.
52| *1835:* child,   *1863:* Thy < > child   *1868:* thy   **54|**   *MS:* right-hand
< > thro'   *1835:* right hand < > through   *1863:* Thy   *1868:* thy

55 Wherein we stumble. God! what shall we say?
How has he sinned? How else should he have done?
Surely he sought thy praise—thy praise, for all
He might be busied by the task so much
As half forget awhile its proper end.
60 Dost thou well, Lord? Thou canst not but prefer
That I should range myself upon his side—
How could he stop at every step to set
Thy glory forth? Hadst thou but granted him
Success, thy honour would have crowned success,
65 A halo round a star. Or, say he erred,—
Save him, dear God; it will be like thee: bathe him
In light and life! Thou art not made like us;
We should be wroth in such a case; but thou
Forgivest—so, forgive these passionate thoughts
70 Which come unsought and will not pass away!
I know thee, who hast kept my path, and made
Light for me in the darkness, tempering sorrow
So that it reached me like a solemn joy;
It were too strange that I should doubt thy love.
75 But what am I? Thou madest him and knowest
How he was fashioned. I could never err

55| *MS:* stumble:—God   *1835:* stumble. God   56| *MS:*——How < >
sinned—how   *1835:* How < > sinn'd—how   *1849:* sinned? How   57| *1863:*
Thy < > Thy   *1868:* thy < > thy   58| *MS:* be wedded to the < > so well
1849: be busied by the < > so much   59| *MS:* As to forget < > end——
1835: end . . .   *1849:* end.   *1868:* As half forget   60| *MS:* Lord? . . . Thou
1835: Lord? Thou   61| *MS:* side . . .   *1849:* side—   63| *MS:*
forth?—hadst Thou   *1835:* forth? Hadst   *1868:* thou   64| *MS:* crowned his
triumph—   *1835:* crown'd   *1849:* have crowned success,   *1863:* Thy   *1868:*
thy   65| *MS:* star——or § written over by § star!—or say he erred,   *1835:* star
. . . Or < > err'd: *1849:* star. Or, say he erred,—   66| *MS:* God—it < >
thee—bathe   *1835:* God; it < > thee: bathe   *1863:* Thee   *1868:* thee
67| *MS:* life! . Thou < > us—   *1835:* life! Thou < > us: *1849:* us;
68| *MS:* be wrath in < > case—but thou § written over by § Thou   *1835:* case;
but   *1849:* be wroth in   *1868:* thou   69| *MS:* Will smile on him! . . . forgive
these   *1835:* him. Forgive < > thoughts,   *1849:* Forgivest—so, forgive   *1863:*
thoughts   70| *1835:* unsought, and < > away.   *1849:* away!   *1863:* unsought
and   71| *MS:* thee—who < > path and   *1835:* thee, who < > path, and
1863: Thee   *1868:* thee   72| *MS:* darkness——tempering   *1835:*
darkness—tempering sorrow,   *1863:* darkness, tempering sorrow   73| *MS:* joy—
—   *1835:* reach'd < > joy;   *1849:* reached   74| *MS:* I < > love . . .   *1835:*
love: *1849:* I   *1863:* Thy love.   *1868:* thy   75| *MS:* I   *1835:* him, and
1849: I   *1863:* him and   76| *MS:* fashioned; I   *1835:* fashion'd. I   *1849:*
fashioned. I

227

That way: the quiet place beside thy feet,
Reserved for me, was ever in my thoughts:
But he—thou shouldst have favoured him as well!

80   Ah! he wakens! Aureole, I am here! 'tis Festus!
I cast away all wishes save one wish—
Let him but know me, only speak to me!
He mutters; louder and louder; any other
Than I, with brain less laden, could collect
85   What he pours forth. Dear Aureole, do but look!
Is it talking or singing, this he utters fast?
Misery that he should fix me with his eye,
Quick talking to some other all the while!
If he would husband this wild vehemence
90   Which frustrates its intent!—I heard, I know
I heard my name amid those rapid words.
Oh, he will know me yet! Could I divert
This current, lead it somehow gently back
Into the channels of the past!—His eye
95   Brighter than ever! It must recognize me!

    I am Erasmus: I am here to pray

77| *MS:* way—the < > feet   *1835:* way: the   *1849:* feet,   *1863:* Thy   *1868:*
thy   **78|**   *MS:* me was < > thoughts;—   *1835:* thoughts;   *1849:* me, was < >
thoughts: **79|**   *MS:* He—Thou   *1835:* he—Thou < > favour'd   *1849:*
favoured   *1863:* well! § end of page §   *1868:* well! § no space §   *1888:* well! /
§ space §   **80|**   *MS:* Ah! he wakens—Aureole < > here,—'tis   *1835:* wakens!
Aureole < > here—'tis   *1849:* wakes   *1863:* here! 'tis   *1868:* wakens
81| *MS:*——I < > wish——   *1835:* I < > wish—   **82|**   *MS:* me, only < >
me!——   *1835:* me—only < > me!   *1863:* me, only   **83|**   *MS:*
mutters—louder and louder:——Any   *1835:* mutters—louder and louder; any   *1863:*
mutters; louder and   **84|**   *MS:* I—with < > laden—would collect   *1835:* I,
with < > laden, would   *1849:* laden, could collect   **85|**   *MS:* forth;—dear
Aureole do   *1835:* forth. Dear Aureole, do   **86|**   *MS:* singing this   *1868:*
singing, this   **87|**   *MS:* Misery! that   *1835:* Misery, that < > eye—   *1863:*
eye,   *1888:* Misery that   **88|**   *MS:* talking——to   *1835:* talking to
89| *1835:* vehemence,   *1863:* vehemence   **90|**   *MS:* intent:—I heard . . . I
1835: intent . . . I heard, I   *1849:* intent!—I heard   **91|**   *MS:* words:—   *1835:*
words: *1863:* words.   **92|**   *MS:* O he will < > could   *1835:* Could   *1863:*
Oh, he   **93|**   *MS:* current——lead   *1835:* current—lead   *1863:* current,
lead   **94|**   *MS:* past . . his   *1835:* past . . . His   *1849:* past!—His   *1863:*
Past   *1868:* past   **95–96|**   *MS:* ever—it < > me! / § space § / I am
Erasmus,—I   *1835:* ever, it < > / § space § / < > Erasmus: I   *1849:* ever! It < >
recognise! / § space § / Let me speak to him in another's name. / I am Erasmus
1863: recognize me!   *1868:* me! / § space § / I am Erasmus

That Paracelsus use his skill for me.
The schools of Paris and of Padua send
These questions for your learning to resolve.
100 We are your students, noble master: leave
This wretched cell, what business have you here?
Our class awaits you; come to us once more!
(O agony! the utmost I can do
Touches him not; how else arrest his ear?)
105 I am commissioned . . . I shall craze like him.
Better be mute and see what God shall send.
PARACELSUS Stay, stay with me!
FESTUS   I will; I am come here
To stay with you—Festus, you loved of old;
Festus, you know, you must know!
PARACELSUS   Festus! Where's
110 Aprile, then? Has he not chanted softly
The melodies I heard all night? I could not
Get to him for a cold hand on my breast,
But I made out his music well enough,
O well enough! If they have filled him full
115 With magical music, as they freight a star
With light, and have remitted all his sin,
They will forgive me too, I too shall know!

97| MS: That Eremita use his wondrous skill . . . . 1835: skill: 1849: That
Paracelsus use his skill for me.   98| MS: . . The 1835: The   99| MS:
resolve . . . 1835: resolve.   100| MS: Master:—leave 1835: master. Leave
1849: master: leave   101| MS: cell,—what 1835: cell; what 1863: cell,
what   102| MS: you— —come 1835: you; come < > more. 1863:
more!   103| MS:— § written over by § (O Agony!—the 1835: (O agony!
the   104| MS: not . . . how 1835: not; how   105| MS: commissioned
. . . . (I < > him— 1835: commission'd . . . I 1849: commissioned 1863: him!
1868: him.   106| MS: I will be 1835: mute, and 1849: Better be mute
1863: mute and   107| MS: Stay—stay < > me! . . . FESTUS —I will—I 1835:
Stay, stay < > me! FESTUS I will; I   108| MS: you . . . . Festus you < > old—
— § written over by § old— 1835: you—Festus < > old; 1849: Festus, you
109| MS: Festus—you know—you < > know . . PARACELSUS Festus . . . where's
1835: Festus, you know, you < > know. PARACELSUS Festus! Where's 1849: must
know!   110| MS: Aprile then? has < > chaunted 1835: Has 1863:
chanted 111| MS: night— —I 1835: night? I   113| MS: enough—
1835: enough,   114| MS: enough . . . . if 1835: enough. If < > fill'd 1849:
O, well enough! If < > filled 1868: O well   115| MS: music as 1849:
music, as   117| MS: too— —I shall Know too!— — 1835: too, I < > know too
. . . 1849: I too shall know!

FESTUS Festus, your Festus!
PARACELSUS   Ask him if Aprile
Knows as he Loves—if I shall Love and Know?
120 I try; but that cold hand, like lead—so cold!
FESTUS My hand, see!
PARACELSUS   Ah, the curse, Aprile, Aprile!
We get so near—so very, very near!
'Tis an old tale: Jove strikes the Titans down,
Not when they set about their mountain-piling
125 But when another rock would crown the work.
And Phaeton—doubtless his first radiant plunge
Astonished mortals, though the gods were calm,
And Jove prepared his thunder: all old tales!
FESTUS And what are these to you?
PARACELSUS   Ay, fiends must laugh
130 So cruelly, so well! most like I never
Could tread a single pleasure underfoot,
But they were grinning by my side, were chuckling
To see me toil and drop away by flakes!
Hell-spawn! I am glad, most glad, that thus I fail!
135 Your cunning has o'ershot its aim. One year,

118| MS: Festus—Festus!— — PARACELSUS —I would have asked if he 1835: Festus,
Festus! PARACELSUS I < > ask'd 1849: Festus, your Festus! PARACELSUS Ask him if
Aprile 119| MS: Loves . . . if < > Love as well § capitalized initials in
print § 1835: KNOWS as he LOVES—if < > LOVE 1849: Knows < > Loves < >
Love and Know? 120| MS: As Know § capitalized initial in print § — —but
< > cold— — —. 1835: KNOW: but < > cold. 1849: I try; but < > cold!
121| MS: Dear Aureole— — PARACELSUS Ah the 1835: Dear Aureole . . . PARACELSUS
Ah, the 1849: My hand, see! PARACELSUS 122| MS: near— —so 1835:
near—so 1849: near! 123| MS:—Tis tale—Jove < > down 1835: 'Tis < >
tale: Jove 1888: down, 124| 1835: mountain-piling, 1868: mountain-
piling 125| MS: crown their work!— 1835: work! 1868: crown the
work. 126| MS:— —And Phaeton . . . doubtless 1835: And
Phæton—doubtless 127| MS: Mortals—but the Gods < > calm 1835:
Astonish'd mortals; but the gods < > calm, 1849: Astonished mortals; though the
1868: mortals, though 128| MS: thunder—all 1835: thunder: all old tales.
1849: tales! 129| MS: Ay, they must 1849: Ay, fiends must 130| MS:
well— — —most 1835: well; most 1888: well! most 131| MS: underfoot
1835: under foot 1849: foot, 1863: underfoot, 132| MS: side— —were
1835: side, were 133| MS: flakes:— 1835: toil, and < > flakes. 1849:
flakes! 1863: toil and 134-135| MS: glad— —most glad that < > fail! /
—Your < > aim;—one year 1835: glad, most glad, that < > / Your < > aim. One
year, 1849: fail! / You that hate men and all who wish their good— / Your 1863:
fail! / Your

One month, perhaps, and I had served your turn!
You should have curbed your spite awhile. But now,
Who will believe 'twas you that held me back?
Listen: there's shame and hissing and contempt,
140 And none but laughs who names me, none but spits
Measureless scorn upon me, me alone,
The quack, the cheat, the liar,—all on me!
And thus your famous plan to sink mankind
In silence and despair, by teaching them
145 One of their race had probed the inmost truth,
Had done all man could do, yet failed no less—
Your wise plan proves abortive. Men despair?
Ha, ha! why, they are hooting the empiric,
The ignorant and incapable fool who rushed
150 Madly upon a work beyond his wits;
Nor doubt they but the simplest of themselves
Could bring the matter to triumphant issue.
So, pick and choose among them all, accursed!
Try now, persuade some other to slave for you,
155 To ruin body and soul to work your ends!
No, no; I am the first and last, I think.

136| *MS:* month perhaps and   *1835:* month, perhaps, and < > turn: *1849:*
turn!   137| *MS:*—You < > awhile:— —but now   *1835:* You < > curb'd < >
awhile. But now,   *1849:* curbed   138| *MS:* You   *1835:* you   139| *MS:*
contempt— —   *1835:* shame, and hissing, and contempt,   *1868:* shame and hissing
and   140| *MS:* me— —none   *1835:* me—none   *1863:* me, none
141| *MS:* me . . . 'tis on *me*   *1835:* me; 'tis on *me*,   *1849:* me—me alone,   *1863:*
me, me   142| *MS:* quack, the liar, the arch-cheat—all on *me!* *1835: me.*
1849: quack, the cheat, the liar,—all on me!   143| *MS:* Mankind   *1835:*
mankind   144| *MS:* In uttermost despair by   *1835:* despair, by   *1849:* In
silence and despair   145| *MS:* truth   *1835:* truth,   146| *MS:* Man < >
failed in all . .   *1835:* man < > fail'd in all—   *1849:* failed no less—
147| *MS:*— —Your plan has proved abortive— —*They* despair?   *1835:* Your < >
abortive. *They*   *1849:* Your wise plan proves abortive. Men despair?
148| *MS:* Ha ha, why they < > empiric   *1835:* Ha, ha! why < > empiric,   *1863:*
why, they   149| *MS:* who thrust   *1849:* who rushed   150| *MS:* Himself
upon < > wits,   *1849:* Madly upon < > wits;   151| *MS:* doubt but the the
§ cancelled by § doubting but the   *1849:* doubt they but the   152| *MS:*
issue!   *1863:* issue.   153| *MS:* So pick < > Accursed!   *1835:* accursed!
1849: Accursed!   *1863:* choose, among < > accursed!   *1868:* So, pick and choose
among   154| *MS:* now,—persuade < > you   *1835:* now, persuade < >
you,   155| *1835:* ends: *1863:* ends!   156| *MS:* No—no! I am < >
think!   *1835:* No, no; I am < > think.   *1849:* think!   *1863:* think.

FESTUS Dear friend, who are accursed? who has done . . .
PARACELSUS What have I done? Fiends dare ask that? or you,
Brave men? Oh, you can chime in boldly, backed
160 By the others! What had you to do, sage peers?
Here stand my rivals; Latin, Arab, Jew,
Greek, join dead hands against me: all I ask
Is, that the world enrol my name with theirs,
And even this poor privilege, it seems,
165 They range themselves, prepared to disallow.
Only observe! why, fiends may learn from them!
How they talk calmly of my throes, my fierce
Aspirings, terrible watchings, each one claiming
Its price of blood and brain; how they dissect
170 And sneeringly disparage the few truths
Got at a life's cost; they too hanging the while
About my neck, their lies misleading me
And their dead names browbeating me! Grey crew,
Yet steeped in fresh malevolence from hell,
175 Is there a reason for your hate? My truths
Have shaken a little the palm about each prince?
Just think, Aprile, all these leering dotards
Were bent on nothing less than to be crowned

157| MS: Sweet friend— —who < > done— — —   1835: friend; who < > done
. . . 1849: Dear friend   1863: friend, who   158| MS: done? you dare < >
You   1835: you,   1849: done? Fiends dare < > you,   159| MS: Brave
Ones— —Oh, you   1835: ones? Oh < > back'd   1849: Brave men? Oh, you < >
backed   160-166| MS: By them— —and what had you to do, wise Peers? /
—Only observe— —why fiends may learn of them § cancelled by § learn from them!
1835: them; and < > peers? / Only observe: why   1849: By the others! What had
you to do, sage peers? / Here stand my rivals, truly—Arab, Jew, / Greek, join dead
hands against me: all I ask / Is, that the world enrol my name with theirs, / And even
this poor privilege, it seems, / They range themselves, prepared to disallow! /
Only   161| 1863: rivals; Latin, Arab   166| 1888: observe! why
167| MS: throes— my   1863: throes, my   168| MS: Aspirings—terrible
watchings each   1835: Aspirings, terrible watchings—each   1863: watchings,
each   169| MS: brain—how   1835: brain; how   171| MS: cost—they
1835: cost; they   172| MS: neck— —their   1835: neck, their < > me,   1863:
me   173-175| MS: Their < > me— —Damned § written over by § me!—Damned
Crew / Is < > hate?— —my   1835: brow-beating me. Wretched crew! / Is < > hate?
My   1849: And their < > me! Grey crew, / Yet steeped in fresh malevolence from
hell, / Is   1863: browbeating   176| MS: each brow?   1849: each head?
1863: each prince?   177| MS: Aprile— —all   1835: Aprile, all   178| MS:
be Kings   1835: kings   1849: than being crowned   1863: than to be crowned

As we! That yellow blear-eyed wretch in chief
180 To whom the rest cringe low with feigned respect,
Galen of Pergamos and hell—nay speak
The tale, old man! We met there face to face:
I said the crown should fall from thee. Once more
We meet as in that ghastly vestibule:
185 Look to my brow! Have I redeemed my pledge?
FESTUS Peace, peace; ah, see!
PARACELSUS   Oh, emptiness of fame!
Oh Persic Zoroaster, lord of stars!
—Who said these old renowns, dead long ago,
Could make me overlook the living world
190 To gaze through gloom at where they stood, indeed,
But stand no longer? What a warm light life
After the shade! In truth, my delicate witch,
My serpent-queen, you did but well to hide
The juggles I had else detected. Fire
195 May well run harmless o'er a breast like yours!
The cave was not so darkened by the smoke
But that your white limbs dazzled me: oh, white,
And panting as they twinkled, wildly dancing!
I cared not for your passionate gestures then,

179| MS: that <> wretch, in chief   1835: That <> wretch in chief,   1863:
chief   180| MS: respect—   1835: feign'd   1849: feigned   1863:
respect,   181| MS: Galen—of <> Hell——nay   1835: Galen, of <> hell;
nay   1863: Galen of <> hell—nay   182–192| MS: man—how we met face to
face . . . ° § footnote § °—He did in effect affirm that he had disputed with Galen in the
vestibule of Hell. / Peace, peace—ah see! PARACELSUS —In truth my   1835: to face
. . . ° § footnote § °He <> hell. / Peace, peace; ah, see! PARACELSUS In   1849: tale,
old man! We met there face to face; § footnote dropped § / I said the crown should
fall from thee; once more / We meet as in that ghastly vestibule: / Look to my brow!
Have I redeemed my pledge? / FESTUS Peace, peace <> see! PARACELSUS Oh,
emptiness of fame! / Oh Persic Zoroaster, lord of stars! / —Who said these old
renowns, dead long ago, / Could make me overlook the living world / To gaze
through gloom at where they stood, indeed, / But stand no longer? What a warm light
life / After the shade! In truth, my   183| 1863: thee. Once   194| MS:
detected———fire   1835: detected. Fire   196| MS: not so darkened § so
inserted above the line §   1835: darken'd   1849: darkened   197| MS: me—
—O white,   1835: me. O   1849: Oh, white,   1863: oh   199| MS: then,—
1835: then,

200 But now I have forgotten the charm of charms,
The foolish knowledge which I came to seek,
While I remember that quaint dance; and thus
I am come back, not for those mummeries,
But to love you, and to kiss your little feet
205 Soft as an ermine's winter coat!
FESTUS   A light
Will struggle through these thronging words at last,
As in the angry and tumultuous West
A soft star trembles through the drifting clouds.
These are the strivings of a spirit which hates
210 So sad a vault should coop it, and calls up
The past to stand between it and its fate.
Were he at Einsiedeln—or Michal here!
PARACELSUS Cruel! I seek her now—I kneel—I shriek—
I clasp her vesture—but she fades, still fades;
215 And she is gone; sweet human love is gone!
'Tis only when they spring to heaven that angels
Reveal themselves to you; they sit all day
Beside you, and lie down at night by you
Who care not for their presence, muse or sleep,
220 And all at once they leave you, and you know them!
We are so fooled, so cheated! Why, even now
I am not too secure against foul play;

200-202| *MS:* now, I < > Charm of Charms / While < > dance;—and   *1835:* now I
< > charm of charms / < > dance; and   *1849:* of charms, / The foolish knowledge
which I came to seek, / While   **204|**   *1835:* feet,   *1863:* feet   **205|**   *MS:*
winter-coat! FESTUS—A   *1835:* winter coat! FESTUS A   *1849:* A sense   *1863:* A
light   **206|**   *MS:* thro < > last,   *1835:* through   *1888:* last.   **207|**   *MS:*
West   *1835:* west   *1863:* West   **208|**   *MS:* thro' < > clouds— —   *1835:*
through < > clouds: *1849:* clouds.   **209|**   *MS:*— —These are the § *are* inserted
above the line §   *1835:* These   **211|**   *MS:* fate: *1863:* Past < > fate.   *1868:*
past   **212|**   *MS:* Einsiedeln—or < > here . . . .   *1835:* Einsiedeln—or < > here
. . .   *1849* here!   **213|**   *MS:* Cruel— —I seek   *1835:* Cruel . . . I seek   *1849:*
Cruel! I seek   **214|**   *MS:* vesture— —but she fades—still fades   *1835:*
vesture—but she fades, still fades;   **215|**   *MS:* gone—sweet Human Love   *1835:*
gone; sweet human love   **216|**   *MS:* Tis < > Angels   *1835:* 'Tis < >
angels   **217|**   *MS:* you— —they   *1835:* you; they   **218|**   *MS:* you and
1835: you, and < > you,   *1863:* by you   **219|**   *MS:* presence—muse or
sleep—   *1863:* presence, muse or sleep,   **220|**   *MS:* you and   *1888:* you,
and   **221|**   fooled—so cheated!—even   *1835:* fool'd, so cheated! Even   *1849:*
fooled, so cheated! Why, even   **222|**   *MS:* play—   *1835:* play: *1868:* play;

The shadows deepen and the walls contract:
No doubt some treachery is going on.
225 'Tis very dusk. Where are we put, Aprile?
Have they left us in the lurch? This murky loathsome
Death-trap, this slaughter-house, is not the hall
In the golden city! Keep by me, Aprile!
There is a hand groping amid the blackness
230 To catch us. Have the spider-fingers got you,
Poet? Hold on me for your life! If once
They pull you!—Hold!
                    'Tis but a dream—no more!
I have you still; the sun comes out again;
Let us be happy: all will yet go well!
235 Let us confer: is it not like, Aprile,
That spite of trouble, this ordeal passed,
The value of my labours ascertained,
Just as some stream foams long among the rocks
But after glideth glassy to the sea,
240 So, full content shall henceforth be my lot?
What think you, poet? Louder! Your clear voice
Vibrates too like a harp-string. Do you ask
How could I still remain on earth, should God
Grant me the great approval which I seek?

223| MS: deepen—and < > contract—   1835: deepen, and   1863: deepen and
1868: contract: 224| MS: on!   1868: on.   225| MS: Tis < > dusk—
—where   1835: 'Tis < > dusk. Where   226| MS: this   1835: This   1849:
murky, loathsome   1868: murky loathsome   227| MS: Death-trap—this
slaughter-house——is   1835: slaughter-house—is   1863: Death-trap, this slaughter-
house, is   228| MS: City!. . keep < > Aprile   1835: city! Keep < >
Aprile,   1849: me, Aprile!   229| MS:——There   1835: There   230| MS:
us——have < > you   1835: us. Have < > you,   231| MS: Dearest?—hold < >
life——if   1835: hold < > life; if   1849: Poet? Hold   1863: life! if   1868:
If   232| MS: you . . Hold——/ Tis < > dream!—no more.   1835: you . . . Hold
. . . / 'Tis < > dream—no   233| MS: still——the < > again   1835: still—the
< > again;   1849: you!—Hold!   1863: still; the   234| MS: happy——all
1835: happy—all   1863: happy: all   235| MS: confer—is   1835: confer:
is   236| MS: of gone-by trouble, this   1835: pass'd,   1849: of trouble < >
passed,   237| 1835: ascertain'd,   1849: ascertained,   239| MS: sea
1835: sea,   241| MS: Poet—Louder! your   1835: poet? Louder! Your
242| MS: harp-string:——is it so?   1835: harp-string. Is   1849: harp-string. Do you
ask   243| MS: "How couldst thou still   1849: How could I still
244| MS: Grant thee the < > approval thou dost seek?   1849: Grant me the < >
approval which I seek?

245 I, you, and God can comprehend each other,
But men would murmur, and with cause enough;
For when they saw me, stainless of all sin,
Preserved and sanctified by inward light,
They would complain that comfort, shut from them,
250 I drank thus unespied; that they live on,
Nor taste the quiet of a constant joy,
For ache and care and doubt and weariness,
While I am calm; help being vouchsafed to me,
And hid from them.—'Twere best consider that!
255 You reason well, Aprile; but at least
Let me know this, and die! Is this too much?
I will learn this, if God so please, and die!

If thou shalt please, dear God, if thou shalt please!
We are so weak, we know our motives least
260 In their confused beginning. If at first
I sought . . . but wherefore bare my heart to thee?
I know thy mercy; and already thoughts
Flock fast about my soul to comfort it,
And intimate I cannot wholly fail,
265 For love and praise would clasp me willingly

245| *MS:* I, thou and God, can *1835:* thou, and God can *1849:* I, you, and
246| *MS:* Men < > murmur and < > enough;— *1835:* men < > murmur, and
< > enough; 247| *MS:* saw thee stainless *1835:* thee, stainless *1849:* saw
me, stainless 249| *MS:* complain 'a comfort shut from us *1835:* complain—' a
< > us, *1849:* complain that comfort, shut from them, 250| *MS:* He drinketh
unespied——for we live on *1835:* unespied; for < > on, *1849:* I drank thus
unespied; that they live 251| *MS:* joy *1835:* joy, 252| *MS:* For ache,
and care < > weariness,— *1835:* care, and doubt, and weariness, *1863:* ache and
care and doubt and 253| *MS:* While He is calm! Help is vouchsafed to Him
1835: he < > him, *1849:* While I am calm; help being vouchsafed to me,
254| *MS:* from us!' ''—twere < > that *1835:* us!' '' 'Twere < > that: *1849:* from
them!—'Twere < > that! *1868:* them.—'Twere 255| *MS:*—You < >
Aprile,—but *1835:* You < > Aprile; but 256| *MS:* die!—is that too *1835:*
die! Is *1849:* Is this too 258| *1863:* Thou < > Thou *1868:* thou < >
thou 259| *MS:* . . . . We are so weak we *1835:* We are *1849:* weak,
we 260| *MS:* beginning; . . . if *1835:* beginning: if *1863:* beginning.
If 261| *MS:* sought . . but *1835:* sought . . . But *1863:* but < > bear < >
Thee? *1868:* bare < > thee? 262| *MS:* mercy—and *1835:* mercy; and
1863: Thy *1868:* thy 263| *1863:* it *1868:* it, 264| *MS:* To intimate
< > fail,— *1835:* fail, *1849:* And intimate 265| *MS:* That love *1849:*
For love

Could I resolve to seek them. Thou art good,
And I should be content. Yet—yet first show
I have done wrong in daring! Rather give
The supernatural consciousness of strength
270 Which fed my youth! Only one hour of that
With thee to help—O what should bar me then!

Lost, lost! Thus things are ordered here! God's creatures,
And yet he takes no pride in us!—none, none!
Truly there needs another life to come!
275 If this be all—(I must tell Festus that)
And other life await us not—for one,
I say 'tis a poor cheat, a stupid bungle,
A wretched failure. I, for one, protest
Against it, and I hurl it back with scorn.

280 Well, onward though alone! Small time remains,
And much to do: I must have fruit, must reap
Some profit from my toils. I doubt my body
Will hardly serve me through; while I have laboured
It has decayed; and now that I demand
285 Its best assistance, it will crumble fast:
A sad thought, a sad fate! How very full

266| MS: them:—Thou art good   1835: them . . . Thou art good,   1849: them:
Thou   1863: them. Thou   267| MS: content, yet,——yet   1835: content;
yet—yet   1863: content. Yet—yet   268| MS: daring!—rather   1835: daring!
Rather   270| MS: That fed my youth——one only hour   1835: youth . . .
one   1849: youth—one   1863: youth! One   1868: Which fed my youth! Only one
hour   271| MS: Thee to help—O <> then!——— 1835: thee to help—O
<> then!   1863: Thee   1868: thee   272| MS: Lost, lost!—thus   1835: Lost,
lost! thus <> order'd <> creatures!   1849: Thus <> ordered <>
creatures,   273| MS: none! none!   1835: none, none!   1863: He   1868:
he   275| MS: that— § written over by § that)   1835: that)   276| MS:
not . . . for one   1835: not—for   1849: one,   277| MS: cheat—a <>
bungle   1835: cheat, a <> bungle,   278| MS: failure . . I   1835: failure.
I   279| MS: it——and <> scorn! . . .   1835: it—and <> scorn!   1863: it,
and   1868: scorn.   280| MS: well—onward tho' alone: small   1835: Well,
onward though   1868: alone! Small   281| MS: do:—I <> fruit—must   1835:
do: I <> fruit, must   282| MS: toils——I   1835: toils. I   283| MS:
through——while   1835: through: while <> labour'd   1849: laboured   1863:
through; while   284| MS: decayed——and   1835: decay'd; and   1849:
decayed   285| MS: fast——   1835: fast: 286| MS: thought—a sad
fate!—how   1835: fate! How   1863: thought, a

Of wormwood 'tis, that just at altar-service,
The rapt hymn rising with the rolling smoke,
When glory dawns and all is at the best,
290 The sacred fire may flicker and grow faint
And die for want of a wood-piler's help!
Thus fades the flagging body, and the soul
Is pulled down in the overthrow. Well, well—
Let men catch every word, let them lose nought
295 Of what I say; something may yet be done.

They are ruins! Trust me who am one of you!
All ruins, glorious once, but lonely now.
It makes my heart sick to behold you crouch
Beside your desolate fane: the arches dim,
300 The crumbling columns grand against the moon,
Could I but rear them up once more—but that
May never be, so leave them! Trust me, friends,
Why should you linger here when I have built
A far resplendent temple, all your own?
305 Trust me, they are but ruins! See, Aprile,
Men will not heed! Yet were I not prepared
With better refuge for them, tongue of mine
Should ne'er reveal how blank their dwelling is:

287| *MS:* Altar-service, *1835:* altar-service, **288|** *MS:*—The *1835:*
The **289|** *MS:* dawns, and < > best,— *1835:* best— *1863:* dawns and
1868: best, **290|** *1835:* faint, *1849:* flicker, and *1863:* flicker and < >
faint **291|** *MS:* die— — —for *1835:* die, for *1863:* die for **293|** *MS:*
overthrow:—well—well— *1835:* pull'd < > overthrow: well, well— *1849:* pulled
1863: overthrow. Well, well— **294|** *MS:* Men < > word—let < > lose
nothing *1835:* men *1849:* lose nought *1863:* word, let **295|** *MS:* say . .
something < > done:— — — *1835:* say; something < > done. **296|** *MS:*
trust *1849:* Trust **297|** *MS:* ruins— —glorious once but < > now— —
1835: ruins—glorious once, but < > now: *1849:* now. *1863:* ruins, glorious
298| *MS:* crouching *1849:* crouch **299|** *MS:* fane— —its arches dim *1835:*
fane; its *1849:* fane; the arches *1863:* fane: the **300|** *MS:* Its crumbling
< > moon— — *1835:* moon: *1849:* The crumbling *1863:* moon— *1868:*
moon, **301|** *MS:* more— —but *1835:* more—but **302|** *MS:*
be—so < > me Friends! *1835:* be, so < > friends, *1849:* me, friends,
304| *MS:* Temple < > own *1835:* temple < > own? **305|** *MS:* me—they
< > ruins!— —see—Aprile *1835:* me, they < > ruins! see Aprile, *1849:* See,
Aprile, **306|** *MS:* They will < > yet *1835:* prepar'd *1849:* Men will < >
Yet < > prepared **307|** *MS:* them, never should tongue *1849:* them, tongue of
mine **308|** *MS:* Of mine reveal < > is— — — *1835:* is; *1849:* Should ne'er
reveal *1863:* is:

I would sit down in silence with the rest.

310 Ha, what? you spit at me, you grin and shriek
Contempt into my ear—my ear which drank
God's accents once? you curse me? Why men, men,
I am not formed for it! Those hideous eyes
Will be before me sleeping, waking, praying,
315 They will not let me even die. Spare, spare me,
Sinning or no, forget that, only spare me
The horrible scorn! You thought I could support it,
But now you see what silly fragile creature
Cowers thus. I am not good nor bad enough,
320 Not Christ nor Cain, yet even Cain was saved
From Hate like this. Let me but totter back!
Perhaps I shall elude those jeers which creep
Into my very brain, and shut these scorched
Eyelids and keep those mocking faces out.

325 Listen, Aprile! I am very calm:
Be not deceived, there is no passion here
Where the blood leaps like an imprisoned thing:
I am calm: I will exterminate the race!

309| MS: rest! 1835: rest. 310| MS: Ha——what? spit at me——and grin
1835: Ha, what < > me, and 1849: what? you spit at me, you grin
312| MS: once—and curse < > why Men, Men, 1835: once, and < > Why men,
men, 1849: once? you 313| MS: it——those 1835: form'd for it; those
1849: formed for it! Those 314| MS: praying 1835: praying; 1849: Follow
me sleeping < > praying God, 1863: Will be before me sleeping < >
praying, 315| MS: die——spare, spare me 1835: die: spare, spare me,
1849: And will < > me. 1863: They will < > die. Spare, spare me,
316| MS:—Sinning < > that— § above § , only 1835: Sinning < > that,
only 317| MS: That horrible scorn——you < > it 1835: scorn; you < >
it, 1863: scorn! You 1888: it. 319| MS: I am——I < > enough——
1835: am. I < > enough, 1849: Cowers thus. I 320| MS: Not Christ——nor
Cain——yet 1835: Not Christ, nor Cain, yet 1863: Christ nor 321| MS:
hate < > this——let < > back—— 1835: this: let < > back, 1863: this. Let
< > back! 1888: Hate 322| MS: shall forget those 1849: shall elude
those 323| 1835: scorch'd 1849: scorched 324| MS: out———
1835: Eyelids, and < > out. 1863: out. § end of page § 1868: out. § end of
page § 1888: out. / § space § 325| MS: Listen Aprile < > calm— 1835:
calm: 1849: Listen, Aprile 326| MS:—Be not deceived—there 1835: Be not
deceived, there < > here, 1863: here 327| MS: thing——— 1835:
imprison'd thing. 1849: imprisoned 1863: thing:

Enough of that: 'tis said and it shall be.
330 And now be merry: safe and sound am I
Who broke through their best ranks to get at you.
And such a havoc, such a rout, Aprile!
FESTUS Have you no thought, no memory for me,
Aureole? I am so wretched—my pure Michal
335 Is gone, and you alone are left me now,
And even you forget me. Take my hand—
Lean on me thus. Do you not know me, Aureole?
PARACELSUS Festus, my own friend, you are come at last?
As you say, 'tis an awful enterprise;
340 But you believe I shall go through with it:
'Tis like you, and I thank you. Thank him for me,
Dear Michal! See how bright St. Saviour's spire
Flames in the sunset; all its figures quaint
Gay in the glancing light: you might conceive them
345 A troop of yellow-vested white-haired Jews
Bound for their own land where redemption dawns.
FESTUS Not that blest time—not our youth's time, dear God!
PARACELSUS Ha—stay! true, I forget—all is done since,
And he is come to judge me. How he speaks,
350 How calm, how well! yes, it is true, all true;

329| MS: be: 1835: be ...   1849: be.   330| MS: merry——safe < > I,
1835: merry—safe   1863: merry: safe < > I   331| MS: thro' < > you,
1835: through   1849: you;   1863: you.   332| MS: rout Aprile!— — —   1835:
Aprile! . . .   1849: rout, Aprile!   333| MS: me   1849: me,   334| MS:
Aureole?—I < > wretched . . . my   1835: Aureole? I < > wretched—my
335| MS: gone——and < > left to me,   1835: gone, and   1868: left me
now,   336| MS: me——take my hand   1835: me—take my hand—   1849: me:
take   1863: me. Take   337| MS: thus . . do < > me Aureole?   1835: thus.
Do   1849: me, thus < > me, Aureole?   1868: me thus   338| MS:
Festus,—my own friend—you < > last?— — —   1835: Festus, my own friend, you
< > last?   339| MS: enterprise— — —   1835: enterprise—   1863:
enterprise;   340| MS: thro' < > it:—   1835: through < > it:
341| MS: Tis < > thank you;——thank < > me   1835: 'Tis < > thank you; thank
< > me,   1863: thank you. Thank   342| MS: Michal!——see   1835: Michal!
See   343| MS: sunset—all   1835: sunset; all   344| MS: light—you
1835: light: you   345-347| MS: yellow-vested, white-haired Jews . . . . . / Not
< > blessed   1835: white-hair'd Jews . . .   1849: white-haired Jews, / Bound for
their own land where redemption dawns! / Not < > blest   1863: yellow-vested
white-haired Jews   1868: dawns.   348| MS: Ha——stay—true I forget——all
< > since!   1835: Ha—stay! true, I forget—all   1868: since,   349| MS:
me:—how he speaks,—   1835: me: how he speaks,   1863: me. How
350| MS: calm—how < > true—all true: 1835: How calm, how < > true, all true;

All quackery; all deceit; myself can laugh
The first at it, if you desire: but still
You know the obstacles which taught me tricks
So foreign to my nature—envy and hate,
355 Blind opposition, brutal prejudice,
Bald ignorance—what wonder if I sunk
To humour men the way they most approved?
My cheats were never palmed on such as you,
Dear Festus! I will kneel if you require me,
360 Impart the meagre knowledge I possess,
Explain its bounded nature, and avow
My insufficiency—whate'er you will:
I give the fight up: let there be an end,
A privacy, an obscure nook for me.
365 I want to be forgotten even by God.
But if that cannot be, dear Festus, lay me,
When I shall die, within some narrow grave,
Not by itself—for that would be too proud—
But where such graves are thickest; let it look
370 Nowise distinguished from the hillocks round,
So that the peasant at his brother's bed
May tread upon my own and know it not;
And we shall all be equal at the last,
Or classed according to life's natural ranks,
375 Fathers, sons, brothers, friends—not rich, nor wise,

351| *MS:* quackery—all deceit! myself   *1835:* quackery; all   *1868:* deceit;
myself   352| *MS:* desire——but   *1835:* desire: but   354| *MS:* nature—
—envy and hate,—   *1835:* nature—envy, and hate—   *1863:* envy and hate,
355| *MS:* opposition,—brutal prejudice—   *1835* opposition—brutal   *1863:*
opposition, brutal prejudice,   356| *MS:* ignorance——what   *1835:*
ignorance—what   357| *MS:* humour them the   *1849:* humour men the
358| *MS:* you   *1835:* palm'd < > you,   *1849:* palmed   359| *MS:* Festus . . .
I   *1835:* Festus. I   *1849:* Festus! I   362| *MS:* will:—   *1835:* will:
363| *MS:* up!—let < > end,—   *1835:* up! let < > end,   *1868:* up: let
364| *MS:* privacy— § above § , an < > me——   *1835:* privacy, an < > me.
365| *MS:* God!   *1868:* God.   366| *MS:* be,——dear < > me   *1835:* be,
dear   *1849:* me,   367| *MS:* grave   *1835:* grave,   368| *MS:*—Not by
itself——for < > proud:——   *1835:* Not by itself—for < > proud—   369| *MS:*
thickest; see it   *1849:* thickest; let it   370| *MS:* round   *1835:* distinguish'd
< > round,   *1849:* distinguished   372| *MS:* Shall tread   *1849:* May
tread   373| *MS:* So we   *1849:* And we   374| *1835:* class'd   *1849:*
classed   375| *MS:* friends——not rich nor wise   *1835:* friends—not rich, nor
wise,

Nor gifted: lay me thus, then say, "He lived
Too much advanced before his brother men;
They kept him still in front: 'twas for their good
But yet a dangerous station. It were strange
380 That he should tell God he had never ranked
With men: so, here at least he is a man."
FESTUS That God shall take thee to his breast, dear spirit,
Unto his breast, be sure! and here on earth
Shall splendour sit upon thy name for ever.
385 Sun! all the heaven is glad for thee: what care
If lower mountains light their snowy phares
At thine effulgence, yet acknowledge not
The source of day? Their theft shall be their bale:
For after-ages shall retrack thy beams,
390 And put aside the crowd of busy ones
And worship thee alone—the master-mind,
The thinker, the explorer, the creator!
Then, who should sneer at the convulsive throes
With which thy deeds were born, would scorn as well
395 The sheet of winding subterraneous fire
Which, pent and writhing, sends no less at last
Huge islands up amid the simmering sea.
Behold thy might in me! thou hast infused

376| _MS:_ thus,—then say "He   _1835:_ thus, then   _1863:_ say, "He   **377|** _MS:_
Men:—   _1835:_ men: _1863:_ men;   **378|** _MS:_ Front——'twas < > good,
_1835:_ front; 'twas   _1863:_ front: 'twas < > good   **379|** _MS:_ But still a < >
station——strange it were   _1835:_ station. Strange   _1849:_ But yet a < > station.
were strange   **380|** _1835:_ rank'd   _1849:_ ranked   **381|** _MS:_ Men:——so
here < > "Man!"   _1835:_ men: so < > man!"   _1849:_ so, here   **382|** _MS:_
PARACELSUS That < > Spirit,   _1835:_ FESTUS That   _1863:_ His < > spirit,   _1868:_
his   **383|** _MS:_—Unto < > sure!——and   _1835:_ Unto < > sure! and   _1863:_
His   _1868:_ his   **384|** _MS:_ forever!   _1835:_ for ever!   _1868:_ ever.
385| _MS:_—Sun!—all < > thee!——what   _1835:_ Sun! all < > thee: what
387| _MS:_ effulgence yet   _1835:_ effulgence, yet   **388|** _MS:_ day?——their < >
bale,   _1835:_ day? their < > bale,   _1849:_ day? Men look up to the sun: _1863:_
day? Their theft shall be their bale: **389|** _MS:_ retrack the beams,   _1835:_ after
ages   _1849:_ after-ages < > retrack thy beams,   **390|** _1835:_ ones,   _1863:_
ones   **391|** _MS:_ alone——the Master mind   _1835:_ alone—the master-
mind,   **392|** _MS:_ Thinker < > Explorer < > Creator—   _1835:_ thinker < >
explorer < > creator;   _1849:_ creator!   **393|** _MS:_ And who   _1849:_ Then,
who   **394|** _MS:_ born— § above § , would   _1835:_ born would   _1849:_ born,
would   **395|** _MS:_ The winding sheet of subterraneous   _1868:_ winding-sheet
_1888:_ The sheet of winding subterraneous   **397|** _MS:_ sea!   _1868:_ sea.
398| _MS:_—Behold   _1835:_ Behold

Thy soul in mine; and I am grand as thou,
400 Seeing I comprehend thee—I so simple,
Thou so august. I recognize thee first;
I saw thee rise, I watched thee early and late,
And though no glance reveal thou dost accept
My homage—thus no less I proffer it,
405 And bid thee enter gloriously thy rest.

PARACELSUS Festus!

FESTUS   I am for noble Aureole, God!
I am upon his side, come weal or woe.
His portion shall be mine. He has done well.
I would have sinned, had I been strong enough,
410 As he has sinned. Reward him or I waive
Reward! If thou canst find no place for him,
He shall be king elsewhere, and I will be
His slave for ever. There are two of us.

PARACELSUS Dear Festus!

FESTUS   Here, dear Aureole! ever by you!

415 PARACELSUS Nay, speak on, or I dream again. Speak on!
Some story, anything—only your voice.
I shall dream else. Speak on! ay, leaning so!

FESTUS   Thus the Mayne glideth
Where my Love abideth.

399| *MS:* mine——and < > thou   *1835:* mine; and < > thou,   **400|**   *MS:*
thee——I so simple   *1835:* thee—I so simple,   **401|**   *MS:* august! I < > thee,
first!   *1835:* thee first;   *1868:* august. I   **402|**   *MS:* rise and I have watched
thee well   *1835:* rise, and < > watch'd < > well,   *1849:* rise, I watched thee early
and late,   **403|**   *MS:* tho' < > reveal that thou acceptest   *1835:* though
1849: reveal thou dost accept   **404|**   *MS:* homage——thus < > it   *1835:*
homage—thus < > it,   **405|**   *MS:* Rest!   *1835:* rest!   *1868:* rest.
406| *MS:*—Festus!——FESTUS——I   *1835:* Festus! FESTUS I   **407|**   *MS:*
woe!   *1868:* woe.   **408|**   *MS:* mine!—He < > well!   *1835:* mine! He   *1868:*
mine. He < > well.   **409|**   *MS:*—I   *1835:* I < > sinn'd   *1849:* sinned
410| *MS:* sinned! Reward   *1835:* sinn'd   *1849:* sinned   *1868:* sinned.
Reward   **411|**   *MS:* Reward!—if   *1835:* Reward! If   *1863:* Thou   *1868:*
thou   **412|**   *MS:* King   *1835:* king   **413|**   *MS:* ever!———there < >
us!—   *1835:* ever! . . . There < > us!   *1849:* ever! There   *1868:* ever. There
414| *MS:* FESTUS—Here   *1835:* FESTUS Here   **415|**   *MS:* Nay speak < >
again—speak   *1835:* Nay, speak < > again. Speak   **416|**   *MS:*—Some
story—anything . . only < > voice—   *1835:* Some story, any thing—only < > voice.
1863: anything   **417|**   *MS:* else—speak on   *1835:* else. Speak on!   *1849:* on!
ay, leaning so!   **418|**   *1849:* Softly the Mayne river glideth   *1863:* Thus the
Mayne glideth   **419|**   *1835:* love abideth;   *1849:* Close by where my love
abideth;   *1863:* Where my Love abideth.

420   Sleep's no softer: it proceeds
On through lawns, on through meads,
On and on, whate'er befall,
Meandering and musical,
Though the niggard pasturage
425   Bears not on its shaven ledge
Aught but weeds and waving grasses
To view the river as it passes,
Save here and there a scanty patch
Of primroses too faint to catch
430   A weary bee.

PARACELSUS More, more; say on!

FESTUS   And scarce it pushes
Its gentle way through strangling rushes
Where the glossy kingfisher
Flutters when noon-heats are near,
435   Glad the shelving banks to shun,
Red and steaming in the sun,
Where the shrew-mouse with pale throat
Burrows, and the speckled stoat;
Where the quick sandpipers flit
440   In and out the marl and grit
That seems to breed them, brown as they:
Nought disturbs its quiet way,
Save some lazy stork that springs,
Trailing it with legs and wings,

421| MS: thro' <> thro' meads   1835: through <> through meads,
422| MS: and on whate'er   1835: and on, whate'er   423| MS: musical
1835: musical,   424| MS: Tho'   1835: Though   1849: pasture's edge   1863:
pasturage   425| MS: shaven edge   1849: shaven ledge   427| MS: To
behold it as   1849: To view the river as   429| 1835: primroses, too   1868:
primroses too   430| MS: bee— —   1835: bee . . .   1863: bee.
431| MS: More,—more—say   1835: More, more; say   1849: FESTUS The river
pushes   1863: FESTUS And scare it pushes   432| MS: thro'   1835: through
<> rushes,   1888: rushes   433| MS: king-fisher   1863: kingfisher
434| MS: near   1835: near,   435| MS: shun   1835: shun,   436| MS:
sun   1835: sun,   438| MS: Burrows—and <> stoat—   1835: Burrows, and
<> stoat,   1863: stoat;   439| MS: sand-pipers   1863: sandpipers
440| MS: the soft and wet   1849: the marl and grit   441| MS: Clay that
breeds   1835: they.   1849: That seems to breed them   1863: they:
442| MS:—Nought <> way   1835: Nought <> way,   1849: disturbs the river's
way,   1863: disturbs its quiet way,   443| MS: springs   1835: springs,
444| MS: wings   1835: wings,

445 Whom the shy fox from the hill
Rouses, creep he ne'er so still.
PARACELSUS My heart! they loose my heart, those simple words;
Its darkness passes, which nought else could touch:
Like some dark snake that force may not expel,
450 Which glideth out to music sweet and low.
What were you doing when your voice broke through
A chaos of ugly images? You, indeed!
Are you alone here?
FESTUS   All alone: you know me?
This cell?
PARACELSUS An unexceptionable vault:
455 Good brick and stone: the bats kept out, the rats
Kept in: a snug nook: how should I mistake it?
FESTUS But wherefore am I here?
PARACELSUS   Ah, well remembered!
Why, for a purpose—for a purpose, Festus!
'Tis like me: here I trifle while time fleets,
460 And this occasion, lost, will ne'er return.
You are here to be instructed. I will tell
God's message; but I have so much to say,
I fear to leave half out. All is confused
No doubt; but doubtless you will learn in time.
465 He would not else have brought you here: no doubt

446| MS: Arouses— — 1835: Arouses . . . 1849: Rouses, creep he ne'er so
still. 447| MS: heart—they < > heart those < > words— 1835: heart! they
< > heart, those < > words; 448| MS: passes which < > touch— 1835:
passes, which < > touch; 1863: touch: 449| MS: expel 1835:
expel, 450| MS: low:— 1835: low. 451| MS: thro' 1835:
through 452| MS: images . . . . It is you indeed! 1835: images? . . . It is you,
indeed! 1849: images? You 453| MS:—Are < > alone:—you 1835: Are
< > alone: you 454| MS:—This < > vault— 1835: This 1863:
vault: 455| MS: stone—the 1863: stone: the 456| MS: in— —a < >
nook:—how 1835: in—a < > nook: how 1863: in: a 457| MS:
PARACELSUS—Ah!— —well remembered:— 1835: PARACELSUS Ah! well remember'd:
1849: remembered: 1863: remembered! 458| MS: purpose— —for 1835:
purpose—for 459| MS: 'Tis < > me . . . here 1835: 'Tis < > me:
here 460| MS: return! 1868: return. 461| MS: instructed— —I
1835: instructed. I 462| MS: Their message— —but < > say 1835: message;
but < > say, 1849: God's message 463| MS: out—all 1835: out: all
1863: out. All 464| MS: Within—but < > time 1835: Within; but < >
time. 1849: No doubt; but 465| MS:— —They would not have despatched
me else— —no 1835: dispatch'd me else: no 1849: He would not else have
brought you here: no

245

I shall see clearer soon.

FESTUS   Tell me but this—
You are not in despair?

PARACELSUS   I? and for what?

FESTUS Alas, alas! he knows not, as I feared!

PARACELSUS What is it you would ask me with that earnest
470 Dear searching face?

FESTUS   How feel you, Aureole?

PARACELSUS   Well:
Well. 'Tis a strange thing: I am dying, Festus,
And now that fast the storm of life subsides,
I first perceive how great the whirl has been.
I was calm then, who am so dizzy now—
475 Calm in the thick of the tempest, but no less
A partner of its motion and mixed up
With its career. The hurricane is spent,
And the good boat speeds through the brightening weather;
But is it earth or sea that heaves below?
480 The gulf rolls like a meadow-swell, o'erstrewn
With ravaged boughs and remnants of the shore;
And now some islet, loosened from the land,
Swims past with all its trees, sailing to ocean;
And now the air is full of uptorn canes,

466| MS: soon:——FESTUS < > this,—   1835: soon. FESTUS < > this—
467| MS: PARACELSUS — —I?—and   1835: PARACELSUS I? and   **468|**   MS: Alas,
alas,—he < > not as I feared— — —   1835: Alas, alas! he < > not, as I fear'd . . .
1849: feared!   **469|**   1835: earnest,   1868: earnest   **470|**   MS: Dear,
searching < > PARACELSUS — — Well;   1835: PARACELSUS Well;   1849: PARACELSUS
Well!   1868: Dear searching < > Well: **471|**   MS: Well:—'tis < >
thing;—I   1835: Well: 'tis < > thing. I   1868: Well. 'Tis < > thing: I
472| MS: now the storm of life is fast subsiding   1849: now that fast the storm of life
subsides,   **473|**   MS: how swift the < > been: 1849: how great the   1863:
been.   **474|**   MS: now,—   1835: now—   **476|**   1835: motion, and mix'd
1849: mixed   1863: motion and   **477|**   MS: career: the   1835: career.
The   **478|**   MS: thro' < > weather   1835: through the bright'ning weather;
1849: brightening   **480|**   MS: meadow-swell—o'erstrewn   1835: meadow-swell,
o'erstrewn   1849: For the < > a meadow, overstrewn   1863: The < > meadow-
swell, o'erstrewn   **481|**   MS: shore   1835: shore.   1849: shore;
482| MS:——And < > islet loosened   1835: And < > islet, loosen'd   1849:
loosened   1888: slet   1889: islet   **483|**   MS: ocean,   1835: ocean.   1849:
ocean;   **484|**   MS:——And canes   1835: And < > up-torn canes,   1863:
uptorn

485 Light strippings from the fan-trees, tamarisks
Unrooted, with their birds still clinging to them,
All high in the wind. Even so my varied life
Drifts by me; I am young, old, happy, sad,
Hoping, desponding, acting, taking rest,
490 And all at once: that is, those past conditions
Float back at once on me. If I select
Some special epoch from the crowd, 'tis but
To will, and straight the rest dissolve away,
And only that particular state is present
495 With all its long-forgotten circumstance
Distinct and vivid as at first—myself
A careless looker-on and nothing more,
Indifferent and amused, but nothing more.
And this is death: I understand it all.
500 New being waits me; new perceptions must
Be born in me before I plunge therein;
Which last is Death's affair; and while I speak,
Minute by minute he is filling me

485| MS: fan-trees— —tamarisks   1835: Like strippings < > fan-trees; tamarisks
1849: Light strippings < > fan-trees, tamarisks   486| MS: Unrooted with < >
them,— —   1835: Unrooted, with < > them,   487| MS: wind:—even   1835:
wind. Even   488| MS: me— —I < > sad   1835: me. I < > sad,   1863: me;
I   489| MS: rest   1835: rest,   490| MS: once!—that is,—those   1835:
once: that is, those   491| MS: Flock back upon me . . . if I choose to single
1835: me. If   1849: Float back at once on me. If I select   492| MS: Some
certain epoch < > crowd— § above § , 'tis   1835: crowd, 'tis   1849: Some special
epoch   493| MS: will—and < > away   1835: will, and < > away,   1863:
away   1868: away,   494| MS: And that < > present only,   1849: And only
that < > present,   1863: present   495| MS: its circumstance forgotten long
1835: long,   1849: its long-forgotten circumstance,   1863: circumstance
496| MS: But now distinct < > first,— 1835: first—   1849: Distinct < >
first—myself   497| MS: I being a < > looker-on—nought more!   1835: looker-
on, nought   1849: A < > looker-on, and nothing more!   1863: looker-on and
1868: more,   498| MS: amused— —but < > more!   1835: amused, but
1863: amused but   1868: more.   1888: amused, but   499| MS: Death;—I
< > all: 1835: death: I < > all.   500| MS: There is new Being waiting
me— § above § , and new   1835: being < > me, and   1849: New being waits me;
new perceptions must   501| MS: Perceptions must be < > before   1849: Be
< > before I plunge therein;   502| MS: I plunge therein,—this last is Deaths
affair,   1835: therein; this < > Death's   1849: Which last < > affair; and while I
speak,   503| MS: And he is filling me, minute by minute,   1835: me minute
by minute   1849: Minute by minute he is filling me

247

With power; and while my foot is on the threshold
505 Of boundless life—the doors unopened yet,
All preparations not complete within—
I turn new knowledge upon old events,
And the effect is . . . but I must not tell;
It is not lawful. Your own turn will come
510 One day. Wait, Festus! You will die like me.
FESTUS 'Tis of that past life that I burn to hear.
PARACELSUS You wonder it engages me just now?
In truth, I wonder too. What's life to me?
Where'er I look is fire, where'er I listen
515 Music, and where I tend bliss evermore.
Yet how can I refrain? 'Tis a refined
Delight to view those chances,—one last view.
I am so near the perils I escape,
That I must play with them and turn them over,
520 To feel how fully they are past and gone.
Still, it is like, some further cause exists
For this peculiar mood—some hidden purpose;
Did I not tell you something of it, Festus?
I had it fast, but it has somehow slipt
525 Away from me; it will return anon.
FESTUS (Indeed his cheek seems young again, his voice
Complete with its old tones: that little laugh

504| MS: With Power— § above § , and 1835: With power, and 1849: power;
and 505| MS: Life—the portals yet unopened— 1835: life—the < >
unopen'd— 1849: the doors unopened yet, 507| MS: Knowledge < >
Events 1835: knowledge < > events, 508| MS: is— — —but < > tell
1835: is . . . But < > tell; 1863: but 509| MS:—It is not fair— —you < >
will arrive 1835: It < > fair. Your < > arrive 1849: not lawful. Your < > will
come 510–511| MS: Some day— —dear Festus you < > me,— / Your turn will
come so that you do but wait!— — / 'Tis < > hear . . . . 1835: day. Dear < > me—
/ < > wait! / 'Tis < > hear . . . 1849: One day. Wait, Festus! You < > me! /
'Tis < > hear! 1868: me. / < > hear. 513| MS: too—what's 1835: too.
What's 514| MS: fire—where'er 1835: fire, where'er 516| MS: Yet I
can not refrain:— —'tis 1835: refrain: 'tis 1849: Yet how can I refrain? 'Tis
517| MS: chances once again;— 1835: again. 1849: chances,—one last
view. 518| MS: escape 1835: escape, 519| MS: over 1835:
over, 520| MS: gone:— 1835: gone. 521| 1835: Still it is like some
1868: Still, it is like, some 522| MS: mood— —some < > purpose— — 1835:
mood—some < > purpose; 524| MS: fast— — —but 1835: fast, but
525| MS: me— —it < > anon.— — 1835: me; it < > anon. 526| MS:
again—his 1835: again, his 527| MS: tones!—that 1835: tones—that 1849:
tones:that

Concluding every phrase, with upturned eye,
As though one stooped above his head to whom
530 He looked for confirmation and approval,
Where was it gone so long, so well preserved?
Then, the fore-finger pointing as he speaks,
Like one who traces in an open book
The matter he declares; 'tis many a year
535 Since I remarked it last: and this in him,
But now a ghastly wreck!)
                              And can it be,
Dear Aureole, you have then found out at last
That worldly things are utter vanity?
That man is made for weakness, and should wait
540 In patient ignorance, till God appoint . . .
PARACELSUS Ha, the purpose: the true purpose: that is it!
How could I fail to apprehend! You here,
I thus! But no more trifling: I see all,
I know all: my last mission shall be done
545 If strength suffice. No trifling! Stay; this posture
Hardly befits one thus about to speak:
I will arise.
FESTUS   Nay, Aureole, are you wild?

528| MS: phrase—with < > eye   1835: phrase; with up-turn'd eye,   1849: phrase,
with up-turned   1863: upturned   529| 1835: stoop'd < > head, to   1849:
stooped   1863: head to   530| MS: approval— —   1835: look'd < >
approval: 1849: looked < > and applause,—   1863: and approval,
531| MS: preserved? . .   1835: preserved?   1849: long, being kept so well?
1863: long, so well preserved?   532| MS: And the forefinger < > speaks
1835: fore-finger < > speaks,   1849: Then, the fore-finger   534| MS:
declares— —'tis   1835: declares; 'tis   535| MS: last:—and < > him   1835:
remark'd it last: and < > him . . .   1849: remarked < > him,   536| MS:
wreck!— § written over by § wreck!) / —And < > be   1835: wreck!) / And < >
be,   537| MS: Aureole? you   1835: Aureole, you   538| MS: The utter
vanity of worldly things?   1849: That worldly things are utter
vanity?   539| MS: Man   1835: man   540| MS: ignorance till God
appoint . . . .   1835: appoint . . .   1888: ignorance, till   541| MS: purpose!
the < > purpose! that   1835: purpose; the < > purpose: that   1863: purpose, the
< > it   1863: it!   542| MS:— —How < > apprehend!— —you   1835: How
< > apprehend! You   543| MS: thus— —but § written over by § thus!—but < >
trifling;—I see all—   1835: thus! But < > trifling; I see all,   1868: trifling: I
544| MS: all;—my   1835: all: my   545| MS: suffice:—no trifling!—stay—this
1835: suffice. No trifling! Stay; this   546| MS: speak—   1835: speak:
547| MS: arise.— FESTUS Dear Aureole— —are you wild? . .   1835: arise. FESTUS
< > Aureole, are you wild?   1849: FESTUS Nay, Aureole

You cannot leave your couch.

PARACELSUS   No help; no help;
Not even your hand. So! there, I stand once more!
550 Speak from a couch? I never lectured thus.
My gown—the scarlet lined with fur; now put
The chain about my neck; my signet-ring
Is still upon my hand, I think—even so;
Last, my good sword; ah, trusty Azoth, leapest
555 Beneath thy master's grasp for the last time?
This couch shall be my throne: I bid these walls
Be consecrate, this wretched cell become
A shrine, for here God speaks to men through me.
Now, Festus, I am ready to begin.
560 FESTUS I am dumb with wonder.

PARACELSUS   Listen, therefore, Festus!
There will be time enough, but none to spare.
I must content myself with telling only
The most important points. You doubtless feel
That I am happy, Festus; very happy.
565 FESTUS 'Tis no delusion which uplifts him thus!
Then you are pardoned, Aureole, all your sin?

PARACELSUS Ay, pardoned: yet why pardoned?

FESTUS   'Tis God's praise

---

⁵⁴⁸| MS: couch— — PARACELSUS —No help! No help!   1835: couch. PARACELSUS No
help; no help;   ⁵⁴⁹| MS: hand!— —so!— —there   1835: hand. So! there
⁵⁵⁰| MS: couch?—why I ne'er < > thus!—   1835: couch? why < > thus.   1849:
couch? I never   ⁵⁵¹| MS: gown— —the < > fur:— —now   1835: gown—the
scarlet, lined < > fur; now   1863: scarlet lined   ⁵⁵²| MS: neck—my   1835:
neck; my   ⁵⁵³| MS: think—even so.   1835: think—even so;   ⁵⁵⁴| MS:—
—Last my < > sword, —ha trusty Azoth? leapest   1835: Last, my < > sword; ha,
trusty Azoth, leapest   1868: sword; ah, trusty   ⁵⁵⁵| MS: masters   1835:
master's   ⁵⁵⁶| MS: bid this cell   1849: bid these walls   ⁵⁵⁷| MS:
consecrate . . this wretched bed become   1835: consecrate; this   1849: wretched cell
become   1863: consecrate, this   ⁵⁵⁸| MS: shrine— —for < > Men thro' me!
1835: shrine; for < > men through   1863: shrine, for   1868: me.   ⁵⁶⁰| MS:
am blind with wonder! PARACELSUS   1835: wonder. PARACELSUS   1849: am dumb
with   ⁵⁶¹| MS: spare . .   1835: spare.   ⁵⁶³| MS: points: you   1835:
points. You   1868: doubtlsss   1888: doubtless   ⁵⁶⁴| MS: Festus?—very
happy?   1835: Festus; very happy.   ⁵⁶⁵| MS: Tis < > thus!—   1835: 'Tis
< > thus . . .   1849: thus!   ⁵⁶⁶| MS: you are pardoned § are inserted above the
line §   1835: pardon'd   1849: pardoned   ⁵⁶⁷| MS: Pardon?— —and
wherefore pardon?— — FESTUS —Tis   1835: Pardon? and < > pardon? FESTUS 'Tis
1849: Ay, pardoned! yet why pardoned? FESTUS   1868: pardoned: yet

That man is bound to seek, and you . . .

PARACELSUS   Have lived!

We have to live alone to set forth well

570   God's praise. 'Tis true, I sinned much, as I thought,

And in effect need mercy, for I strove

To do that very thing; but, do your best

Or worst, praise rises, and will rise for ever.

Pardon from him, because of praise denied—

575   Who calls me to himself to exalt himself?

He might laugh as I laugh!

FESTUS   But all comes

To the same thing. 'Tis fruitless for mankind

To fret themselves with what concerns them not;

They are no use that way: they should lie down

580   Content as God has made them, nor go mad

In thriveless cares to better what is ill.

PARACELSUS No, no; mistake me not; let me not work

More harm than I have worked! This is my case:

If I go joyous back to God, yet bring

585   No offering, if I render up my soul

Without the fruits it was ordained to bear,

If I appear the better to love God

568| *MS:* Man < > to seek,—and you . . . PARACELSUS ——Have   *1835:* man < >
seek, and you . . . PARACELSUS Have   569| *MS:* live, alone, to   *1835:* live alone
to   570| *MS:* praise: 'tis < > thought—   *1835:* praise. 'Tis < > sinn'd < >
thought,   *1849:* sinned   571| *MS:* And, in effect, need mercy——for   *1835:*
And in effect need mercy, for   572| *MS:* thing . . but   *1835:* thing; but
573| *MS:* worst—praise rises and < > ever!   *1835:* worst, praise rises, and < >
ever.   *1888:* ever   *1889:* ever.   574| *MS:* Him?——who call me to Himself
1835: Him, who   *1849:* Him, because of praise denied—   *1868:* him
575| *MS:* To teach me better, and exalt me higher? . . . .   *1835:* better and < >
higher!   *1849:* Who calls me to Himself to exalt Himself?   *1868:* himself < >
himself?   576| *MS:* laugh, as < > all this comes   *1835:* laugh as I laugh.
FESTUS   *1849:* I laugh! FESTUS Then all comes   *1863:* FESTUS But all
577| *MS:* thing——'tis < > Mankind   *1835:* thing. 'Tis < > mankind
578| *MS:* not: *1835:* not;   579| *MS:* way——they   *1835:* way: they
581| *MS:* better their condition:—   *1835:* condition.   *1849:* better what is
ill.   582| *MS:* No, No! mistake me not——let   *1835:* No, no; mistake me not;
let   583| *MS:* have done!—this < > case:——   *1835:* done. This < > case:
1849: done! This   *1868:* have worked! This   585| *MS:* offering—if   *1835:*
offering; if   *1849:* offering, if   586| *MS:* bear,—   *1835:* ordain'd to bear;
1849: ordained to bear,   587| *MS:* appear to love God better for   *1849:* appear
the better to love God

For sin, as one who has no claim on him,—
Be not deceived! It may be surely thus
590 With me, while higher prizes still await
The mortal persevering to the end.
Beside I am not all so valueless:
I have been something, though too soon I left
Following the instincts of that happy time.
595 FESTUS What happy time? For God's sake, for man's sake,
What time was happy? All I hope to know
That answer will decide. What happy time?
PARACELSUS When but the time I vowed myself to man?
FESTUS Great God, thy judgments are inscrutable!
600 PARACELSUS Yes, it was in me; I was born for it—
I, Paracelsus: it was mine by right.
Doubtless a searching and impetuous soul
Might learn from its own motions that some task
Like this awaited it about the world;
605 Might seek somewhere in this blank life of ours
For fit delights to stay its longings vast;
And, grappling Nature, so prevail on her
To fill the creature full she dared thus frame
Hungry for joy; and, bravely tyrannous,

588| MS: My sins— —as   1835: sins, as < > him,   1849: For sin < > him,—
1863: Him,—   1868: him,—   **589|** MS: deceived;—it may be only thus   1835:
deceived: it   1849: be surely thus   **590|** MS: me— —or higher prizes may
await   1835: me; or   1849: me, while higher prizes still await   **591-593|** MS:
end:— / Beside < > valueless / I have < > tho'   1835: end. / Beside, I < >
valueless; / < > though   1849: end. / For I too have been something, though too
soon   1863: end. / Beside I am not all so valueless: / I have been something, though
too soon I left   **594|** MS: time . . . .   1835: time . . .   1849: I left the < >
time!   1863: Following the   1868: time.   **595|** MS: time?— —for < > sake—
—for Man's sake   1835: time? For < > sake, for man's sake,   **596|** MS: all
1835: All   **597|** MS: decide . . . what   1835: decide. What   **598|** MS:
Man?   1835: vow'd < > man.   1849: vowed my help to man?   1863: vowed
myself to   **599|** 1863: Thy   1868: thy   **600|** MS: Yes— —it < > me—
—I < > it:—   1835: Yes, it < > me; I < > it—   **601|** MS: I . . .
Paracelsus:—it < > right:—   1835: I, Paracelsus: it < > right.   **602|** MS:
impetuous spirit   1849: impetuous soul   **604|** MS: world— — —   1835:
world;   **606|** MS: vast,   1835: vast;   **607|** MS: grappling strenuously
with Fate, compel her   1849: grappling Nature, so prevail on her   **608|** MS:
full, whom she dared frame   1835: full whom   1849: full she dared to frame
1868: dare thus frame   **609|** MS: joy:—and—bravely tyrannous—   1835: joy,
and, bravely tyrannous,

252

610 Grow in demand, still craving more and more,
And make each joy conceded prove a pledge
Of other joy to follow—bating nought
Of its desires, still seizing fresh pretence
To turn the knowledge and the rapture wrung
615 As an extreme, last boon, from destiny,
Into occasion for new covetings,
New strifes, new triumphs:—doubtless a strong soul,
Alone, unaided might attain to this,
So glorious is our nature, so august
620 Man's inborn uninstructed impulses,
His naked spirit so majestical!
But this was born in me; I was made so;
Thus much time saved: the feverish appetites,
The tumult of unproved desire, the unaimed
625 Uncertain yearnings, aspirations blind,
Distrust, mistake, and all that ends in tears
Were saved me; thus I entered on my course.
You may be sure I was not all exempt
From human trouble; just so much of doubt
630 As bade me plant a surer foot upon
The sun-road, kept my eye unruined 'mid

610| *MS:* demand—still < > and more— — — *1835:* demand, still < > and
more, 611| *MS:* make the joy *1849:* make each joy 612| *MS:* Of
further joy to follow— — —bating nothing *1835:* follow—bating *1849:* Of other joy
< > bating nought 613| *MS:* desires, but seizing all pretence *1849:* desires,
still seizing fresh pretence 615| *MS:* From Destiny as an extreme, last boon,
1849: As an extreme, last boon, from Destiny, *1863:* destiny, 617| *MS:*
triumphs: doubtless a strong spirit *1835:* triumphs. Doubtless *1849:*
triumphs:—doubtless a strong soul *1888:* soul, 618| *MS:* Might do all this
unaided and alone, *1849:* Alone, unaided might attain to this, 619| *MS:*
nature— —so *1835:* nature, so 620| *MS:* impulses— — — *1835:*
impulses— *1849:* impulses, 622| *MS:*—But it was < > me! I < > so:
1835: But < > me: I < > so: *1849:* But this was < > me; I < > so;
623| *MS:* saved—the < > appetites— *1835:* saved: the < > appetites,
624| *MS:* desire—the aimless *1835:* desire, the *1849:* desire, the unaimed
625| *MS:* yearnings—near-sighted ambition, *1835:* yearnings, near-sighted *1849:*
yearnings, aspirations blind, 626| *MS:* mistake—and *1835:* mistake,
and 627-628| *MS:* me, tho' the lion-heart repines not / At working thro' such lets
its purpose out: / . . . . You *1835:* though the lion heart < > / < > through < >
out. / You *1849:* me; thus I entered on my course! / You *1868:* course.
629| *MS:* trouble,—just *1835:* trouble: just 631| *MS:* sun-road— —kept
1835: sun-road—kept < > unruin'd mid *1849:* unruined *1863:* sun-road, kept < >
'mid

The fierce and flashing splendour, set my heart
Trembling so much as warned me I stood there
On sufferance—not to idly gaze, but cast
635 Light on a darkling race; save for that doubt,
I stood at first where all aspire at last
To stand: the secret of the world was mine.
I knew, I felt, (perception unexpressed,
Uncomprehended by our narrow thought,
640 But somehow felt and known in every shift
And change in the spirit,—nay, in every pore
Of the body, even,)—what God is, what we are,
What life is—how God tastes an infinite joy
In infinite ways—one everlasting bliss,
645 From whom all being emanates, all power
Proceeds; in whom is life for evermore,
Yet whom existence in its lowest form
Includes; where dwells enjoyment there is he:
With still a flying point of bliss remote,
650 A happiness in store afar, a sphere
Of distant glory in full view; thus climbs
Pleasure its heights for ever and for ever.
The centre-fire heaves underneath the earth,
And the earth changes like a human face;

632| *MS:* splendour—set   *1863:* splendour, set   633| *1835:* warn'd   *1849:*
warned   634| *MS:* sufferance— —not < > but have   *1835:* sufferance—not
1849: but cast   635| *MS:* Remembrance of a darkling Race— —save that,
1835: race; save   *1849:* Light on a darkling race; save for that doubt,
637| *MS:* To reach: the secret   *1835:* To reach—the   *1849:* To stand: the
638–639| *MS:* felt . . not as one knows or feels / Aught else— —a vast perception
unexpressed, / Uncomprehended   *1835:* felt, not < > / < > else; a < >
unexpress'd,   *1849:* felt, perception unexpressed, / Uncomprehended
641–642| *MS:* spirit I bear— —nay, dare I say / In every pore of this fast-fading frame
/ I felt, I knew what God < > are° § footnote § °"Paracelse faisait profession du
Pantheisme le plus grossier." *Renauldin.*   *1835:* bear—nay < > say, // < > are, °
°Panthéisme   *1849:* spirit,—nay, in every pore / Of the body, even,)—what < > are,
§ footnote dropped §   643| *MS:* Life is . . . how   *1835:* life is—how
644| *MS:* ways— —one < > Bliss   *1835:* ways—one < > bliss,   645| *MS:*
Being < > Power   *1835:* being < > power   646| *MS:* Proceeds— —in < >
Life   *1835:* Proceeds; in < > life   647| *MS:* Existence   *1835:*
existence   648| *MS:* Includes— —where < > Enjoyment < > He!   *1835:*
Includes; where < > enjoyment   *1868:* he: 649| *MS:* remote—   *1849:*
remote,   650| *MS:* afar—a   *1849:* afar, a   651| *MS:* view— —thus
1835: view; thus   652| *MS:* forever and forever!   *1835:* for ever and for
ever!   *1868:* ever.

655 The molten ore bursts up among the rocks,
Winds into the stone's heart, outbranches bright
In hidden mines, spots barren river-beds,
Crumbles into fine sand where sunbeams bask—
God joys therein. The wroth sea's waves are edged
660 With foam, white as the bitten lip of hate,
When, in the solitary waste, strange groups
Of young volcanos come up, cyclops-like,
Staring together with their eyes on flame—
God tastes a pleasure in their uncouth pride.
665 Then all is still; earth is a wintry clod:
But spring-wind, like a dancing psaltress, passes
Over its breast to waken it, rare verdure
Buds tenderly upon rough banks, between
The withered tree-roots and the cracks of frost,
670 Like a smile striving with a wrinkled face;
The grass grows bright, the boughs are swoln with blooms
Like chrysalids impatient for the air,
The shining dorrs are busy, beetles run
Along the furrows, ants make their ado;
675 Above, birds fly in merry flocks, the lark
Soars up and up, shivering for very joy;
Afar the ocean sleeps; white fishing-gulls
Flit where the strand is purple with its tribe

655| MS: rocks   1835: rocks—   1849: rocks,   656| MS: heart—
—outbranches   1835: heart-outbranches   1849: heart, outbranches   657| MS:
mines . . spots < > river-beds . .   1835: mines—spots < > river-beds—   1849:
mines, spots < > river-beds,   658| MS: bask——.   1835:
bask—   659| MS: therein!—the   1835: therein! The   1868: therein. The
660| MS: foam white   1835: foam, white < > Hate: 1849: Hate,   1863:
hate,   661| MS: When in < > waste strange   1849: When, in < > waste,
strange   662| MS: cyclops-like   1835: cyclops-like,   663| MS: flame . . .
1835: flame,   1849: flame;—   1863: flame—   664| MS: pride!   1868:
pride.   665| MS: still: earth < > clod,   1835: clod;   1863: still; earth < >
clod: 667| MS: it——rare   1835: it; rare   1863: it, rare   668| MS:
Buds here and there upon   1849: Buds tenderly upon   669| MS: frost   1835:
wither'd < > frost,   1849: withered   670| MS: face,   1835: face;
671| MS: swollen   1835: swoln < > blooms,   1863: blooms   672| MS: air.
1835: air;   1863: air,   673| MS: busy——beetles   1835: busy; beetles   1863:
busy, beetles   674| MS: furrows . . ants < > ado . .   1835: furrows, ants < >
ado;   675| MS: Above birds < > flocks——the   1835: flocks—the   1849:
Above, birds   1863: flocks, the   677| MS: sleeps . . . white fishing gulls   1835:
sleeps; white fishing-gulls

Of nested limpets; savage creatures seek
680 Their loves in wood and plain—and God renews
His ancient rapture. Thus he dwells in all,
From life's minute beginnings, up at last
To man—the consummation of this scheme
Of being, the completion of this sphere
685 Of life: whose attributes had here and there
Been scattered o'er the visible world before,
Asking to be combined, dim fragments meant
To be united in some wondrous whole,
Imperfect qualities throughout creation,
690 Suggesting some one creature yet to make,
Some point where all those scattered rays should meet
Convergent in the faculties of man.
Power—neither put forth blindly, nor controlled
Calmly by perfect knowledge; to be used
695 At risk, inspired or checked by hope and fear:
Knowledge—not intuition, but the slow
Uncertain fruit of an enhancing toil,
Strengthened by love: love—not serenely pure,
But strong from weakness, like a chance-sown plant
700 Which, cast on stubborn soil, puts forth changed buds

679| MS: limpets: savage   1835: limpets; savage   680| MS: plain:— —and
1835: plain; and   1863: plain—and   681| MS: rapture! Thus He   1868:
rapture. Thus he   682| MS: Life's   1835: life's   683| MS: Man < >
Scheme   1835: man < > scheme   684| MS: Being—the < > Sphere   1835:
being < > sphere   1849: being, the   685| MS: Life   1835: life
686| 1835: scatter'd   1849: scattered   687| MS: combined . . . dim   1835:
combin'd—dim   1849: combined   1863: combined, dim   688| MS:
Whole,—   1835: whole—   1863: whole,   689| MS: Creation   1835:
creation,   690–693| MS: Creature < > make . . . / —(So would a Spirit deem,
intent on watching / The purpose of the world from its faint rise / To its mature
development)—some point / Whereto those wandering rays should all converge— — —
§ written over by § converge— / Might: neither   1835: creature < > make— / (So
< > // < > developement)—some < > // < > controll'd   1849: make— / Some
point where all those scattered rays should meet / Convergent in the faculties of man.
/ Power; neither < > controlled   690| 1863: make,   693| 1863:
Power—neither   694| MS: knowledge—to   1849: knowledge; to
695| MS: risk—inspir'd < > fear:—   1835: inspir'd or check'd < > fear—   1849:
risk, inspired or checked < > fear: 696| MS: Knowledge:—not   1835:
Knowledge: not   1849: Knowledge; not   1863: Knowledge—not   697| MS:
inhancing toil   1835: enhancing toil,   698| MS: love; Love:—not   1835:
Strengthen'd by love—love: not   1849: Strengthened by love: love; not   1863: love:
love—not   699| MS: But power from   1849: But strong from   700| MS:
Which cast < > soil puts   1835: Which, cast < > soil, puts < > buds,   1863: buds

And softer stains, unknown in happier climes;
Love which endures and doubts and is oppressed
And cherished, suffering much and much sustained,
And blind, oft-failing, yet believing love,
705 A half-enlightened, often-chequered trust:—
Hints and previsions of which faculties,
Are strewn confusedly everywhere about
The inferior natures, and all lead up higher,
All shape out dimly the superior race,
710 The heir of hopes too fair to turn out false,
And man appears at last. So far the seal
Is put on life; one stage of being complete,
One scheme wound up: and from the grand result
A supplementary reflux of light,
715 Illustrates all the inferior grades, explains
Each back step in the circle. Not alone
For their possessor dawn those qualities,
But the new glory mixes with the heaven
And earth; man, once descried, imprints for ever
720 His presence on all lifeless things: the winds
Are henceforth voices, wailing or a shout,

701| *MS:* stains unknown < > climes . . . *1835:* stains, unknown < > climes:
1849: climes; 702| *MS:* endures, and doubts, and *1835:* oppress'd *1849:*
oppressed, *1863:* endures and doubts and is oppressed 703| *MS:*
cherished—suffering < > sustained,— *1835:* cherish'd—suffering < >
sustain'd— *1849:* cherished, suffering < > sustained, *1863:* much and much
704| *MS:* A blind, unfailing and devoted Love:— *1835:* unfailing, and < > love:
1849: blind, oft-failing, yet believing love, *1868:* And blind 705| *MS:* And
half-enlightened < > Trust:—— *1835:* half-enlighten'd, often-chequer'd trust:
1849: A half-enlightened, often-chequered trust:— 706| *MS:* Anticipations,
hints of these and more *1849:* Hints and previsions of which faculties,
707| *MS:* everywhere—all seek *1849:* everywhere about 708| *MS:* An object
to possess and stamp their own, *1835:* own; *1849:* The inferior natures; and all
lead up higher, *1863:* natures, and 709| *MS:* the forthcoming race, § written
over by § Race, *1835:* race, *1849:* the superior race, 711| *MS:* Man < >
last: so *1863:* man < > last. So 712| *MS:* Life: one < > Being *1835:* life
< > being *1849:* life; one 713| *MS:* Scheme *1835:* scheme < > up;
and *1863:* up: and 714| *MS:* light *1835:* light, 716| *MS:*
circle:—not *1835:* circle: not *1849:* circle. Not 717| *MS:* The clear dawn of
those qualities shines out, *1849:* For their possessor dawn those qualities,
719| *MS:* earth—Man *1835:* earth. Man *1849:* earth: Man *1863:* earth;
man 720| *MS:* things—the *1849:* things; the *1863:* things: the
721| *MS:* voices—wailing *1835:* voices, wailing, or *1849:* voices, in a wail or
shout, *1868:* voices, wailing or a shout,

257

A querulous mutter or a quick gay laugh,
Never a senseless gust now man is born.
The herded pines commune and have deep thoughts,
725 A secret they assemble to discuss
When the sun drops behind their trunks which glare
Like grates of hell: the peerless cup afloat
Of the lake-lily is an urn, some nymph
Swims bearing high above her head: no bird
730 Whistles unseen, but through the gaps above
That let light in upon the gloomy woods,
A shape peeps from the breezy forest-top,
Arch with small puckered mouth and mocking eye.
The morn has enterprise, deep quiet droops
735 With evening, triumph takes the sunset hour,
Voluptuous transport ripens with the corn
Beneath a warm moon like a happy face:
—And this to fill us with regard for man.
With apprehension of his passing worth,
740 Desire to work his proper nature out,
And ascertain his rank and final place,
For these things tend still upward, progress is
The law of life, man is not Man as yet.
Nor shall I deem his object served, his end
745 Attained, his genuine strength put fairly forth,

722| MS: laugh,— 1835: mutter, or < > laugh— 1863: laugh, 1868: mutter
or 723| MS: Man is born: 1835: man 1849: born! 1868: born.
724| MS: commune, and 1863: commune and 1888: thoughts 1889:
thoughts, 725| MS: discuss 1835: discuss, 1863: discuss 728| MS:
urn some 1835: urn, some 730| MS: thro' 1835: through 731| MS:
woods 1835: woods, 732| MS: Shape 1835: shape 733| MS: eye:
pucker'd 1849: puckered 1868: eye. 734| MS: enterprise—deep 1863:
enterprise, deep 735| MS: evening;——triumph when the sun takes rest,—
1835: evening—triumph < > rest— 1849: evening; triumph takes the sun-set hour,
1863: evening, triumph < > sunset 736| MS: transport when the cornfields
ripen 1835: corn-fields 1849: transport ripens with the corn 737| MS:
face:——— 1835: face: 738| MS: And < > Man, 1835: man,
1849:—And 1868: man. 739| MS: Deep apprehension 1849: With
apprehension 741| MS: To ascertain < > place— 1835: place, 1849: And
ascertain < > place; 1863: place, 742| MS: For all these < > tend
upward—progress 1849: For these things tend still upward 1863: upward,
progress 743| MS: Life—Man is not Man as yet: 1835: man < > man
1849: man's self is not yet Man! 1863: life, man's 1868: man is not Man as
yet. 745| MS: fairly out, 1835: Attain'd 1849: Attained < > fairly forth,

While only here and there a star dispels
The darkness, here and there a towering mind
O'erlooks its prostrate fellows: when the host
Is out at once to the despair of night,
750 When all mankind alike is perfected,
Equal in full-blown powers—then, not till then,
I say, begins man's general infancy.
For wherefore make account of feverish starts
Of restless members of a dormant whole,
755 Impatient nerves which quiver while the body
Slumbers as in a grave? Oh long ago
The brow was twitched, the tremulous lids astir,
The peaceful mouth disturbed; half-uttered speech
Ruffled the lip, and then the teeth were set,
760 The breath drawn sharp, the strong right-hand clenched stronger,
As it would pluck a lion by the jaw;
The glorious creature laughed out even in sleep!
But when full roused, each giant-limb awake,
Each sinew strung, the great heart pulsing fast,
765 He shall start up and stand on his own earth,
Then shall his long triumphant march begin,
Thence shall his being date,—thus wholly roused,

747| *MS:* darkness—here < > Mind   *1835:* mind   *1849:* darkness, here
748| *MS:* its crawling fellows:—when the host § written over by § Host   *1835:*
fellows: when the host   *1849:* its prostrate fellows   **749|** *MS:* night,—   *1835:*
night;   *1849:* night,   **750|** *MS:* Mankind is perfected alike,   *1835:* mankind
1849: mankind alike is perfected,   **751|** *MS:* then—not < > then   *1835:* then,
not < > then,   **752|** *MS:* Begins the general infancy of Man;   *1835:* man;
1849: I say, begins man's general infancy!   *1868:* infancy.   **754|** *MS:* Whole
1835: whole—   *1863:* whole,   **755|** *MS:* Body   *1835:* body   **756|** *MS:*
O   *1849:* O, long   *1868:* Oh long   **757|** *MS:* twitched—the < > astir—
1835: twitch'd, the < > astir,   *1849:* twitched   **758|** *MS:* disturbed—half
uttered   *1835:* disturb'd—half-utter'd   *1849:* disturbed; half-uttered   **759|** *MS:*
lip . . . sometimes the teeth set hard   *1835:* lip; sometimes the teeth were set,   *1849:*
lip, and then the   **760|** *MS:* right hand   *1835:* right-hand clench'd
stronger—   *1849:* clenched stronger,   **761|** *MS:* the maw . . .   *1835:* maw:
1849: the jaw;   **762|** *1835:* laugh'd   *1849:* laughed   **763|** *MS:* when
aroused—each < > awake—   *1835:* arous'd < > awake,   *1849:* when full
roused   **764|** *MS:* strung—the < > fast—   *1835:* strung, the   *1849:*
fast,   **765|** *MS:* up, and < > earth   *1835:* earth—   *1849:* earth,   *1863:* up
and   **766|** *MS:* begin—   *1849:* And so begin his < > march,   *1863:* Thence
shall his < > march begin,   **767|** *MS:* date—what thus collected   *1835:* date;
what   *1849:* And date his being thence,—thus wholly roused,   *1863:* Thence shall
his being date,—thus

What he achieves shall be set down to him.
When all the race is perfected alike
770 As man, that is; all tended to mankind,
And, man produced, all has its end thus far:
But in completed man begins anew
A tendency to God. Prognostics told
Man's near approach; so in man's self arise
775 August anticipations, symbols, types
Of a dim splendour ever on before
In that eternal circle life pursues.
For men begin to pass their nature's bound,
And find new hopes and cares which fast supplant
780 Their proper joys and griefs; they grow too great
For narrow creeds of right and wrong, which fade
Before the unmeasured thirst for good: while peace
Rises within them ever more and more.
Such men are even now upon the earth,
785 Serene amid the half-formed creatures round
Who should be saved by them and joined with them.
Such was my task, and I was born to it—
Free, as I said but now, from much that chains
Spirits, high-dowered but limited and vexed
790 By a divided and delusive aim,

768| MS: He shall achieve, shall < > him! 1849: What he achieves shall 1868:
him. 770| MS: Man < > is:—all < > Mankind 1835: man < > is: all < >
mankind 1849: Man < > mankind, 1863: is; all 1868: man 771| MS:
Man < > § all < > end inserted above the line § < > far; 1835: man 1863:
far: 772| MS: Man 1835: man 773| MS: God: prognostics 1835:
God. Prognostics 774| MS: Man's 1835: man's 776| 1835: before,
1863: before 777| MS: In the eternal < > Life pursues: 1835: life 1849:
In that eternal circle run by life: 1863: life. 1868: circle life pursues.
778| MS: bound 1835: bound, 779| MS: To have new 1849: And find
new 780| MS: griefs—they 1835: griefs; they 1849: griefs; and outgrow
all 1863: griefs; they outgrow 1868: they grow too great 781| MS: wrong
which 1835: wrong, which 1849: The narrow 1868: For narrow
782| MS: Before unmeasured < > good, while 1835: unmeasur'd < > good;
while 1849: Before the unmeasured 1863: good: while 783| MS: more
1835: more. 784| MS:—Such 1835: Such < > earth— 1849: earth,
785| half-form'd < > round, 1849: half-formed 1863: round 786| MS:
Whom they should save and join with them at last; 1835: last: 1849: Who should
be saved by them and joined with them. 787| MS: Task < > it 1835: task
< > it— 789| MS: Spirits high-dowered 1835: high-dower'd, but < >
vex'd 1849: Spirits, high-dowered < > vexed 1863: high-dowered but
790| MS: Aim, 1835: aim— 1849: aim,

A shadow mocking a reality
Whose truth avails not wholly to disperse
The flitting mimic called up by itself,
And so remains perplexed and nigh put out
795 By its fantastic fellow's wavering gleam.
I, from the first, was never cheated thus;
I never fashioned out a fancied good
Distinct from man's; a service to be done,
A glory to be ministered unto
800 With powers put forth at man's expense, withdrawn
From labouring in his behalf; a strength
Denied that might avail him. I cared not
Lest his success ran counter to success
Elsewhere: for God is glorified in man,
805 And to man's glory vowed I soul and limb.
Yet, constituted thus, and thus endowed,
I failed: I gazed on power till I grew blind.
Power; I could not take my eyes from that:
That only, I thought, should be preserved, increased
810 At any risk, displayed, struck out at once—
The sign and note and character of man.
I saw no use in the past: only a scene

793| *MS:* mimic which itself has bred, *1849:* mimic called up by itself,
794| *1835:* perplex'd *1849:* perplexed 795| *MS:* gleam . . . *1835:*
gleam; *1849:* gleam. 796| *MS:* But, from the first the cheat could lure me
not: *1835:* But, from the first, the *1849:* I, from the first, was never cheated so;
1863: cheated thus; 797| *1835:* fashion'd *1849:* fashioned 798| *MS:*
Man's—a < > done *1835:* man's; a < > done— *1849:* done,
799| *MS:*—A *1835:* A < > minister'd unto, *1849:* ministered *1868:* unto.
1888: unto 800| *MS:* Man's expence *1835:* man's expense 801| *MS:*
behalf a *1835:* behalf; a 802| *MS:* Reserved that < > him: I ne'er cared
1849: Denied that < > him! I cared not *1863:* him. I 804| *MS:*
Elsewhere—for < > Man, *1835:* Elsewhere: for < > man, 805| *MS:* And
thereto I devoted soul and limb. *1835:* And to man's glory vow'd I soul *1849:* glory,
vowed *1868:* glory vowed 806| *1835:* endow'd, *1849:* endowed,
807| *MS:* Power < > blind *1835:* fail'd < > power < > blind. *1849:* failed < >
blind— *1863:* blind. 808| *MS:* Power: I < > that *1835:* that— *1849:* On
power; I *1863:* that: *1868:* Power 809| *MS:*—That only was to be
preserved—increased *1835:* That < > preserved, increased *1849:* That only, I
thought, should be preserved *1849:* risk, displayed 810| *MS:* once *1835:* risk, display'd < >
once— *1849:* risk, displayed 811| *MS:* Man *1835:* The sign, and note, and
< > man. *1863:* sign and note and 812| *MS:* Past— —only *1835:* past:
only *1863:* Past *1868:* past

Of degradation, ugliness and tears,
The record of disgraces best forgotten,
815 A sullen page in human chronicles
Fit to erase. I saw no cause why man
Should not stand all-sufficient even now,
Or why his annals should be forced to tell
That once the tide of light, about to break
820 Upon the world, was sealed within its spring:
I would have had one day, one moment's space,
Change man's condition, push each slumbering claim
Of mastery o'er the elemental world
At once to full maturity, then roll
825 Oblivion o'er the work, and hide from man
What night had ushered morn. Not so, dear child
Of after-days, wilt thou reject the past
Big with deep warnings of the proper tenure
By which thou hast the earth: for thee the present
830 Shall have distinct and trembling beauty, seen
Beside that past's own shade when, in relief,
Its brightness shall stand out: nor yet on thee
Shall burst the future, as successive zones

813| *MS:* tears   *1835:* ugliness, and tears;   *1849:* degradation, imbecility—   *1863:* imbecility,   *1868:* degradation, ugliness and tears,   814| *MS:*—The < > forgotten;   *1835:* The   *1849:* forgotten,   816| *MS:* To be erased: I < > Man   *1835:* man   *1849:* Fit to erase   *1863:* erase. I   817| *MS:* not be all-sufficient   *1835:* now;   *1868:* not stand all-sufficient < > now,   819| *1835:* light about   *1849:* light, about   820–821| *MS:* world was < > spring, / Although my own name led the brightness in: / I < > have had § had inserted above the line § one night— § above § , one § cancelled by § one day—one   *1835:* seal'd < > // < > day, one < > space,   *1849:* world, was sealed < > spring: / I   *1863:* spring: 822| *MS:* Man's condition—push   *1835:* man's condition, push   823| *MS:* To mastery   *1863:* Of mastery   824| *MS:* maturity,—then   *1835:* maturity: then   *1849:* maturity, then   825| *MS:* o'er its work and < > Man   *1835:* work, and < > man   *1849:* o'er the tools, and   *1888:* the work, and   826| *MS:* morn—not < > child § written over by § Child   *1835:* usher'd morn. Not < > child   *1849:* ushered   827| *MS:* Past *1835:* Past,   *1868:* past   829| *MS:* earth— —for < > Present   *1835:* earth: for   *1849:* earth: the Present for thee   *1868:* present   *1888:* earth: for thee the present   831| *MS:* Beside its shadow whence in strong relief   *1835:* shadow—whence, in < > relief,   *1849:* Beside that Past's own shade, whence, in relief,   *1863:* shade whence   *1868:* past's own shade when, in   832| *MS:* Its features shall stand out—nor   *1835:* out: nor   *1849:* Its brightness shall stand out: nor on thee yet   *1888:* nor yet on thee   833| *MS:* Future as   *1835:* Future, as   *1866:* future

Of several wonder open on some spirit
835 Flying secure and glad from heaven to heaven:
But thou shalt painfully attain to joy,
While hope and fear and love shall keep thee man!
All this was hid from me: as one by one
My dreams grew dim, my wide aims circumscribed,
840 As actual good within my reach decreased,
While obstacles sprung up this way and that
To keep me from effecting half the sum,
Small as it proved; as objects, mean within
The primal aggregate, seemed, even the least,
845 Itself a match for my concentred strength—
What wonder if I saw no way to shun
Despair? The power I sought for man, seemed God's.
In this conjuncture, as I prayed to die,
A strange adventure made me know, one sin
850 Had spotted my career from its uprise;
I saw Aprile—my Aprile there!
And as the poor melodious wretch disburthened
His heart, and moaned his weakness in my ear,
I learned my own deep error; love's undoing
855 Taught me the worth of love in man's estate,
And what proportion love should hold with power

834| *MS:* Spirit   *1835:* spirit   **835–837|**   *MS:* to heaven, / But Hope and Fear
and Love < > Man!   *1835:* to heaven: / But hope, and fear, and love, shall < >
man!   *1849:* to heaven: / But thou shalt painfully attain to joy, / While hope
1863: to heaven: // < > hope and fear and   **839|**   *1835:* circumscribed—
1849: circumscribed,   **840|**   *MS:* The actual < > decreased   *1835:* As actual
< > decreased,   **841|**   *1835:* that,   *1863:* that   **842|**   *MS:* sum   *1835:*
sum,   **843|**   *MS:* proved: as   *1849:* proved; as   **844–845|**   *MS:* aggregate,
remained alone / Of all the company, and, even the least, / More than a < >
strength— — — —   *1835:* remain'd alone // < > strength . . .   *1849:* aggregate,
seemed, even the least, / Itself a < > strength—   **847|**   *MS:* Despair?
§ above §—for Power seemed shut from Man forever.   *1835:* Despair? for power
seem'd < > man for ever.   *1849:* Despair? The power I sought for man, seemed
God's!   *1863:* God's.   **848|**   *1835:* pray'd   *1849:* prayed   **849|**   *MS:*
know one sin   *1835:* One Sin   *1849:* know, One Sin   *1863:* one sin
850–852| *MS:* uprise / And   *1835:* uprise; / < > disburthened   *1849:* uprise; / I
saw Aprile—my Aprile there! / And < > disburthened   **853|**   *MS:* heart and
< > ear   *1835:* heart, and moan'd < > ear,   *1849:* moaned   **854|**   *MS:* error:
Love's   *1835:* learn'd < > love's   *1849:* learned   **855|**   *MS:* Love in Man's
estate   *1835:* love in man's estate,   **856|**   *MS:* Love < > Power   *1835:* love
< > power

In his right constitution; love preceding
Power, and with much power, always much more love;
Love still too straitened in his present means,
860 And earnest for new power to set love free.
I learned this, and supposed the whole was learned:
And thus, when men received with stupid wonder
My first revealings, would have worshipped me,
And I despised and loathed their proffered praise—
865 When, with awakened eyes, they took revenge
For past credulity in casting shame
On my real knowledge, and I hated them—
It was not strange I saw no good in man,
To overbalance all the wear and waste
870 Of faculties, displayed in vain, but born
To prosper in some better sphere: and why?
In my own heart love had not been made wise
To trace love's faint beginnings in mankind,
To know even hate is but a mask of love's,
875 To see a good in evil, and a hope
In ill-success; to sympathize, be proud
Of their half-reasons, faint aspirings, dim
Struggles for truth, their poorest fallacies,
Their prejudice and fears and cares and doubts;

857| *MS:* constitution .... Love   *1835:* constitution: love   *1849:* constitution;
love   858| *MS:* Power——with < > Power always < > Love   *1835:*
Power—with < > power < > love;   *1849:* Power, and with < > power,
always   859| *MS:* in its present means   *1835:* straiten'd < > means,   *1849:*
straitened   *1868:* in his present   860| *MS:* Power to set it free.   *1835:*
power   *1888:* set love free.   861| *1835:* learn'd < > learn'd: *1849:* learned
< > learned: 862| *MS:* thus when Men   *1835:* thus, when men
863| *MS:* revealings and would worship me   *1835:* revealings—would have
worshipp'd me—   *1849:* revealings, would < > worshipped me,
864| *MS:*—And   *1835:* And < > proffer'd praise;   *1849:* proffered
praise—   865| *MS:*—When   *1835:* When awaken'd   *1849:* awakened
867| *MS:* knowledge—and < > them ....   *1835:* them—   *1849:* knowledge,
and   868| *MS:* Man   *1835:* man,   870| *1835:* display'd   *1849:*
displayed   872| *MS:* Love   *1835:* love   873| *MS:* Love's < >
Mankind;   *1835:* love's < > mankind—   *1849:* mankind,   874| *MS:* Hate
< > Love's;   *1835:* hate < > love's;   *1849:* love's,   876| *MS:* In ill
success——to sympathize—be   *1835:* In ill-success. To   *1849:* ill-success; to
sympathize, be   877| *MS:* aspirings, struggles   *1849:* aspirings, dim
878| *MS:* Dimly for   *1835:* truth—their   *1849:* Struggles for truth, their
879| *MS:* And prejudice, and < > doubts—   *1835:* fears, and cares, and doubts;
1849: Their prejudice   *1863:* prejudice and fears and cares and

264

880 All with a touch of nobleness, despite
Their error, upward tending all though weak,
Like plants in mines which never saw the sun,
But dream of him, and guess where he may be,
And do their best to climb and get to him.
885 All this I knew not, and I failed. Let men
Regard me, and the poet dead long ago
Who loved too rashly; and shape forth a third
And better-tempered spirit, warned by both:
As from the over-radiant star too mad
890 To drink the life-springs, beamless thence itself—
And the dark orb which borders the abyss,
Ingulfed in icy night,—might have its course
A temperate and equidistant world.
Meanwhile, I have done well, though not all well.
895 As yet men cannot do without contempt;
'Tis for their good, and therefore fit awhile
That they reject the weak, and scorn the false,
Rather than praise the strong and true, in me:
But after, they will know me. If I stoop
900 Into dark tremendous sea of cloud,
It is but for a time; I press God's lamp

880| *MS:* nobleness for all   *1835:* nobleness, for   *1849:* Which all touch upon
nobleness, despite   *1868:* All with a touch of nobleness   881| *MS:* error, all
ambitious, upward tending   *1835:* tending,   *1849:* all tend upwardly though
weak,   *1868:* error, upward tending all though   882| *MS:* sun   *1835:*
sun,   884| *1835:* him: *1849:* him.   885| *MS:* not and I failed:—let
Men   *1835:* not, and I fail'd; let men   *1849:* failed. Let   886| *MS:* Poet
1835: poet   887| *MS:* rashly— —and < > Third   *1835:* rashly; and < >
third,   *1849:* Who once loved rashly   *1863:* Who loved too rashly < > third
888| *MS:* better tempered spirit warned by both,   *1835:* temper'd spirit, warn'd by
both;   *1849:* tempered < > warned by both: *1863:* better-tempered
889|, *MS:* overradiant   *1835:* over-radiant   890| *MS:* the light-springs   *1868:*
the life-springs   891| *MS:* abyss   *1835:* abyss,   892| *MS:* Ingulphed
< > night— § above § , might   *1835:* Ingulf'd < > night, might   *1849:* Ingulfed
< > night,—might   893| *MS:* World: *1835:* world: *1849:* world.
894| *MS:* Meanwhile I < > tho' < > well:—   *1835:* Meanwhile, I < > though
< > well.   895| *MS:* Men < > contempt   *1835:* men < > contempt—
1863: contempt;   896| *MS:*—'Tis < > good,—tis § cancelled by § good, and
therefore   *1835:* 'Tis   897–899| *MS:* reject me and speak scorn of me, / But
< > well: I stoop   *1835:* me, and < > of me;   *1849:* reject the weak, and scorn
the false, / Rather than praise the strong and true, in me. / But < > know me! If I
1863: me: / < > me. If   900| *MS:* cloud   *1835:* cloud,   901| *MS:* But
tis but   *1835:* 'tis   *1849:* It is but

265

Close to my breast; its splendour, soon or late,
Will pierce the gloom: I shall emerge one day.
You understand me? I have said enough?

905 FESTUS Now die, dear Aureole!

PARACELSUS   Festus, let my hand—
This hand, lie in your own, my own true friend!
Aprile! Hand in hand with you, Aprile!

FESTUS And this was Paracelsus!

902| *MS:* breast,—its splendour soon or late   *1835:* breast—its splendour, soon or
late,   *1863:* breast; its   903| *MS:* gloom . . I < > day   *1835:* gloom: I < >
day.   *1849:* day!   *1863:* day.   904| *MS:* me,—I § written over by § me?—I
< > enough! § written over by § enough?   *1835:* me? I   905| *MS:*
Festus—let   *1835:* Festus, let   906| *MS: This* hand—lie < > own— —my
own   *1835:* hand, lie < > own . . . my   *1849:* This < > own—my   *1863:* own, my

NOTE

The liberties I have taken with my subject are very trifling; and the reader may slip the foregoing scenes between the leaves of any memoir of Paracelsus he pleases, by way of commentary. To prove this, I subjoin a popular account, translated from the "Biographie Univer-
5   selle, Paris," 1822, which I select, not as the best, certainly, but as being at hand, and sufficiently concise for my purpose. I also append a few notes, in order to correct those parts which do not bear out my own view of the character of Paracelsus; and have incorporated with them a notice or two, illustrative of the poem itself.

10 "PARACELSUS (Philippus Aureolus Theophrastus Bombastus ab Hohenheim) was born in 1493 at Einsiedeln,[1] a little town in the canton of Schwyz, some leagues distant from Zurich. His father, who exercised the profession of medicine at Villach in Carinthia, was nearly related to George Bombast de Hohenheim, who became after-
15 ward Grand Prior of the Order of Malta: consequently Paracelsus could not spring from the dregs of the people, as Thomas Erastus, his sworn enemy, pretends.[2] It appears that his elementary education was much neglected, and that he spent part of his youth in pursuing the life common to the travelling *literati* of the age; that is to say, in

---

1| *MS:* trifling and § ? §   *1835:* trifling; and   2| *MS:* the foregoing scenes § *foregoing* inserted above the line §   4| *MS:* Account translated < > *Biographie Universelle, Paris 1822,*   *1835:* "Biographie < > Paris, 1822."   *1863:* 'Biographie Universelle, Paris, 1822.'   *1888:* "Biographie < > Paris," 1822,   6| *MS:* hand and   *1835:* hand, and   7| *MS:* notes in < > § *correct* < > *not* inserted above the line §   *1835:* notes, in   8| *MS:* Paracelsus, and   *1835:* Paracelsus; and   9| *MS:* two illustrative   *1835:* two, illustrative   10–11| *MS:* (Philippus < > Hohenheim) § *Aureolus* inserted above the line §   *1863:* (Philippus < > Hohenheim)   12| *MS:* Schwitz   *1888:* Schwyz   13| *MS:* Medecine   *1835:* medicine at Villach, in   *1868:* Villach in   14–15| *MS:* became in the event Grand   *1849:* became afterward Grand   15| *1835:* Malta; consequently   *1868:* Malta: consequently   16–17| *MS:* Erastus his < > enemy pretends   *1835:* Erastus, his < > enemy, pretends   18–19| *MS:* the § inserted above the line §   19| *MS:* Literati < > age, that   *1835:* literati < > age; that

267

20 wandering from country to country, predicting the future by astrol-
ogy and cheiromancy, evoking apparitions, and practising the differ-
ent operations of magic and alchemy, in which he had been initiated
whether by his father or by various ecclesiastics, among the number of
whom he particularizes the Abbot Tritheim,[3] and many German
25 bishops.

"As Paracelsus displays everywhere an ignorance of the rudiments of
the most ordinary knowledge, it is not probable that he ever studied
seriously in the schools: he contented himself with visiting the Uni-
versities of Germany, France and Italy; and in spite of his boasting
30 himself to have been the ornament of those institutions, there is no
proof of his having legally acquired the title of Doctor, which he
assumes. It is only known that he applied himself long, under the
direction of the wealthy Sigismond Fugger of Schwatz, to the discov-
ery of the Magnum Opus.

35 "Paracelsus travelled among the mountains of Bohemia, in the
East, and in Sweden, in order to inspect the labours of the miners, to
be initiated in the mysteries of the oriental adepts, and to observe the
secrets of nature and the famous mountain of loadstone.[4] He professes
also to have visited Spain, Portugal, Prussia, Poland, and Transyl-
40 vania; everywhere communicating freely, not merely with the physi-
cians, but the old women, charlatans and conjurers of these several
lands. It is even believed that he extended his journeyings as far as
Egypt and Tartary, and that he accompanied the son of the Khan of
the Tartars to Constantinople, for the purpose of obtaining the secret
45 of the tincture of Trismegistus from a Greek who inhabited that
capital.

20-21| MS: future from § *from* inserted above the line § the inspection of the stars and
the lines of the hand, evoking apparitions and repeating the   1835: apparitions, and
< > alchemy in   1849: future by astrology and cheiromancy, evoking apparitions, and
practising the   22| MS: alchemy in   1835: alchemy, in   23| MS: father,
or < > ecclesiastics,   1835: father or < > ecclesiastics,   24| MS: Tritheim
and   1835: Tritheim, and   25| MS: Bishops.   1835: bishops.   27| MS:
he should have ever   1849: he ever   28| MS: Schools   1835: schools
29| MS: France, and Italy   1868: France and Italy   33| 1835: Fugger, of
1868: Fugger of   37| MS: Oriental Adepts, and § , probable; concealed by
binding §   1835: oriental adepts, and   39-40| MS: Transsylvania— § above §
where he communicated freely not   1835: Transylvania, where < > freely, not
1849: Transylvania; everywhere communicating   47| MS: but with the   1835:
charlatans, and conjurors, of   1849: but the < > conjurers   1868: charlatans and
conjurers of   44| MS: Constantinople for   1835: Constantinople, for
45| MS: Trismegistus, from   1868: Trismegistus from

268

"The period of his return to Germany is unknown: it is only certain that, at about the age of thirty-three, many astonishing cures which he wrought on eminent personages procured him such a celebrity, that he was called in 1526, on the recommendation of Œcolampadius,[5] to fill a chair of physic and surgery at the University of Basil. There Paracelsus began by burning publicly in the amphitheatre the works of Avicenna and Galen, assuring his auditors that the latchets of his shoes were more instructed than those two physicians; that all Universities, all writers put together, were less gifted than the hairs of his beard and of the crown of his head; and that, in a word, he was to be regarded as the legitimate monarch of medicine. 'You shall follow me,' cried he, 'you, Avicenna, Galen, Rhasis, Montagnana, Mesues, you, gentlemen of Paris, Montpellier, Germany, Cologne, Vienna,[6] and whomsoever the Rhine and Danube nourish; you who inhabit the isles of the sea; you, likewise, Dalmatians, Athenians; thou, Arab; thou, Greek; thou, Jew: all shall follow me, and the monarchy shall be mine.'[7]

"But at Basil it was speedily perceived that the new Professor was no better than an egregious quack. Scarcely a year elapsed before his lectures had fairly driven away an audience incapable of comprehending their emphatic jargon. That which above all contributed to sully his reputation was the debauched life he led. According to the testimony of Oporinus, who lived two years in his intimacy, Paracelsus scarcely ever ascended the lecture-desk unless half drunk, and only dictated to his secretaries when in a state of intoxication: if summoned to attend the sick, he rarely proceeded thither without previously drenching himself with wine. He was accustomed to retire

---

47| *MS:* unknown; it   *1835:* unknown: it   48| *MS:* 33   *1849:* thirty-
three   49| *MS:* personages, procured   *1835:* personages procured
51| · *MS:* Physic and Surgery   *1835:* physic and surgery   52| *MS:*
Amphitheatre   *1835:* amphitheatre   54–55| *MS:* Physicians—that all the
Universities, all the writers   *1835:* physicians; that   *1849:* all Universities, all
writers   55| *MS:* together were   *1835:* together, were   56| *MS:* crown of
his head, and that, finally, he § *crown of his head* replaces four illegible words §
1849: that, in a word, he   58–59| *MS:* me' cried he 'you < > Mesue,—you,
Gentlemen   *1835:* me,' cried he, 'you < > Mesue; you   *1849:* Mesues, you   *1863:*
gentlemen   60| *MS:* and all soever whom the   *1840:* and whomsoever
the   61| *MS:* sea—you likewise, < > Arab—   *1835:* sea; you, likewise, < >
Arab,   62| *MS:* Greek—thou Jew—all   *1835:* Greek; thou, Jew; all   *1863:* Jew.
all   65| *MS:* Quack: scarcely had a   *1835:* quack. Scarcely   *1849:* Scarcely
a   67| *MS:* their § cancels *his* §   69| *MS:* Oporinus   *1835:*
Oporinus,   70| *MS:* lecture— § inserted above the line §   72| *MS:* sick
he   *1835:* sick, he

269

to bed without changing his clothes; sometimes he spent the night in
75 pot-houses with peasants, and in the morning knew no longer what
he was about; and, nevertheless, up to the age of twenty-five his only
drink had been water.[8]

"At length, fearful of being punished for a serious outrage on a
magistrate,[9] he fled from Basil towards the end of the year 1527, and
80 took refuge in Alsatia, whither he caused Oporinus to follow with his
chemical apparatus.

"He than entered once more upon the career of ambulatory theos-
ophist.[10] Accordingly we find him at Colmar in 1528; at Nuremberg
in 1529; at St. Gall in 1531; at Pfeffers in 1535; and at Augsburg in
85 1536: he next made some stay in Moravia, where he still further
compromised his reputation by the loss of many distinguished pa-
tients, which compelled him to betake himself to Vienna; from thence
he passed into Hungary; and in 1538 was at Villach, where he dedi-
cated his 'Chronicle' to the States of Carinthia, in gratitude for the
90 many kindnesses with which they had honoured his father. Finally,
from Mindelheim, which he visited in 1540, Paracelsus proceeded to
Salzburg, where he died in the Hospital of St. Stephen (*Sebastian* is
meant), Sept. 24, 1541."—(Here follows a criticism on his writings,
which I omit.)

95   [1]*Paracelsus* would seem to be a fantastic version of *Von Hohenheim;* Einsi-
edeln is the Latinized Eremus, whence Paracelsus is sometimes called, as in the
correspondence of Erasmus, Eremita; Bombast, his proper name, probably ac-
quired, from the characteristic phraseology of his lectures, that unlucky signifi-
cation which it has ever since retained.

75| *MS:* peasants and   *1835:* peasants, and   76| *MS:* and nevertheless < >
25   *1835:* and, nevertheless   *1849:* twenty-five   79| *MS:* Basil, towards < >
year 27 and   *1835:* Basil towards < > year 27, and   *1849:* year '27   *1863:* year
1527   81| *MS:* chymical   *1863:* chemical   82| *MS:* Theosophist   *1835:*
theosophist   83-84| *MS: 1528:* at < > 1529:   *1835:* 1528/ at < > 1529;
1868: 1529: at Nuremburg   *1888:* 1529; at Nuremberg   84| *MS:* 1531: at < >
1535: at Augsburg   *1835:* 1531; at < > 1535; at Augsburg   *1849:* 1535; and at
Augsburg   88| *MS:* Hungary, and   *1849:* Hungary; and   89| *MS:*
Chronicle < > Carinthia, in § ? §   *1835:* 'Chronicle' < > Carinthia, in
91| *MS:* Mindelheim, where he was in   *1849:* Mindelheim, which he visited in
92-93| *MS: (Sebastian,* he means.) Sept. 24, 151. (Here   *1835:* means), Sept. 24,
1541"—(Here § MS does not put translation in quotes §   *1849:* (*Sebastian,* is
meant)   95-99| *MS:* § Complete Note 1 § Hohenheim, Einsiedeln and the latin
§ *the latin* inserted above the line § Eremus, (whence Paracelsus is sometimes called, as
in the correspondence of Erasmus, § *in* < > *Erasmus,* inserted above the line §
Eremita,) are I suppose one and the same town.   *1835:* Einsiedeln, and the Latin
Eremus (whence < > are, I suppose, one   *1849:* § as in 1888 except § Latin < >
name, originally acquired   *1863:* name probably acquired   *1868:* Latinized

100   ²I shall disguise M. Renauldin's next sentence a little. "Hic (Erastus sc.)
Paracelsium trimum a milite quodam, alii a sue exectum ferunt: constat imber-
bem illum, mulierumque osorem fuisse." A standing High-Dutch joke in those
days at the expense of a number of learned men, as may be seen by referring to
such rubbish as Melander's "Jocoseria," etc. In the prints from his portrait by
105   Tintoretto, painted a year before his death, Paracelsus is *barbatulus*, at all
events. But Erastus was never without a good reason for his faith—*e.g.* "Helve-
tium fuisse (Paracelsum) vix credo, vix enim ea regio tale monstrum ediderit."
(De Medicina Nova.)
        ³Then Bishop of Spanheim, and residing at Würzburg in Franconia; a town
110   situated in a grassy fertile country, whence its name, Herbipolis. He was much
visited there by learned men, as may be seen by his "Epistolæ Familiares," Hag.
1536: among others, by his staunch friend Cornelius Agrippa, to whom he dates
thence, in 1510, a letter in answer to the dedicatory epistle prefixed to the
treatise De Occult. Philosoph., which last contains the following ominous allu-
115   sion to Agrippa's sojourn: "Quum nuper tecum, R. P. in cœnobio tuo apud
Herbipolim aliquamdiu conversatus, multa de chymicis, multa de magicis, multa
de cabalisticis, cæterisque quæ adhuc in occulto delitescunt, arcanis scientiis
atque artibus una contulissemus," etc.
        ⁴"Inexplebilis illa aviditas naturæ perscrutandi secreta et reconditarum
120   supellectile scientiarum animum locupletandi, uno eodemque loco diu persistere
non patiebatur, sed Mercurii instar, omnes terras, nationes et urbes perlustrandi
igniculos supponebat, ut cum viris naturæ scrutatoribus, chymicis præsertim, ore
tenus conferret, et quæ diuturnis laboribus nocturnisque vigiliis invenerant una
vel altera communicatione obtineret." (Bitiskius in Præfat.) "Patris auxilio
125   primum, deinde propria industria doctissimos viros in Germania, Italia, Gallia,
Hispania, aliisque Europæ regionibus, nactus est præceptores; quorum liberali

---

100| *MS:* disguise < > a § cancel illegible words §   101| *MS:* à < > à   *1863:*
a < > a   102| *MS:* illum et § illegible cancelled by § μισογυταιον fuisse." < >
joke of those   *1835:* μισογυταιον· < > joke in those   *1849:* illum fuisse." A   *1863:*
illum, mulierumque osorem fuisse." A   103| *MS:* days at the expence of a vast
number of learned men as § *at* < > *men,* inserted above the line §   *1835:* expense
1849: of a number   104| *MS:* Jocoseria, &c &c.   *1845:* Jocoseria, &c. &c.
1863: 'Jocoseria," etc.   *1888:* "Jocoseria,"   105| *MS:* painted a year before his
death § inserted above the line §   107| *MS:* fuisse (P) vix < > ediderit."   *1835:*
fuisse (P.) vix < > ediderit."—   *1849:* fuisse (Paracelsum) vix   *1863:* ediderit:
1868: ediderit."   108| *MS: De Med. Novâ.*   *1835:* (De Medicina Nova.)
109| *MS:* Franconia,—a   *1835:* Franconia, a   *1849:* Franconia: a   110| *MS:*
its Latin name Herbipolis. He   *1849:* its name, Herbipolis. He   111–112| *MS:*
Epistolae familiares. Hag. 1536.   *1835:* 1536:   *1863:* 'Epistolae Familiares, Hag. *1888:*
"Epistolae Familiares."   112–113| *MS:* Among others by < > Cor. < > dates
from thence   *1849:* others, by < > Cornelius < > dates thence,   *1863:* among
113| *MS:* 1510 a   *1849:* 1510, a   114| *MS:* de Occult. Phil. which last § *last*
inserted above the line §   *1863:* De Occult. Philosoph.,   115| *MS:* to his
sojourn: < > P, in   *1835:* P. in   *1849:* to Agrippa's sojourn: 118| *MS:*
contulissemus" &c &c   *1835:* contulissemus," &c &c.   *1863:* contulissemus,"
etc.   120| *MS:* loco, diu   *1868:* loco diu   121| *MS:* mercurii   *1868:*
Mercurii   122| *MS:* supponebat et cum   *1868:* supponebat, ut cum
123| *1849:* unâ   *1863:* una   124| *MS: Bitiskius in praefat.*   *1835:* Praefat.
1849: alterâ   *1863:* altera < > (Bitiskius in Praefat.)   125| *MS:* primùm < >
propriâ industriâ < > Germaniâ, Italiâ, Galliâ,   *1863:* primum < > propria industria
< > Germania, Italia, Gallia,

doctrina, et potissimum propria inquisitione ut qui esset ingenio acutissimo ac fere divino, tantum profecit, ut multi testati sint, in universa philosophia, tam ardua, tam arcana et abdita eruisse mortalium neminem." (Melch. Adam. in Vit.
130 Germ. Medic.) "Paracelsus qui in intima naturæ viscera sic penitus introierit, metallorum stirpiumque vires et facultates tam incredibili ingenii acumine exploraverit ac perviderit, ad morbos omnes vel desperatos et opinione hominum insanabiles percurandum; ut cum Theophrasto nata primum medicina perfectaque videtur." (Petri Rami Orat. de Basilea.) His passion for wandering is best
135 described in his own words: "Ecce amatorem adolescentem difficillimi itineris haud piget, ut venustam saltem puellam vel fœminam aspiciat: quanto minus nobilissimarum artium amore laboris ac cujuslibet tædii pigebit?" etc. ("Defensiones Septem adversus æmulos suos." 1573. Def. 4ta. "De peregrinationibus ex exilio.")
140 5The reader may remember that it was in conjunction with Œcolampadius, then Divinity Professor at Basil, that Zuinglius published in 1528 an answer to Luther's Confession of Faith; and that both proceeded in company to the subsequent conference with Luther and Melanchthon at Marpurg. Their letters fill a large volume.—"D.D. Johannis Œcolampadii et Huldrichi Zuinglii Epistolarum
145 lib. quatuor." Bas. 1536. It must be also observed that Zuinglius began to preach in 1516, and at Zurich in 1519, and that in 1525 the Mass was abolished in the cantons. The tenets of Œcolampadius were supposed to be more evangelical than those up to that period maintained by the glorious German, and our brave Bishop Fisher attacked them as the fouler heresy:—"About this time arose out of
150 Luther's school one Œcolampadius, like a mighty and fierce giant; who, as his master had gone beyond the Church, went beyond his master (or else it had been impossible he could have been reputed the better scholar), who denied the real presence; him, this worthy champion (the Bishop) sets upon, and with five books (like so many smooth stones taken out of the river that doth always run
155 with living water) slays the Philistine; which five books were written in the year of our Lord 1526, at which time he had governed the see of Rochester twenty years." (Life of Bishop Fisher, 1655.) Now, there is no doubt of the Protestantism

127| MS: doctrinâ, et potissimùm propriâ   1863: doctrina, et potissimum propria   128| MS: tantùm <> philosophiâ   1849: universâ   1863: tantum <> universa philosophia   129| MS: neminem," Melch. <> Vit.   1863: neminem," (Melch. <> Vit.   130| MS: Medic. "Paracelsus <> penitùs   1863: Medic.) "Paracelsus <> penitus   132| MS: perviderit; ad <> disperatos   1849: desperatos   1868: perviderit, ad   133| MS: primùm   1863: primum   134| MS: videtur." Petri <> Basileâ. His   1863: videtur." (Petri <> Basilea.) His   135| MS: words. "Ecce   1835: words: "Ecce   137–139| MS: pigebit? &c. Defensiones <> exilio."   1835: pigebit?" &c.— <> 1573. Def. 4ta. "De   1863: pigebit?" etc. ('Defensiones <> suos.' 1573. Def. 4ta. 'De <> exilio.') 1888: ("Defensiones <> suos." <> "De <> exilio.")   140| MS: reader will remember   1849: reader may remember   141| MS: Divinity-Professor   1868: Divinity Professor   142| MS: Faith, and that he accompanied him to   1849: Faith; and that both proceeded in company to   144| MS: volume—   1835: volume.—   144–145| MS: D D Johannis <> Bas. 1536.   1835: D. D. Johannis <> 1536.   1863: D. D. Johannis <> Epistolarum' <> Bas.   1888: "D. D. Johannis <> Epistolarum lib. quatuor." Bas.   148| MS: those at that   1849: those up to that   151| MS: church   1849: Church   152| MS: scholar) who   1863: scholar), who   156| MS: 20   1888: twenty   157| MS: years."—Life of Bp. Fisher. 1655. Now there   1835: 1655.   1849: Now, there   1863: years." (Life of Bishop Fisher. 1655.)

272

of Paracelsus, Erasmus, Agrippa, etc., but the nonconformity of Paracelsus was always scandalous. L. Crasso ("Elogj d'Huomini Letterati," Ven. 1666) informs us that his books were excommunicated by the Church. Quenstedt (de Patr. Doct.) affirms "nec tantum novæ medicinæ, verum etiam novæ theologiæ autor est." Delrio, in his Disquisit. Magicar., classes him among those "partim atheos, partim hæreticos" (lib. i. cap. 3). "Omnino tamen multa theologica in ejusdem scriptis plane atheismum olent, ac duriuscule sonant in auribus vere Christiani." (D. Gabrielis Clauderi Schediasma de Tinct. Univ. Norimb. 1736.) I shall only add one more authority:—"Oporinus dicit se (Paracelsum) aliquando Lutherum et Papam, non minus quam nunc Galenum et Hippocratem redacturum in ordinem minabatur, neque enim eorum qui hactenus in scripturam sacram scripsissent, sive veteres, sive recentiores, quenquam scripturæ nucleum recte eruisse, sed circa corticem et quasi membranam tantum hærere." (Th. Erastus, Disputat. de Med. Nova.) These and similar notions had their due effect on Oporinus, who, says Zuingerus, in his "Theatrum," "longum vale dixit ei (Paracelso), ne ob præceptoris, alioqui amicissimi, horrendas blasphemias ipse quoque aliquando pœnas Deo Opt. Max. lueret."

⁶Erastus, who relates this, here oddly remarks, "mirum quod non et Garamantos, Indos et *Anglos* adjunxit." Not so wonderful neither, if we believe what another adversary "had heard somewhere,"—that all Paracelsus' system came of his pillaging "Anglum quendam, Rogerium Bacchonem."

⁷See his works *passim*. I must give one specimen:—Somebody had been styling him "Luther alter." "And why not?" (he asks, as he well might). "Luther is abundantly learned, therefore you hate him and me; but we are at least a match for you.—Nam et contra vos et vestros universos principes Avicennam,

---

¹⁵⁸| *MS:* Agrippa &c but <> of P was   *1835:* Agrippa, &c. but <> of Paracelsus was   *1868:* Agrippa, etc., but   ¹⁵⁹| *MS:* (*Elogj d'Huomini Letterati. Ven. 1666*)   *1835:* 1666   *1863:* ('Elogj <> Letterati.' Ven. 1666)   *1888:* ("Elogj <> Letterati," Ven. 1666)   ¹⁶⁰⁻¹⁶¹| *MS:* church. Quenstedt (*de Patr. Doct.*)   *1835:* Church   *1868:* (de Patr. Doct.)   ¹⁶¹| *MS:* Medicinae <> Theologia   *1835:* tantùm <> medicinae <> theologiae   *1863:* tantum   ¹⁶²| *MS:* Delrio in his Disquisit. Magicar.   1835: Delrio, in   1863: Disquisit. Magicar.,   ¹⁶³| *MS:* (*lib 1. cap 3*). <> Theologica   *1835:* 1. *cap.* 3.) <> theologica   *1863:* (lib. 1. cap. 3). 1888: lib. i. cap. 3).   ¹⁶⁴| *MS:* Scriptis <> Atheismum <> Christiani"— *1835:* scriptis planè <> atheismum <> Christiani."   *1863:* plane   ¹⁶⁵| *MS:* D. Gabrielis <> 1736.   *1835:* 1736.   *1863:* (D. Gabrielis <> 1736.)   ¹⁶⁶| *MS:* se (P) aliquando   *1835:* se (Paracelsum) aliquando   ¹⁶⁷| *MS: 1835:* minùs   *1863:* minus   ¹⁶⁹| *MS:* rectè   *1863:* recte   ¹⁷⁰⁻¹⁷¹| *MS: Th. Erastus. Disputat. de Med. Novâ.*   *1863:* (Th. Erastus, Disputat. de Med. Nova.)   ¹⁷²| *MS:* Zuingerus in his "*Theatrum,*" <> ei (P) ne   *1835:* Zuingerus, in his *Theatrum,* <> ei (Paracelso) ne   *1863:* 'Theatrum,'   *1888:* "Theatrum,"   ¹⁷³| *MS:* praeceptoris alioqui   *1835:* praeceptoris, alioqui   ¹⁷⁵| *MS:* Erastus who <> remarks "mirum   *1835:* Erastus, who <> remarks, "mirùm   *1863:* mirum   ¹⁷⁶⁻¹⁷⁸| *MS:* adjunxit."   *1849:* § adds § Not <> Bacchonem."   ¹⁷⁹| *MS:* specimen: somebody   *1835:* specimen:—Somebody 1888: specimen: Somebody   *1889:* specimen:—Somebody   ¹⁸⁰| *MS:* not?" he asks, as he will might,—"Luther   *1835:* alter:" "and <> might; "Luther   *1849:* not?" (he <> might), "Luther   *1863:* might,) "Luther   *1868:* might.) "Luther   *1888:* alter." "And <> might), "Luther   ¹⁸²| *MS:* you"—"Nam <> Principes   *1835:* you." <> principes   *1849:* you.—Nam

Galenum, Aristotelem, etc. me satis superque munitum esse novi. Et vertex iste
meus calvus ac depilis multo plura et sublimiora novit quam vester vel Avicenna
185 vel universæ academiæ. Prodite, et signum date, qui viri sitis, quid roboris
habeatis? quid autem sitis? Doctores et magistri, pediculus pectentes et fricantes
podicem." (Frag. Med.)
    [8]His defenders allow the drunkenness. Take a sample of their excuses:
"Gentis hoc, non viri vitiolum est, a Taciti seculo ad nostrum usque non inter-
190 rupto filo devolutum, sinceritati forte Germanæ coævum, et nescio an aliquo
consanguinitatis vinculo junctum." (Bitiskius.) The other charges were chiefly
trumped up by Oporinus: "Domi, quod Oporinus amanuensis ejus sæpe narravit,
numquam nisi potus ad explicanda sua accessit, atque in medio conclavi ad
columnam τετυφωμένος adsistens, apprehenso manibus capulo ensis, cujus
195 κοίλωμα hospitium præbuit, ut aiunt, spiritui familiari, imaginationes aut con-
cepta sua protulit:—alii illud quod in capulo habuit, ab ipso Azoth appellatum,
medicinam fuisse præstantissimam aut lapidem Philosophicum putant." (Melch.
Adam.) This famous sword was no laughing-matter in those days, and it is now a
material feature in the popular idea of Paracelsus. I recollect a couple of
200 allusions to it in our own literature, at the moment.
        Ne had been known the Danish Gonswart,
        Or Paracelsus with his long sword.
                                    'Volpone' act ii. scene 2.

        Bumbastus kept a devil's bird
205   Shut in the pummel of his sword,
        That taught him all the cunning pranks
        Of past and future mountebanks.
                        'Hudibras,' part ii. cant. 3.

    This Azoth was simply "*laudanum suum.*" But in his time he was commonly
210 believed to possess the double tincture—the power of curing diseases and trans-
muting metals. Oporinus often witnessed, as he declares, both these effects, as
did also Franciscus, the servant of Paracelsus, who describes, in a letter to
Neander, a successful projection at which he was present, and the results of

---

[183] *MS:* Aristotelem *&c 1835:* Aristotelem, *&c. 1863:* etc.   [184] *MS:*
quàm   *1863:* quam   [185] *MS:* Academiae   *1835:* academiae   [187] *MS:*
podicem."   *1835:* podicem."—*Frag. Med. 1863:* podicem." (Frag. Med.)
[188] *MS:* allow this:— take § cancelled by § allow the drunkenness:—take   *1835:*
drunkenness. Take   [191] *MS: Bitiskius. 1863:* junctum." (Bitiskius.)
[192] *MS:* Oporinus: § two thirds of a line cancelled § Domi   *1835:* saepè   *1863:*
saepe   [195] *MS:* praebuit ut aiunt spiritui   *1888:* praebuit, ut aiunt,
spiritui   [196] *MS:* appellatum   *1888:* appellatum,   [197-198] *MS:*
Medicinam < > *Melch. Adam. 1835:* Putant."—*Melch. 1863:* medicinam < >
putant." (Melch. Adam.)   [198] *MS:* laughing matter < > days and   *1835:* days,
and   *1863:* laughing-matter   [201] *MS:* Gonswart   *1835:* Gonswart,
[203] *MS: Volpone, Act 2. sc. 2   1835: Act* 2. sc. 2.   *1849: Act* ii, *sc.* 2.   *1863:*
'Volpone,' Act ii. Scene 2.   *1888:* 'Volpone, act ii, scene 2.   [204] *MS:* Devil's
1868: devil's   [206] *MS:* Pranks   *1835:* pranks,   *1868:* pranks   [208] *MS:*
Hudibras. Part ii. Cant. 3.   *1835: Part* 2. *Cant.* 3.   *1849: Part* ii, *Cant.* 3.   *1863:*
'Hudibras,' Part ii. Cant. 3.   *1888:* part ii, cant. 3.   [209] *MS:* § no ¶ § < >
suum:" But   *1835: suum.*" But   [210] *MS:* Double Tincture   *1835:* double
tincture < > diseases, and   *1868:* diseases and   [212-213] *MS:* Franciscus the
< > Paracelsus who < > Neander a   *1835:* Franciscus, the < > Paracelsus, who < >
Neander, a

which, good golden ingots, were confided to his keeping. For the other quality,
215 let the following notice vouch among many others:—"Degebat Theophrastus
Norimbergæ procitus a medentibus illius urbis, et vaniloquus deceptorue pro-
clamatus, qui, ut laboranti famæ subveniat, viros quosdam authoritatis summæ in
Republica illa adit, et infamiæ amoliendæ, artique suæ asserrendæ, specimen ejus
pollicetur editurum, nullo stipendio vel accepto pretio, horum faciles præbentium
220 aures jussu elephantiacos aliquot, a communione hominum cæterorum segregatos,
et in valetudinarium detrusos, alieno arbitrio eliguntur, quos virtute singulari
remediorum suorum Theophrastus a fœda Græcorum lepra mundat, pristinæque
sanitati restituit; conservat illustre harum curationum urbs in archivis suis testi-
monium." (Bitiskius.)° It is to be remarked that Oporinus afterwards repented of
225 his treachery: "Sed resipuit tandem, et quem vivum convitiis insectatus fuerat
defunctum veneratione prosequutus, infames famæ præceptoris morsus in remorsus
conscientiæ conversi pœnitentia, heu nimis tarda, vulnera clausere exanimi quæ
spiranti inflixerant." For these "bites" of Oporinus, see Disputat. Erasti, and
Andreæ Jocisci "Oratio de Vit. ob. Opora;" for the "remorse," Mic. Toxita in pref.
230 Testamenti, and Conringius (otherwise an enemy of Paracelsus), who says it was

*The premature death of Paracelsus casts no manner of doubt on the fact of
his having possessed the Elixir Vitæ: the alchemists have abundant reasons to
adduce, from which I select the following, as explanatory of a property of the
Tincture not calculated on by its votaries:—"Objectionem illam, quod Para-
(5) celsus non fuerit longævus, nonnulli quoque solvunt per rationes physicas: vitæ
nimirum abbreviationem fortasse tallibus accidere posse, ob Tincturam fre-
quentiore ac largiore dosi sumtam, dum a summe efficaci et penetrabili hujus
virtute calor innatus quasi suffocatur." (Gabrielis Clauderi Schediasma.)

214| MS: his trust: for < > quality   1835: trust. For < > quality,   1849: his
keeping. For   215| MS: following vouch < > others: "Degebat   1835:
others:—"Degebat   1849: following notice vouch   216| MS: prociscus à
Medentibus   1863: procitus a medentibus   218| MS: Reipublicâ illâ   1835: Rei
publicâ   1863: Republica illa   220| MS: à   1863: a   222| MS: à fœdâ
< > leprâ   1863: a foeda < > lepra   223-224| MS: Urbs in Archivis < >
testimonium."—Bitiskius.   1839: urbs in archivis   1863: testimonium."
(Bitiskius.)   225| MS: treachery "Sed   1835: treachery: "Sed
226-227| MS: fuerat, defunctum < > conversi, pœnitentiâ heu < > tarda vulnerâ
1835: fueratu defunctum < > conversi pœnitentiâ   1863: pœnitentia < > tarda,
vulnera   227| MS: clausêre   1863: clausere   228| MS: Oporinus see
"Disputat Erasti"—   1835: Oporinus, see "Disputat. Erasti,"   1863: Disputat.
Erasti,   229-230| MS: Andreas Jociscus "Oratio de vit. et. ob. Opi:—for < >
Toxitus in praef. Testamenti   1835: Opori;" for < > Toxites   1849: Toxita   1863:
'Oratio de vit. et ob. Opori, < > in pref. Testamenti,   1868: Andreae Jocisci   1888:
"Oratio de Vit ob. Opori;"

°1| MS: of P. casts   1835: of Paracelsus casts   2| MS: Alchemists   1835:
alchemists   3| MS: adduce—from   1835: adduce, from   4| MS: votaries.
"Objectionem   1863: votaries:—'Objectionem   5| MS: Physicas   1835:
physicas   8| MS: Gabrielis Clauderi Schediasma   1835: suffocatur."—Gabrielis
< > Schediasma.   1863: suffocatur." (Gabrielis Clauderi Schediasma.)

contained in a letter from Oporinus to Doctor Vegerus.†
Whatever the moderns may think of these marvellous attributes, the title of
Paracelsus to be considered the father of modern chemistry is indisputable.
Gerardus Vossius, "De Philosa et Philosum sectis," thus prefaces the ninth section
235 of cap. 9, "De Chymia"—"Nobilem hanc medicinæ partem, diu sepultam avorum
ætate, quasi ab orco revocavit Th. Paracelsus." I suppose many hints lie scattered
in his neglected books, which clever appropriators have since developed with
applause. Thus, it appears from his treatise "De Phlebotomia," and elsewhere,
that he had discovered the circulation of the blood and the sanguification of the
240 heart; as did after him Realdo Colombo, and still more perfectly Andrea Cesal-
pino of Arezzo, as Bayle and Bartoli observe. Even Lavater quotes a passage
from his work "De Natura Rerum," on practical Physiognomy, in which the
definitions and axioms are precise enough: he adds, "though an astrological
enthusiast, a man of prodigious genius." See Holcroft's translation, vol. iii. p.
245 179—"The Eyes." While on the subject of the writings of Paracelsus, I may
explain a passage in the third part of the Poem. He was, as I have said,
unwilling to publish his works, but in effect did publish a vast number. Valentius
(in Præfat. in Paramyr.) declares "quod ad librorum Paracelsi copiam attinet,

†For a good defence of Paracelsus I refer the reader to Olaus Borrichius'
treatise—"Hermetis etc. Sapientia vindicata," 1674. Or, if he is no more learned
than myself in such matters, I mention simply that Paracelsus introduced the
use of Mercury and Laudanum.

231| *MS:* from O. to   *1835:* from Oporinus to   232-234| *MS:* attributes they
have confirmed P's title to < > chymistry. Gerardus   *1835:* attributes, they < >
P.'s   *1849:* attributes, the title of Paracelsus to be considered the father of modern
chemistry, is indisputable. Gerardus   *1888:* Chemistry is   234| *MS:* Vossius "De
Philosâ. et Philosum. sectis   *1835: sectis,"*   *1863:* Vossius, 'De Philosa et Philosum
sectis,'   *1888:* "De < > sectis,"   235| *MS: Cap.* 9 "De Chymia."—Nobilem < >
sepultam, avorum   *1835:* Cap. 9, *"De Chymiâ"*—"Nobilem < > sepultam avorum
1863: cap. 9, 'De Chymia'   *1888:* "De Chymia"   236| *MS:* aetate quasi ab ⌐
Orco   *1835:* orco   *1888:* aetate, quasi   238| *MS:* applause: thus < > *"De
Phlebotamiâ"*   *1835:* applause. Thus < > Phlebotamiâ,"   *1863:* 'De Phlebotamia,'
1888: "De Phlebotamia,"   240-241| *MS:* heart: as did after him Andreas
Cesalpinus of Arezzo, who died 1603 aged 83, as Bayle observes. Even   *1835:* heart; as
< > 1603, aged   *1849:* after him Realdo Columbo, and still more perfectly Andrea
Cesalpino of Arezzo, as Bayle and Bartoli observe. Even   242| *MS: "De naturâ
Rerum,"   1835:* work, *"De   1863:* 'De Natura Rerum,'   *1868:* work 'De   *1888:* "De
Natura Rerum,"   243| *MS:* enough < > tho'   *1835:* enough: < >
though   244-245| *MS: Translation Vol. 3. p* 179. *"The eyes."   1835:* Translation,
vol. iii. p. 179—*"The Eyes."*   245| *MS:* of P, I   *1835:* of Paracelsus, I
246| *MS:* Part   *1835:* part   248| *MS: (in præfat. In Paramyr.)* < > Pi.   *1835:*
(in Præfat in Paramyr)   1849: (in Præfat. in Paramyr.) < > Paracelsi   *1863:* (in
Praefat. in Paramyr.)

†2| *MS:* treatise "Hermetis *&c* sapientia vindicata. 167."   *1835:* Treatise—"Hermetis
&c.   1863: 'Hermetis etc. Sapientia vindicata,' 1674.   *1888:* "Hermetis < >
vindicata." 1674.

audio, a Germanis prope trecentos recenseri." "O fœcunditas ingenii!" adds he,
250 appositely. Many of these, were, however, spurious; and Fred. Bitiskius gives his
good edition (3 vols. fol. Gen. 1658) "rejectis suppositis solo ipsius nomine
superbientibus quorum ingens circumfertur numerus." The rest were "charissi-
mum et pretiosissimum authoris pignus, extorsum potius ab illo quam obtentum."
"Jam minime eo volente atque jubente hæc ipsius scripta in lucem prodisse
255 videntur; quippe quæ muro inclusa ipso absente, servi cujusdam indicio, furto
surrepta atque sublata sunt," says Valentius. These have been the study of a host
of commentators, amongst whose labours are most notable, Petri Severini, "Idea
Medicinæ Philosophiæ. Bas. 1571"; Mic. Toxetis, "Onomastica. Arg. 1574";
Dornei, "Dist. Parac. Franc. 1584"; and "Pi Philosæ Compendium cum scholiis
260 auctore Leone Suavio. Paris." (This last, a good book.)
    ⁹A disgraceful affair. One Liechtenfels, a canon, having been rescued *in
extremis* by the *"laudanum"* of Paracelsus, refused the stipulated fee, and was
supported in his meanness by the authorities, whose interference Paracelsus
would not brook. His own liberality was allowed by his bitterest foes, who found
265 a ready solution of his indifference to profit in the aforesaid sword-handle and
its guest. His freedom from the besetting sin of a profession he abhorred—(as he
curiously says somewhere, "Quis quæso deinceps honorem deferat professione
tali, quæ a tam facinorosis nebulonibus obitur et administratur?")—is recorded in
his epitaph, which affirms—"Bona sua in pauperes distribuenda collocandaque
270 erogavit," *honoravit*, or *ordinavit*—for accounts differ.
    ¹⁰"So migratory a life could afford Paracelsus but little leisure for applica-
tion to books, and accordingly he informs us that for the space of ten years he
never opened a single volume, and that his whole medical library was not
composed of six sheets: in effect, the inventory drawn up after his death states
275 that the only books which he left were the Bible, the New Testament, the
Commentaries of St. Jerome on the Gospels, a printed volume on Medicine, and
seven manuscripts."

---

²⁵⁰| *MS:* he appositely: Many of these were   *1835:* appositely. Many   *1849:* he,
appositely   *1888:* these, were   ²⁵¹| *MS: (3 vols. fol. Gen. 1658)*   *1835:* (3 vols.
fol. Gen. 1658)   *1849:* suppositas   *1863:* suppositis   ²⁵²| *1835:* ingeus   *1849:*
ingens   ²⁵³| *MS:* Authoris < > quam   *1835:* authoris piguus < > potiùs
1849: pignus   *1863:* potius < > quam   ²⁵⁵| *MS:* absente servi   *1888:* absente,
servi   ²⁵⁷| *MS:* among   *1888:* amongst   ²⁵⁷⁻²⁶⁰| *MS: Idea Medicinæ
Philosophiæ. Bas. 1571.* Mic. Toxetis *Onomastica. Arg.* 1574. Dornei *Dict. Parac. Franc.*
1584. and *Pi. Philosæ Compendium um scholiis auctore Leone Suavio. Paris.*   *1835:*
Severini, *Idea* < > 1571; Mic. Toxetis, *Onomastica.* Arg. 1574: Dornei, *Dict.* < >
1584; and   *1863:* 'Idea Medicinæ Philosophiæ Bas. 1571;' Mic. Toxetis, 'Onomastica.
Arg. 1574;' Dornei, 'Dict. Parac. Franc. 1584;' and 'Pi Philosæ Compendium cum
scholiis auctore Leone Suavio. Paris.'   *1888:* "Idea < > 1571;" < > "Onomastica. Arg.
1574;" < > "Dict. < > 1584:" and "Pi < > Paris."   ²⁶¹| *MS:* Liechtenfels a
canon, having   *1835:* Liicetenfels, a   ²⁶²| *MS:* of P, refused to come down with
the stipulated   *1835:* of Paracelsus, refused   *1849:* refused the stipulated
²⁶³| *MS:* Authorities < > interference P   *1835:* authorities < > interference
Paracelsus   ²⁶⁶| *MS:* guest: his < > abhorred (as   *1835:* guest. His < >
abohorred—(as   ²⁶⁸| *MS:* à < > administratur?) is § written over by §
administratur?") is   *1849:* administratur?,"—is   *1863:* a   ²⁶⁹| *MS:* epitaph
which affirms   *1835:* epitaph, which affirms—   ²⁷⁰| *MS:* erogavit"—honoravit—or
ordinavit   *1835:* erogavit" honoravit, or   *1849:* erogavit," honoravit   *1863:*
honoravit, or ordinavit

277

PAULINE

Pauline; A Fragment of a Confession was written in 1832 and published in March, 1833, London: Saunders and Otley, Conduit Street. At the end of the poem appears the note "Richmond, October 22, 1832." John Forster's copy of the poem has a note in B's hand explaining his presence in Richmond and suggesting that as the date of his conception of the poem: "Kean was acting there: I saw him in Richard III that night, and conceived the childish scheme already mentioned: there is an allusion to Kean, page 47 [11. 669–75]. I don't know whether I had not made up my mind to *act,* as well as to make verses, music, and God knows what,—*que de châteaux en Espagne* [what castles in Spain]!"

The John Forster copy, originally owned by John Stuart Mill, is now in the Forster Collection at the Library of the Victoria and Albert Museum, South Kensington. It contains notes which Mill wrote in anticipation of a review which he either never finished or failed to publish. Mill's annotated copy found its way back to B who responded to Mill's comments by remarks of his own. B later gave the book to Forster.

After its initial publication, the poem did not appear again until 1868. In the introductory note to the 1868 edition Browning felt it necessary to apologize for *Pauline* [See prefatory material to the editions of 1868, 1888, and 1889 included in this edition].

Title Page] "*Plus ne* . . . The quotation is from a poem called "De lui-même". Because of its thematic relevance to *Pauline,* it is translated here in its entirety:

I am no longer that which I was,
Nor will I ever know how to be so again;
My beautiful springtime and my summer
Have gone out the window.
Love, thou hast been my master,
I have served thee above all the gods.
O if I could be born a second time
How much better would I serve thee!

279

Title Page] *Marot* Clément Marot (c. 1496–1544), a French court poet of the early Renaissance, was born at Cohors in Quercy. His career would have held some interest for B. He lived for a time in Italy (and died there), he was critical of the established theology, the friars, and the papacy. His early collection of poetry, *Adolescence Clementine* (1532), bears some resemblance to *Pauline* in its confessional tone.

Reverse Title Page] *Non dubito . . .* I am sure that the title of my book, because of its rarity, will entice very many to read it. Among those will be some whose opinions are hostile, whose minds are weak—many of these are even malicious—, who are unable to accept my genius, and who, rash in their ignorance, will create a clamor after scarcely even glancing at the title. They will say that I teach forbidden things, lay the seeds of heresies, offend pious ears, and corrupt pure minds. . . . They are so full of care for their consciences that neither Apollo, nor all the Muses, nor even an Angel from heaven could free me from their curses. Now I too am full of care for them—that they not read my book, nor understand it, nor remember it; for it is harmful and very poisonous. In this book is the gateway to hell; it speaks hard words. Let them beware that it not shake their understanding out of them. But you, who come to read it with fair minds, if only you use as much discretion and prudence as bees use in gathering honey, go ahead and read it free from anxiety. I think that you will obtain from it no little utility and much pleasure. If you find anything which displeases you, reject it and do not use it. FOR I AM NOT SAYING THAT THESE THINGS ARE GOOD FOR YOU, I AM ONLY SAYING THEM. But do not reject the others. . . . So, if anything has been said too freely, forgive my youth since I, the writer of this work, am less than a youth.

Reverse Title Page] *H. Cor Agrippa, . . .* Henry Cornelius Agrippa of Nettesheim (1486–1535), writer and physician, wrote on occult philosophy, particularly that ascribed to the tradition of Hermes Trismegistus. His *De occulta philosophia* was written around 1510 and published in revised form in Antwerp in 1531. The work is a mixture of Neoplatonic and Christian belief in which magic emerges as the means by which man most readily achieves knowledge of God.

Reverse Title Page] *V.A. XX Vixi annos viginti.* I was twenty years old.

48] *Northern night* In northern latitudes, as in Lapland, unbroken daylight in summer and darkness in winter last for several months each.

142] *His award* A note in B's hand found in John Forster's copy of *Pauline* reads "The award of fame to him—the late acknowledgement of Shelley's genius."

151] *Sun-treader* Undoubtedly a reference to Percy Bysshe Shelley. In the John Forster copy, Mill wrote in the margin along side the lines beginning "I ne'er had ventured . . ." (141) the comment "Only at the fourth reading of this poem I found out what this meant." B replied at the bottom of the page (ending with line 153) with the comment quoted above (l. 142n). For young B's indebtedness to Shelley, see F. A. Pottle, *Shelley and Browning: A Myth and Some Facts* (Chicago, 1923).

321-322] *a god/Wandering after beauty* . . . Possibly a reference to Apollo whose love for and pursuit of Daphne is the most famous of his many amours. Ovid in his *Metamorphoses* tells the story of his pursuit of Daphne who, a devotee of Artemis and thus vowed to chastity, was changed into a laurel tree in order to avoid the embraces of her lover. The passage might also refer to Pan who pursued many nymphs, one of whom, Syrinx, was transformed into a bed of reeds from which Pan cut the first Pan-pipe. It is conceivable that B left the reference intentionally ambiguous so as to suggest recurring classical themes.

322] *a giant* Perhaps Atlas whom Homer describes as one who kept the pillars which hold heaven and earth asunder. The pillars which he supported were thought to rest in the sea beyond the most Western horizon. Hence, the image which B employs.

323] *an old hunter* P-C suggests that the old hunter is possibly Peleus on the grounds that he participated in the Calydonian boar hunt and that the gods were present for his marriage to the sea nymph Thetis. He appears in conversation with Thetis as an old man at the end of Euripides' *Andromache*. Orion, on the other hand, is identified primarily as a hunter and was in constant converse with the gods. He was beloved of the dawn goddess Eos and is most frequently associated with Artemis (or Diana), goddess of wild animals and the hunt. According to the most popular account of his death, Artemis, who loved him, was tricked by the jealous Apollo into shooting him with arrows. It is true that he appears nowhere in Greek legend as a particularly old man but then Browning may be using the word less to describe the hunter's age than to emphasize that he is a hunter from the remote past. Moreover, age was a very relative thing in Greek myth.

324] *high crested chief* In Book III of Homer's *Odyssey*, old Nestor, king of Pylos, tells Telemachus, son of Odysseus, that following the downfall of Troy the Argive army was divided among those who remained in Troy with Agamemnon, hoping by sacrifice to appease the wrath of Athene, and those who departed immediately for home. The latter sailed first to the island of Tenedos. Among the most illustrious of the crew, in addition to Nestor himself, were Odysseus, Diomedes, and Menelaus.

325] *Tenedos* An island about seven miles in length situated in the Aegean Sea off the Troad. The island is called Bozcaada today.

331] *Dim clustered isles* Islands in the Aegean Sea, east of Greece.

334] *Swift-footed* Hermes, messenger of the gods.

335] *Proserpine's* The daughter of Zeus and Demeter, who with the consent of Zeus was abducted by Hades and became his wife. Because of Demeter's anger Zeus sent Hermes to rescue Proserpine from Hades.

403] *White way* Milky way.

479] *Arab birds* Whether or not B had a specific bird in mind is not clear. Of all the possible identifications of a particular bird that have been offered that of the pelican is most convincing. The pelican is found in Arabia and also fits B's description in its habits of flight.

488] *vanity of vanities! Ecclesiastes* 1:2.

527-528] *One branch from the gold forest, like the knight/Of old tales,* At the command of the Cumaean sybil, Aeneas must find and pluck a golden bough if he wishes to visit Anchises in the Underworld. The story appears in Vergil's *Aeneid,* IV.

567-568] *that king/Treading the purple calmly to his death* On page 30 in the John Forster copy of *Pauline,* B prints in Greek the following quotation from Aeschylus' *Agamemnon,* lines addressed by Agamemnon to Clytemnestra: "Since I have been overbourn to harken to thee in this, I will tread upon the purple pathway as I pass to my palace halls." (The translation is from The Loeb Classical Library, Aeschylus II, *Agamemnon,* ll. 956-957.)

572] *And him sitting alone in blood* On page 40 in the John Forster copy of the poem, B prints in Greek the following quotation from Sophocles' *Ajax,* indicating that it elucidates line 572:

But now, confounded in his [Ajax'] abject woe,
Refusing food or drink, he sits there still,
Just where he fell amid the carcases
Of the slain sheep and cattle . . .
Ho Teucer! [Brother of Ajax] where is Teucer? Will his raid
End never? And the while I am undone!

(The translation is from The Loeb Classical Library, Sophocles II, *Ajax,* 11.322-324, 342-343.)

573] *and the boy* Orestes who says in the *Libation Bearers,* "But—since I would have you known—for I know not how 'twill end. . . . But while I still retain reason, I proclaim to those who hold me dear and declare that not without justice did I slay my mother, polluted murderess of my father, and a thing loathed of Heaven." (The translation is from The Loeb Classical Library, Aeschylus II, *The Libation Bearers,* ll. 1021–23, 1026-27.)

656] *Andromeda* In Greek legend the daughter of Cepheus and Cassiopeia. Cepheus, in order to appease the anger of Poseidon, chained Andromeda to a rocky cliff at the edge of the sea. Perseus rescued her. According to Mrs. Sutherland Orr (*Hbk.,* London, 1896, p. 21) "The 'Andromeda' described . . . is that of Polidori di Caravaggio, of which Mr. Browning possessed an engraving, which was always before his eyes as he wrote his earlier poems. The original was painted on the wall of a garden attached to the Palazzo Bufalo—or del Bufalo—in Rome."

669-675] *I will . . . through decay.* A reference to Edmund Kean (1787-1833). See note on text. Kean was one of the most famous tragic actors of all times, known particularly for his Shakespearean roles. He scored his first important public triumph when he played with great emotional fervor the part of Shylock at Drury Lane in 1814. In March, 1833, shortly after B saw him at Richmond, he collapsed on the stage of Covent Garden where he was playing Othello.

811] *aims* *Je crains . . .* I fear indeed that my poor friend may not always be perfectly understood in what remains to be read of this strange fragment, but he is less suitable than any other to make clear that which of its very nature can never be any more than dream and confusion. Moreover, I do not know whether in trying better to coordinate certain parts, one would not run the risk of destroying the only merit which such a unique work might claim, that of giving a fairly precise idea of the genre of which it is only a rough sketch. This unpretentious beginning, this stirring of passion, which at first increases and then by degrees subsides, these transports of the soul, the sudden return upon the self, and above all, that way of thinking which is peculiar to my friend, make changes almost impossible. Reasons which he has caused to be esteemed elsewhere, and others even more powerful, have won my indulgence for this work which I would otherwise have advised him to throw in the fire. I do not believe less, because of this, in the great principle of all composition, a principle of Shakespeare, of Raphael, of Beethoven, from which it follows that the concentration of ideas is due much more to their conception than to their execution. I have every reason to fear that the first of these qualities is still alien to my friend, and I doubt very strongly that a redoubling of effort would cause him to acquire the second. The best thing would be to burn this—but what am I to do?

I think that in that which follows he alludes to a particular examination which he once made of the soul, or rather his own soul, to discover the sequence of objects that it would be possible for him to achieve, each of which, having been obtained, was to form a kind of plateau, from which he could perceive other ends, other projects, other pleasures, which, in their turn, were to be surmounted. What resulted was that unconsciousness and sleep would put an end to everything. This conception, which I do not fully understand, is perhaps as unintelligible to him as it is to me.

851] *Olivet* The mountain facing Jerusalem on the east. At the foot of the mount of Olives in the garden of Gethsemane, the place where Jesus went with his disciples the night before the crucifixion. A tradition identifies Olivet with the Mount of Transfiguration. Luke 22: 39.

920] *And the crew wandered in its bowers* In Book IX of Homer's *Odyssey,* Odysseus and his men stop at the island of the Lotos Eaters where part of the men eat of the lotus and, because of its narcotic effect, lose their will to return home.

964] *the fair pale sister, went to her chill grave* Antigone, whose story is told in Sophocles' play of that name, chose to be put to death rather than accept Creon's arbitrary decree that her slain brother be denied the customary rites of burial.

1020] *Sun-treader* See l. 151 n.

PARACELSUS

The Manuscript

The MS is in the Victoria and Albert Museum Library, in the Forster collection. It is now bound in reddish-brown leather, in rather good condition, elaborately decorated in gold. John Forster's bookplate is attached to the inside of the front cover. The cover measures 11⅜" by 8¼". The pages are 10¾" by 8¼". Compressed, the MS is about ½" thick. The paper is watermarked "J. Whatman" and the date "1834." The obverse of the first used leaf is blank; on the reverse is pasted a print of the full-length portrait of Paracelsus. Above the print is written, almost certainly in B's hand, "Parturiunt madido quae nixu proela, recepta: Sed quis scripta manu sunt—veneranda magis." "The offspring which issued forth out of intoxicated effort, has been accepted; but whatever is written by hand ought to be venerated." At the side is "To *John Forster Esq* (my early understander) with true thanks for his generous and seasonable public Confession of Faith in me. RB. *Hatcham, Surrey*, 1842." The next leaf, obverse and reverse, headed PARACELSUS: by RBT. BROWNING, contains the preface cancelled after the first edition. It is followed by the "Persons." The next 103 pages contain the poem itself. The Note and notes follow, in considerable disorder, with numerous interleavings.

The MS presents several puzzling features. It is written throughout in B's very clear hand, but the punctuation is corrected in both pencil and ink, as follows. In Act I, the leaf containing lines 704–792 has been corrected in pencil, not, it would seem, in B's hand; on the upper left-hand corner of the obverse is written in pencil "Stock." This leaf is reversed in the present condition of the MS. The second page of Part III is the obverse of its leaf. At this point the corrections in pencil are resumed. In the upper left-hand corner is written in ink "J. Riggs." "J. Riggs" appears twice more in this Part, as does "Stock." The pencil corrections continue through the page that ends with l. 1009, the obverse of its leaf. The next page is corrected in ink, and "Stock" is written in the upper right-hand corner. The first leaf, i.e., the first two pages, of Part IV is corrected in pencil, possibly in B's hand. As the variants indicate, there are punctuation corrections throughout the MS in what is evidently B's hand. A small number of substantive corrections are obviously in B's hand, but the corrections described above are exclusively of punctuation. Another oddity of the MS is that B has pasted in portraits of Paracelsus not only as a Frontispiece, but also at the ends of Parts III and IV. Although we have not been able to reproduce B's discriminations among dashes of differing length we have attempted to indicate in the variants other oddities of punctuation that occur in the MS. The effect of the original punctuation is to give the poetry a spontaneity, a feeling of rapidity of thought not to be found in the 1835 text. It is hoped that something of this effect survives in the conventionalized approximation adopted for the variants; but a reading of *Paracelsus* in the Forster MS is an instructive and vivifying experience.

The Text

B's principal source was Frederick Bitiskius' edition of the works of Paracelsus (Note: l. 119n), and the article on Paracelsus in the *Biographie Universelle,* which B is said to have read through. Most of the information about the various proper names in both text and B's notes is taken from the latter work. For additional information, the principal source has been Walter Pagel, *Paracelsus: An Introduction To Philosophical Medicine in the Era of the Renaissance,* (S. Karger: Basel and New York, 1958). For translations from the Latin we are indebted to Professor K. Don Morris of the University of South Carolina.

Dedication] Comte Amédée de Ripert-Monclar, who was a quasi-official representative of the Bourbons to the French exiles in England, met B through B's half-uncle, William Shergold Browning, of Rothschild's bank in Paris. De Ripert-Monclar suggested Paracelsus to B as the subject for a poem.

Persons] *Paracelsus* See B's Note, which follows the text of the poem, and the present annotations to the poem and the Note.

PART I

Scene] *Würzburg* A town in central Germany on the Main River. In 1512 it was the seat of the Prince-Bishop of Würzburg, an independent principality, part of the Holy Roman Empire. Since 1815 it has been part of the kingdom and then the State of Bavaria.

1512] 1507, the date B first used, is as probable for Paracelsus' association with Trithemius (l. 241n) as 1512.

60] *Saint Saviour's.* Probably the Cathedral. The first Cathedral, begun in 788, was dedicated to the Holy Savior; the second, begun in the latter half of the ninth century, was dedicated to St. Kilian; the third, begun in the eleventh century, is a Romanesque building with two towers, badly damaged in World War II and currently being restored.

120] *Einsiedeln* A town in Switzerland, twenty mi. SE of Zurich and five

286

mi. S of Lake Zurich, in the Canton of Schwyz. Since the early middle ages it has been a famous place of pilgrimage.

241] *Trithemius* John Tritheim, historian, theologian, and writer on alchemy and secret writing. He was born in 1462 at Trittenheim, in the Electorate of Trier, a town in W Germany near the border of Luxembourg. In the sixteenth century it was part of the Rhenish Palatinate and was ruled by an archbishop. Tritheim learned to read at the age of fifteen and studied at Trier. In 1482, returning to Trittenheim, he spent the night at the Benedictine abbey at Spanheim, or Sponheim. He decided to take orders and shortly after was elected abbot. Finding the abbey in a deplorable condition, he set the monks to copying and caring for MSs, and formed a remarkable library of more than 2000 volumes, in many languages, especially Greek, Hebrew, and Latin. He rapidly acquired considerable fame. In 1505, returning from a visit to Heidelberg, the seat of the Prince Palatine, he learned that the monks had rebelled against his discipline and had deposed him. His prince appointed him abbot of the Abbey of St. James in Würzburg, and he entered on his appointment October 15, 1506. He died there December 26, 1516. He was one of the most voluminous of all writers, as famous for his piety as for his learning, and contributed greatly to the revival of learning in Germany.

347] *geier-eagle* Leviticus 11:18 (King James version) mentions the giereagle (see variants). The Revised Standard uses "vulture;" *geier* is German for hawk.

357–358] *Black Arts, Great Works, the Secret and Sublime* The first refers to Black Magic, or sorcery; the other terms are from alchemy. The Great Work or *Magnum Opus*, was the process by which the Philosopher's Stone was formed, which could turn base metals into gold or silver. The materials used for the Stone were sublimed in the course of the Magnum Opus, which was the ultimate ambition and secret of the alchemists. The historical Paracelsus was deeply learned in alchemy, and his important achievements were made in an alchemical context. The alchemists used a veiled and allegorical language in their writings.

417] *Stagirite* Aristotle, the Greek philosopher (384–323 B.C.) was born at Stagira, Macedon.

481] *riveled* Shriveled, or wrinkled, as by heat.

609] *commissary* One to whom some charge, duty, or office has been committed.

651] *gold and apes* Solomon "had at sea a navy of Tharshish with the navy of Hiram; once in three years came the navy of Tharshish, bringing gold, and silver, ivory, and apes, and peacocks." I Kings 10:22.

811] *Mayne* River flowing through N. Bavaria, generally in a western direction. It flows into the Rhine at Mainz. Würzburg is built on both sides of it.

812 *schistous* Schistose.

25] *arch-genethliac* An astrologer in the modern sense; one who foretells the course of a life by studying the influences of the stars at the moment of birth. Here, *arch* means "of the highest eminence."

265] *fire-labarum* . . . *old founder of these walls* Eusebeius of Caesarea (270–340), the biographer of the Roman Emperor Constantine, relates that the latter saw a fiery cross in the sky during one of his marches in the campaign against his rival Emperor, Maxentius, whom he defeated in 312 B.C. He subsequently adopted as his banner the labarum, a long streamer of silk hanging from the cross-pole of a long staff. The banner displayed images of the reigning emperor and his children, and the summit of the staff was crowned with a monogram consisting of the first two letters, in Greek, of the name of Christ. Constantine delayed his baptism until he was near death, but established Christianity as the official religion of the Empire. He decided to make the ancient Byzantium the capital of the Empire in 324, and dedicated the city in 330 or 334.

471] *tent-tree* A tall screw pine, confined to Lord Howe Island, between Australia and New Zealand.

PART III

Scene] *Basel* A city in N Switzerland, situated on both sides of the Rhine. In 1526 a center of humanism, publishing, and religious reform, with an important university, it was one of the most cultivated of German cities.

1526 The historical Paracelsus was in Basel by November, 1526, having gone there from Strassburg by way of Tübingen and Freiburg. His students followed him to Basel. Oecolampadius (l. 293n) seems to have been responsible for his appointment, which was a difficult one for Paracelsus, since it was a municipal and not a University appointment, yet carried with it the right to lecture at the University. Oecolampadius was a friend of the reformers at Strassburg whom Paracelsus had known there. The appointment took place in March, 1527, and Paracelsus left in January or February 1528. See annotations to B's Note.

128] *pansies** **Citrinula* . . . Dorn. "Citrinula (flammula), a herb very familiar to Paracelsus." Gerhard Dorn, a German chemist and alchemist lived in the middle of the sixteenth century. He was an early Paracelsean and was one of the group who published their master's works, very few of which had been printed during Paracelsus' lifetime. Perhaps Dorn's most important achievement was his *Dictionary of the Chemistry of Theophrastus,* Frankfurt, 1583, in which he attempted to define and explain Paracelsus' obscure terminology.

211] *Rhasis* Razes, Rhazes, or Rasis. Arabian physician of the tenth century, principally in Bagdad. His various treatises were translated into Latin and used throughout the middle ages and after. His treatise on small-pox and measles was still considered valuable in the nineteenth century.

222] *fallen prince of morning* Lucifer, or morning-star, the leader of the rebellion of the angels against God.

293] *Oecolampadius* John Oecolampadius or, in German, Hausschien. Born in 1482 at Weinsberg in Franconia, Germany, his family was originally from Basel. His interest in theology led him to study Greek and Hebrew, and in 1515 he went to preach at Basel, where he became acquainted with Erasmus, then publishing his edition of the New Testament in Greek (l. 480). After an interim as a monk, his interest in the new theological opinions of the oncoming Reformation led him back to Basel, where, given a chair of theology at the University, he openly attacked the dogma and the rites of Roman Catholicism. He thus became one of the leaders of the Reformation, signalizing his freedom by marrying in 1521. He took part in the great quarrel between Carlstadt and Luther (l. 295n) and declared himself on the side of Zwingli (l. 956n), towards whom he had the same relation as that of Melancthon to Luther, a kind of lieutenant or chief assistant. After further successes, against both Catholics and Anabaptists (l. 993n), he died in 1531.

294] *Castellanus* Pierre Duchatel, born towards the end of the fifteenth century, he eventually became Bishop of Orleans, Grand Almoner of France, and favorite of Francis I of France. He was educated at the then famous College of Dijon. He taught himself Greek and began publishing at the age of sixteen. Attracted to Basel by the reputation of Erasmus (l. 480n), he became an assistant to Frobenius, the printer-publisher (l. 295n), as corrector of the press; thus he had an important and honorable position in the publication of the Greek and Latin editions Erasmus was bringing out. He left Basel in 1529, when Catholicism was officially suppressed.

295] *Munsterus* Sebastian Munster, born in 1489 at Ingelheim in the Palatinate, was a Hebrew scholar, a geographer, and a mathematician. He completed his studies at the University of Tübingen in SW Germany and became a Franciscan in order to work in quiet. Luther's writings led him to break with the Roman Catholic church, and in 1529 he went to Basel, where he taught theology and Hebrew in the University. He died in 1552.

295] *Frobenius* Johannes Froben, born in the last half of the fifteenth century at Hermelburg in Franconia, Germany, went to the University of Basel and established himself there as a printer. He was one of the first German printers to use roman type. He was learned and connected with the principal scholars of the day, especially Erasmus (l. 294n, and l. 480n). He printed a series of the Latin Fathers of the Church and Erasmus' New Testament, which appeared in 1516. In 1526 Paracelsus cured him of an illness, but his sudden death in October, 1527, seriously undermined Paracelsus' position in Basel.

344] *Luther* By 1526 the great Reformer (1483–1546) had abandoned the traditional interpretation of the Bible in favor of the new grammatical-historical interpretation, had developed his new concept of grace as a force that operated not through the sacraments but through the individual, had made his attack on indulgences, in his ninety-five theses had published his belief that man is justified, or attains to value before God, by his joyous belief in God and in Christ, had been condemned, in 1521, at the Imperial Diet, or Council, at Worms, had been placed under the Imperial Ban, and had gone into hiding at the Wartburg, the ancient castle near Eisenach, in central Germany, had returned to Wittenberg, and had definitely broken with the Roman Catholic church.

391] *rear-mice* Rere-mice, or bats.

394] *Lachen* A village on the shore of Lake Zürich, NE of Einsiedeln.

437] *sudary* A square of linen carried by the upper classes of ancient Rome to wipe sweat off one's face.

441] *suffumigation* The medical application of smoke to the body.

480] *Erasmus* The great Humanist of Northern Europe, he contributed powerfully to the Renaissance in the North, and to the Reformation, though he never accepted it. He was probably born in or near Rotterdam in 1467. In 1514–1516 he was in Basel to publish his Greek New Testament. In 1521 he settled there to supervise the publication of his work by Frobenius (l. 295n). In 1526 he consulted Paracelsus by letter, on the recommendation of Frobenius, asking for advice about how to treat his bladder stones. In 1529, when Roman Catholicism was suppressed in Basel, he left for Freiburg, Germany, some thirty-five mi. N of Basel. In 1535, in the hopes of recovering his health, which had been permanently damaged by his poverty when he was a student in Paris, he returned to Basel, where he died in July, 1836. Erasmus' request and Paracelsus' reply are to be found in Bitiskius (Note: l. 119n).

714] *addressed* Made ready.

801] *News from Lucern or Zurich* Such news would have to do with the growing Reformation in Switzerland.

867] *Praeclare! Optime!* "Excellent! Very well (said)!"

907] *Ulysses' bow, Achilles' shield* The bow is proverbially efficacious because with it Ulysses slew Penelope's many suitors; the shield was the most splendid, since it was forged by *Hephaeistos,* the god of fire and smiths. (*Odyssey,* xxi; *Iliad,* xviii.)

915] *Frobenius' press* See l. 295n.

946] *Aetius* Physician of Amida, Roman city in Mesopotamia, towards the end of the fifth century and the beginning of the sixth. His *Tetrabiblos,* a compilation of earlier physicians, was widely copied and known through the middle ages and, in part, printed in the sixteenth century.

946] *Oribasius* Famous Greek physician of the fourth century, born at Pergamum. He had the friendship of the Emperor Julian the Apostate, who attempted to restore paganism. His works are in part compilations and in part original. About a third were known through the middle ages and were printed in the sixteenth century.

946] *Galen* The greatest physician of antiquity, after Hippocrates, lived in the second century. No author of antiquity was so productive, though more than half of his works are lost. He was known through the middle ages, and the printing of his works began in the fifteenth century.

947] *Serapion* A Syrian physician of the tenth century. Two of his works survive.

947] *Avicenna* The greatest of Arabian physicians, born in Persia in 980. He died in 1037. He was an alchemist and a metaphysician as well. His *Canons,* translated into Latin, were used through the middle ages and into the eighteenth century, dominating medical study. He was primarily a compiler of Greek and Roman medical treatists, and his works were among the first of those of the traditional physicians to be printed, beginning in the fifteenth century.

947] *Averröes* Arabian physician and philosopher, born at Cordova, Spain, in the twelfth century. He died in Morocco in 1198. He was primarily a theoretical physician, rather than a practical one, and particularly dependent on Aristotle and Galen.

955–961] *Zwuinglius . . . Zurich . . . Luther . . . Wittenberg . . . Carolostadius* Ulrich Zwingli, the principal Swiss reformer, was born at Wildhaus, in the Toggenburg valley in NE Switzerland, January 1, 1484, and was killed in battle in 1531. He studied at Basel, Berne, and Vienna. At the age of eighteen he began teaching at Basel. In 1506 he was given the benefice at Glaris, in the bishopric of Constance. He devoted his study to Greek and the New Testament, the fathers of the church, and such moderns as the heretics Wycliffe and Hus. In 1515 he was appointed to Einsiedeln. He began to reform this ancient place of pilgrimage, the birthplace of Paracelsus, by burying relics, and the like, and discouraging pilgrims. In 1516 he was called to Zürich, which he made one of the chief centers of the Reformation. In 1520 he renounced his pension from Rome and began to teach nothing but the Gospel. By 1525, a year in which he became involved in a quarrel with Luther, he had married and had established the Reformation in Zürich. Carolostadius (Andrew Bodenstein, called Carlstadt (c. 1480–1541) originally the Greek tutor of Luther at the University of Wittenberg, and later his colleague) continued Luther's reforms while Luther was in refuge and hiding in the Wartburg, when he had been placed under the Ban of the Empire and his books had been condemned as heretical (l. 344n). Luther returned to Wittenberg in 1522 in defiance of the Ban and continued the reform, though more conservatively. Carlstadt, who had come to the conclusion that the Lord's supper was a commemorative rite only, denied the Real Presence in the consecrated bread and wine, a radical position which Luther rejected. Luther forced Carlstadt to leave Wittenberg for Strassburg, but his doctrines caught the attention of Zwingli and Oecolampadius (l. 293n). By 1525 Erasmus (l.

48on) was impressed, and did not see how the new doctrine could be refuted, though he preferred that the Old Catholic doctrine be preserved for the sake of peace. The argument centered on the word "is" in such Gospel passages as that found in Matthew 26:26–28, "And as they were eating, Jesus took bread and blessed it, and brake it, and gave it to the disciples, and said, Take, eat; this *is* my body. And he took the cup, and gave thanks, and gave it to them, saying, Drink ye all of it; for this *is* my blood of the new testament, which is shed for many for the remission of sins." Luther's doctrine, sometimes called consubstantiation, asserted that the body and blood were present, though the bread and wine were not transmuted, just as, in the simile often used, fire is present in red-hot iron, though the iron remains iron. The Carlstadt-Zwingli-Oecolampadius interpretation was that "is" in such statements is properly interpreted as "is a sign of." A pamphlet war began between Zwingli and Luther in 1526, but an open break did not occur until the following year.

993] *gangs of peasants . . . Suabia . . . Münzer . . . the duke, the landgrave and the elector* These lines refer to the Peasant's War. This revolt, the last of a series of such revolts in Germany, was inspired by the revolutionary and democratic character of the Reformation ideas. It began in the SW part of the Black Forest in June, 1524, and spread rapidly through SW Germany, i.e., Suabia and Württemberg. By the end of the year it had spread N to Saxony and Thuringia, in central Germany, the area in which Luther had his headquarters, was most powerful, and was under the protection of the Electoral Dukes of Saxony, first Frederick the Wise and then his brother John the Constant, who became Duke in 1525. ("Electoral" indicates the right to participate in the election of the Holy Roman Emperor; there were also non-electoral Dukes of another area of Saxony.) Here Thomas Müntzer, the Anabaptist, had set up a theocratic state in Mühlhausen, in central Germany. Anabaptism, which had many forms, started in Switzerland and was suppressed there in 1525 by Zwingli, and its leaders either killed or driven out; thus its ideas spread to N Germany. The heart of the position was an absolutely free church, one unconnected with any state or ecclesiastical system. In its extreme forms it was apocalyptic and communistic, anticipating the Last Judgement. This was the form it took when it combined with Müntzer's belief in ecstatic visions and freedom even from the Bible. He was attacked by Duke Henry of Brunswick (who was not sympathetic with the reforms and remained Catholic, but whose territories were not far from Mühlhausen); by Philip, the Landgrave of Hesse, sympathetic with the Reformation; and by Duke John, the Elector of Saxony. Müntzer was defeated and beheaded at Mühlhausen in May, 1525. The revolt did not last much longer; it was repressed with great brutality and slaughter. Luther's opposition to the Peasants cost him popular support and was in part responsible for the establishment of Lutheranism as a state religion.

PART IV

Scene] *Colmar* A town in E France forty mi. SSE of Strassburg. In 1528 it was an Imperial City, free from all feudal lords except the Holy Roman Emperor.

1] *Oporinus* John Herbst (in Latin, Oporinus) was born in Basel Jan. 25, 1507. Educated in Strassburg, he returned to Basel and went to work for Frobenius on the latter's edition of the Greek fathers of the church (III:1. 295n). He decided to study medicine and attached himself to Paracelsus, who promised to prepare him to receive the doctorate in a year. He followed him when he left Basel for Colmar, hoping to learn from him to prepare laudanum (Note: 1. 209n), the composition of which was a secret. Wearied of losing his time with such a master, he solicited employment as a teacher, and the scholar Grunaeus obtained for him at the University of Basel the chair of Greek, which he filled with distinction. In 1539, being required to have the degree at least of Master of Arts, he left the University and founded a printing establishment. Despite poverty, he subsequently published excellent editions of the classics which he himself prepared for the press and also the work of Vesalius, the first modern anatomist. He died July 6, 1568, and was buried next to Erasmus. (See also B's Note, and his note 8).

1–7] *Von Visenburg . . . Torinus . . . Pütter* These names are apparently B's invention.

5] *Liechtenfels* See B's Note and his note 9.

82] *Saul* The first king of Israel. After Samuel had anointed him, "a company of prophets met him; and the Spirit of God came upon him, and he prophesied among them. And it came to pass, when all that knew him beforetime saw that, behold, he prophesied among the prophets, then the people said one to another, What is this that is come unto the son of Kish? Is Saul also among the prophets? And one of the same place answered and said, But who is their father? Therefore it became a proverb, Is Saul also among the prophets?" I Samuel 10:10–12.

112] *St. John* The fourth Gospel.

114] *stone* Bladder, kidney, or gall-bladder stones.

115] *Quid multa?* "Why many words?"

190] *sandal* The fruit of the Indo-Malayan sandal tree is cultivated for preserves and pickles.

190] *stripes* Strips.

192] *nard* An ointment made partly from nard, or spikenard.

199] *Egyptian's fine worm-eaten shroud* Mummy wrappings were much valued in the middle ages and later for medicinal purposes, principally for reasons given in 1. 198.

213] *Luther's psalms* Luther (III:1. 344) wished to make congregational singing an important and dignified part of church service, thus signifying the believer's direct relation to God and God's Grace. To this end he composed a number of hymns, some original, some adapted from earlier Catholic hymns, and some based on the Psalms of the Bible. Of the last, the best known is "A mighty fortress is our God," derived from Psalm 46.

310] *Fiat . . . vili.* Let the experiment be performed on a body of no value.

588] *serviceable spirits . . . lamp's rubbing* In the *Arabian Nights* Aladdin procures a lamp by rubbing which he summons spirits, or genii, who do his bidding.

PART V

Scene] *Salzburg* A town in Austria, just over the border of Bavaria, seventy-five mi. E and a little S of Munich. At this time the Archbishop of Salzburg was a virtually independent prince within the Holy Roman Empire, and ruled a considerable territory, mostly to the S of the city.

St. Sebastian Paracelsus requested burial in the almshouse of St. Sebastian, but there is no evidence that he died there.

96] *Erasmus* See III:l. 480n.

97] *schools* The medical schools of Paris and Padua were among the most famous of the Medieval and Renaissance periods, particularly that of Padua.

123] *Jove strikes the Titans down* In Greek mythology the Titans were the children of Heaven and Earth, and Zeus (Jove) was himself a child of Titans. When he rebelled against his father, the other Titans came to his father's aid, but were defeated by Zeus. Subsequently Earth brought forth another race, the Giants, who attacked Zeus, piling the mountains Pelion and Ossa on one another in order to reach Olympus, or at least threatening to do so. The Titans and the Giants are often, indeed ordinarily, confused.

126] *Phaeton* Phaëthon, the son of Helios (Apollo) persuaded his father, against the latter's judgment, to let him drive the horses of the sun. He lost control, the chariot of the sun was swept close to the earth, which was in danger of being consumed by its fire, and on the appeal of Gaea (Earth) Zeus (Jove) killed Phaëthon with a thunderbolt; Helios resumed control of the horses.

161] *Latin, Arab, Jew, Greek* See III:ll. 946–947n.

181] *Galen of Pergamos and hell* Paracelsus "gloried in passing as a magician; he even boasts of having received from Hell letters from Galen, and of having had, in the vestibule of Hades, lively disputes with Avicenna about potable gold, the tincture of the philosophers, the quintessence, the mithridate, the philosopher's stone, etc." From the article in the *Biographie Universelle* part of which B translates in his Note. (Note: l. 92n)

187] *Zoroaster* The Greek form of Zarathustra, or Zarathushtra, the Persian religious prophet, founder of the Parsee or Magian religion, who lived perhaps around 600 B.C., perhaps as early as 1000 B.C. The heart of his teaching was that the world was divided between two principles of light and darkness, or good and evil. Various forms of this belief have penetrated to Europe and have been responsible for numerous Christian heresies. For B the best account of Zoroaster was probably in Chapter VIII of Gibbon's *Decline and Fall of the Roman Empire* (1776–1788).

320] *Cain* The son of Adam, who killed his brother Abel and was the first murderer. God put a mark upon him to protect him from all enemies. Genesis 4.

554] *Azoth* See B's Note: note 8, and annotations.

The Note

[B uses three kinds of notes to his Note: * and † for notes at the foot of the page; numbered notes printed after the Note; and * and † footnotes for his note 5. He re-arranged them slightly in 1849. Because of the complexities involved in presenting variants on the same page, in this edition the first two have been re-arranged in a single series. The following table shows B's changes and the changes made here.

This edition
1835
1849–1889

Line	Note number	Note number	Note number
11	1	* (p. 203)	1
16	2	* (p. 204)	* (1888, p. 179)
23	3	1	2
36	4	2	3
47	5	3	4
56	6	* (p. 206)	* (1888, p. 180)
59	7	† (pp. 206–7)	† (1888, p. 181)
72	8	4	5
74	9	5	6
78	10	* (p. 208)	* (1888, p. 181)
209	*	* (p. 214)	* (1888, p. 185)
216	†	† (p. 214)	† (1888, p. 185)]

4] B does not translate the entire *Biographie Universelle* article. The more important omitted passages are translated below.

10] *Paracelsus* probably means "surpassing Celsus" (the Roman writer on medicine, first century A.D., or the opponent of Christianity, second century A.D.); the name was not used in print until 1536. It seems probable that the name was not self-invented but was given to him by his drinking companions at Colmar (1528). The name Theophrastus is not documented before 1526, and Philipp first appears on his tombstone.

11] *Hohenheim* famous alchemist and enthusiast of the sixteenth century, *was born in 1493"* He was probably born May 1, 1494.

14] *nearly related* Actually George Bombast, the Grand Prior, was Paracelsus' grandfather.

16] *Thomas Erastus* Thomas Liebler, called Erastus (1528–1583), Swiss physician and theologian, principally remembered for his doctrine that the church must be subordinate to the state. He attacked Paracelsean theories and teachings in his *Disputations on the New Medicine of Paracelsus,* in four parts, 1572–1573. He was professor at the University of Basel from 1580 until his death.

17] *"pretends.* The latter also relates (*Disput. de medic. nova Paracelsi,* Part I, p. 237) that Paracelsus suffered castration at the age of three years. Others say that he lost his virility as a consequence of the bite of a pig. What is certain is that he had no beard and that he detested women. *It appears"*

24] *Tritheim* See I:l. 241n.

24] *many German bishops* should be "several German bishops."

33] *Sigismond Fugger* Sigmund Fueger. Schwaz in Austria E of Innsbruck was the site of Frueger's mines. Paracelsus was also at the mining school of the Fuggers at Hutenberg near Villach, in Carinthia, south central Austria, where his father had been a physician.

34] *Magnum Opus* See I:ll. 351–358.

35] "Following the custom of alchemists, *Paracelsus travelled"*

43] *Khan of the Tartars* The Tartars, or Tatars, were remnants of the Empire of the Golden Horde of Chingis-khan or Genghis Khan 1167–1227). The Tartar Khanate of the Crimea, in Southern Russia, was a rich and powerful independent nation in the sixteenth century.

45] *Trismegistus* Certain sacred books of the last centuries before Christ, dealing with such divers matters as geology, astrology, medicine, temple ritual, and hymns in honor of the Gods, were believed to have been written by an ancient Egyptian priest, Hermes Trismegistus. Hermeticism was revived in the early Renaissance and mingled with alchemical tradition, which supposed itself derived from the writings of Hermes Trismegistus. The *tincture* was probably the oxide obtained from employing quicksilver in the process of separating gold and silver from the native matrix.

50] *Oecolampadius* See III:l. 293n.

51] *Basil* Basel. See III: Scene n.

53] *Avicenna* and *Galen* See III:ll. 946–947n. The sources indicate that only Avicenna was burned.

58] *Rhasis* See III:l. 211n. *Montagnana* Bartolommeo Montagnana, died 1470, one of the earliest collectors of *consilia,* descriptions of medical cases in a form meaningful to modern medicine. *Mesues* Arabian physician of the ninth century. By origin a Nestorian Christian, he supervised translations from Greek, Syrian, and Persian for Haroun-al-Raschid, the great Caliph of Bagdad. His medical writings were translated into Hebrew and Latin, and his works were printed in Venice and elsewhere before 1500.

59] *Paris, Montepellier,* etc. Seats of schools of medicine.

63] *"be mine.* The novelty of his doctrines, the emphasis with which he spoke of his success, the power he claimed to prolong life and to cure even incurable diseases, his practice of lecturing the vulgar, all these circumstances combined attracted to Basel a crew of the credulous, idlers and enthusiasts. We still possess the lectures that he gave on practical medicine: their language is a mixture of German and barbarous Latin; and they offer nothing but empirical remedies, recommended with the greatest pretentions possible. So much impudence, far from diminishing his fame, only made it grow, according to the witness of Ramus [Petrus Ramus or Pierre de la Rameé (1515–1572) French humanist and anti-Scholastic and anti-Aristotelian] to the point that Erasmus (III:l. 480n) himself, who had suffered a long time from the gravel, invoked the aid of Paracelsus; and this led to a correspondence between these two men, so differently famed, which has come to us. *But at Basil"*

69] *Oporinus* See IV:l. 1n.

80] *Alsatia* The present Alsace on the French side of the Rhine. Paracelsus fled to Colmar (IV:*Scene* n).

84] *St. Gall* St. Gallen, a city in NE Switzerland. *Pfeffers* Pfäfers near Bad Ragaz, a city twenty-five mi. S of St. Gallen, site of a monastery and an ancient spa. *Augsburg* City in S Germany.

85] *Moravia* Province in what is now central Czechoslovakia, in the sixteenth century a Margravate of the Holy Roman Empire which in 1526 became part of the Archduchy of Austria.

91] *Mindelheim* Town in S Germany, SW of Augsburg.

92] *"St. Stephen* (Sebastian *is meant*), (V:*Scene* n.) *September 24, 1541.* Thus ended his life, when he was only forty-eight, and well-nigh poverty-stricken, he who pretended to possess the double secret of transmuting metals and of prolonging life for several centuries.

His philosophical and medical system is interesting by its very absurdity. A summary follows. He takes as his first support religion and the sacred writings. He asserts that the contemplations of the perfections of Divinity is enough to procure all intelligence and wisdom; that the Holy Scripture leads to all truths; that the Bible is the key to the theory of sickness; that it is necessary to consult the Apocalypse to know what magical medicine is. The man who blindly obeys the will of God and succeeds in identifying himself with the celestial intelligences possesses the philosophic stone; he can cure all ills, and prolong life at his will, because he possesses the tincture which Adam and the patriarchs used before the flood to live for eight or nine centuries. Paracelsus professed the grossest pantheism; he owned the existence of pure spirits without soul. According to him, all beings, even minerals and fluids, partook of food and drink and expelled excrement. His physiologic theory, a confused heap of the most incoherent ideas, is built on the application of the laws of the Cabala to the demonstration of the functions of the human body. Thus the vital force is an emanation of the stars. The sun is *en rapport* with the heart, *etc.* . . . . Paracelsus is not less absurd in his theory of pathology. Turning back always to magic, he asserts that it is the art of arts, that here one must find medical wisdom. He gloried in passing as a magician; he even boasts of having received from Hell letters from Galen, and of having had, in the vestibule of Hades, lively disputes with Avicenna about potable gold, the tincture of the philosophers, the quintessence, the mithridate, the philosopher's stone, *etc.* . . . . In particular he explains every ill with the aid of his three principles out of chemical entities, which he substitutes for the four elements of the ancients (salt, sulphur, and mercury), *etc.* . . . . One cannot dispute, however, the value of the effort he made to introduce into medicine the use of preparations of antimony, mercury, salt, and iron-bearing substances, which have so efficacious an effect on our organs. One cannot deny that alchemy, which has ruined so many adepts, was advantageous for the medical sciences, because of important discoveries of which it was the source. Paracelsus published very few works in his lifetime. Since those which are attributed to him offer numerous contradictions, one is led to the conclusion that several were composed by his students. If we wished to cite the titles of all of his writings, they would require several pages; we limit ourselves therefore to listing several complete collections. I. German editions: Basel, 1574, octavo; ibid. 1589–1590, ten volumes in quarto, edited by J. Huser: Strasburg, 1608–1618, four volumes in folio, also by J. Huser, who died after having published the first two volumes. The fourth is confined to apocryphal writings. II. Latin editions. *Opera omnia medico-chymico chirurgica,* Frankfurt, 1630, ten volumes in quarto; Geneva, 1658, three volumes in folio. III. French editions: *La Grande Chirurgie de Paracelse,* translated from the Latin edition of J. Dalhem, by Cl. Dariot, Lyon, 1593, quarto, 1603, quarto; Montbéliard, 1608, octavo.—*La petite chirurgie,* the same, Paris, 1623, octavo. These are almost the only works which have appeared in our tongue. For information about Paracelsus, and for his life, one can consult the following books. Michael Toxitis, *Onomasticum medicum et explicatio verborum* Paracelsi; P. Severini, *Ideae medicinae philosophicae;* D. Leclerc, *Histoire de la Médicine; Histoire Littéraire de Paracelse,* with a facsimile of his writings (in Volume 2, pp. 177–285, of the *Nouveau Journal des Arts et de la Littérature,* by The. de Murr); Adelung, *Histoire de la Folie Humaine,* Vol. 7; Sprengel, *Histoire Pragmatique de la Médicine,* Vol. III.

R——D——N"

In 1835 B purchased Oswald Croll, *Philosophy Reformed in Four Profound Tractates. The I. Discovering the great and deep mysteries of nature: by that learned chymist and physician Osw. Crollius. The other III. Discovering the wonderful mysteries of the creation, by Paracelsus: being his Philosophy to the Athenians.* Both made English by H. Pinnell. London, Lloyd, 1657. Croll (1580–1609) was one of the early Paracelseans. In these works Paracelsus discusses his theory that all matter (which he thought of as living) and all living things emanated in four stages from the Great Mystery, and did not come into existence by the special creation of God. These ideas may have been B's justification for Paracelsus' evolutionary vision in Part V, just before his death.

91] *Paracelsus* See l. 10n.

97] In 1941 H. E. Sigerist published an article in the *Bulletin of the History of Medicine* proving that the pejorative use of the term "Bombastic" does not refer to Paracelsus but derives from the Greek bombyx, silkworm, and designates its product silk and later cotton and cotton wadding. The first recorded metaphorical use of the word is from 1589.

100] *Hic . . . fuisse.* "This man (Erastus) says that Paracelsus was castrated as a three year old by a certain soldier, some others that it was done by a boar; at any rate he was beardless and hated women."

104] *Melander's "Jocoseria"* A collection of jokes and anecdotes by Otto Melander, *1597.*

105] *Tintoretto* Bitiskius (l. 119n.) used an engraving of a portrait he said was by Tintoretto (1518–1594) as his frontispiece. He refers to it on p. [2] of his Preface. I have been unable to confirm the existence of such a portrait.

106] *Helvetium . . . ediderit* "I can scarcely believe that Paracelsus was Swiss, for I can hardly imagine that region producing such a monster." For *Erastus* see l. 16n.

112] *Cornelius Agrippa* Henry Cornelius Agrippa of Nettesheim, physician and philosopher (1486–1535). An associate of Paracelsus, he wrote on the occult philosophy, particularly that ascribed to the tradition of Hermes Trismegistus (l. 42n), and on *The Uncertainty and Vanity of the Sciences,* Cologne, 1527, and elsewhere. His *On Occult Philosophy* was published at Antwerp and Paris in 1531. This contains both the dedicatory epistle to Tritheim and the latter's answer. He is perhaps best known today for his panegyric in praise of women, *On the Nobility and Pre-excellence of the Feminine Sex,* Antwerp, 1529, a declamation made to please Margaret of Austria, Regent of Flanders.

115] *Quum . . . contulissemus* "When recently the Reverend Father was with you in your cloister in Würzburg, a great many things were said about chemistry, magic, the occult, and other things which up to now lurked in secret, as well as the arcane science and art in which we had a common interest."

119] *Inexplebilis . . . obtineret* "The insatiable desire to scrutinize the secrets of nature and to fill the mind with the material of arcane science was his; he could not persist in any one place for any length of time but yet he mastered mercury and scattered the sparks of his knowledge gained from wandering many lands, nations, and cities. When he was with men of an observant nature, especially chemists, he attracted them, and obtained in one way or another those who had discovered something in the process of assiduous work." Bitiskius, Preface, p. [4]. The full title of Bitiskius' edition of the works of Paracelsus is, Aur. Philip Theoph. Paracelsi Bombast ab Hohenheim, medici et philosophi celeberrimi, chemicorumque principis, *Opera omnia medico-chemico-chirurgica, tribus voluminibus comprehensa.* Editio novissma et emendatissima, ad Germanica & Latina exemplaria accuratissimè collata: Variis tractatibus & opusculis summâ hinc inde diligentiä conquisitis, ut in voluminis primi praefatione indicatur, locupletata: Indicibusque; exactissimis instructa. Genevae, Sumptibus Ioan. Antonii, & Samuelis De Tournes. M. DC. LIIX. On p. [11] of his Preface Bitiskius identifies himself as a Polish knight, a "mystes naturae," and one justly known as a citizen of the world.

124] *Patris* . . . *neminem* "First with the aid of his father and then by his own industry, he acquired a set of followers, the most learned men in Germany, Italy, France, Spain, and other regions of Europe; men who by a liberal doctrine and through appropriate searching managed to accomplish so much, that many were willing to say that no mortal had ever been able to master in general philosophic terms, problems so arduous, so arcane, and so hidden." The passage is to be found on p. 28 of one of B's sources, Melchior Adam, *Vitae Germanorum medicorum: qui secula superiori, et quod excurrit, claruerunt: congestae & ad annum usque M DC XX deductae a Melchiore Adama. Cum indice triplici: personarum gemino, tertio rerum.* Haedelbergae, impensis heredum Jonae Rosae, exaudit Johannes Georgius Geyder, Acad. Typogr. Anno M. DC. XX.

130] *Paracelsus* . . . *videtur* "Paracelsus entered so deeply into the vitals of nature; the strengths of plants and animals; explored and understood with such incredible talent the powers and faculties of metals and plants; healing completely all dread diseases which in ordinary opinion were either hopeless or considered incurable; that it would have seemed that with Theophrastus the science of medicine was not only discovered but perhaps even concluded." This excerpt from Peter Ramus' *Oration on Basel* is to be found in Bitiskius, Preface, p. [6] and in Melchior Adam, p. 29 (ll. 111n and 116n). For *Ramus,* see l. 63n.

135] *Ecce* . . . *pigebit?* "And yet it did not bother this youthful lover of difficult journeys that he should catch a glimpse of a pretty girl or woman. Should it shame him that the labor and tedium of the most noble of arts should be alleviated by love?" *Seven Defenses against the Calumnies of his enemies.* "Fourth defense: Concerning my far wanderings." This work is, of course, in Bitiskius.

145–149] See III:1. 956n.

157] *Life of Bishop Fisher,* by Thomas Bayly, written in the sixteenth century but not published until the seventeenth.

159] *Crasso* Lorenzo Crasso, Italian of the seventeenth century. His *Elogies of Men of Letters* was published in Venice and elsewhere in 1656. For each there is a portrait, several pieces in prose and verse, in his praise, and a list of his works, both printed and manuscript.

160] *Quenstedt* Jean André Quenstedt (1617–1688), a learned Protestant theologian of Germany. In 1644 he started teaching geography and history at the University of Wittenberg, and in 1647 succeeded to the chair of theology. In 1654 he published a kind of literary history, *Dialogus de patriis illustrium doctrine et scriptis virorum, omnium ordinam ac facultatum, qui ab initio mundi per universum terrarum orben usque ad annum 1600 claruerunt.*

162] *Delrio* Martin-Antoine del Rio, born in Antwerp, died in Louvain, 1608; he taught in Styria and Spain, as well as the Low Countries, and was a learned man, though credulous. His most famous book, to which B refers, was his *Disquisition on Magic,* published in Louvain in 1599 and often reprinted.

162] *partim . . . haereticos* "in part atheists, in part heretics"

163] *Omnino . . . . Christiani* "Although there is a great deal of theology in his writings, they smell almost entirely atheistic, and sound rather harshly on truly Christian ears."

165] *Clauderi* Daniel Gabriel Clauder, 1633–1691, German physician and chemist. His *Dissertation on the Universal Tincture, Vulgarly Called the Philosopher's Stone,* etc. was published in Altenburg, 1678.

166] *Oporinus . . . haerere* "Oporinus (IV:l. 1n) says that Paracelsus said that he could by some means reconcile the Pope and Luther, just as he had Galen and Hippocrates, for none of them up to this point had written anything on the scriptures, either old or new, that had in any way destroyed its basis. They seemed only to be stuck fast upon the outer and superficial surface of things." *Erastus,* see l. 16n. This quotation is from the famous letter of Oporinus to Rainerus Solenander and Johann Weyer. B could have found it in Daniel Sennert's *De chymicorum cum Aristotelcis et Galenicis consensu ac dissensu liber,* etc. Wittenberg, 1629. Solenander (1524–1601) was a follower of Johannes Argenterius (1513–1572), whose attack on Galenic medicine was quite independent of Paracelsus'. Johannes Wier or Weyer, called Vigerus (1515–1588), was a physician of the Low Countries and for a time in France. He was most famous for his demonstration that it was wrong to believe in the powers of witches and sorcerers. The first edition of his most famous work on the subject was printed in Basel, 1563. Daniel Sennert (1572–1637) attempted to reconcile the new chemical medicine, which owed much to Paracelsus, with the theory of the humors of the Galenic tradition.

171] *Oporinus* See IV:l 1n.

172] *Zuingerus* Theodore Zwinger, the elder, the first of a family of distinguished physicians and scientists, was born at Basel in 1533. He was the nephew of Oporinus (IV:l 1n). After study in France and Italy, he returned to Basel in 1559. At the University he taught in succession Greek, moral philosophy, and theoretical medicine. He died from attending and studying the poor victims of the plague in 1588. He published his *Theatrum vitae humanae* in Basel in 1565; it continued for a number of years, even after his death, and is a vast compilation of historical anecdotes and facts.

172] *longum . . . lueret* "And so he said a final farewell to him lest he also should pay the penalty someday to God on high for these horrendous blasphemies of his mentor, otherwise a very good friend."

175] *Erastus* See l. 16n.

175] *mirum . . . adjunxit* "It is a wonder that he did not add Africans, Indians, and English."

178] *anglum . . . Bacchonem* "A certain Englishman, Roger Bacon." (1214–1292) One of the first great medieval scientists.

182] *Nam . . . podicem* "Indeed I know that I have armed myself more and more against you and your mentors, Avicenna, Galen, Aristotle, etc. The peak of my bald head knows far, far more than either your Avicenna or all the followers of your whole profession. Come now, give us a sign what kind of men you are, what strength you have. Just what are you? Learned men and teachers, combing lice and scratching your ass." The passage may be found in Paracelsus' *Fragmenta ad operum medicorum,* Bitiskius, I, p. 346. (l. 119n.)

189] *Gentis . . . junctum* "This is but a trifling vice of the race, not really of this man. From the age of Tacitus to our own this vice has continued in an uninterrupted thread. Perhaps it is inherent in a true German, possibly linked indelibly, although I cannot guess how, by consanguinity." Bitiskius, p. [4]. (l. 119n.)

192] *Domi . . . putant* "As Oporinus his secretary has frequently said, he never left his house to go to his lectures unless drunk; and standing in the midst of the hall, he leaned blearily against a column; grasping the hilt of his sword in his hands, the hospitality of the hollow of which he offered, so they say, to his familiar spirit; he put forth his ideas and concepts:—some think that the hollow of his sword contained either a superb medicine or the philosopher's stone, which he called Azoth. Melchior Adam, p. 35 (l. 116n).

202] *Volpone* Play by Ben Jonson, acted in 1605 and published in 1607. The passage comes from a song, Act II, Scene ii, ll. 131–132 (ed. Herford-Simpson, Vol. V, Oxford, 1937, 1954).

208] *Hudibras* By Samuel Butler (1612–1680), Part I, 1662; Part II, 1663; Part III, 1678. The passage comes from Part II, Canto III, ll. 627–630.

209] *Azoth . . . laudanum suum* "Azoth" is a word used in later alchemical literature; it combines the first and last letter of the alphabet with the last letters of the Greek and Hebrew alphabets; it indicates the world-soul, penetrating and enlivening the universe. Current opinion surmises that it was related to the "Laudanum" which Paracelsus carried in the hilt of his famous long sword; the usual pictures of the sword shows "Azoth" inscribed on the pommel. This laudanum was not, as in modern times, an opiate, but the gum Laudanum of the pharmacopea or a compound remedy that contained pearls among its ingredients.

212] *Franciscus . . . Neander.* This information comes from Bitiskius p. [5] (l. 119n). Michael Neander published his *Orbis terrae partium succincta explicatio* at Leipzig in 1536. In it may be found a letter by Neander about Paracelsus.

215] *Degebat . . . testimonium* "While Theophrastus was in Nürnberg he was challenged by the healers of that city and called a boaster and a liar. In order to correct this slander he went to the governing officials of the Republic [Nürnberg was then an Imperial City, subject only to the Holy Roman Emperor] to remove the stain upon his reputation and to acquaint them with his skill and art; he promised that he would produce a specimen of it with no stipend or fee. At their order, and on the choice of another doctor, certain individuals were selected with obviously diseased elephantine ears which separated them from the community of other men and had thrust them aside into invalidism. And Theophrastus through the singular skill of his remedies cleansed them of this foul leprosy of the Greeks and restored their earlier health. That city has preserved an illustrious testimony to these cures in its archives." Bitiskius, Preface p. [5] (l. 119n).

224] Note* *Objectionem . . . suffocatur* "The argument that Paracelsus died fairly young some attribute to physical reasons. Perhaps so short a life was due to frequent overdoses of Tincture of which the greatest and most lasting effect would arise from a strength and an amount that would be fatal." *Clauderi* See l. 165n.

224] *Oporinus* See IV:1. 1n.

225] *Sed . . . inflixerant* "Finally he reconsidered, and the man whom he had reviled while still alive and in association with his intimates, he respected after he died, and the disrespect he paid to his mentor turned into stings of conscience, a penitence too late to heal the wounds of the dead which he had inflicted upon him living." Bitiskius, Preface, p. [3] l. 119n.

228] *Disput. Erasti.* See l. 16n.

229] *Andreae Jocisci* Jociscus, *Life of Oporinus,* Strassburg, 1569.

229] *Toxita* Michael Schütz, or, in Latin, Toxites. One of the early Paracelseans, author of *Onomastica* [specialized lexicon] *medicum et explicatio verborum Paracelsi,* Strassburg, 1574; and compiler of the *Testamentum Paracelsi,* Strassburg, 1574, which includes various documents, such as Paracelsus' will and his epitaph, also a preface, in which Toxites refers to Oporinus' (IV:1. 1) regret at having written as he did to Vigerus (l. 166n) and at having given away the books and preparations of Paracelsus. The *Testamentum* is incorporated at the end of the Vol. III of Bitiskius (l. 119n), with separate pagination.

230] *Conringius* Hermann Conring (1606–1681), an East Frisian, who spent most of his productive years at Helmstaedt in N Central Germany. He was one of the most learned and illustrious men of the seventeenth century, publishing over two hundred books on a great variety of subjects, including medicine. In 1648 he attacked Borrichius (see following note) for his defense of Paracelsus in *De hermetica Aegyptiorum veter et Paracelsicorum nova medicina liber.* A second edition (1669) defended his position against Borrichius' attacks.

231] Note† *Borrichius* Olaus Borrichius, chemist and physician of Denmark (1626–1690). He followed the principles of Paracelsus and of revived alchemy, but made important discoveries. He continued the Hermetic tradition (l. 42n) and was an opponent of Conring (see the preceding note). His principal attacks were published in 1668 and 1674. The second was *Hermetis, Aegyptiorum et chimicorum sapientia.* However fancifully developed, Paracelsus' great achievement, according to modern scholarship, was replacing the four humors by chemical entities in speculating about disease. That is, he conceived that man should be studied in his relation to his organic and inorganic environment. *Laudanum* See l. 209n.

234] *Vossius* Gerard-Jean Vossius (1577–?). Born in Heidelberg of Dutch parents, he grew up in Holland, and lived principally at Leyden and Amsterdam. Admired by Laud, archbishop of Canterbury, he was made Canon of Canterbury and granted a pension by Charles I, although he continued to live in Holland. He was one of the most learned and sensible men of letters of the seventeenth century, writing on a multitude of subjects. His *De philosophia et philosophorum sectis,* edited by his son Isaac, was published at the Hague in 1658. It was concerned with both speculative and practical philosophy, including medicine.

235] *Nobilem . . . Paracelsus* "This noble part of medicine, so long buried in the age of our fathers, has been recalled, as if from Hell, by Theophrastus Paracelsus."

238] *De Phlebotamia* The reference to the discovery of the circulation of the blood comes from Bitiskius' Preface to his second volume, p. [4] (l. 119n).

240] *Realdo Colombo* Famous Italian anatomist of the sixteenth century. He may have died in 1577. He studied living animals and observed that the heart contracts when the arteries dilate, and vice versa.

240] *Andrea Cesalpino of Arezzo,* Italy (1519–1603). A physician, botanist, and professor of medicine, as well as philosopher, he discovered the circulation of the blood, and, according to Bayle (see following note) was the first to do so.

241] *Bayle* Pierre Bayle (1647–1706), author of the famous *Dictionnaire Critique et Historique,* 2 vols., 1696, 2nd ed., 1720, subsequent editions revised and issued by others. The work was one of the principal sources for the anti-ecclesiastical struggle of the Enlightenment, and Bayle is usually identified with scepticism.

241] *Bartoli* Daniel Bartoli, Italian scholar (1608–1685), a Jesuit. He wrote about the history of the Jesuits and various other subjects, including freezing and coagulation, and tension and pressure.

241] *Lavater* Johann Kasper Lavater (1741–1801), Swiss writer, pastor, theologian, etc. He was most famous for his theories of physiognomy, his science of the soul, which had a wide-spread influence throughout Europe, and led to the founding of the pseudo-science of phrenology. His principal works on physiognomy appeared 1775–1778. Thomas *Holcroft* (1745–1809), English miscellaneous writer and dramatist, published his translation, *Essays on Physiognomy,* in 1789(?).

247] *Valentius (in Praefat. in Paramyr.)* Paracelsus' *Opus Paramirum (Work beyond Wonder)* was completed in 1531, when he was at St. Gallen (see B's Note). It contained his basic medical doctrines, but was not published until after his death. Valentius' Preface is in Bitiskius (l. 119n).

248] *quod . . . ingenii* "As far as the corpus of Paracelsus' work is concerned, I understand that the Germans have collected nearly three hundred works attributed to him. What productivity! How fertile his talent!"

250] *Bitiskius . . . good edition* See l. 119n.

251] *rejectis . . . numerus* "Those which fundamentally took pride only in his name have been rejected. There are a great many in circulation." Bitiskius, Preface, p. [1] (l. 119n.).

252] *"charissimum . . . obtentum"* "That priceless and invaluable author's mark which has been gleaned internally rather than merely alleged." Bitiskius, Preface, p. [1] (l. 119n).

254] *Jam . . . sunt* "And now indeed even without his aid or help the writings came to light; those shut up in a wall, in his absence, at the direction of some servant, were secretly removed and carried off."

256] *Valentius* See l. 247n.

258] *Petri Severini* Peter Soerenssen (1542–1602), an early Paracelsean, author of *Idea medicinae philosophicae fundamenta,* Basel, 1571 (l. 92n).

258] *Toxetis* See l. 229n.

259] *Dornei* See III l. 128n.

260] *Suavio* Leo Suavius, pseudonym of Jacques Gohorry, French translator, poet, historian, and alchemist of the 16th century. He had little learning, and less in the way of critical powers. In 1568 he published in Paris his *Theophrasti Paracelsi philosophiae et medicinae utriusque universae compendium, ex optimis quibus cumque eus libris, cum scholiis in libros iv ejusdem de vita larga.* It was vehemently attacked by Dorn (see III:l. 128) and other German Paracelseans.

261] *Liechtenfels* Modern scholarship tends to accept B's interpretation of this affair, that it was a deliberate trap set by Paracelsus' enemies. He had to flee because he had publicly insulted a judge, and thus made himself liable to arrest and severe—perhaps capital—punishment.

267] *Quis . . . administratur* "Who, may I ask, could possibly gain honor from a profession manipulated and controlled by such criminal rascals." The works of Paracelsus are studded with hundreds of insults to the medical profession. B probably noted this from Bitiskius (l. 119n) and was unable to find it again. After considerable search, the present editor has not been able to find it either.

269] *Bona . . . erogavit* "He simply asked that his worldly possessions be collected and distributed among the poor." The alternative readings for *erogavit* come from Adam (l. 124n). The *Testamentum* (l. 230n) has "honoravit."

271] Note *10* also comes from the *Biographie Universelle,* as the variant for the first edition indicates. (l. 92n.)